★★★ THE ★★★ CIVIL WAR PAINTINGS OF MORT KÜNSTLER

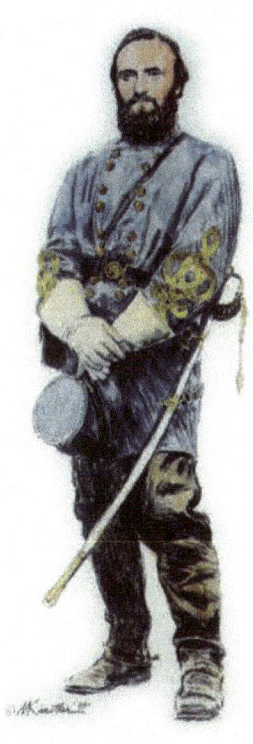

MKüns

★★★ THE ★★★
CIVIL WAR
PAINTINGS OF
MORT KÜNSTLER

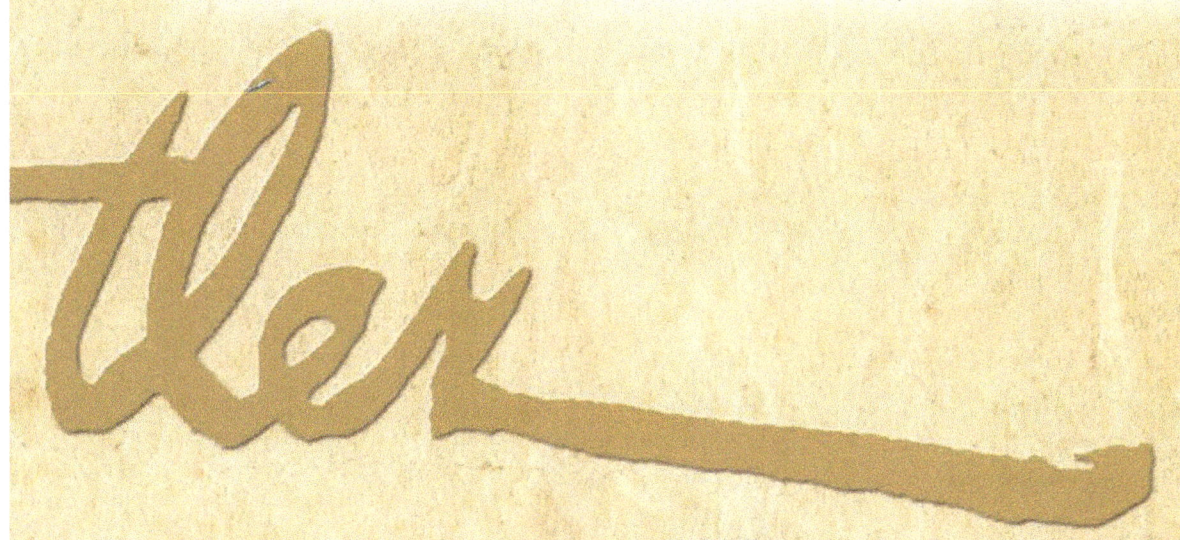

CUMBERLAND HOUSE
NASHVILLE, TENNESSEE

THE CIVIL WAR PAINTINGS OF MORT KÜNSTLER
VOLUME 2: FROM FREDERICKSBURG TO GETTYSBURG
PUBLISHED BY CUMBERLAND HOUSE PUBLISHING, INC.
431 Harding Industrial Drive
Nashville, Tennessee 37211

Text based on the writings of Rod Gragg, Mort Künstler, James M. McPherson, and James I. Robertson Jr. All art dimensions are presented height x width in inches.

Cover design by Gore Studio, Inc., Nashville, Tennessee

Library of Congress Cataloging-in-Publication Data

Künstler, Mort.
  The Civil War paintings of Mort Künstler / Mort Künstler.
      v.   cm.
   Contents: v. 2. Fredericksburg to Gettysburg.
   ISBN- 97-8-1-168442-833-5 (hc)
   1. United States—History—Civil War, 1861–1865—Pictorial works—Catalogs. 2. United States—History—Civil War, 1861–1865—Art and the war—Catalogs. 3. Künstler, Mort—Catalogs. I. Title.
E468.7.K844 2006
759.13—dc22   2006015631

1 2 3 4 5 6 7 8 9 10—10 09 08 07

To the memory of those who started me
on my journey as an artist—
my parents, Tom and Rebecca Künstler

CONTENTS

FOREWORD

FOLLOWING ANTIETAM, Northern leaders implored Gen. George B. McClellan to strike the weakened Confederate army again. McClellan responded with six weeks of excuses and inaction. Abraham Lincoln thereupon replaced him with Gen. Ambrose E. Burnside. The new commander devised a plan to move secretly and quickly around Lee's right flank and force a battle on open ground south of Fredericksburg, Virginia.

The Union movement, however, stalled in front of that river port. Robert E. Lee pulled Thomas J. "Stonewall" Jackson's divisions from the Shenandoah Valley and placed the reunited Confederate army in a strong position on high ground behind Fredericksburg. With secrecy and speed now gone, Burnside lacked the mental agility to employ a different strategy. On December 13 he blindly sent waves of Union soldiers across an open plain against Lee's lines. Thirteen times the Federals attacked; thirteen times Confederates blasted the ranks into bloody pieces. Burnside's stubbornness cost him almost thirteen thousand men; Lee's casualties were forty-five hundred soldiers.

At one point in the lopsided battle, Lee commented sadly, "It is well that war is so terrible; else we should grow too fond of it."

February 1863 saw Gen. Joseph Hooker take command of the Union army. A skilled organizer, he rebuilt the Army of the Potomac into a gigantic, highly disciplined force. Hooker also formulated an almost perfect battle strategy. With a two-to-one advantage in numbers, Hooker was going to split his army. A third of his troops, under Gen. John Sedgwick, would remain at Fredericksburg to face Lee; Hooker and seventy thousand men were to march twenty miles west, cross the Rappahannock and Rapidan rivers, then curl around the flank of the Southern army. Lee would then seem to have but two choices: stand and fight on two fronts at Fredericksburg or fall back and do battle on ground of Hooker's choosing.

The two wings of the Union army were in place by the end of April 1863. Yet because Lee was so outnumbered, he could take daring risks. He left a small detachment in front of Sedgwick at Fredericksburg and moved speedily with his main force to confront Hooker. Meanwhile, the Union commander had halted at Chancellorsville, a crossroads deep in an area of thick woods and dense undergrowth known as the Wilderness. Worse, Hooker, suddenly lost the driving energy that had been his greatest asset.

Confederate cavalry discovered that Hooker's western flank was unanchored. Lee and Jackson resolved that the flanked would become the flanker. Jackson, with the bulk of the Southern army, would execute a sweeping march around the Union right while Lee held Hooker's attention with a small force in the center.

This audacity by Lee worked brilliantly. Jackson's late-afternoon attack on May 3 drove the Federals three miles and bent Hooker's line into a hairpin shape. Shortly after nightfall, Jackson was accidentally shot by his own men. Three days of desperate fighting then ensued, both around Chancellorsville and back near Fredericksburg. Lee deftly shifted his forces from one sector to another to meet the Union threats. The offensive that Hooker thought was unbeatable became Lee's most stunning victory. However, with Jackson's death, Lee lost not only his principal lieutenant but also the element of mobility so essential to success for his ill-equipped, ever-diminishing army.

From the beginning of the war, Lee had maintained that the South lacked the resources to conduct a long, defensive contest. The key to victory, he felt, was to strike a decisive blow—possibly on Northern soil—that would break the Union will to continue the war. Chancellorsville had certainly demoralized a large segment of the Northern population. Virginia badly needed respite from being the war's major battleground. The time for a Southern offensive was ripe.

Confederate soldiers began filing across the Potomac River in mid-June. A feeling of invincibility surged through the ranks. "Marse Robert" was at their head, and another great victory might well bring peace.

Among the handful who truly sense the human, indelible element of this war is Mort Künstler. That alone goes far in explaining why he is the premier Civil War artist of our time.

Künstler possesses much more than extraordinary artistic talent. He has become one of the greatest popularizers of Civil War history. His subjects are always widely appealing to the eye and to the mind. Next, Künstler pursues accuracy to an extent that would make some historians blush. He once made a journey halfway across the continent to learn from an individual exactly how one hooked together a forty-horse team.

Then comes the painting. Not only is his work a breathtaking blend of color, lights, and shadows, but a moment in time is portrayed so realistically that history comes alive on canvas. Whether the subject is an iconic leader, an ordinary soldier, a horse, a home, or a church steeple, it is brought into focus with all the care and actuality that a brush can achieve.

Civil War artists have existed for 140 years, yet there is only one Mort Künstler. To go through the pages of these volumes will readily reveal the reasons for the popularity of his original paintings as well as his widely collected limited-edition prints and canvas reproductions. More important, studying this superb collection is a first-class excursion into art and history at their best. Every Civil War likeness Künstler creates is a reminder to us all that while we can call the United States our nation, we must never forget those countrymen who gave it to us.

James I. Robertson Jr.

★★★ THE ★★★ CIVIL WAR PAINTINGS OF MORT KÜNSTLER

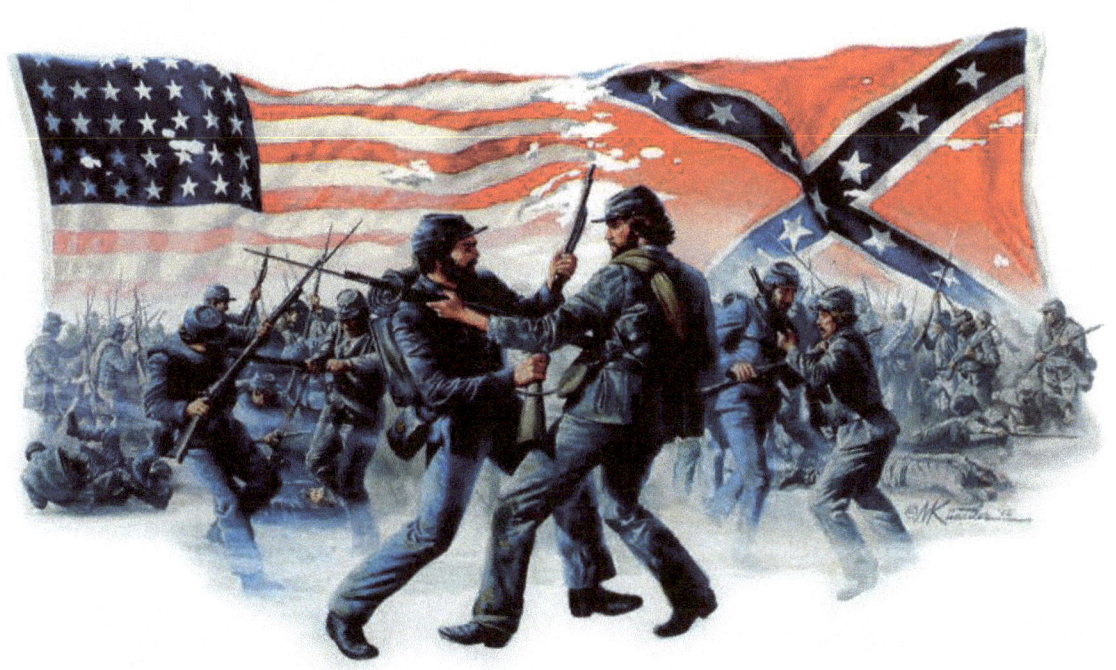

THE PALACE BAR

WINCHESTER, VIRGINIA
OCTOBER 18, 1862

1997, oil, 30 x 44

IN 1988, I met Wil Feltner, at the time the CEO of F&M Bank in Winchester, Virginia. This relationship produced some of my most popular paintings. The bank owned several old buildings in town that dated back to the Civil War. Many of these structures were renovated for offices and a gallery, and Wil asked me if I might be interested in doing a painting that would incorporate one of the buildings in the composition. When I received a packet of photographs and other information about the building, I was thrilled with the possibilities.

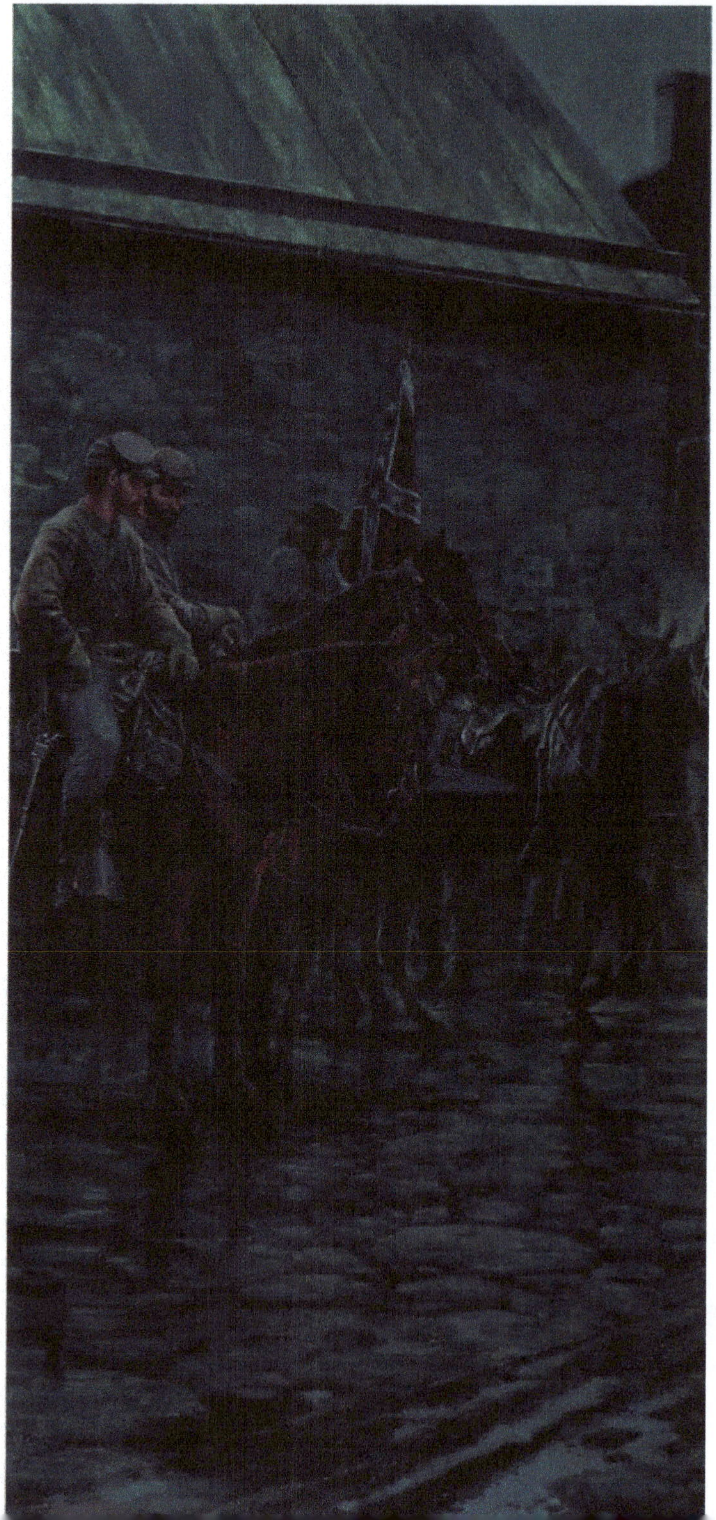

14

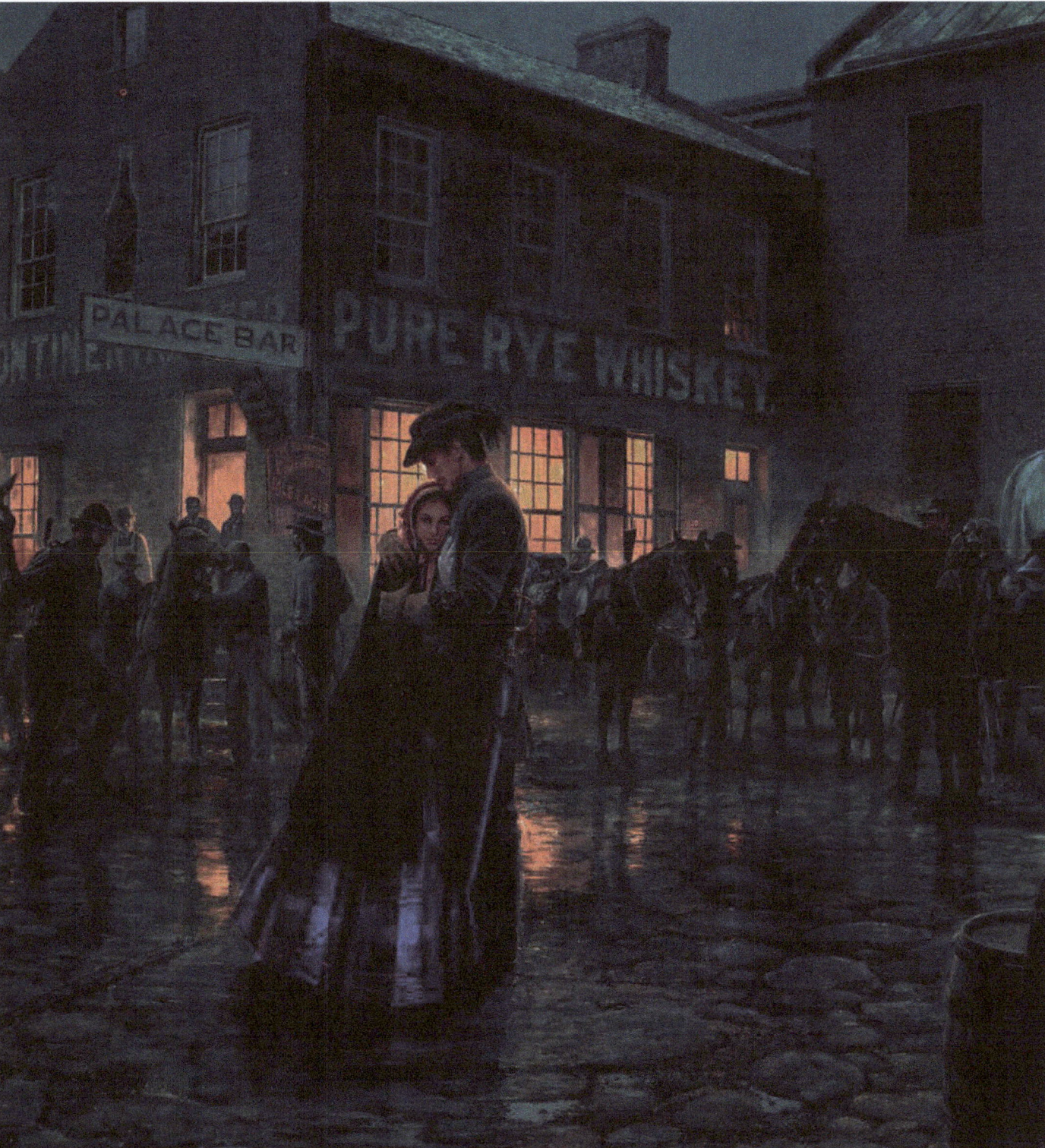

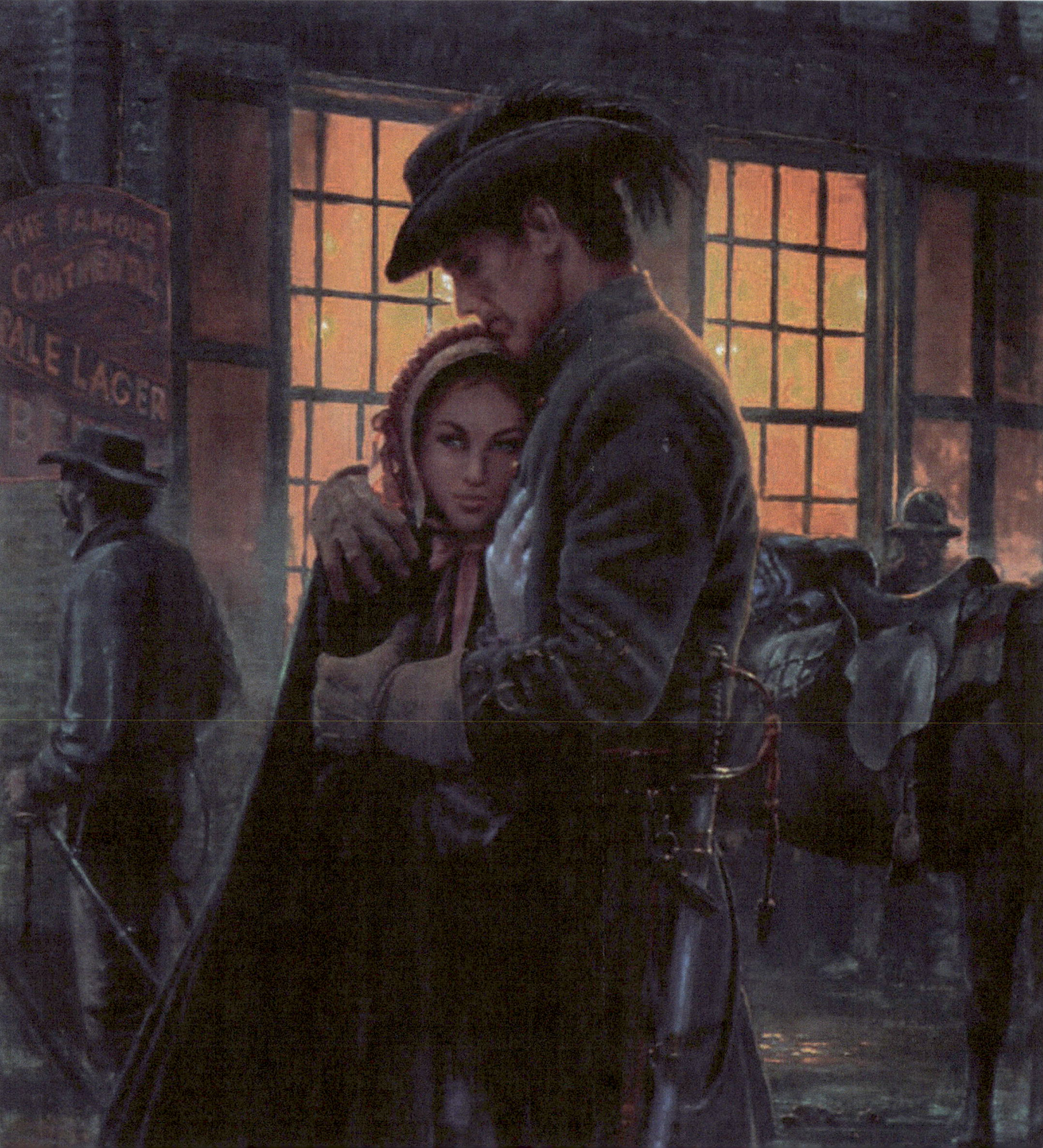

During the war, the building had been a bar, and that subject lent itself to the use of colorful outdoor signs in the painting. The structure was brick with interesting windows and shutters. Furthermore, it was situated, not on a street, but adjacent to a courtyard that was used as a parking and staging area for horses, carriages, and other conveyances.

The bar theme immediately led me to consider a night scene. I had recently finished *Wayside Farewell*, a night snow scene, which is also in the bank's collection, so I did not want to do another snow scene. Instead, I settled on the idea of a rainy night. With the lights on in the bar, I felt I could get some interesting reflections in the damp setting. The proximity of the open courtyard led me to depict another farewell scene. To make it different from my previous romantic pieces, I chose to include an active group of cavalrymen checking their mounts, accouterments, saddles, and such.

In my romantic paintings, I seem to always position the man on the right. This allows me to show swords and sashes, which I find very interesting.

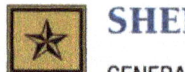

SHENANDOAH AUTUMN

GENERALS STUART AND JACKSON
MILLWOOD, VIRGINIA
NOVEMBER 4, 1862

2003, oil, 22 x 36

detail, right

BY LATE 1862, Gens. Thomas J. Jackson and J. E. B. Stuart were giants in gray. Only Robert E. Lee was held in higher esteem. Now, Lee's army was regrouping and preparing to repel an imminent Northern assault.

On November 3, 1862, Stonewall Jackson established his headquarters on the grounds of the Carter Hall plantation near Millwood, Virginia, about eleven miles east of Winchester. The next day, Jackson received a visit from Stuart, who was fresh from battle and a hard night's ride. Jackson promptly ordered his cooks to feed the weary warriors. "Nothing was better calculated to restore our good spirits than the summons to the General's large breakfast-table," recalled Maj. Johann Heros von Borcke. Within hours, Stuart and his staff were back in the saddle and bidding good-bye to their host.

Carter Hall stands almost unchanged today. I chose it as the backdrop for *Shenandoah Autumn* because of its elegant beauty, which is rarely seen by the public, and to depict two near-mythic Southern leaders. The setting also gave me the chance to paint the beautiful autumn colors of the Shenandoah Valley.

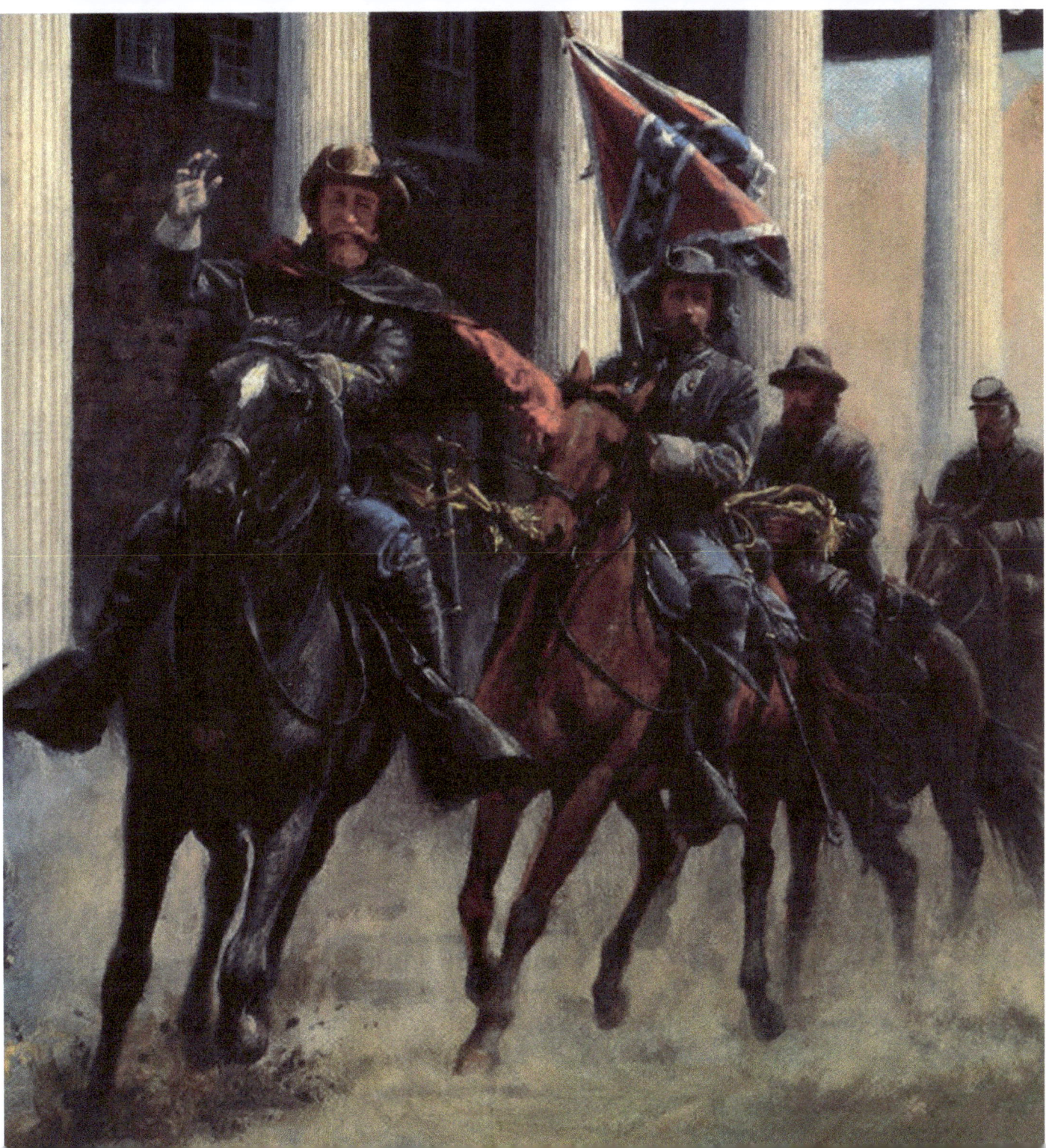

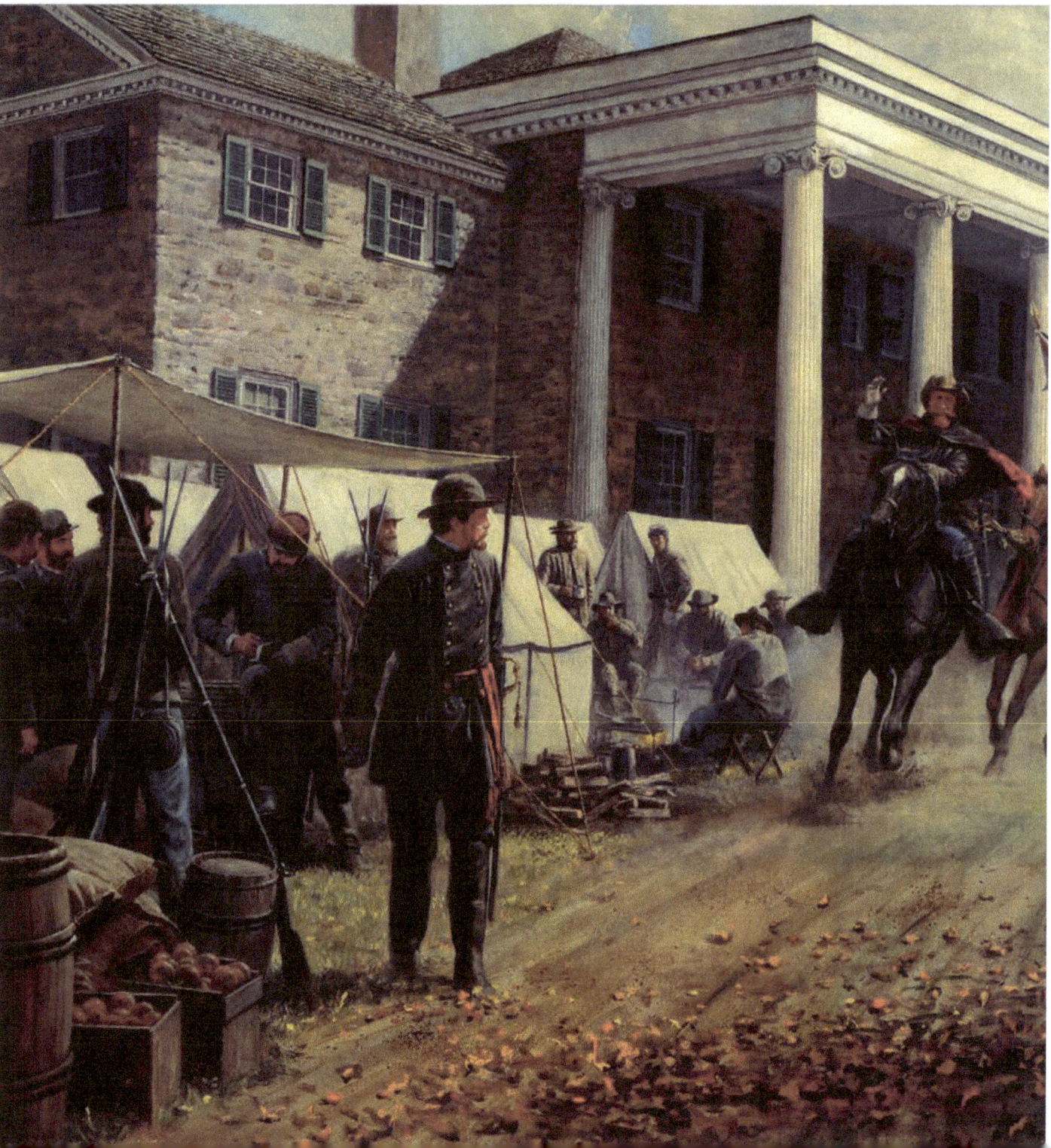

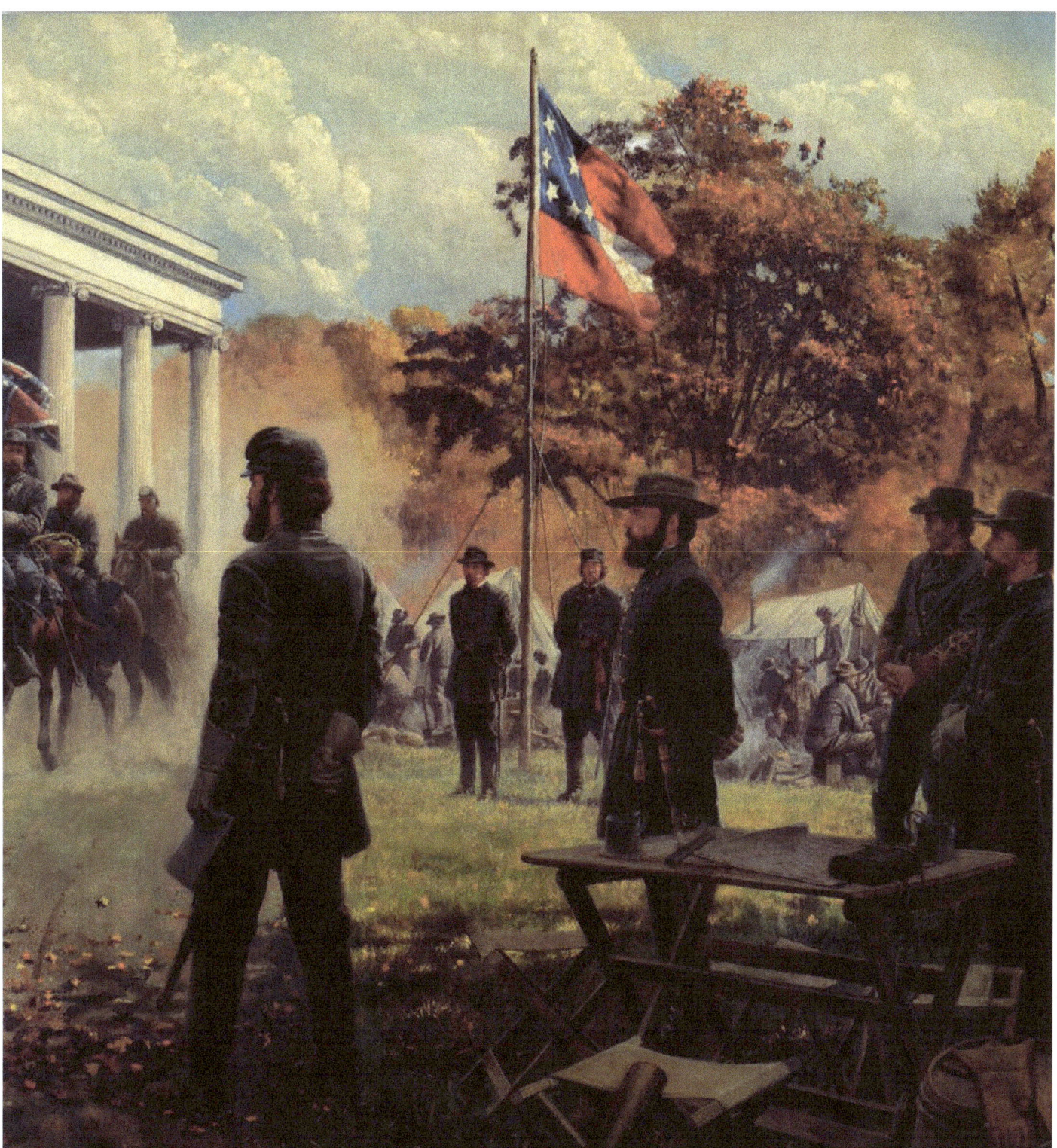

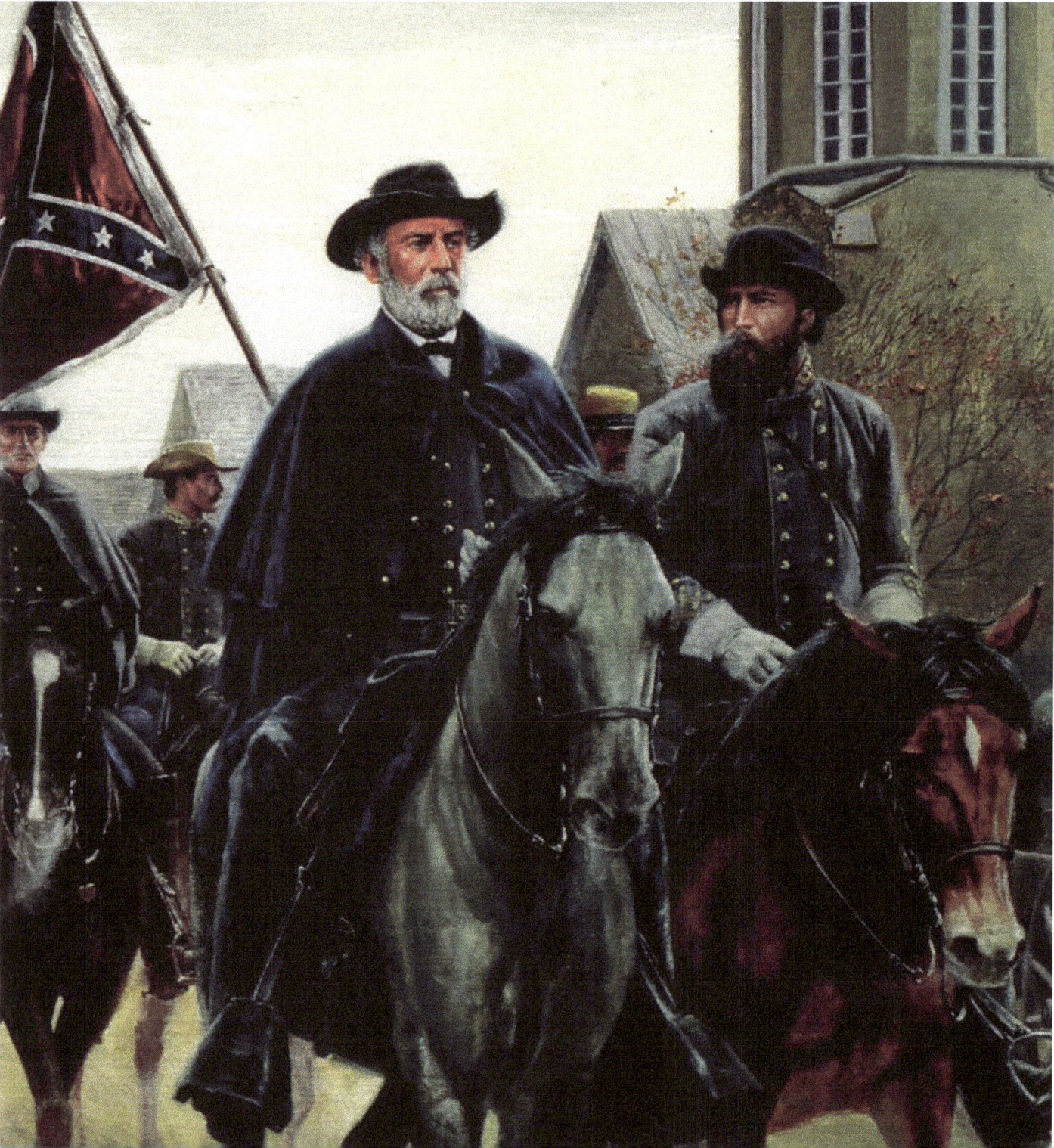

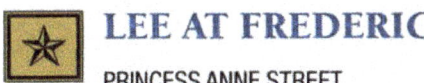

LEE AT FREDERICKSBURG

PRINCESS ANNE STREET
NOVEMBER 20, 1862, 9:40 A.M.

1990, oil, 34 x 56

detail, left

THE TOWN of Fredericksburg, situated roughly halfway between Washington and Richmond, became the focal point of the approaching Union offensive. Rather than wait for the spring, when offenses were usually begun, the new commander of the Army of the Potomac, Ambrose E. Burnside, devised a clever plan to seize the critical city on the Rappahannock River and its railroad junction as part of his march on Richmond. The Confederate army was in winter quarters west of the town and might not be able to intercept the Federals if Burnside's army moved quickly, which it did. But the military bureaucracy was ten days late in delivering the pontoon boats necessary for the river crossing. While the Union army waited on the northern bank of the Rappahannock, Lee's army began to entrench on the southern bank. Lee himself arrived on November 20.

I had wanted to do a painting of Fredericksburg for some time. When I learned that no artist had ever painted Lee and James Longstreet at Fredericksburg, that was the extra impetus that I needed to begin this project.

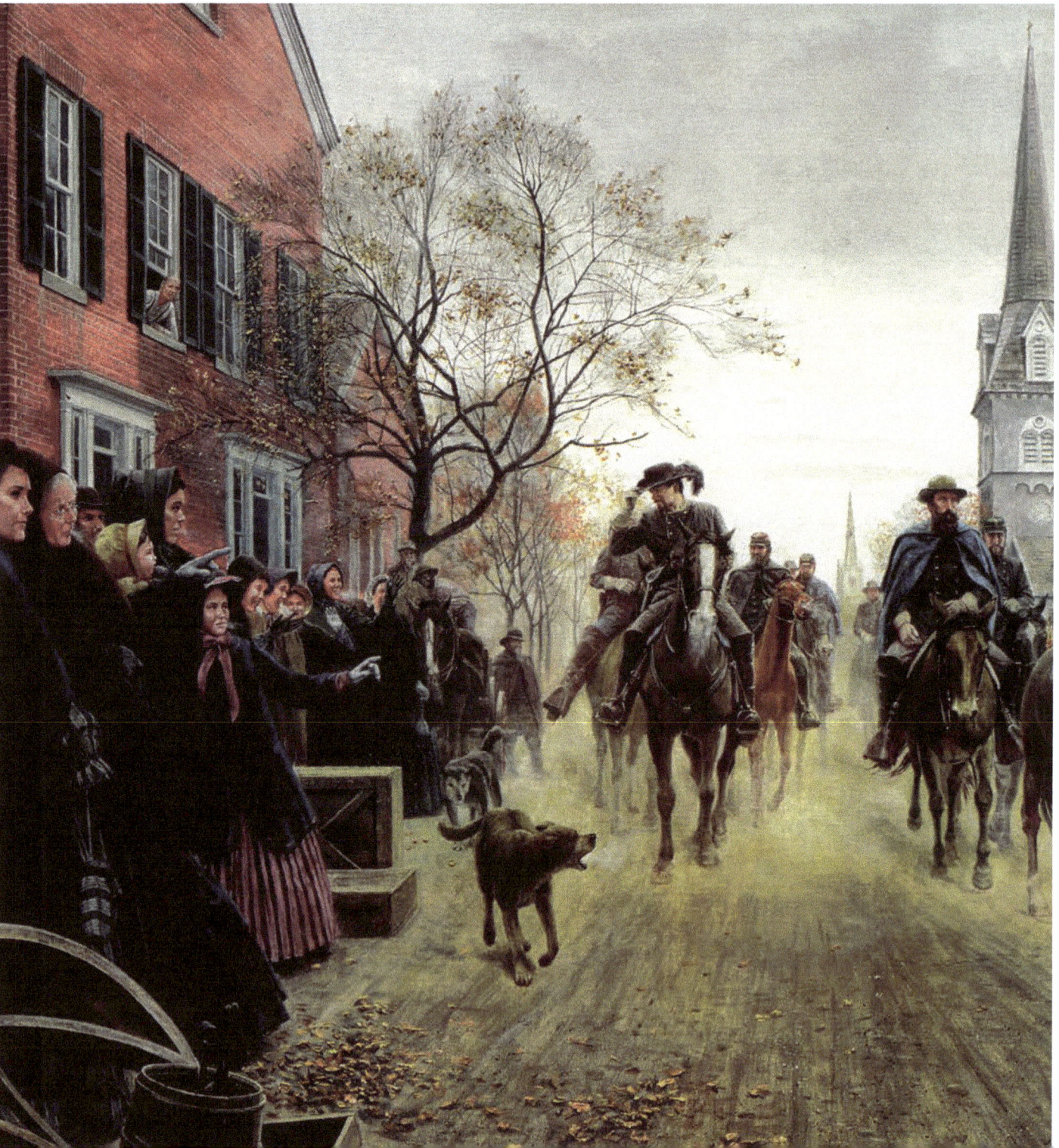

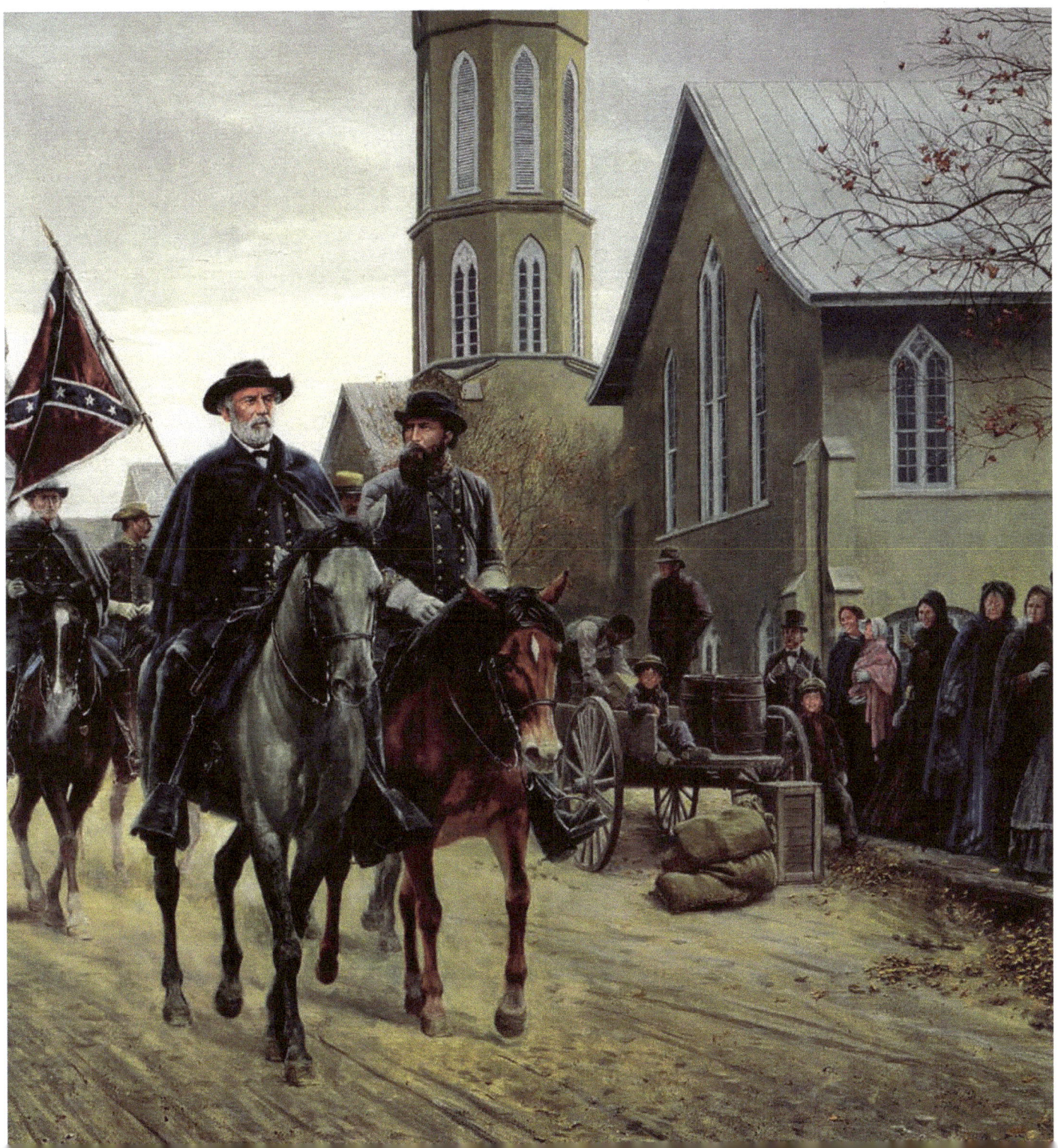

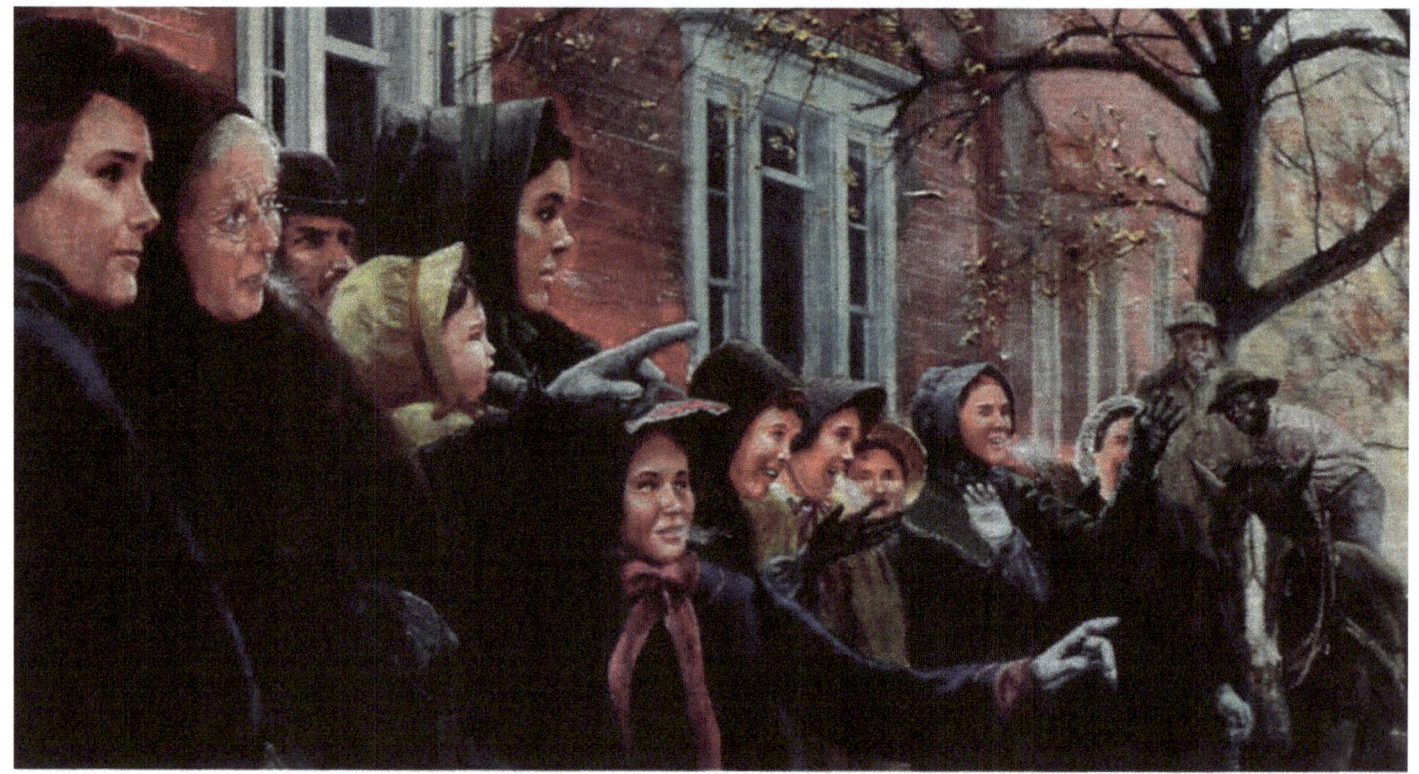

When I visited the town, I was immediately impressed with the appeal and beauty of the city. The steeples of Princess Anne Street pulled me like a magnet. Once I had strolled down this main street, I knew this would be the setting for my painting.

By facing north, near Mason's Hall, I could get all three steeples into view. On the right is the steeple of the brick courthouse. Farther down the street, in the center of the painting, is the towering steeple of St. George's Episcopal Church, which is virtually unchanged since the war. In the far distance, one sees the Baptist church steeple. The building on the extreme left was a residence at the time and still exists, almost the same as it was in 1862.

I decided to depict Lee and Longstreet together on their arrival during the morning of November 20, when both generals rode down Princess Anne

Street with their entourages. The citizenry—made up primarily of women, children, and old men—was surprised and delighted to see the famous legends in person and felt confident that the Union threat would be repelled.

The center of interest is, of course, Lee and his horse Traveller. To the right is Longstreet, whom he had ordered to join him in Fredericksburg. Immediately behind them is a trooper carrying a battle flag. Directly under the flag is Col. Charles Marshall, Lee's aide-de-camp throughout the war. Behind the flag, between Marshall and Lee, is Col. James Corley, chief quartermaster. To the left of the clock on the St. George's steeple is Lee's medical director, Lafayette Guild. Riding in front of him and to the left of the steeple is Maj. Charles Venable. To Venable's left and tipping his hat to a group of young women is Col. Walter Taylor. To Taylor's right and directly behind him is Col. Briscoe Baldwin, chief of ordnance. Other officers of both staffs and escort troopers follow.

The mood of the civilians changed dramatically during the next forty-eight hours. Union Gen. Edwin V. Sumner sent an ultimatum to the townspeople to evacuate the city or endure a bombardment. Lee had no military alternative to thwart the gunners on the high ground across the river, and so he suggested that the citizens should seek safety. During the night of November 22, despite a freezing sleet storm, the civilians evacuated. Twenty days later, on the morning of December 11, the first Union shells crashed into the houses and shops of the colonial city. Fredericksburg would never be the same.

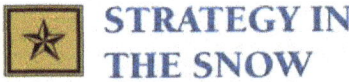

STRATEGY IN THE SNOW

FREDERICKSBURG, VIRGINIA
NOVEMBER 29, 1862

1994, oil, 27 x 35

Since the completion of *Confederate Christmas*, I have regularly contemplated other snow paintings. While reading Douglas Southall Freeman's masterful biography of Lee, I came across a description of Jackson's arrival at Lee's headquarters at Fredericksburg during the evening of November 29, 1862. Possibilities for a painting of this meeting immediately came into focus for me.

Jackson's corps was among the last elements of Lee's army to arrive at Fredericksburg. When Sumner's threatened bombardment did not occur, Lee was not sure that Burnside

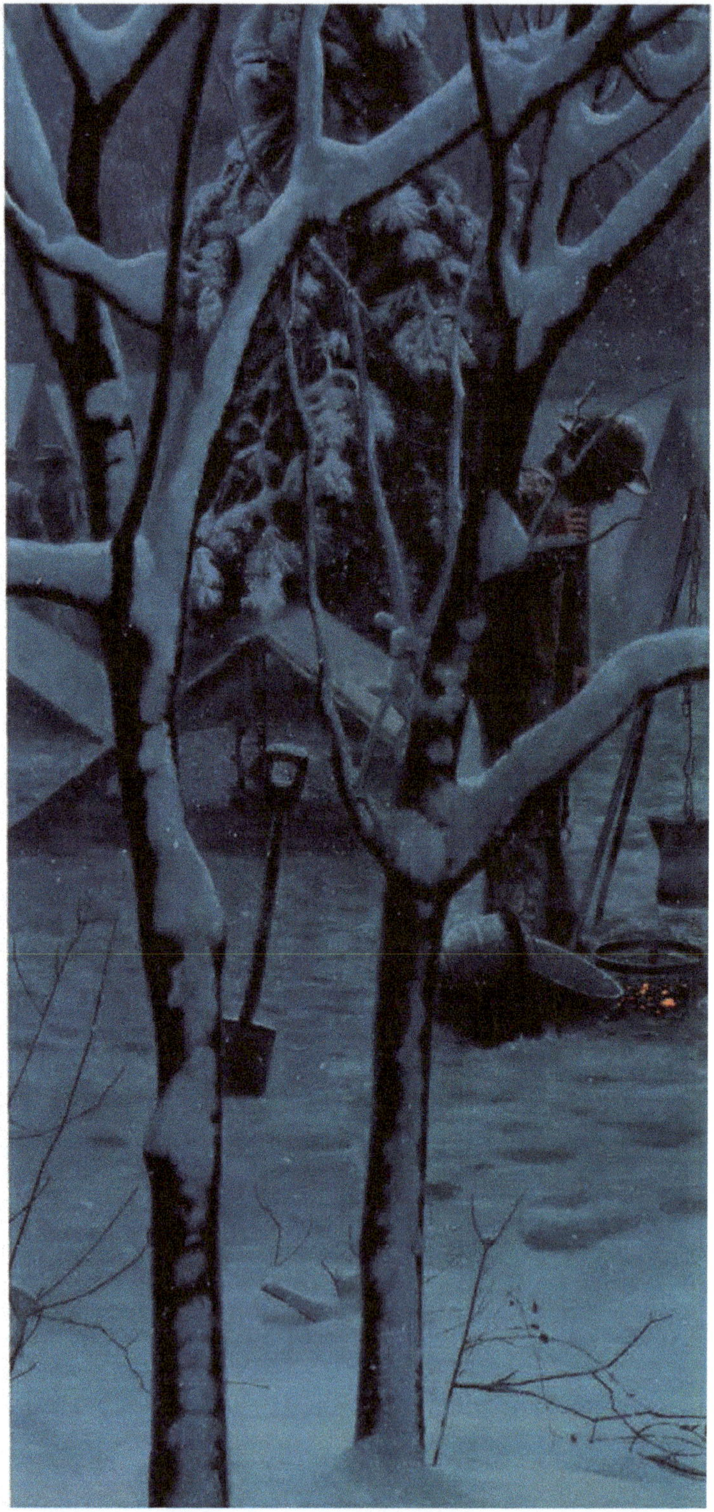

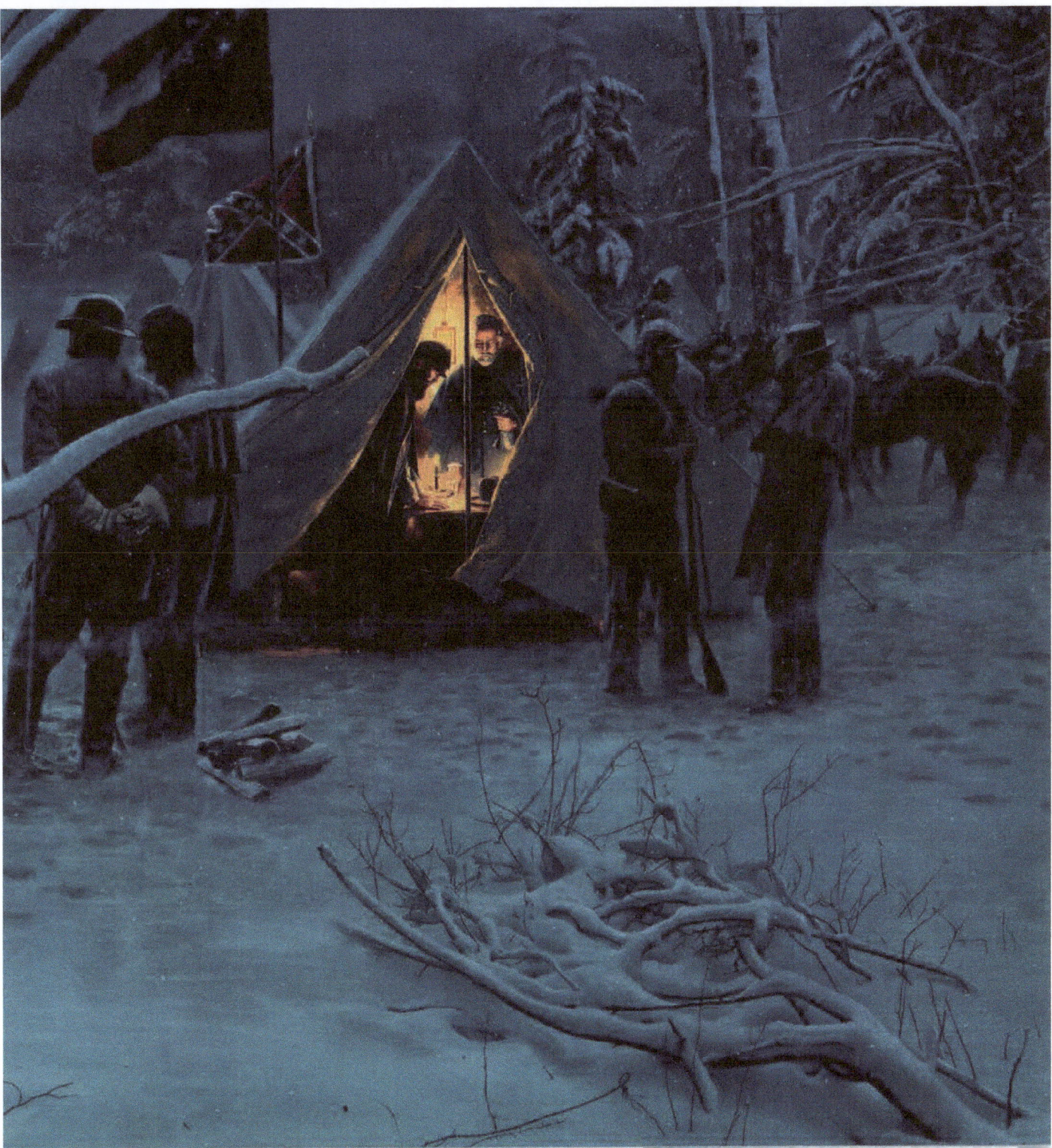

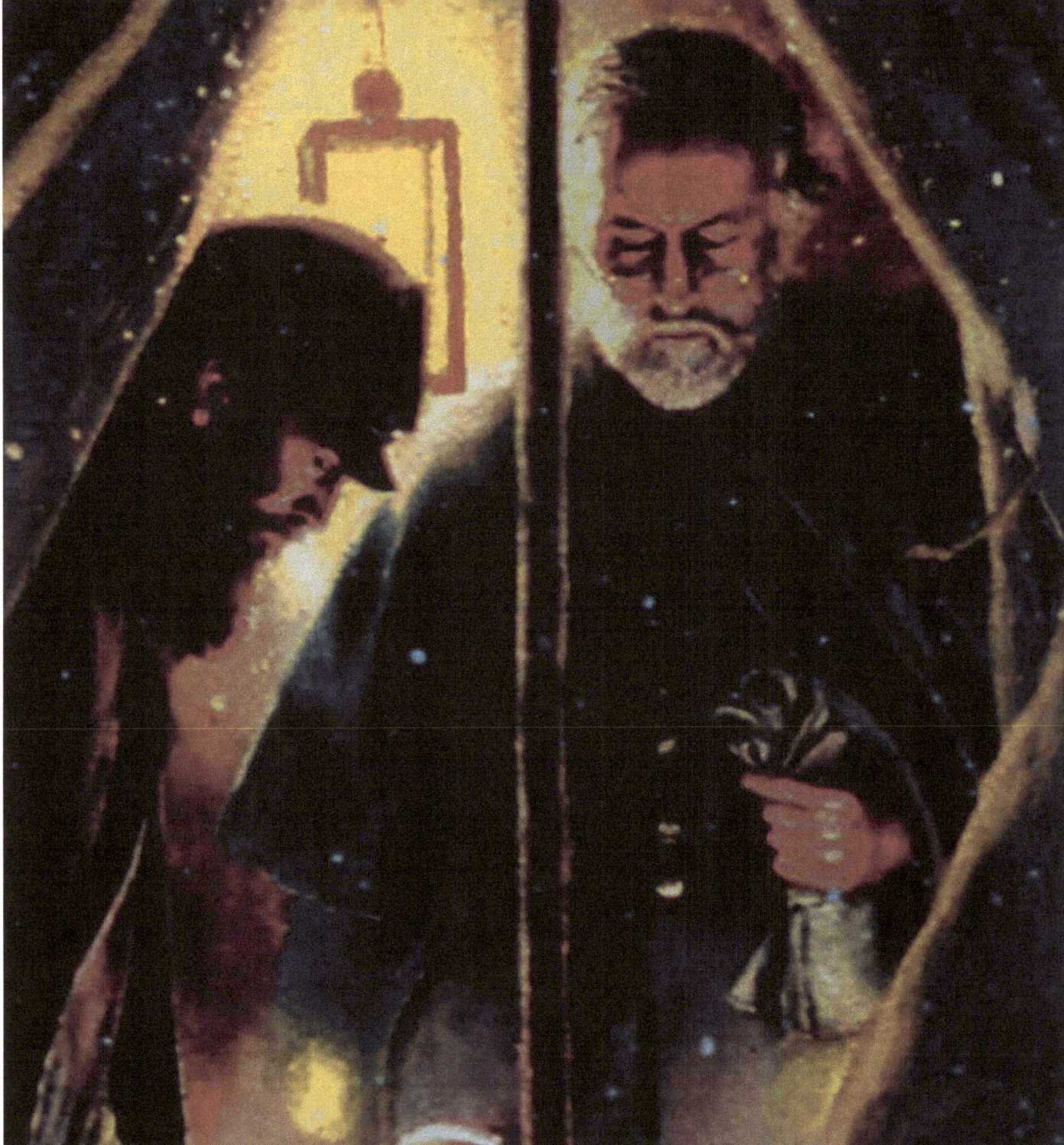

would attack him here, and so he gave Jackson tremendous discretion in responding to the threat. When Lee clearly understood the Federal commander's intentions, his orders for Jackson to move quickly to join him had been anticipated: Jackson was already on the march.

On the morning of November 29, Jackson rode ahead of his corps, with aide James Power Smith and four couriers, to cover the last forty miles of the trek. The day before, Jackson learned that his wife had given birth to a daughter. Yet he told no one—not even Lee, when he saw him that night.

It was dark when Jackson's party reached the cluster of tents that made up Lee's headquarters near Hamilton's Crossing. Their arrival, Smith noted, "created quite a stir." The commotion brought Lee out of his tent, and a short while later, the two generals had supper together. Either during the meal or afterward, Lee conveyed his plans that Jackson should occupy the right side of the Confederate line, to the south of the town, so that he could move up to support Longstreet or advance farther down the Rappahannock, should Burnside shift his attack in that direction.

I liked the idea of showing the two generals in Lee's tent and using candlelight to focus attention on them. I realized that tent flaps would be closed during the winter, but gusts of wind would likely reveal the two men in thoughtful conversation over a campaign table. The blowing flags and capes and the officer holding onto his hat all emphasize air in motion.

There are wonderful contemporary descriptions of winter camps, including the placement of Lee's flags and the tents of his aides, which I was able to draw upon to create this painting. The terrain and trees are typical of the site of the camp on that cold November 1862 night.

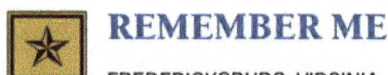

REMEMBER ME

FREDERICKSBURG, VIRGINIA

NOVEMBER 30, 1862

1997, oil, 26 x 42

detail, right

FREDERICKSBURG IS one of the oldest communities in the Old Dominion. The picturesque city was founded in 1671 and has a rich colonial history. George Washington grew up here and allegedly hurled a Spanish silver dollar across the nearby Rappahannock. The city was home to John Paul Jones, and James Madison began his law practice here.

I wanted to use the city as a backdrop—before its devastation during the 1862 battle—for a romantic painting representing a scene acted out countless times: a soldier saying good-bye to his sweetheart, knowing that this might be the last time they would see each other.

I again chose Princess Anne Street as the setting for my painting. By moving up the street, farther north from the viewpoint of my painting *Lee at Fredericksburg*, I was able to feature St. George's Episcopal Church again, but this time in a more prominent role. I also included the wonderful cast-iron fence that surrounds the Presbyterian church diagonally across from St. George's and also featured the National Bank of Fredericksburg on the other corner. This building was a bank even during the war and is still a town landmark.

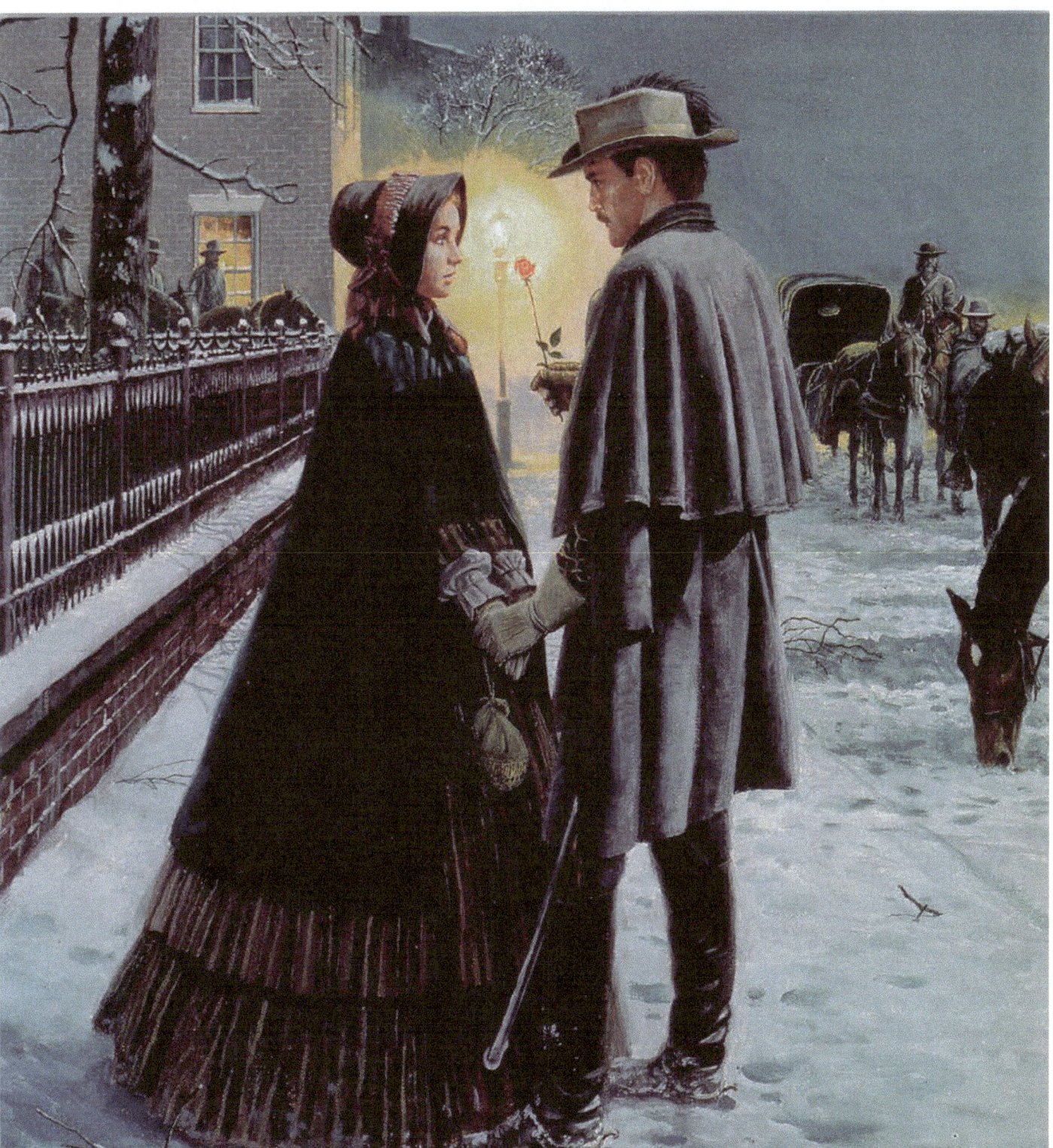

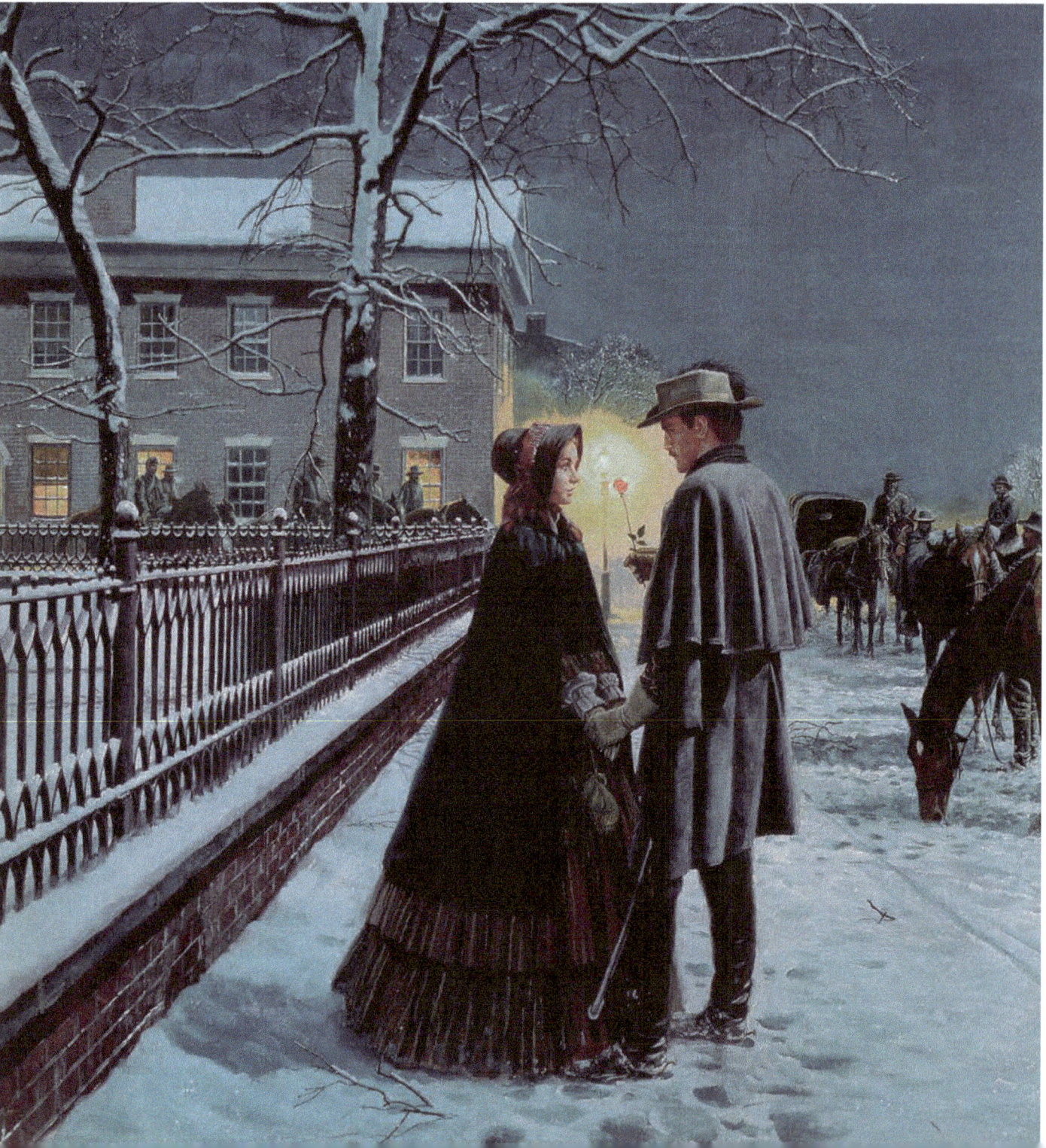

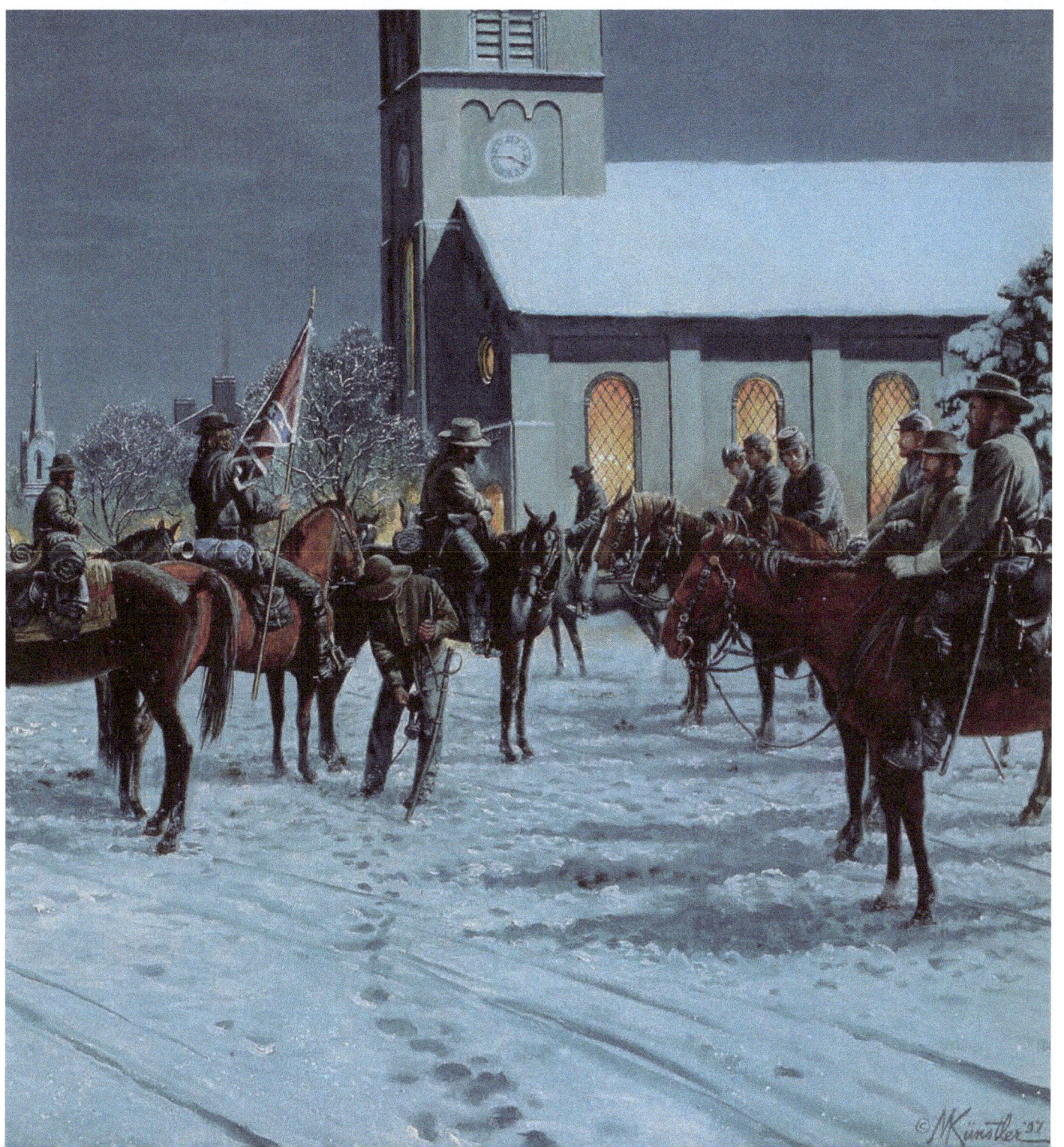

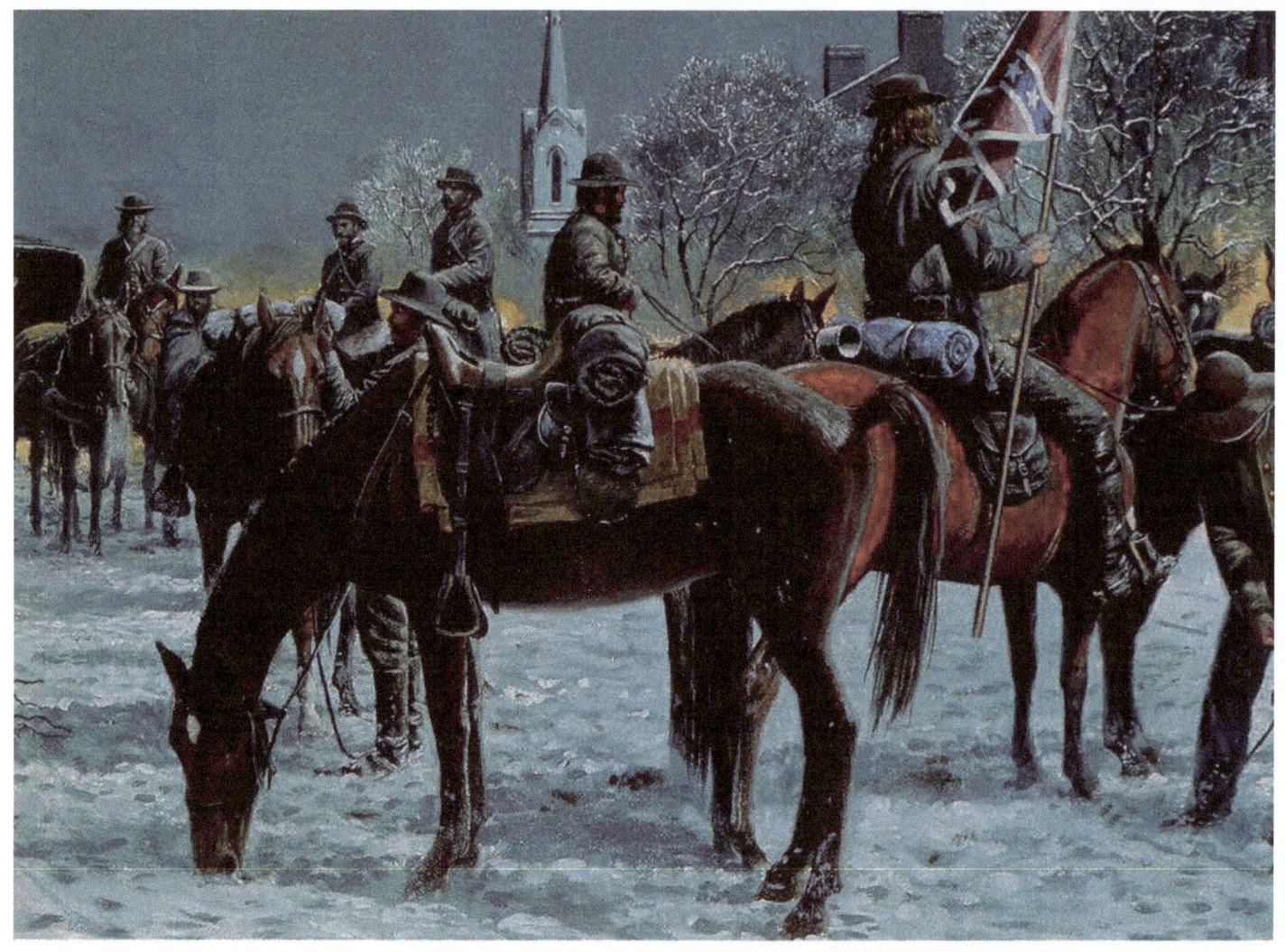

Both Abraham Lincoln and Jefferson Davis gave speeches on the steps of this building. Lincoln spoke at the side entrance; Davis delivered his from the front steps on Princess Anne Street.

St. George's was built in 1849. The central tower and steeple, long a city landmark, have survived the ravages of time and war. The clock in the tower was set in place in 1850 by the city government, which is still respon-

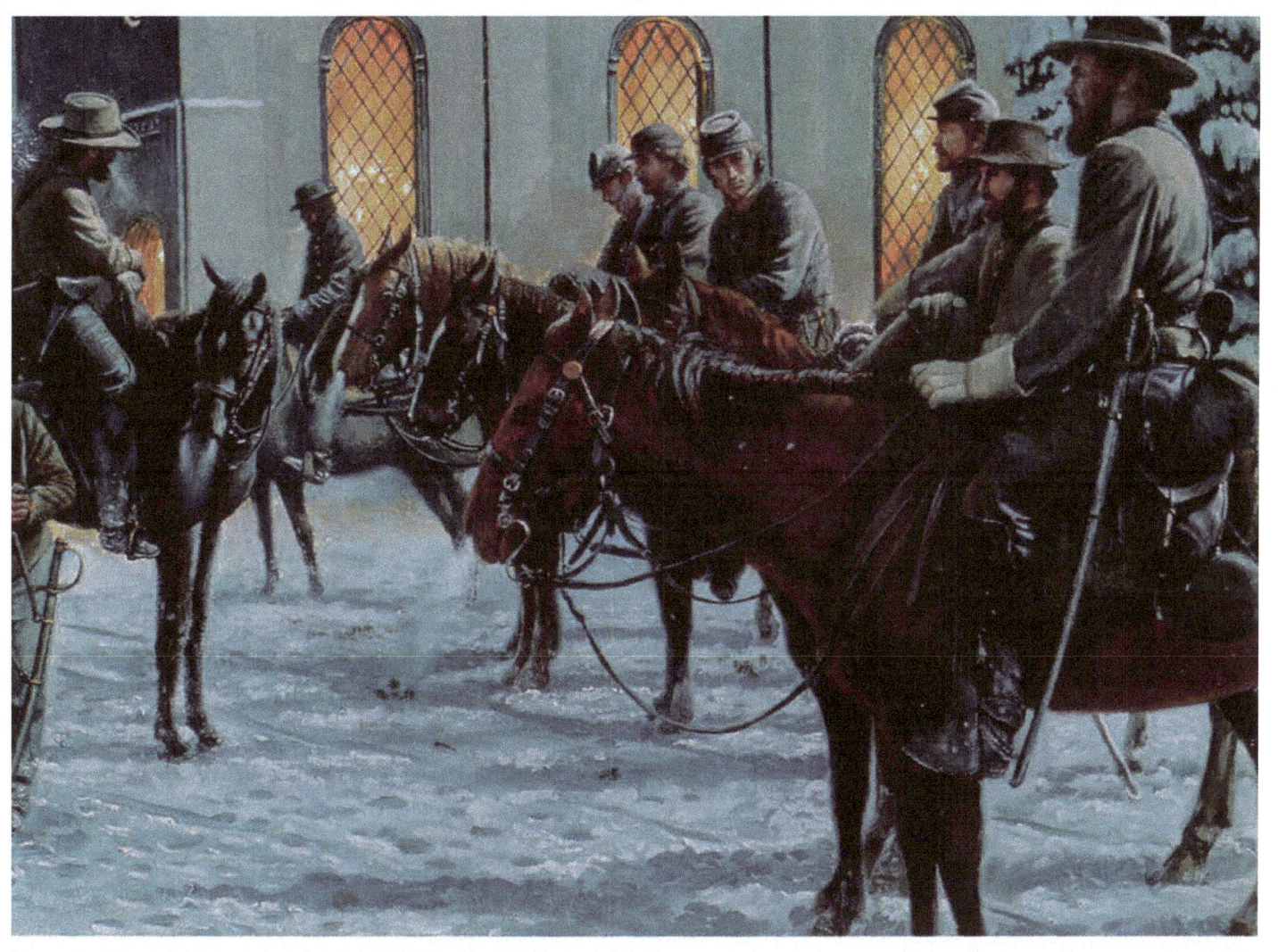

sible for its maintenance. Not until the end of the nineteenth century did stained-glass church windows become popular. During the war, the glass panes were diamond shaped, which is how I depicted them in the painting. In order to accurately present the town before it was damaged during the battle, I consulted original drawings done by E. Sachs and Co. of Baltimore in 1856.

THE FIGHTING 69TH

GENERAL MEAGHER AND THE IRISH BRIGADE
FREDERICKSBURG, VIRGINIA
DECEMBER 2, 1862

1998, oil, 26 x 48

detail, right

AMID THE ranks of the Army of the Potomac on the northern bank of the Rappahannock was the famed Irish Brigade. I had first painted the brigade in action at Antietam. So it was only logical that I should select a Fredericksburg scene for my next painting of the Irish troops in the Civil War. Among the brigade's regiments was the Sixty-ninth New York.

The Federals had been in camp across from Fredericksburg since November 17. After waiting for days for orders to advance, many believed there would be no battle and on November 29 began building winter quarters.

While researching the painting, I learned that the Sixty-ninth had no green flag during the ensuing battle, because the green regimental flag had been sent to New York to be replaced. The colors, however, were not retired until December 2. So I used that date to set the story line for this image.

In the painting, the color guard and officers of the Sixty-ninth report to brigade headquarters to formally return the colors. Meanwhile, a staff officer points out where the long-awaited pontoons have been placed.

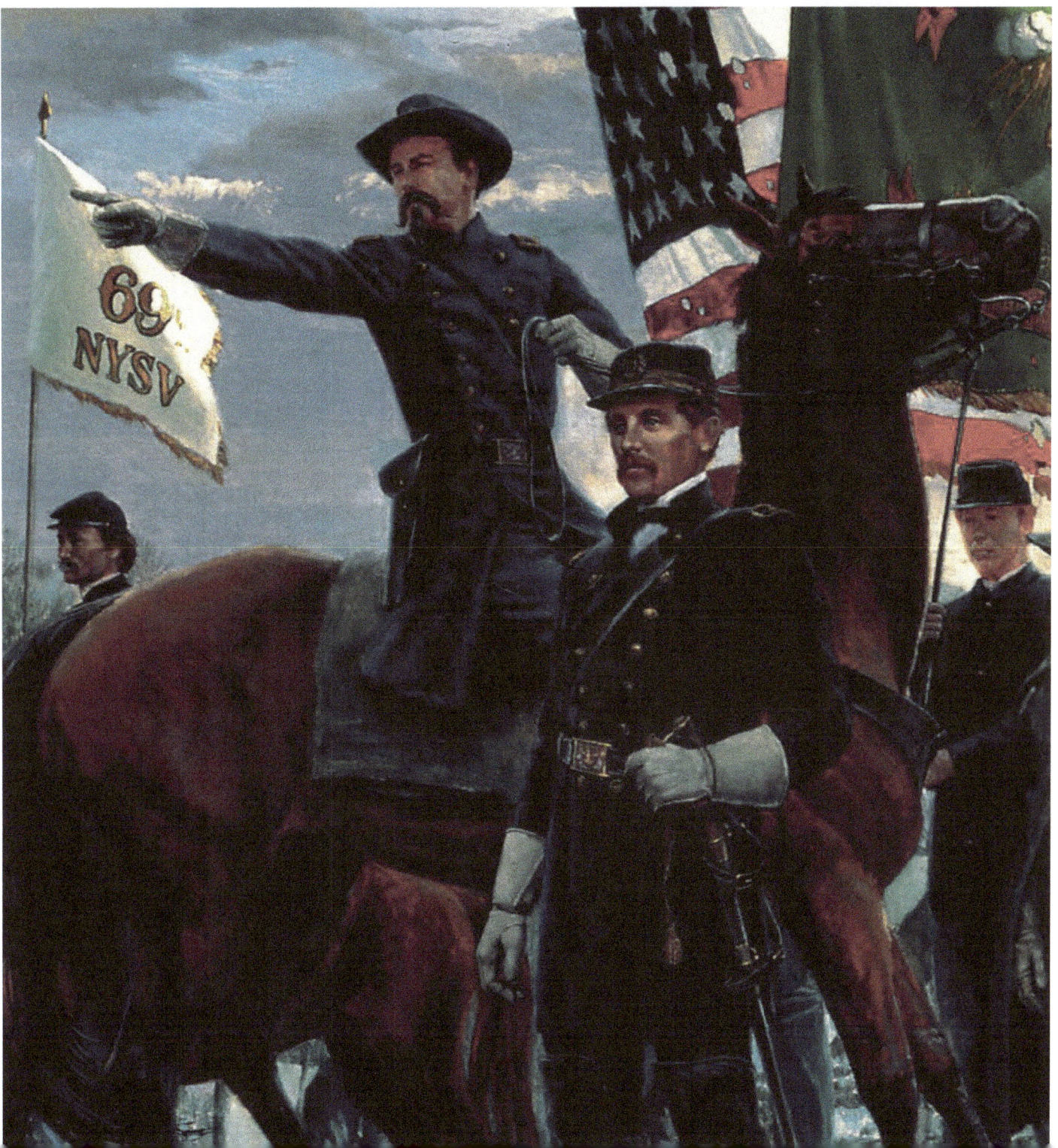

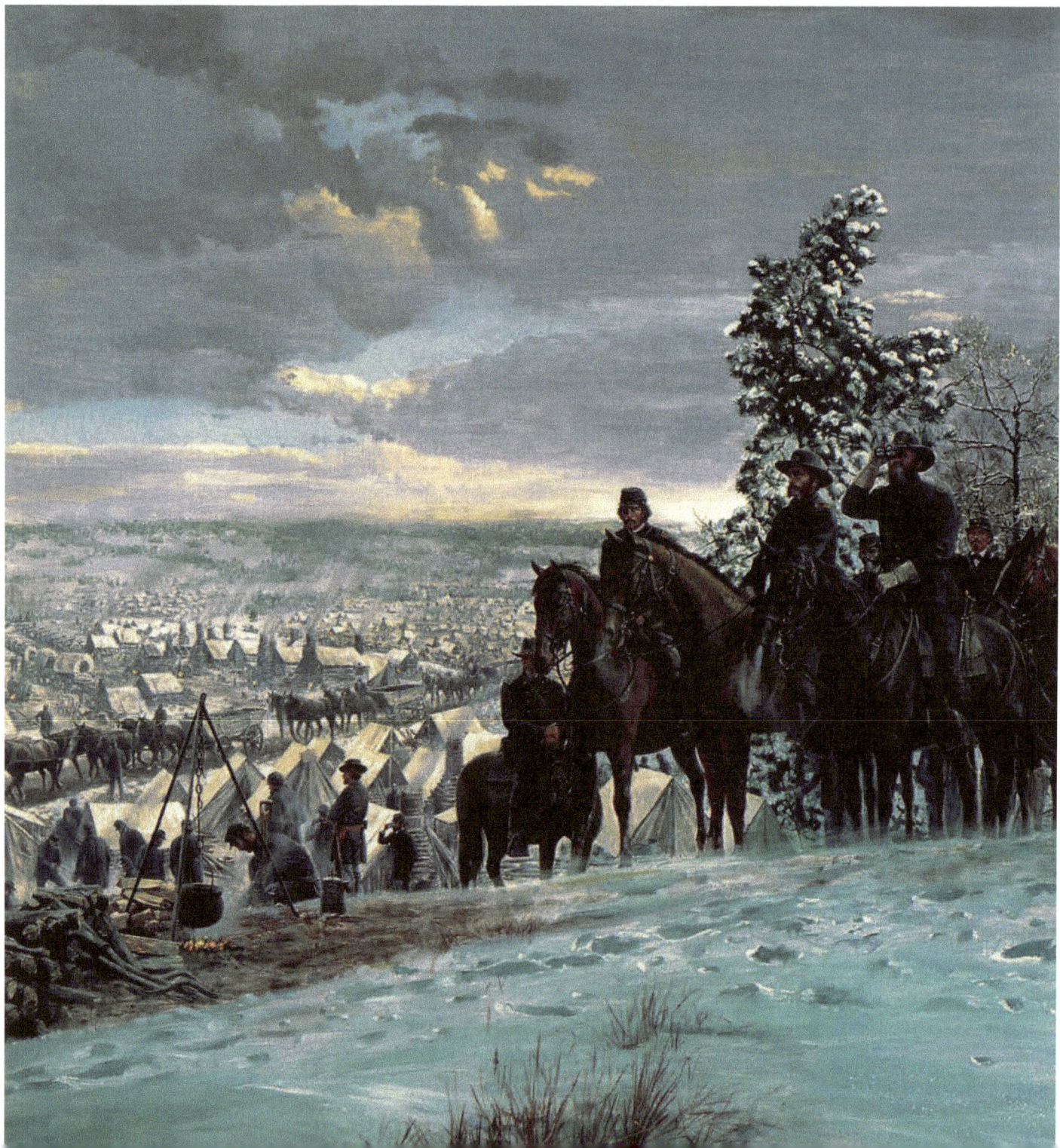

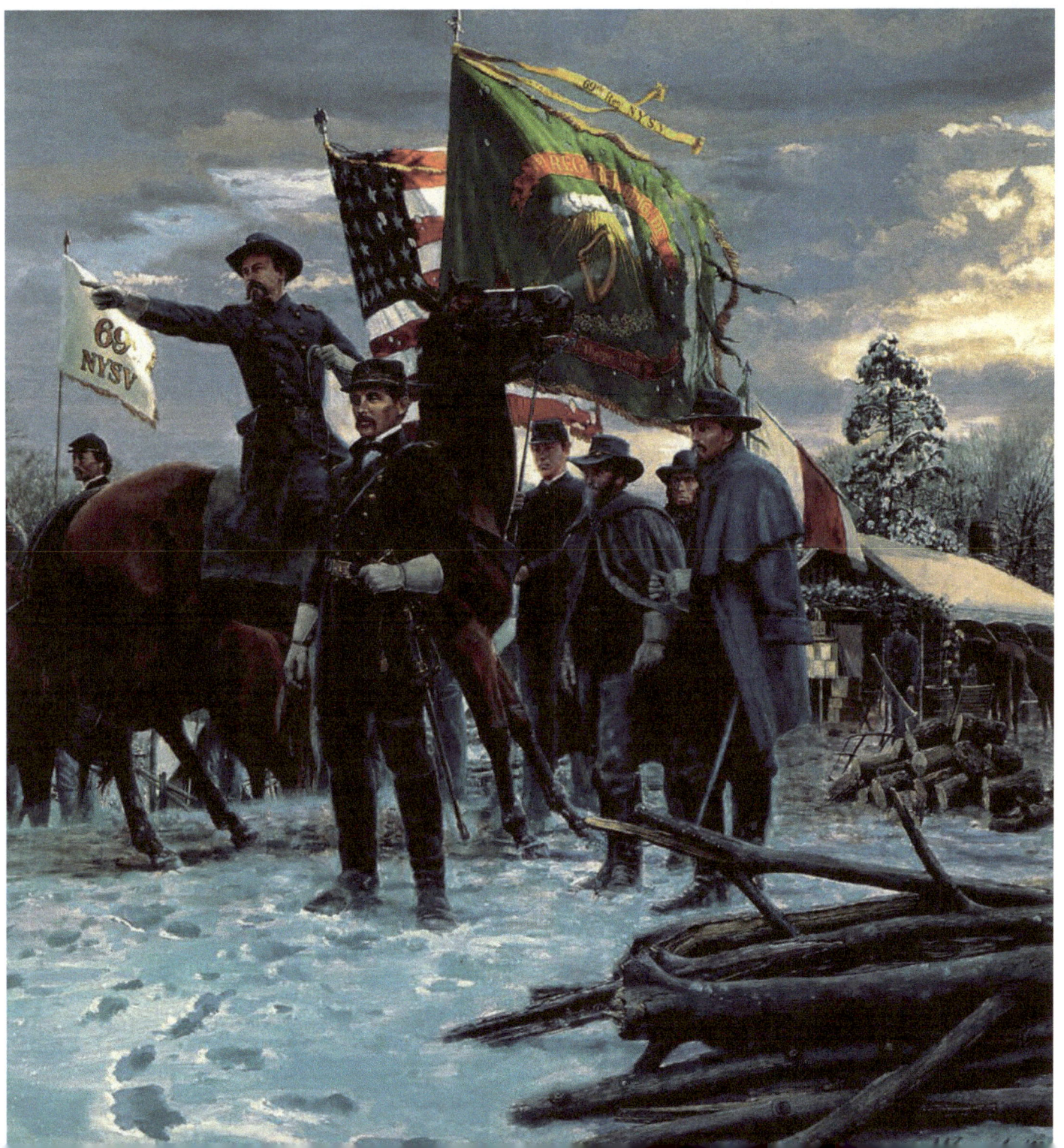

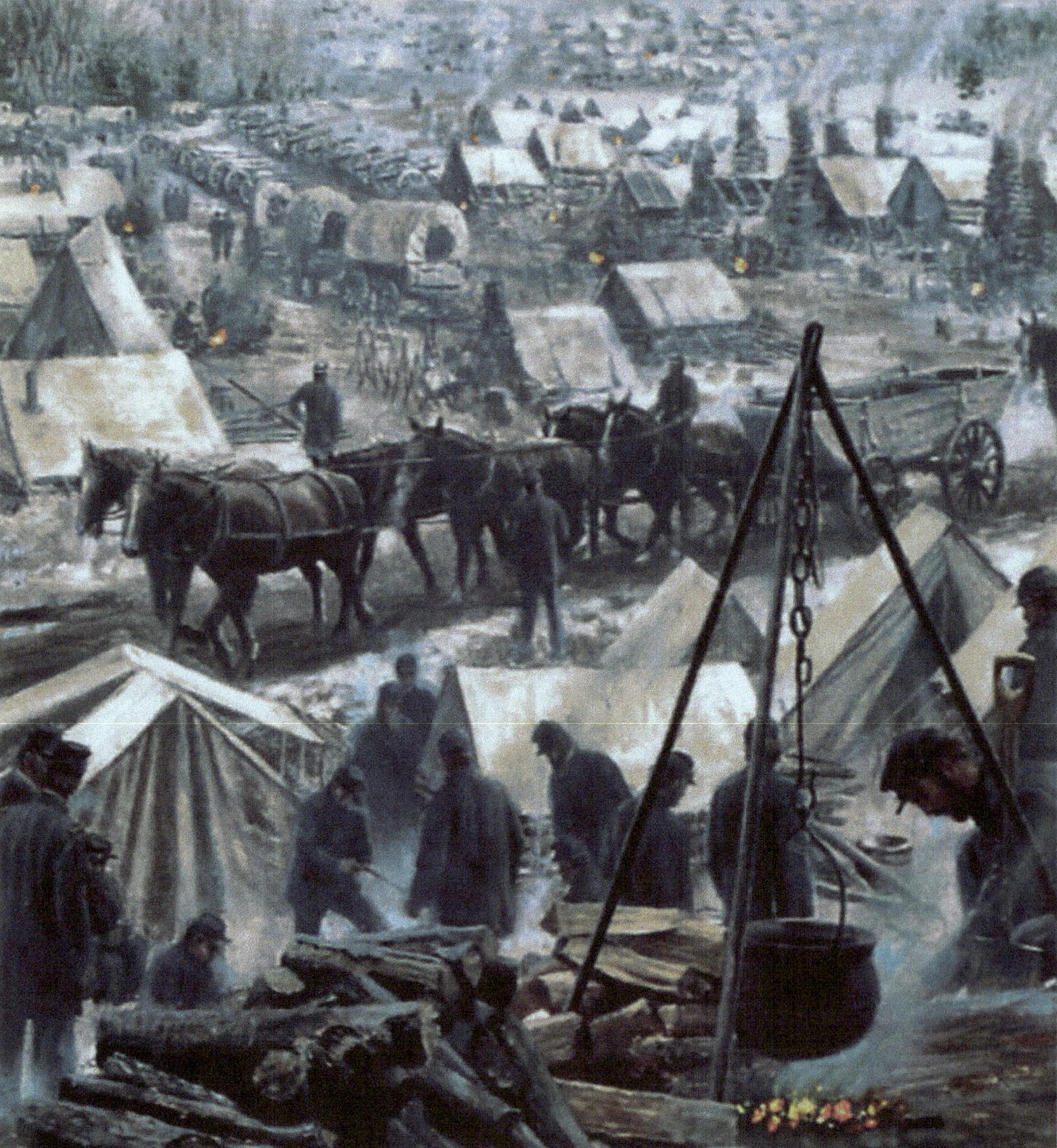

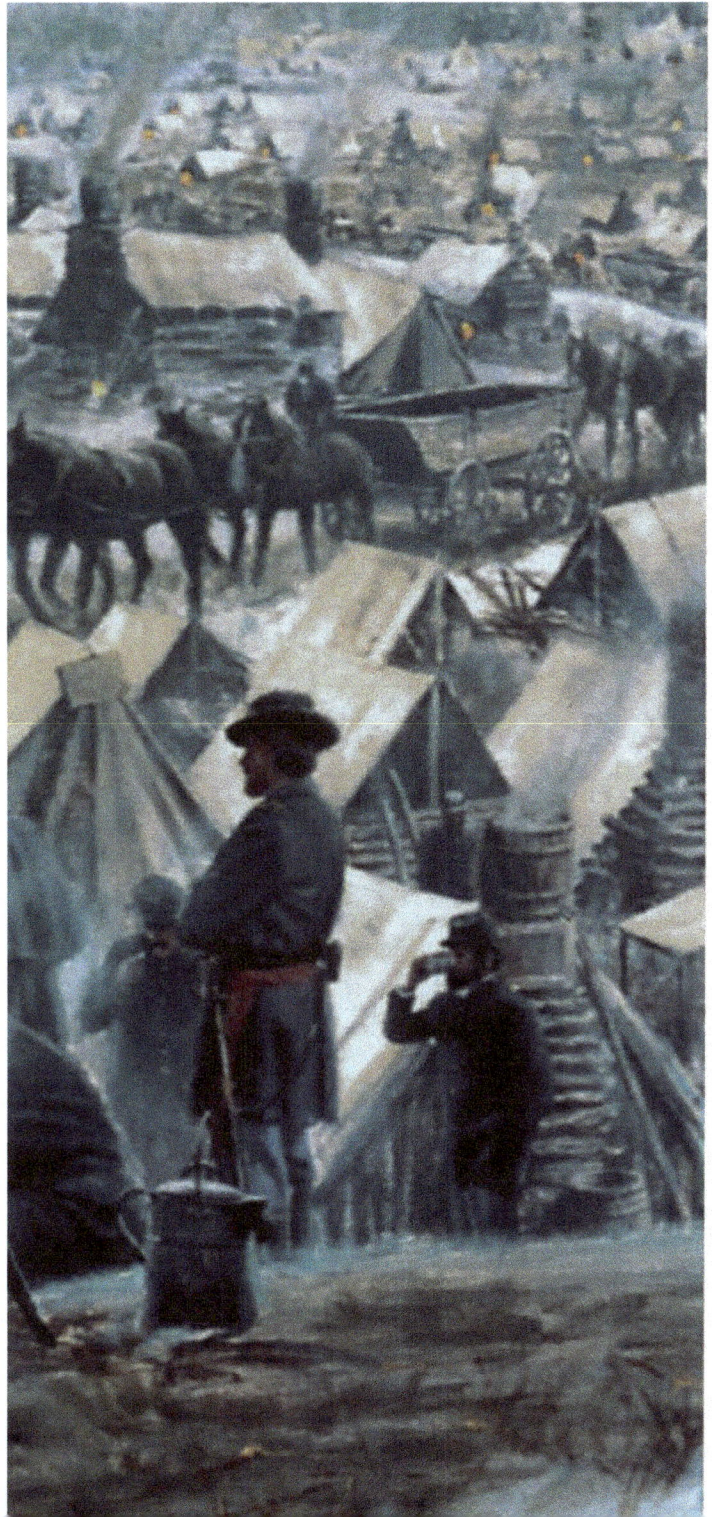

The tears and bullet holes depicted in the green regimental flag are based on the actual flag, which still exists, as do the ribbons. An interesting note is that the flag bears the inscription of the First Regiment; the Sixty-ninth New York was considered the first regiment of the Irish Brigade. The white-and-red headquarters flag replicates the banner of the Second Brigade, First Division, Second Corps. The white marker with the gold "69th NYSV" also still exists.

The new regimental colors were scheduled to be presented in a formal ceremony on December 13, and the brigade's carpenters built a large log hall in their encampment for the festivities. General Burnside had other plans, however. The battle of Fredericksburg commenced on that day, and the Irish Brigade made its deadly assault on Marye's Heights with green sprigs of boxwood in their headgear in place of the missing flags.

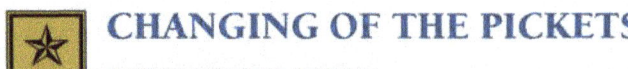

CHANGING OF THE PICKETS

FREDERICKSBURG, VIRGINIA
DECEMBER 6, 1862

2001, oil, 22 x 36

detail, right

IN EARLY December, as winter draped the riverside town in a white cloak, Fredericksburg's residents made do with the ways of war. To avoid attracting Federal artillery fire into the city, Lee maintained a reduced urban presence. Even the few troops detailed for picket duty were careful not to provoke enemy fire. So I devoted this painting to the townspeople of Fredericksburg, because they represented in many ways townspeople both North and South. All Americans made sacrifices during this terrible conflict, and all of them valiantly moved forward with life, enduring sacrifice, and persevered.

To convey this, I chose an ordinary event: the changing of the picket guard. The townspeople are seen gathering at the churches for evening services. Two young boys admire the couriers posed to deliver dispatches to the various commands in the area, and a group of young women make inquires. As darkness descends, the pickets undergoing inspection soon will be en route to relieve the pickets on duty near the river, and the women and children of Fredericksburg—encouraged by their evening worship experiences—will return home to resume their lives between two armies soon to collide.

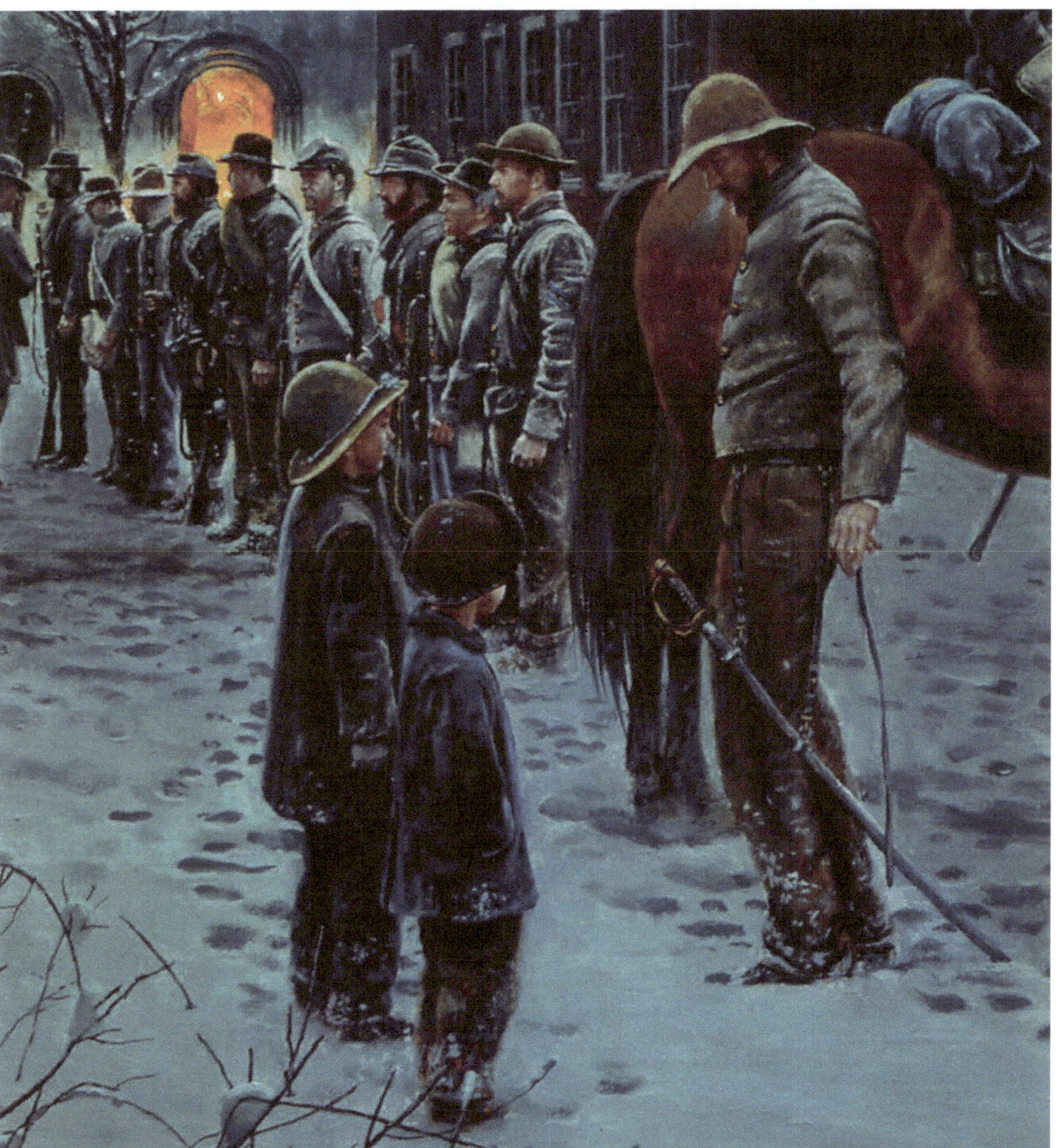

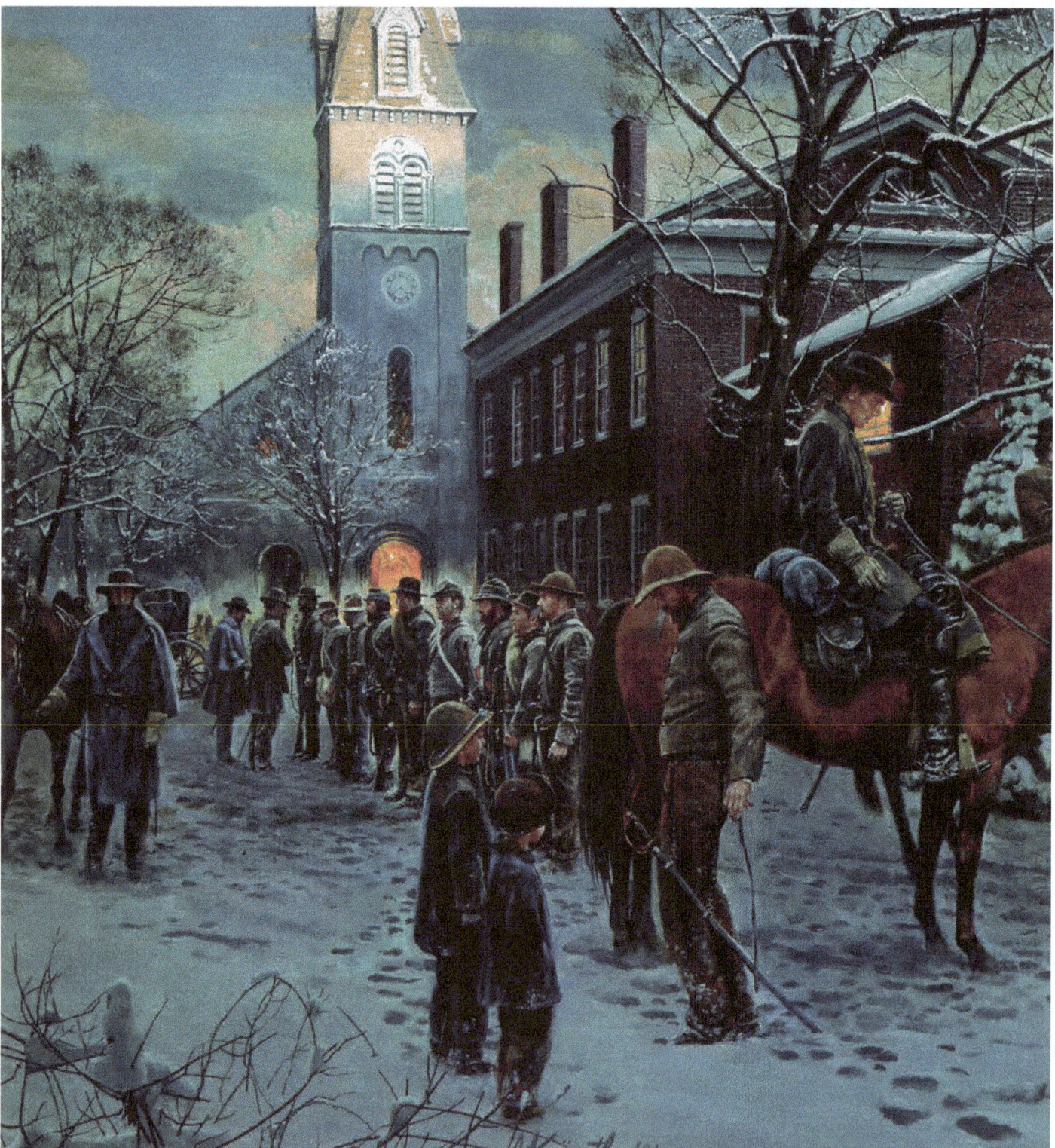

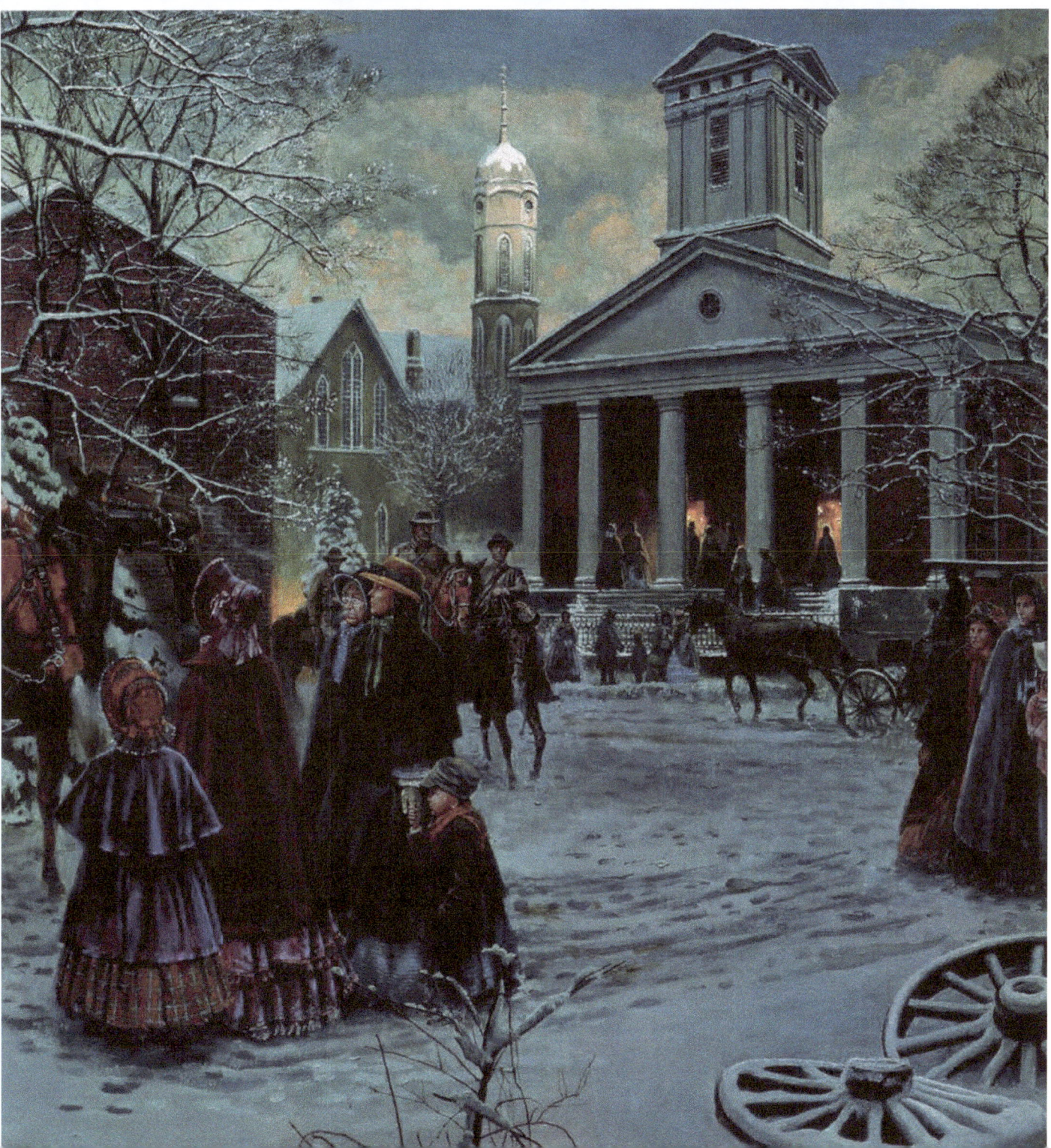

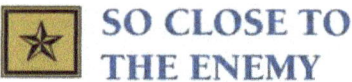

SO CLOSE TO THE ENEMY

FREDERICKSBURG, VIRGINIA
DECEMBER 12, 1862

2006, oil, 26 x 36

ON DECEMBER 12, Robert E. Lee concluded that he needed additional reconnaissance of the enemy—and decided to do it himself. Accompanied by Stonewall Jackson and Maj. Johann Heros von Borcke, Lee moved to within four hundred yards of the Federal line. The three were "so close to the enemy," von Borcke noted, that a vigilant Northern observer could have changed the outcome of the battle.

Most of my snow scenes are set at night. Lee's excursion occurred near midday, after the morning mist had cleared, which enabled me to paint the scene in bright sunlight.

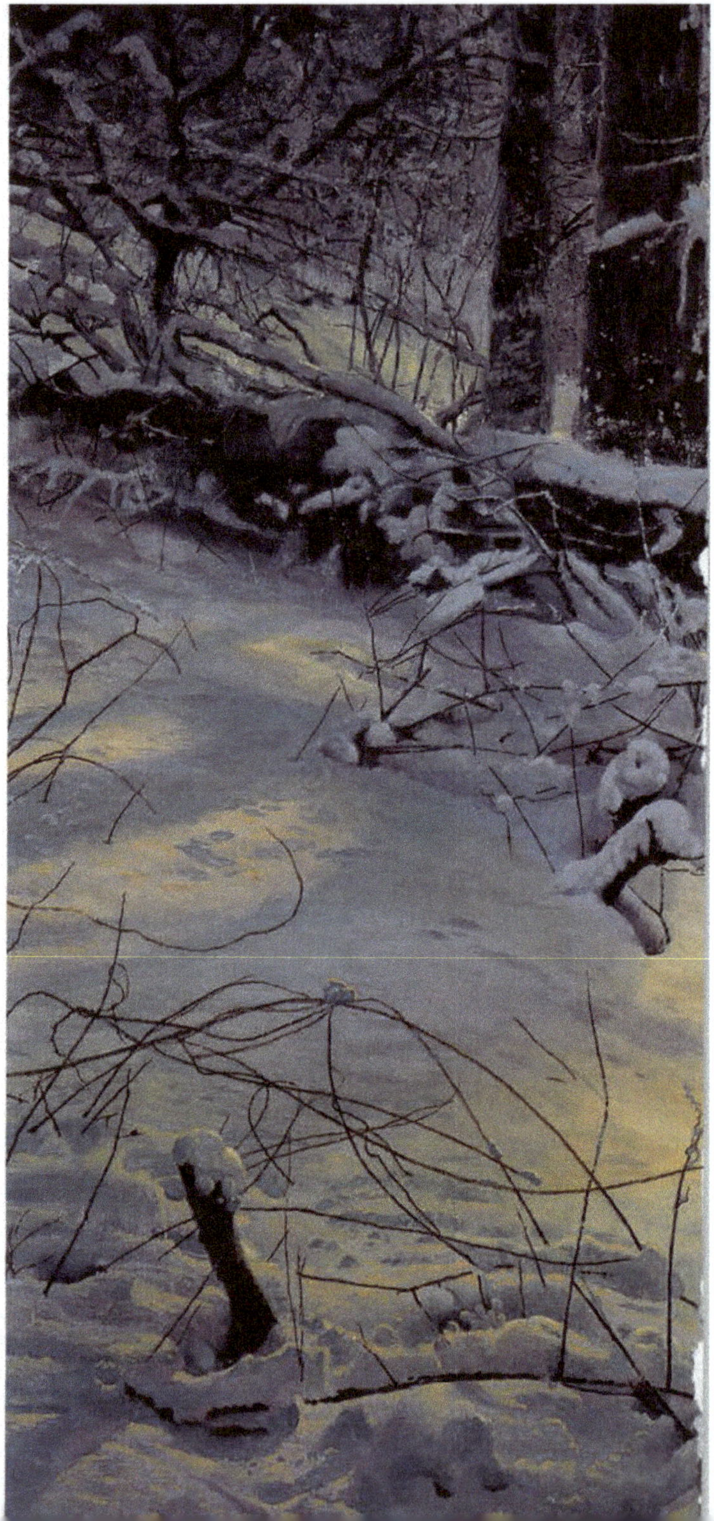

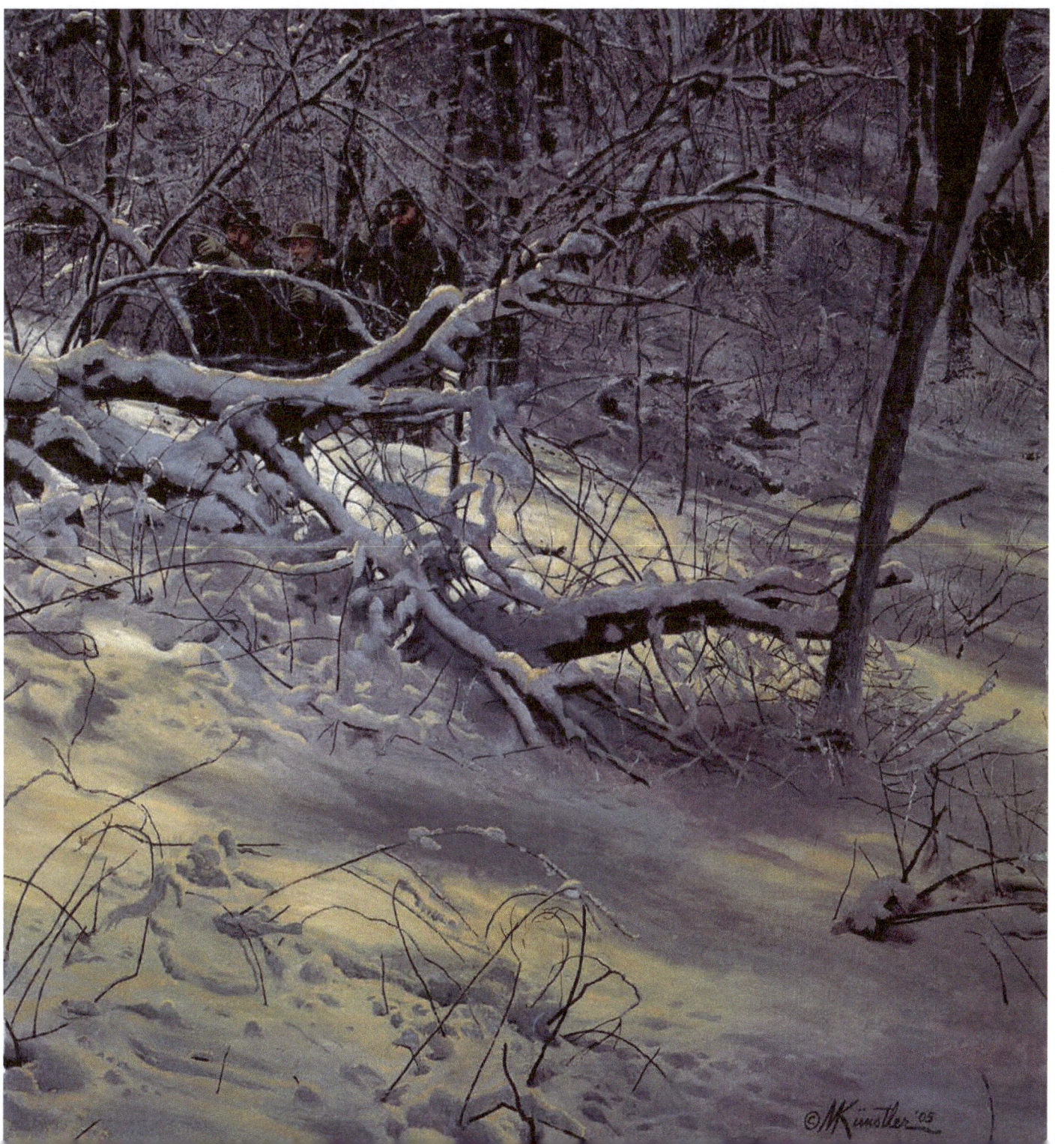

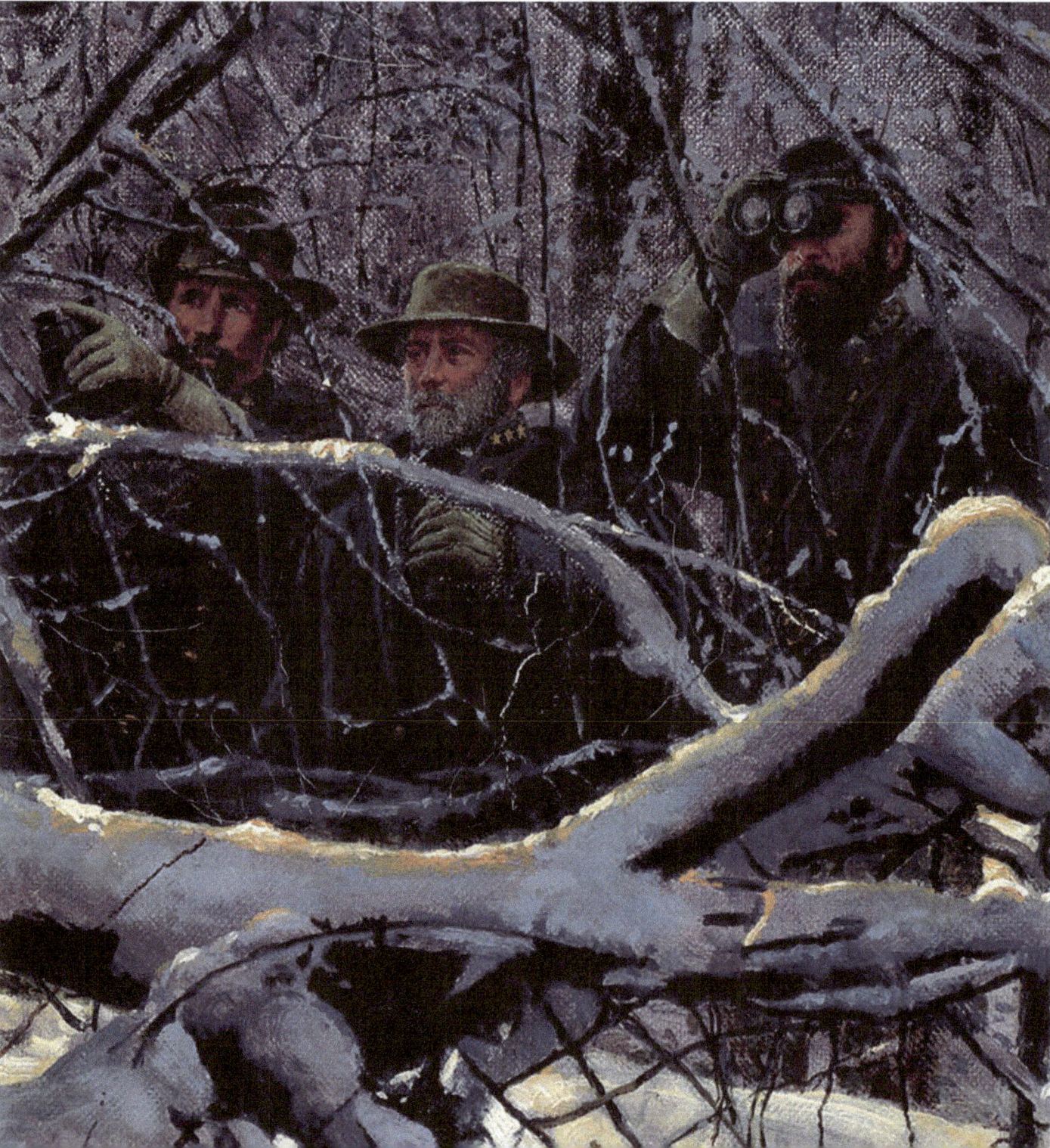

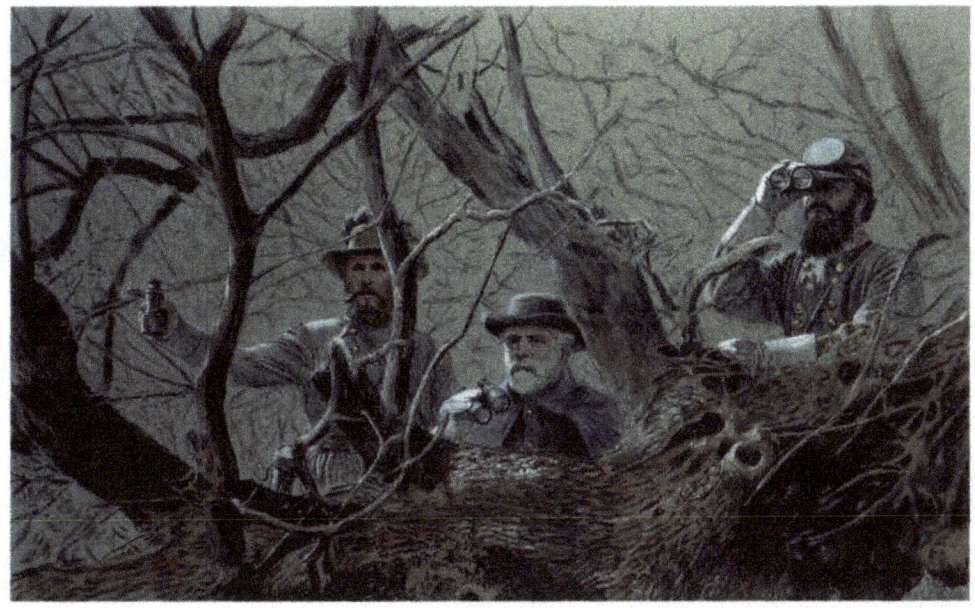

THE SCOUTS OF FREDERICKSBURG

STUDY

1995, mixed media, 17 x 24

I decided to feature the snowy landscape and camouflage the three officers in the shadows of the woods. I used the warmer tones of the three figures to contrast with the cool colors of the snow and trees, which gradually leads the viewer's eye to the trio. Lee is the central figure and the focus of attention, thus I designed the branches to point toward him. As viewers are drawn into the painting, they eventually see the mounted escorts in the background.

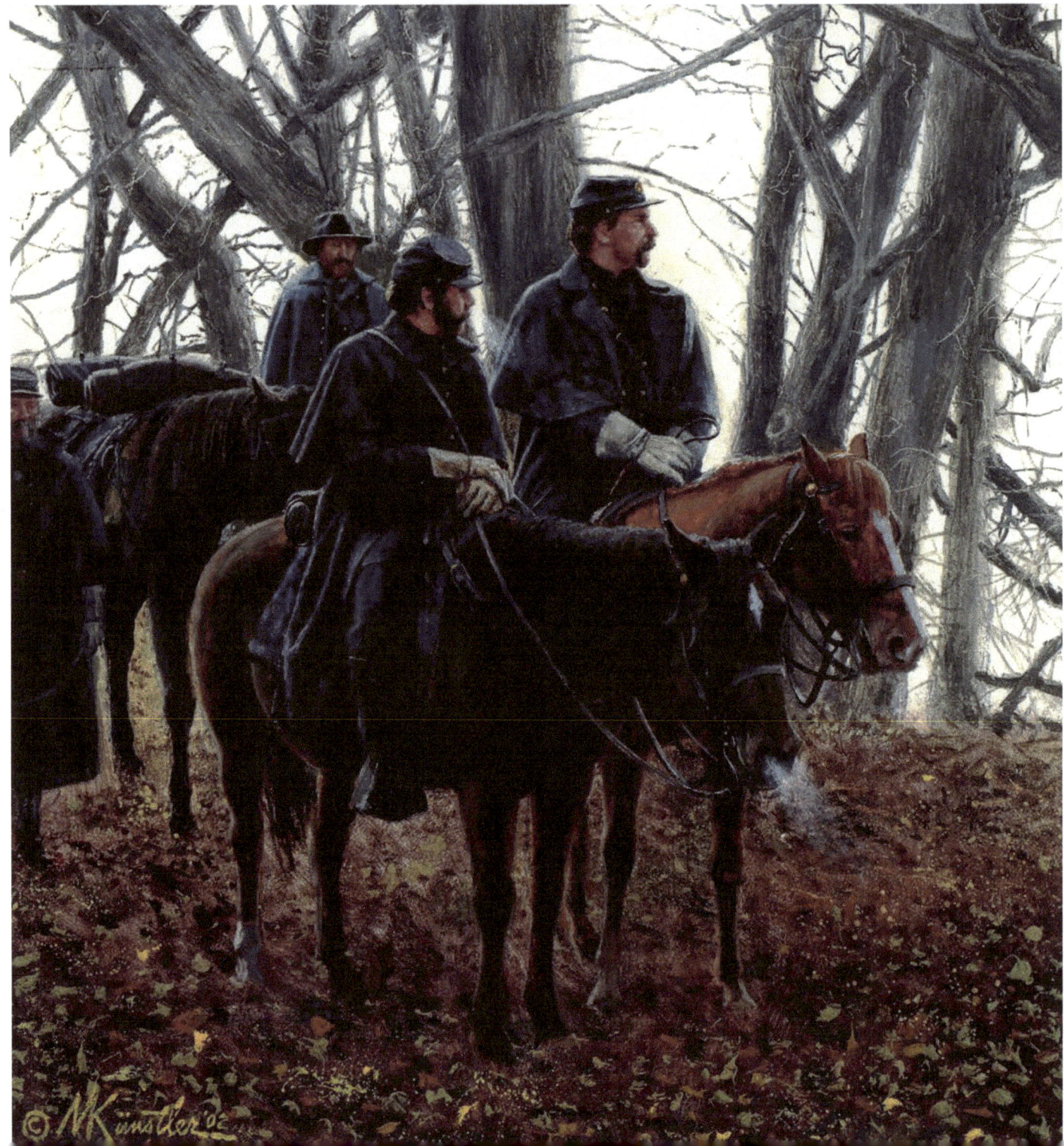

LIEUTENANT COLONEL J. L. CHAMBERLAIN AND STAFF

DECEMBER 1862

2002, oil, 11 x 9¼

JOSHUA LAWRENCE CHAMBERLAIN was one of the least likely Union heroes of the war. And I find him to be one of my most fascinating subjects. In 1862, he was the lieutenant colonel of the Twentieth Maine Infantry, which that winter found its camp about three miles from Fredericksburg.

In the predawn hours of December 11, Chamberlain's men from Maine marched five miles to Burnside's headquarters, which overlooked the city. A misty fog offered slim protection to the Union engineers at work on the pontoon bridges the troops needed to cross the Rappahannock. Confederate sharpshooters hindered their progress, and Federal gunners fired on the buildings from which the snipers were targeting the engineers.

Chamberlain and an aide ventured to the nearby heights. As the fog lifted, they glimpsed artillery shells bursting over the scenic city and scattered fires generating billowing columns of smoke. Waterfront warehouses exploded into splinters as Chamberlain saw riflemen scurry in the streets. Beyond the city, he saw a rolling plain with scattered houses rise and become a range of hills. And on the closest ridge, he saw Lee's silent gun batteries and waiting army.

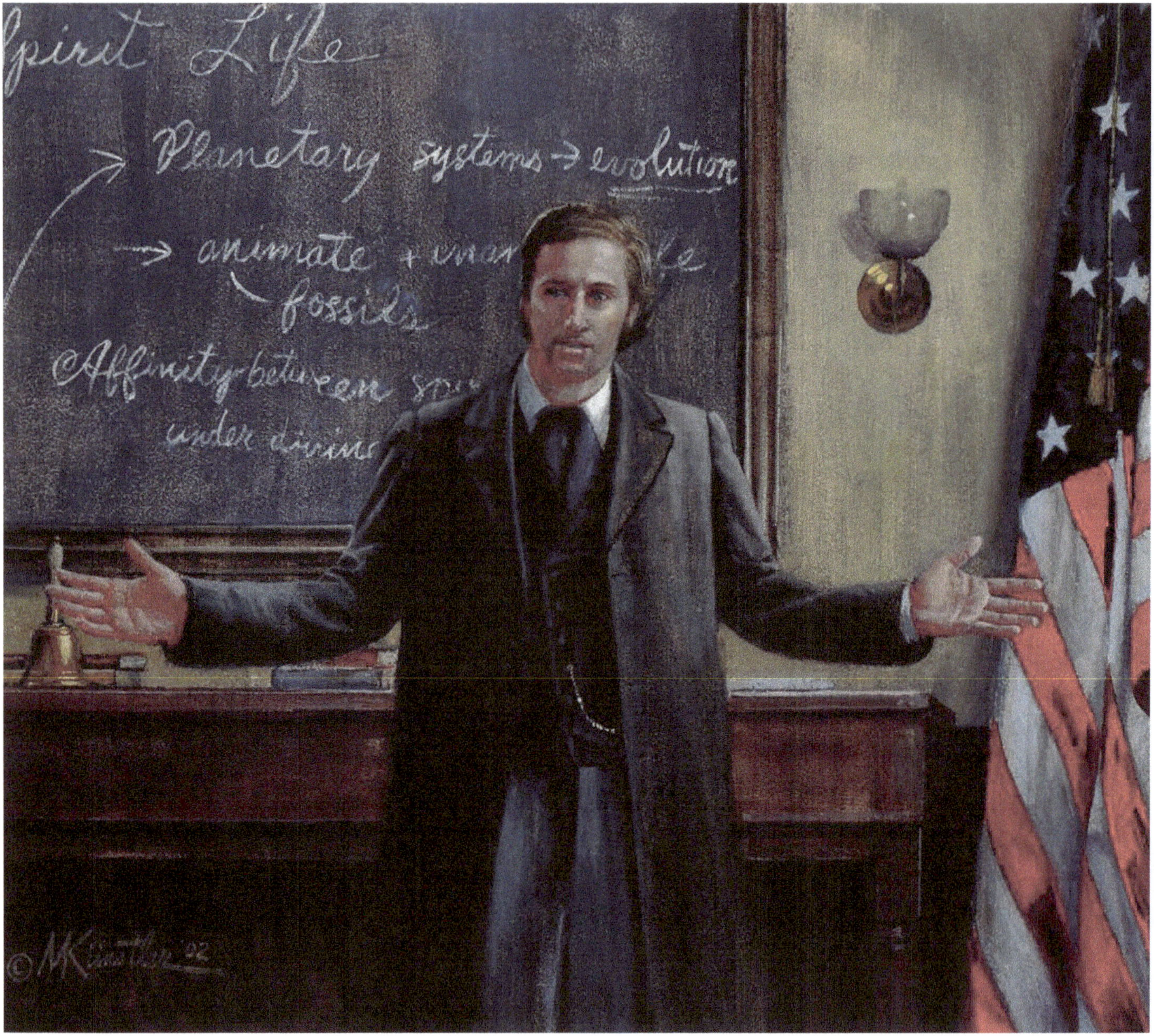
pirit Life
Planetary systems → evolution
fossils
Affinity between

THE PROFESSOR FROM MAINE

JOSHUA L. CHAMBERLAIN AT BOWDOIN COLLEGE

2002, oil on board, 9¼ x 10¾

CHAMBERLAIN WAS like many men who surprised their colleagues with their accomplishments during the war. A stammering speech impediment early in life made him somewhat of a loner who lacked self-assurance and self-assertion when around strangers. As was the case with Thomas J. Jackson, Chamberlain preferred solitude.

He was born in Maine in 1828, and school lessons and farmwork occupied his early years. In school, he demonstrated a gift for languages, eventually mastering nine.

His father wanted him to go to West Point; his mother wanted him to enter the ministry. Chamberlain wanted neither. So he delayed making a decision by entering Bowdoin College. It was a typical liberal arts institution that stressed classical languages and mathematics. After his graduation in 1855, Chamberlain joined the faculty. By 1860, he was chair of the department of modern languages and contemplating a leave of absence to study in Europe.

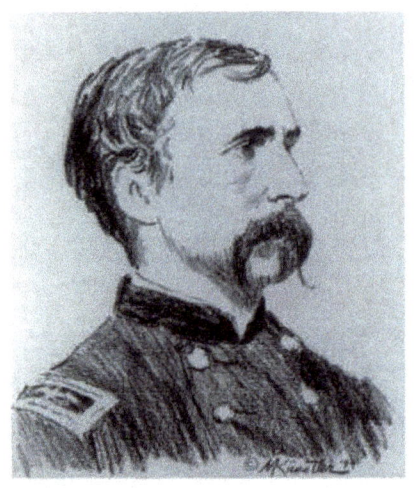

When the war erupted in 1861, Chamberlain did not answer the initial call for volunteers. But he became increasingly anxious when the war continued into 1862, and his conscience burned at his doing nothing for the Union cause.

In the summer of 1862, he visited Governor Israel Washburn and tendered his services. Washburn offered him the colonelcy of one of the new regiments being formed, but Chamberlain knew that he did not yet know how to command. He knew how to learn, and so he requested the position of a second-in-command. A week later, he accepted appointment as lieutenant colonel of the Twentieth Maine.

The regiment's colonel was Adelbert Ames, a high graduate in the West Point Class of May 1861 who had been wounded in the battle of First Manassas and awarded the Medal of Honor for his actions that day. Ames drilled the regiment by day and devoted his nights to tutoring Chamberlain on regulations, strategy, and tactics. A month after its formation, the Twentieth Maine arrived in Washington and became part of the Fifth Corps, which then marched to Maryland and was held in reserve during the September 14–17 Antietam campaign. Although not engaged in the battle, the sights of the battlefield were unsettling.

Chamberlain's baptism under fire came later. At Fredericksburg.

FACING ➤

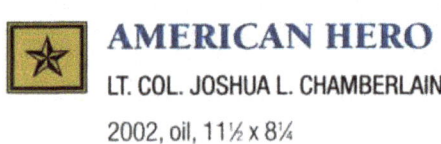

AMERICAN HERO
LT. COL. JOSHUA L. CHAMBERLAIN
2002, oil, 11½ x 8¼

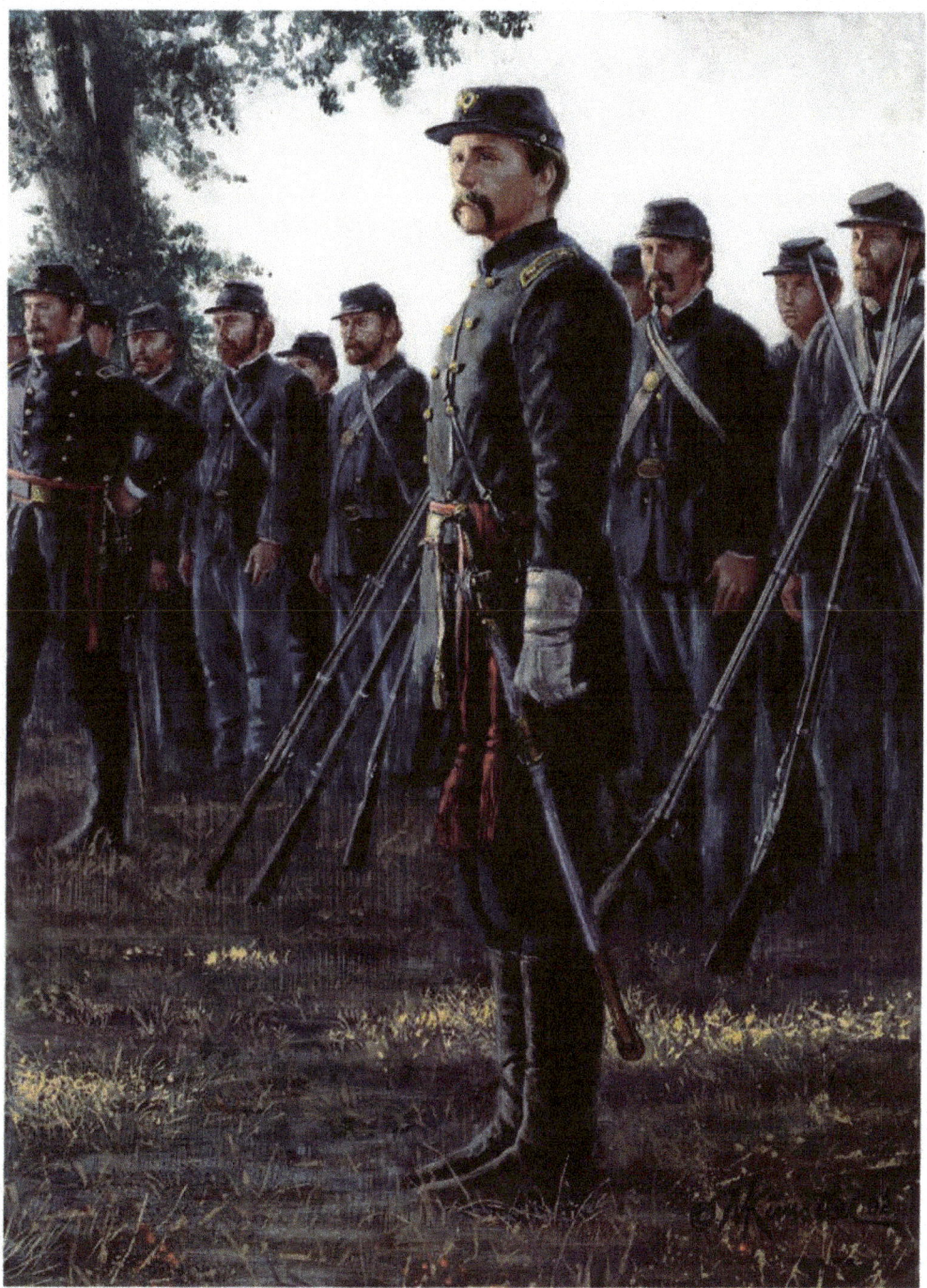

LEE'S LIEUTENANTS

FREDERICKSBURG, VIRGINIA
DECEMBER 13, 1862

1997, oil, 30 x 34

detail, right

O N THE morning of December 13, Stonewall Jackson surprised everyone by wearing a new uniform. The gold-trimmed coat was a gift from Stuart; new trousers and boots had been given to him by several grateful people of the Shenandoah Valley; and a new cap with a wide gold band had been sent by his wife, Anna. The general also wore a new sword and spurs. Thus attired, he inspected his troops, garnering scrutiny from men long accustomed to seeing their general less finely attired. One feared that Jackson "wouldn't get down to work" because he was so well dressed. Another said, "He looked so unlike our 'Old Jack' that very few noticed him and none recognized him until he had passed." Still, the vast majority cheered at the striking sight of their commander as he departed for Lee's headquarters and a final briefing with Longstreet and Stuart.

Stuart genially complimented Jackson on his appearance. When others made similar comments, Jackson muttered, "I believe it was some of my friend Stuart's doing."

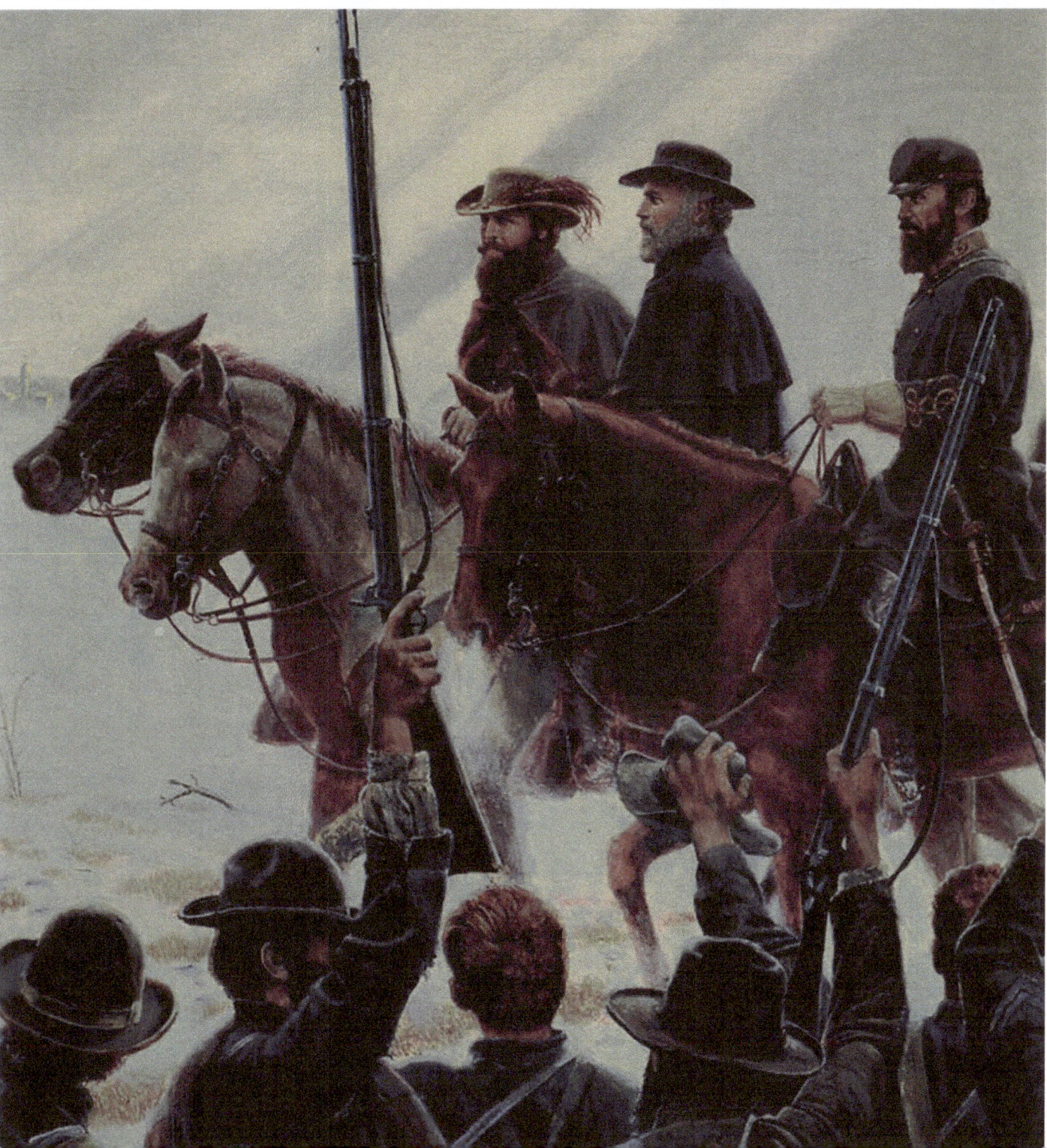

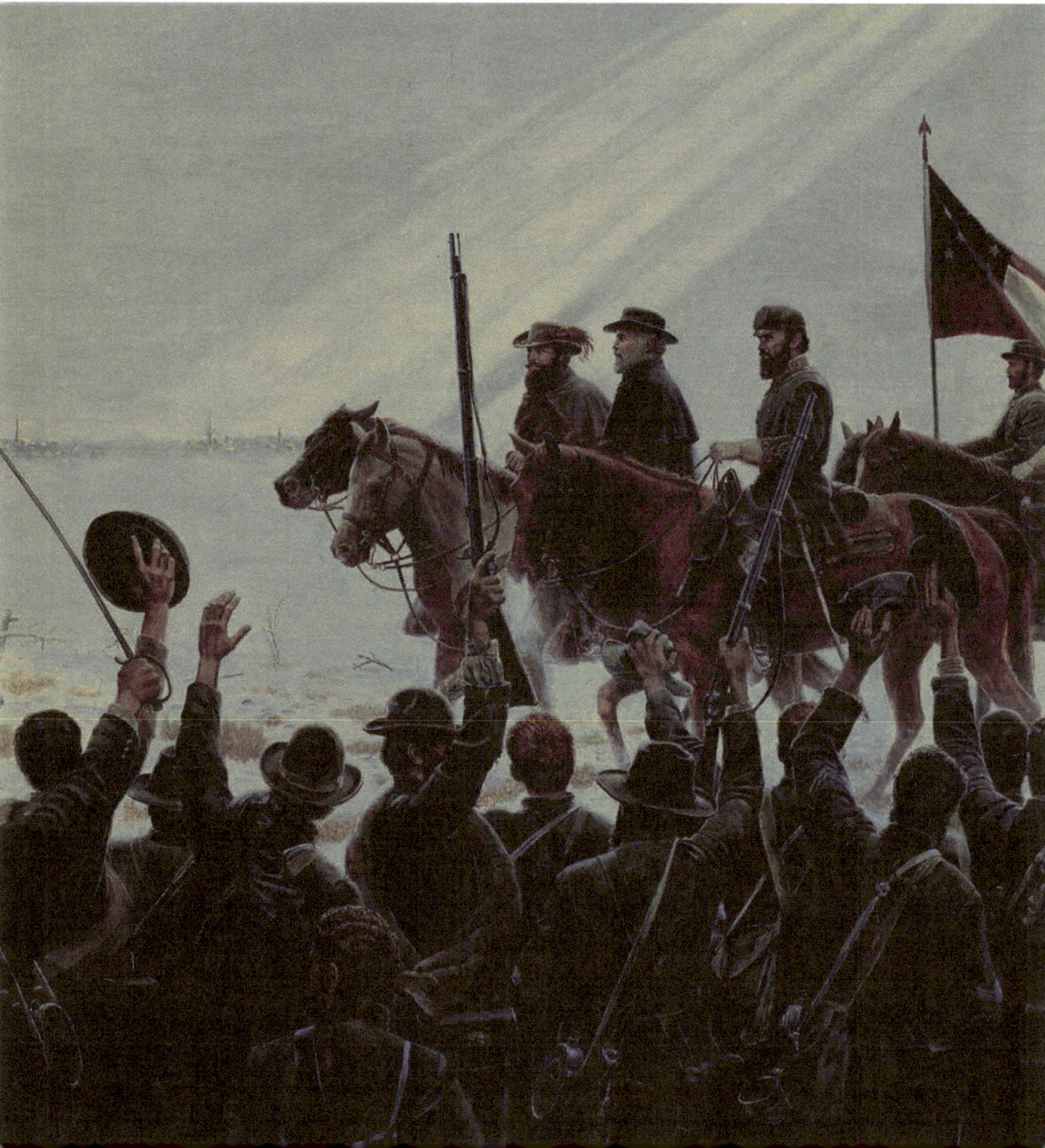

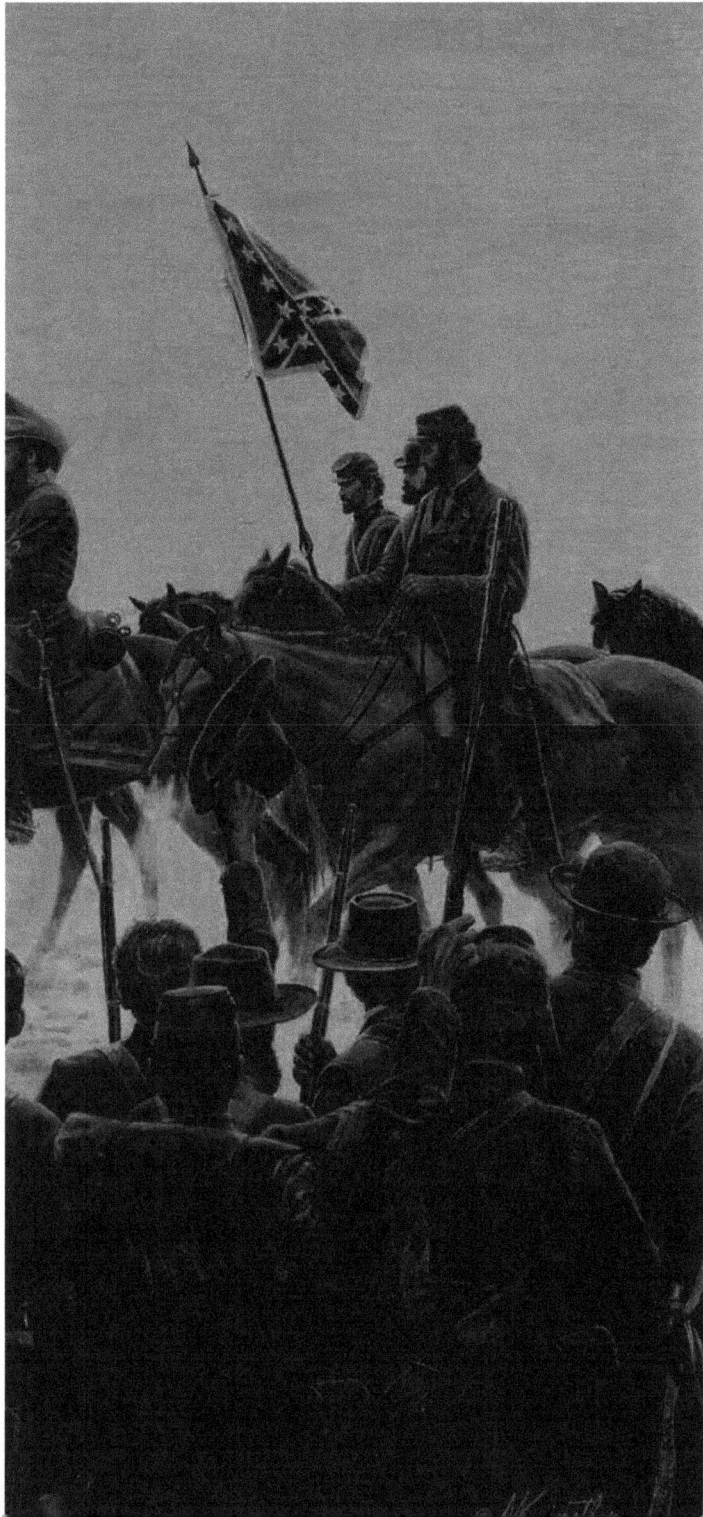

The four men reviewed their options, weighing the strengths and weaknesses of their positions. Both Jackson and Stuart urged Lee to attack. A dense fog hung over the city, and both commanders saw it as a veil through which they could surprise the Federals. But Lee appreciated the strength of his position on the high ground overlooking the city and saw that the numerically superior Union troops would not erode it. A counterattack would be in order after the enemy had exhausted themselves.

Longstreet announced his suspicions that the assault would begin against the right side of the line: Jackson's position. Jackson concurred. And so Lee indicated that he would inspect the area shortly.

When the council concluded and the generals began to return to their commands, in the words of Douglas Southall Freeman, "drab daylight began to soften into gold under the rays of a mounting sun." Fredericksburg's church steeples emerged in the distance above the morning mist. I had seen this lighting effect myself when I visited Lee's Hill, the site of the general's headquarters.

For the first time since painting *"I Will Be Moving Within the Hour,"* I was able to paint Lee with Stuart, Jackson, and Longstreet together. The back view of the Confederate troops was chosen deliberately so that no faces are showing, which keeps the focus on the generals. I also wanted to show the respect and affection that Lee's men held for their commander and their field commanders. The painting depicts Lee's lieutenants as they appeared as well as the boundless confidence in which the rank and file held them.

Jackson returned to his lines around 9:00 a.m. One of his men recalled: "He suddenly appeared in our front with his cap pulled down over his forehead, almost hiding his eyes. The troops cheered him wildly. He gave us a sharp, searching, but not unkindly look, raised his cap, and rode rapidly on. His eyes seemed to be on fire, so eager was he for the fray."

The battle of Fredericksburg began around 10:00 a.m. against Jackson's position south of the city. He held.

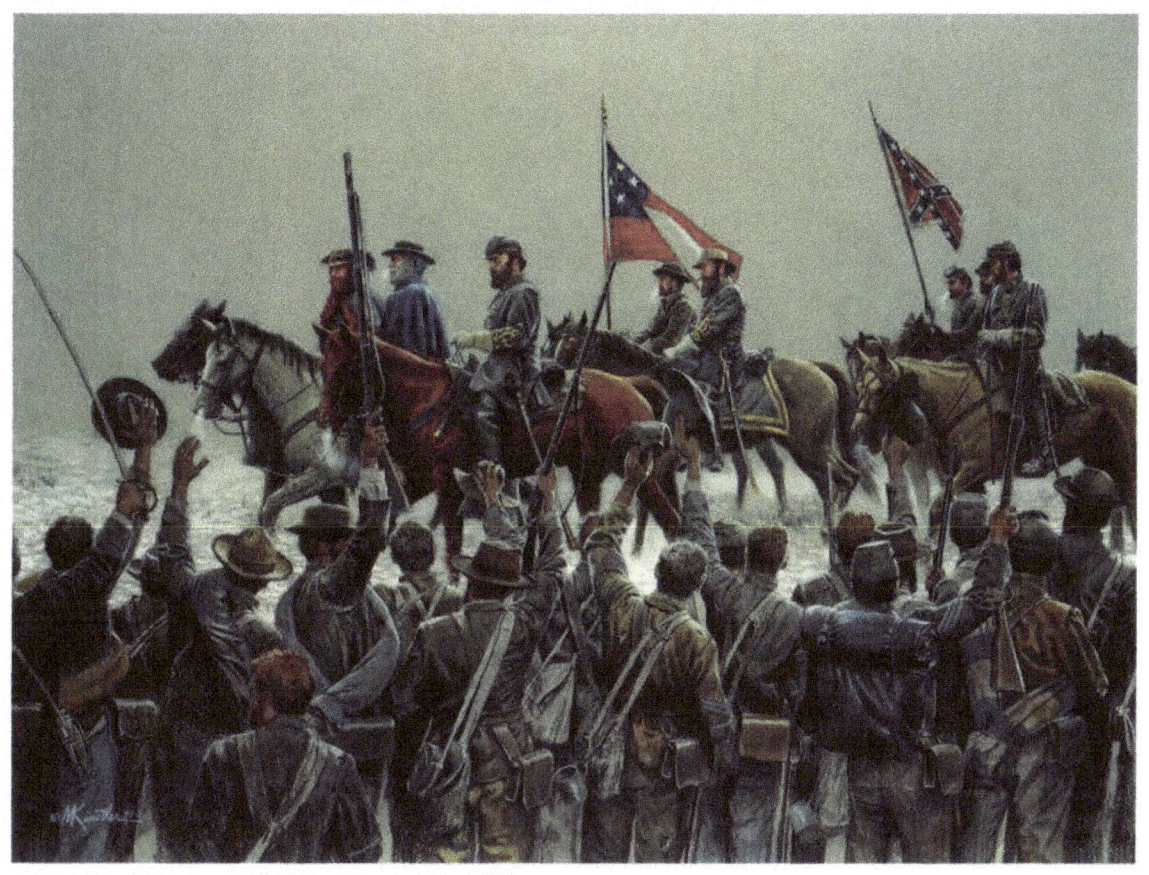

LEE'S LIEUTENANTS

STUDY

1997, oil, 30 x 34

"... WAR IS SO TERRIBLE"

LONGSTREET AND LEE
FREDERICKSBURG, VIRGINIA
DECEMBER 13, 1862

1995, oil, 22 x 34

detail, right

ROBERT E. LEE viewed the battle from a small hill near the center of the Confederate line. Afterward known as Lee's Hill, the eminence offered the commanding general a clear view of Longstreet's position to the left and Jackson's command to the right.

From his vantage point, Lee witnessed the initial action of the morning. The fog lifted first to his right, and three Union divisions advanced in parade fashion. In reply, two horse-drawn guns began to maneuver and fire from various positions in front of Jackson's line, targeting the Federals' left flank. Union batteries opened on the duo of Confederate guns, but the Southerners continued to fire and move and fire and move, even after one weapon had been disabled. The single gun retired only after the gunners had exhausted their ammunition. Lee viewed all of this through his field glasses then said to those around him, "It is glorious to see such courage in one so young!"

The Union guns opened on Jackson's line while the infantry regrouped, attacked, and were then repelled. As they fell back, an attack began on the left, against Longstreet's corps, beginning the first of many futile charges to-

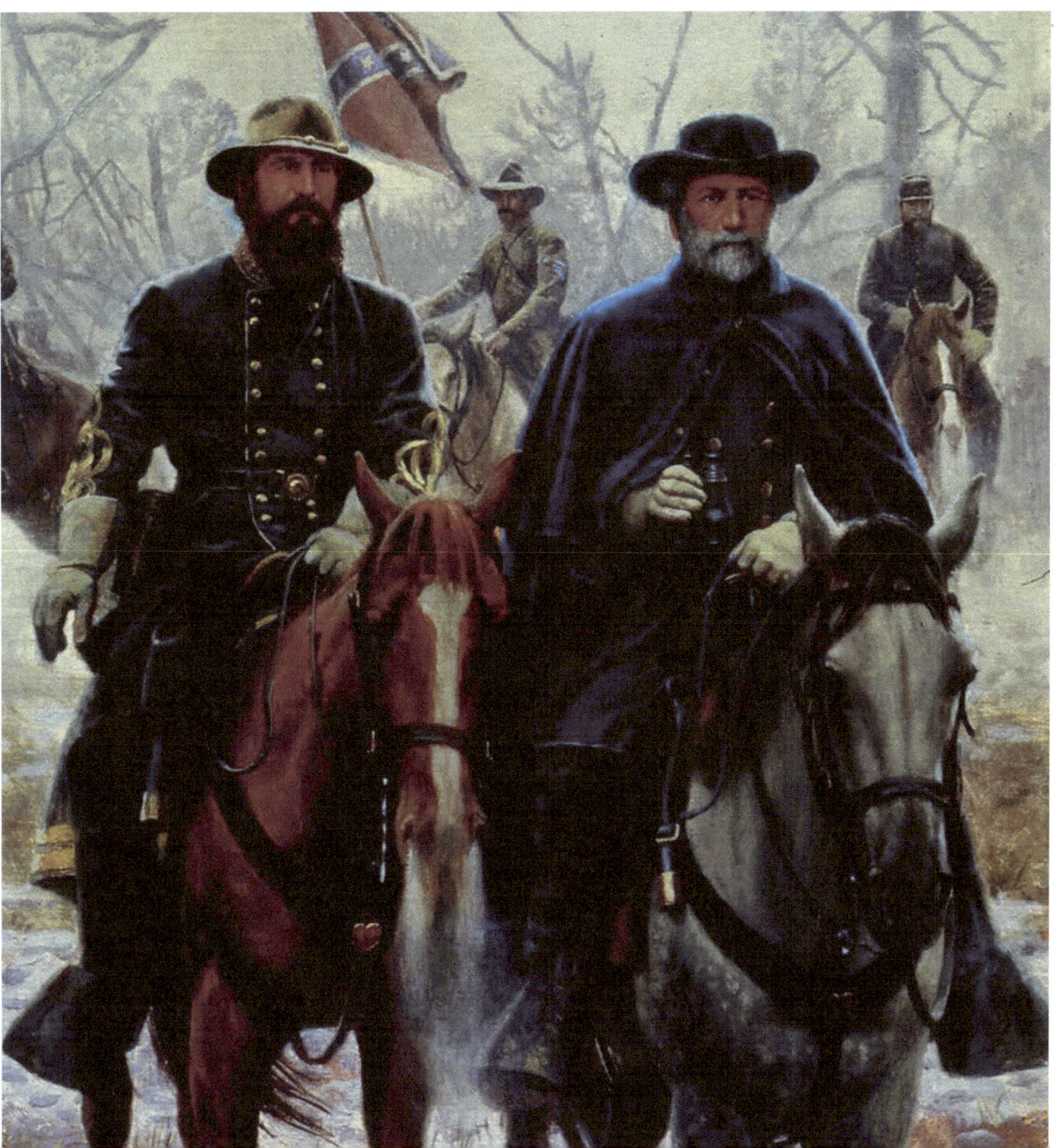

ward Marye's Heights. After the third assault, Lee said to Longstreet, "They are massing very heavily and will break your line, I am afraid." But the corps commander replied, "General, if you put every man now on the other side of the Potomac in that field to approach me over that same line, and give me plenty of ammunition, I will kill them all before they reach my line. Look to your right; you are in some danger there. But not on my line."

To the right, just before 1:00 p.m., Lee saw Union artillery begin a new shelling of Jackson's corps and swarms of Federal troops rush the Confederate position and then concentrate on a wooded area. With the fighting out of view, Lee could only wonder how Jackson was faring. Another assault then began against Marye's Heights, and Union gunners opened fire across the whole front. A shell thudded into the ground close to Lee, but it did not

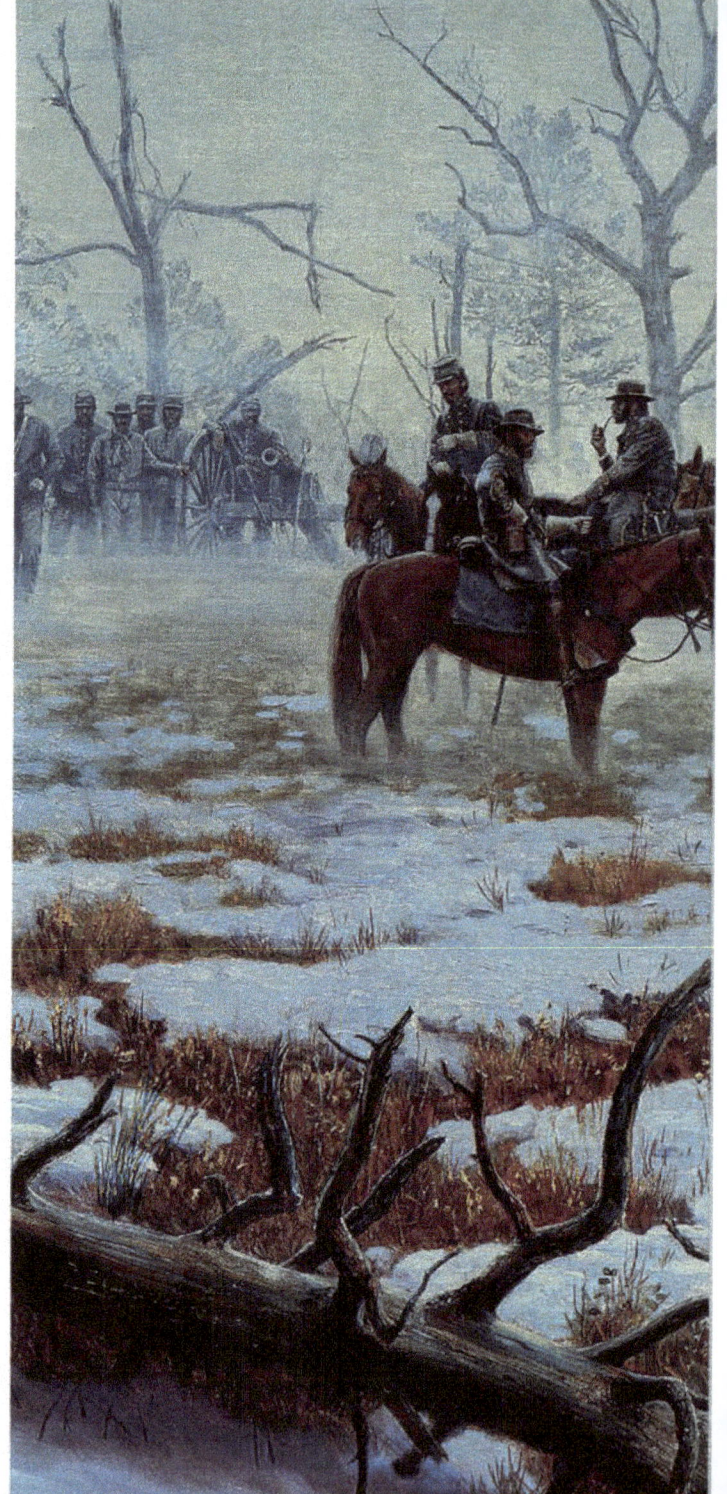

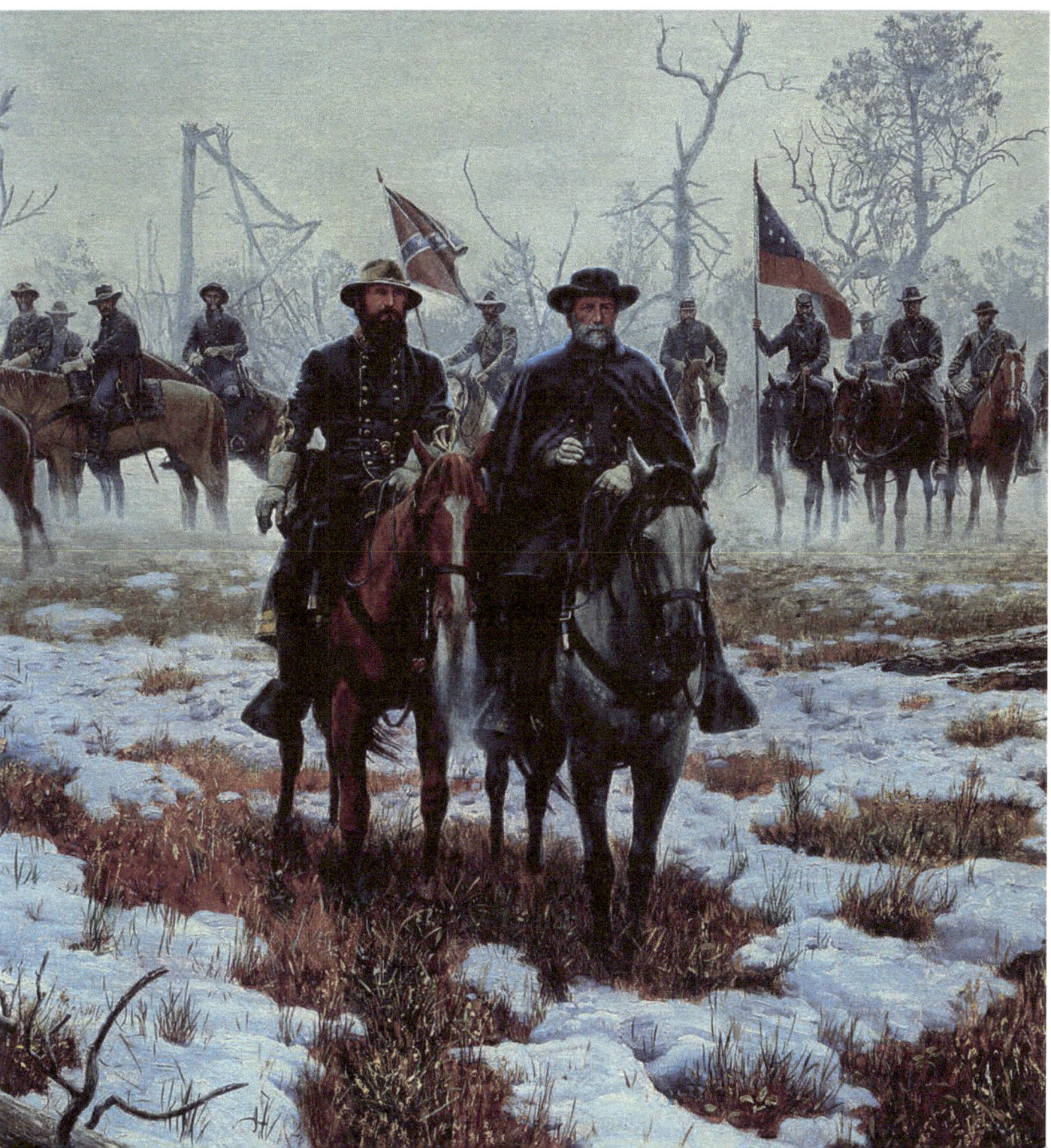

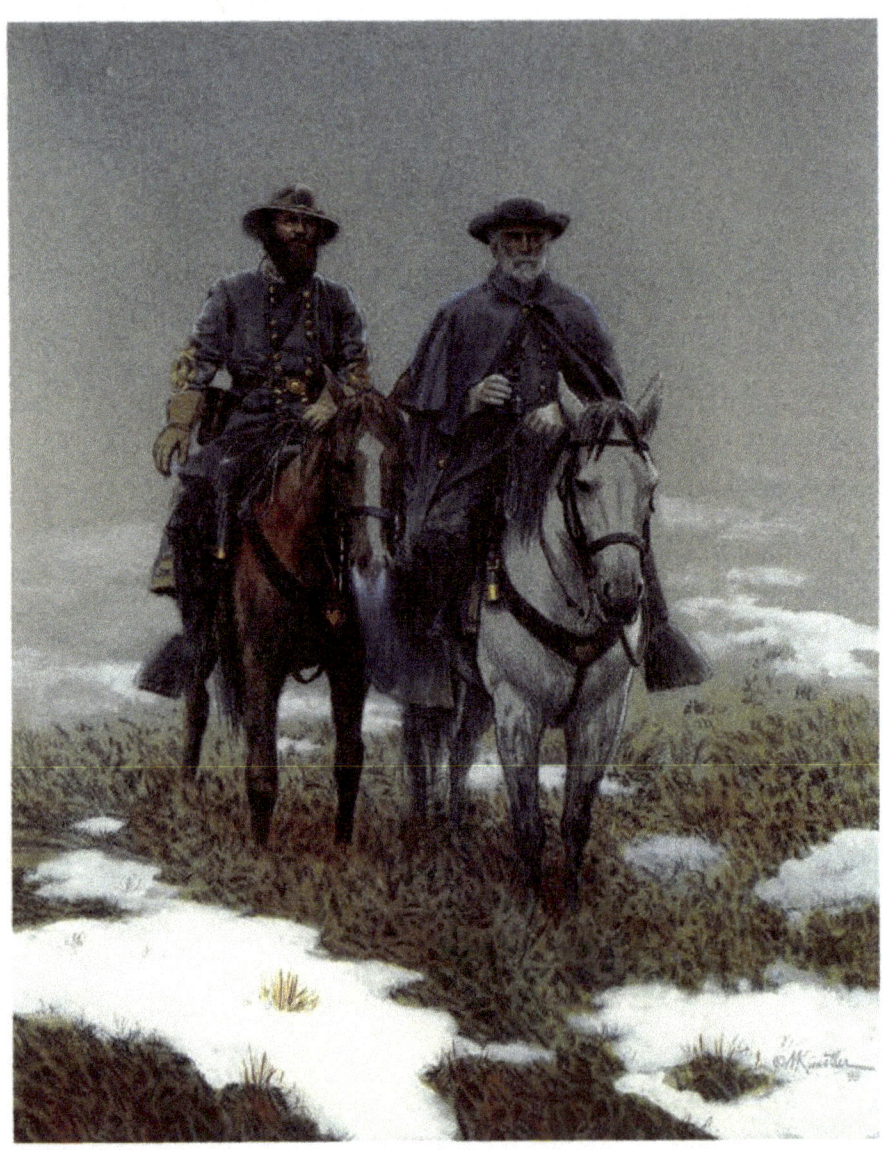

". . .WAR IS SO TERRIBLE"

STUDY

1995, mixed media,

24 x 18½

explode. A nearby cannon burst, its breech fragmenting and filling the air with shrapnel. None of the gunners or the generals were injured.

There was still the question of how the fighting was going on the right, and then the Rebel Yell could be heard over the deafening sound of artillery. A few minutes later, Union troops were fleeing from the woods they had entered, with Jackson's men in pursuit.

At this moment, Lee biographer Douglas Southall Freeman says, "Lee's eyes flashed as he saw them, and the blood of 'Light-Horse Harry' [his father] fought in his veins with the calmer strain of the peace-loving Carters [his mother's family]. Turning to Longstreet he revealed the whole man in a single brief sentence: 'It is well that war is so terrible—we should grow too fond of it.'"

These words sum up the man's character. In spite of the success his army was having, he never overlooked the horrors of war. For this reason, I chose to depict Lee and Longstreet as they looked out over the battlefield from Lee's Hill. In addition to the generals and their attending staffs, I also included the gun positions and crews in the painting. Federal artillery had shelled Lee's Hill, so I placed the twisted and wrecked trees in the picture to add depth, authenticity, and the feeling of imminent danger.

This is one of the few paintings I've done that incorporates fog, a difficult effect to achieve. In the end, I tried to faithfully capture an unforgettable moment of the war, one that characterizes Lee. It also complements my earlier work, *Lee at Fredericksburg,* in which the general arrives with Longstreet. It seemed only fitting to have the two of them together in this depiction of the climax of the battle.

IN THE HANDS OF PROVIDENCE

CHAMBERLAIN AT FREDERICKSBURG

DECEMBER 13, 1862

2003, oil, 24 x 38

detail, right

By 2:00 p.m. Burnside shifted his attack to Longstreet's front on Marye's Heights and sent wave after wave against that bulwark. For hours, Lt. Col. Joshua L. Chamberlain and the Twentieth Maine awaited the command to enter the fray.

In the late afternoon they moved forward in the final charge of the battle. Artillery raked their ranks as they ran "over fences and through hedges," Chamberlain remembered, "over bodies of dead men and living ones, past four lines that were lying on the ground." On these plains of death, the men from Maine—and Chamberlain—forged a reputation for coolness and courage.

I painted this charge from an angle that allowed me to show the sun setting on the spires of the city. A shell burst silhouettes Chamberlain and makes him the center of interest. The numbers D21 and 48 on the caps in the foreground are from the Twenty-first Massachusetts and the Forty-eighth Pennsylvania regiments that had charged across the ground earlier. I based the title of the painting on Alice Rains Trulock's biography of Chamberlain because it sums up the man's personality: he treasured character, duty, charity, courage, and faith and lived what he believed.

70

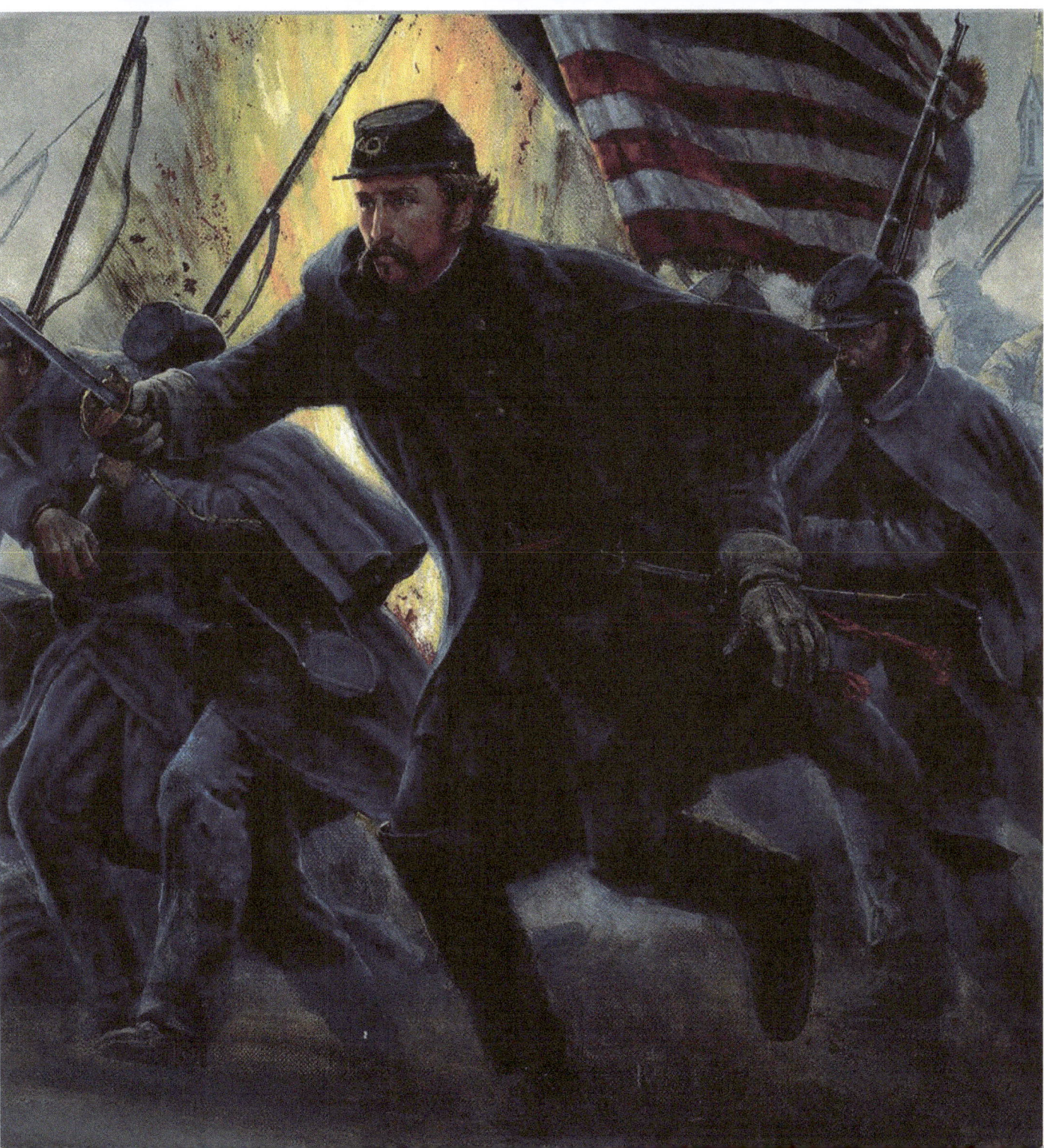

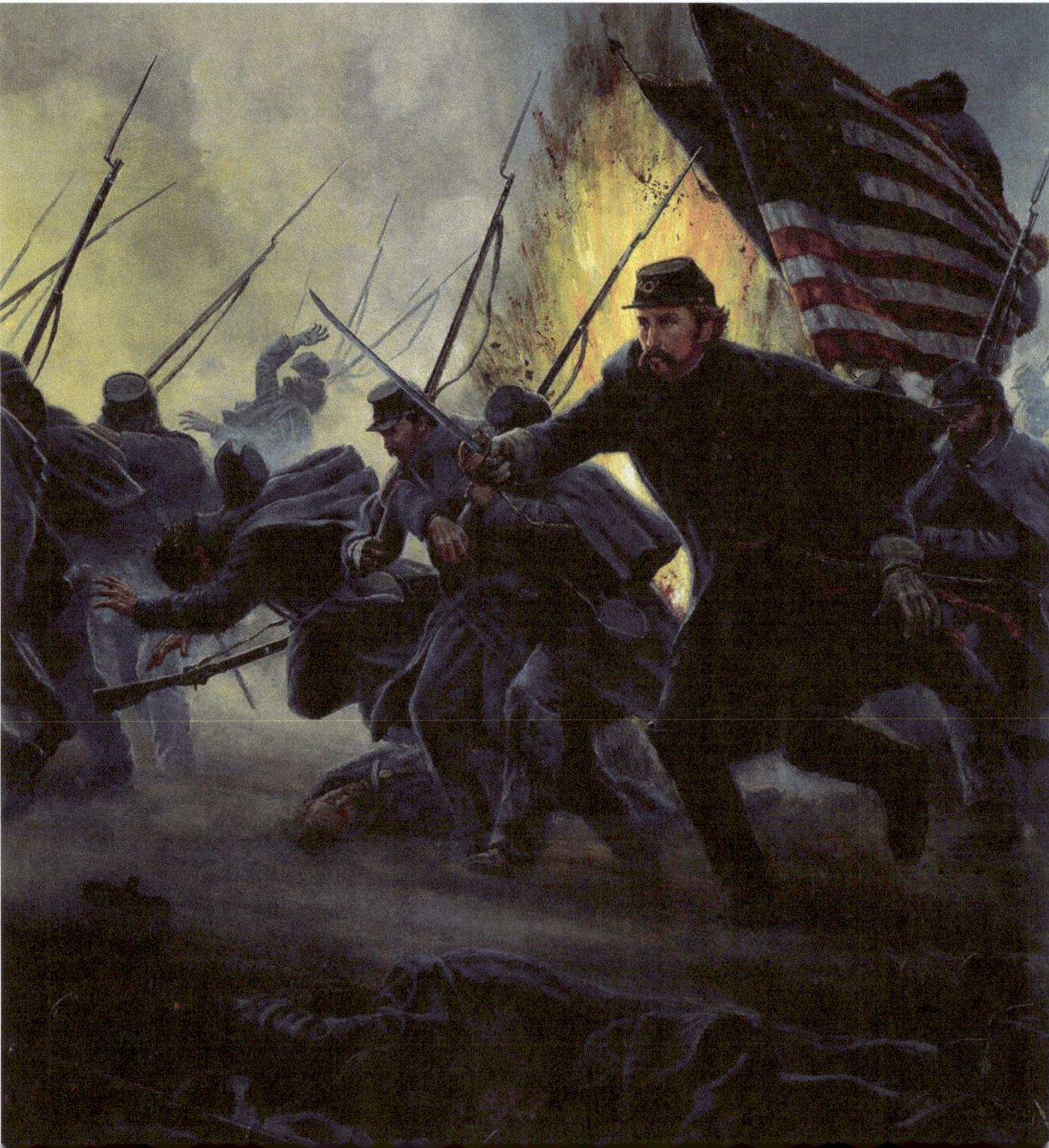

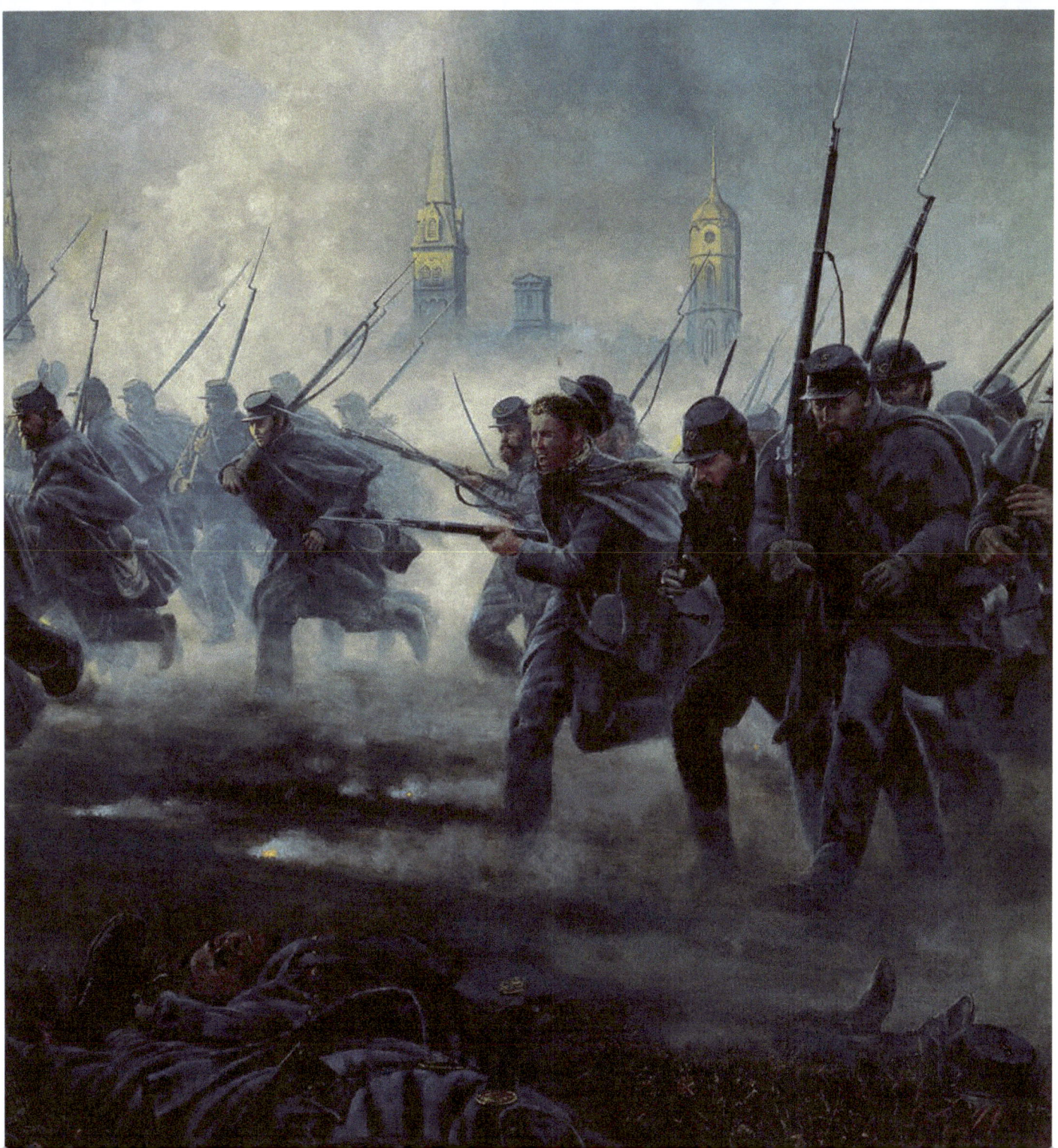

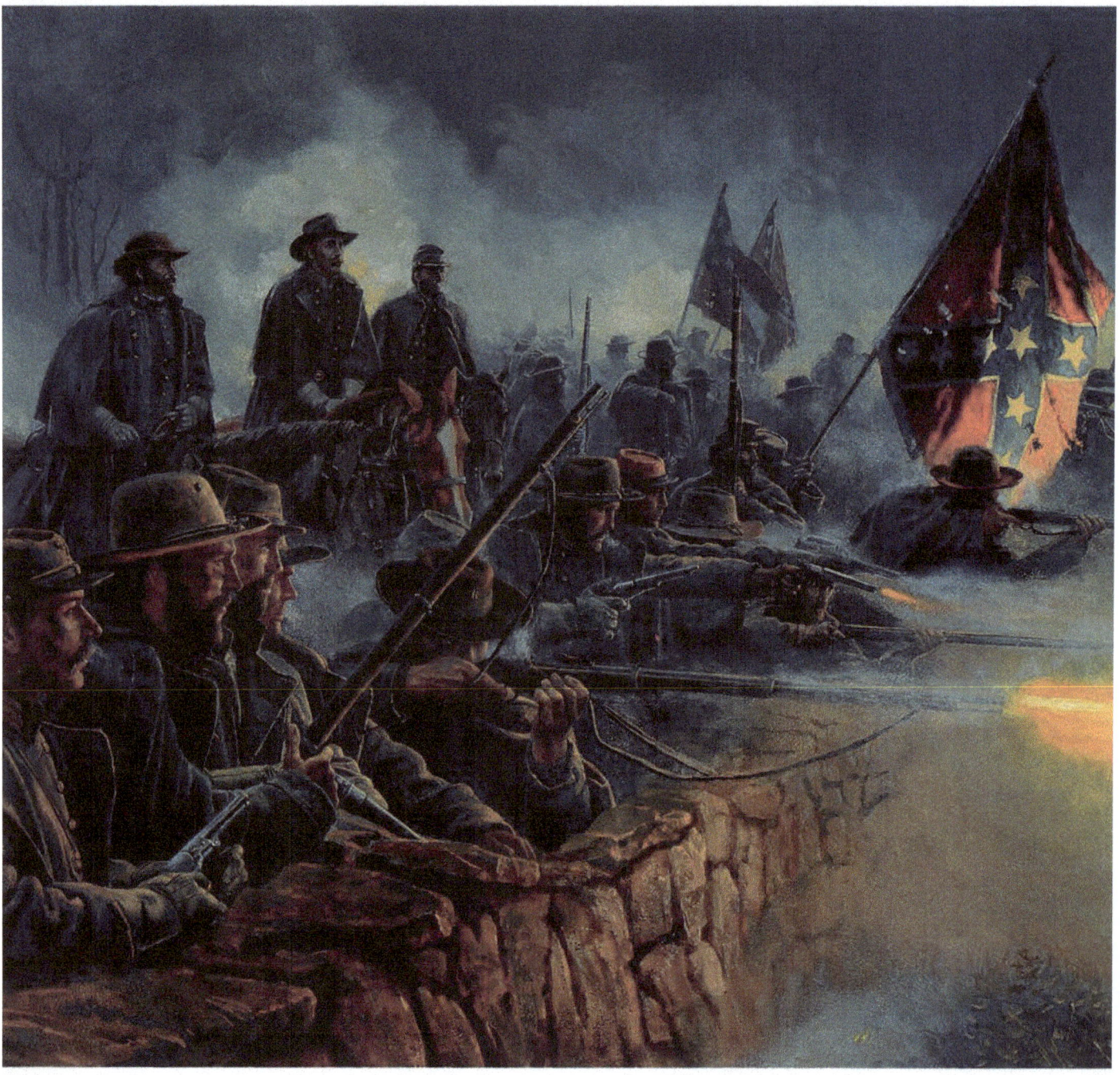

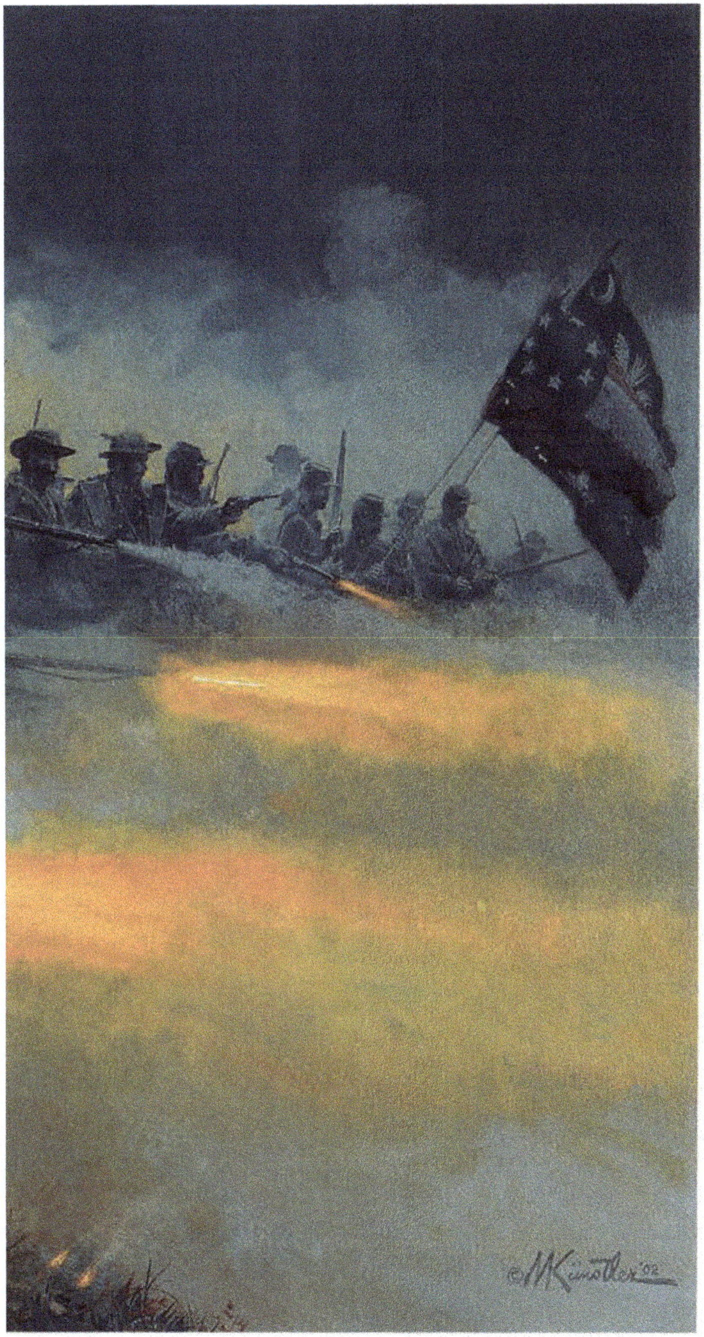

VALOR IN GRAY

KERSHAW'S BRIGADE AT FREDERICKSBURG,
DECEMBER 13, 1862

2002, oil, 14¼ x 23⅛

Atop Marye's Heights, the Southerners held an almost impregnable
position that was anchored in a
sunken road behind a stone wall.
Meanwhile, the advancing Northerners had to assault uphill over a long
and open plain. Defending the
sunken road were troops from Georgia, North Carolina, and South Carolina commanded by Brig. Gen. Joseph
B. Kershaw. He kept the brigade in
place, and they poured a terrible fire
into the charging Federals.

Kershaw is mounted on horseback
in the painting, between two of his

aides. I deliberately show a good deal of gunfire in this painting to demonstrate the overwhelming fire that the Union troops endured. I use gun flashes to dramatically light the battle flag in the center of the painting. The First National flag can be seen in the background, as well as South Carolina's Palmetto flag.

The various figures in the extreme left foreground and the perspective down the line behind the stone wall to the right background show all the steps involved in firing a rifle, from loading to firing. I was also able to show that the two sides were so close to each other that the officers were firing their pistols.

This is a companion piece to the next painting, *Courage in Blue*. Together they movingly express the extraordinary bravery evident on both sides during this engagement as well as throughout the war.

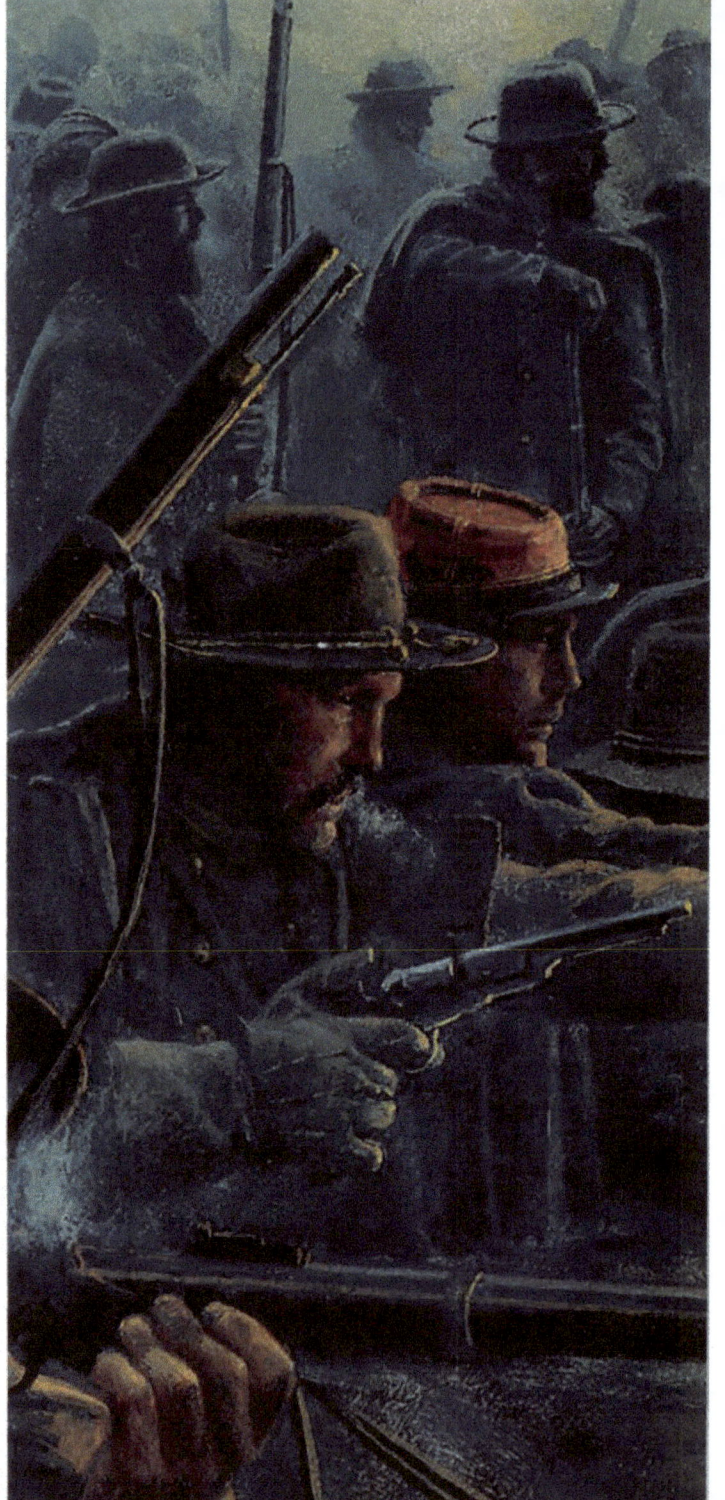

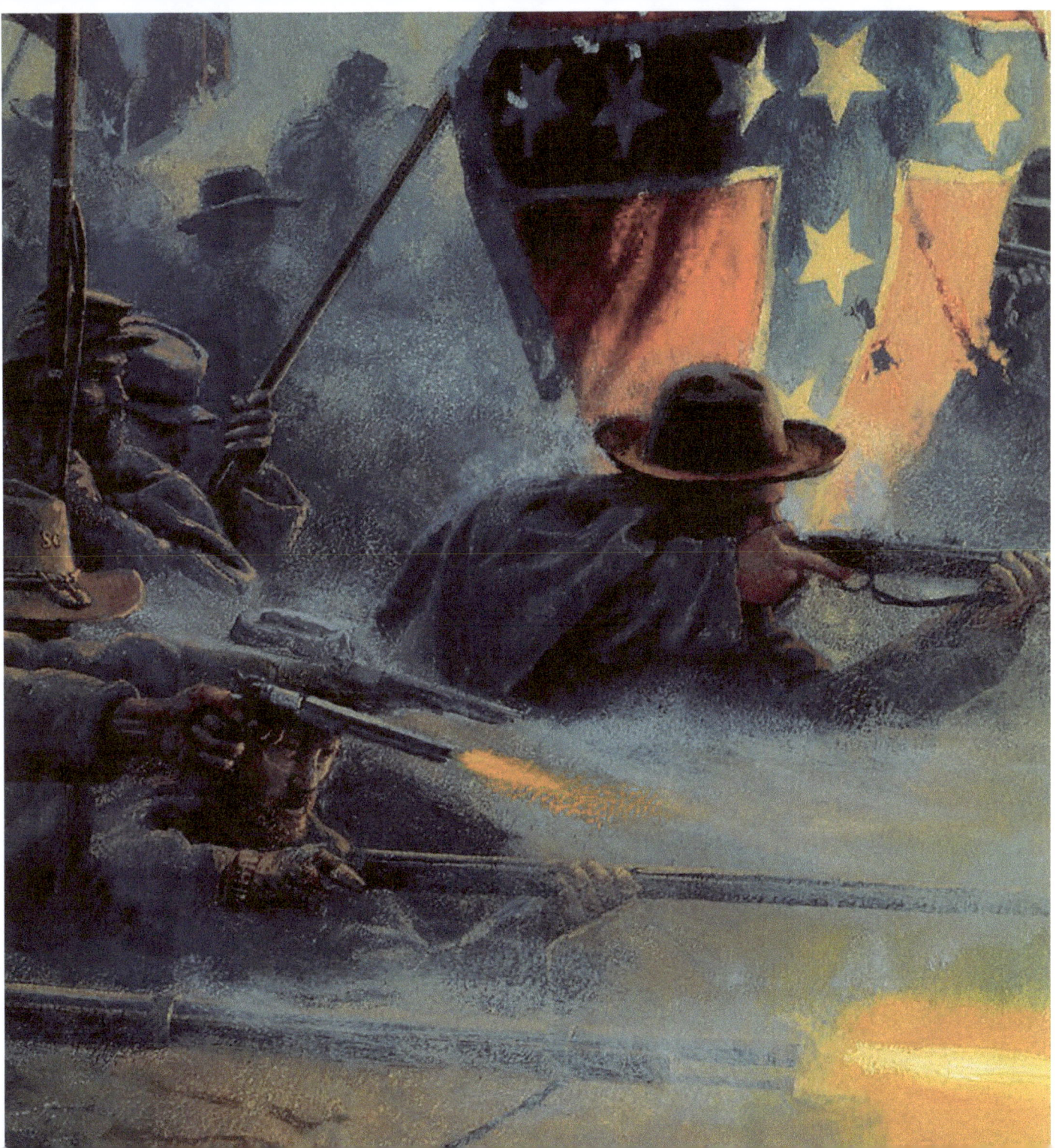

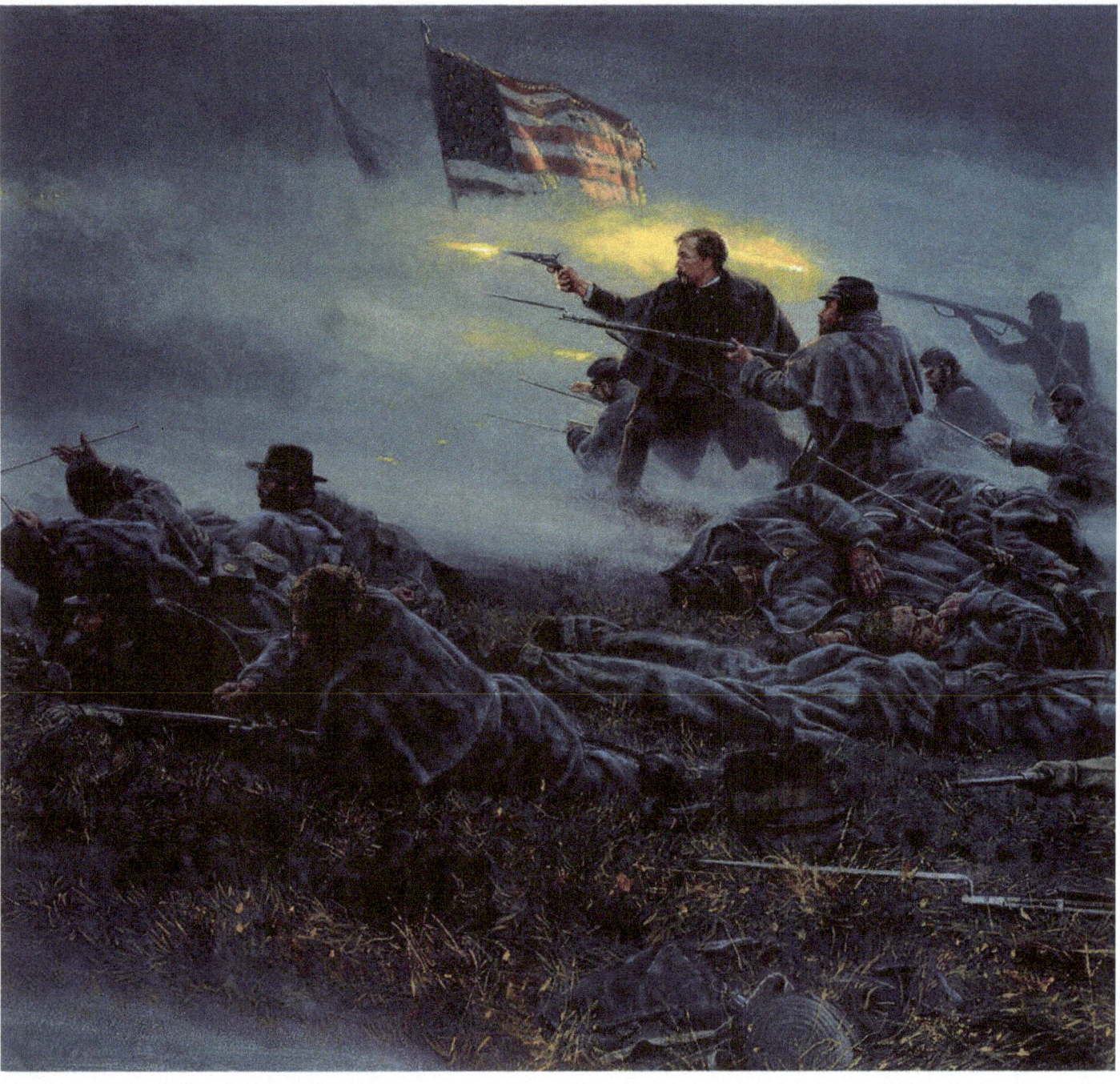

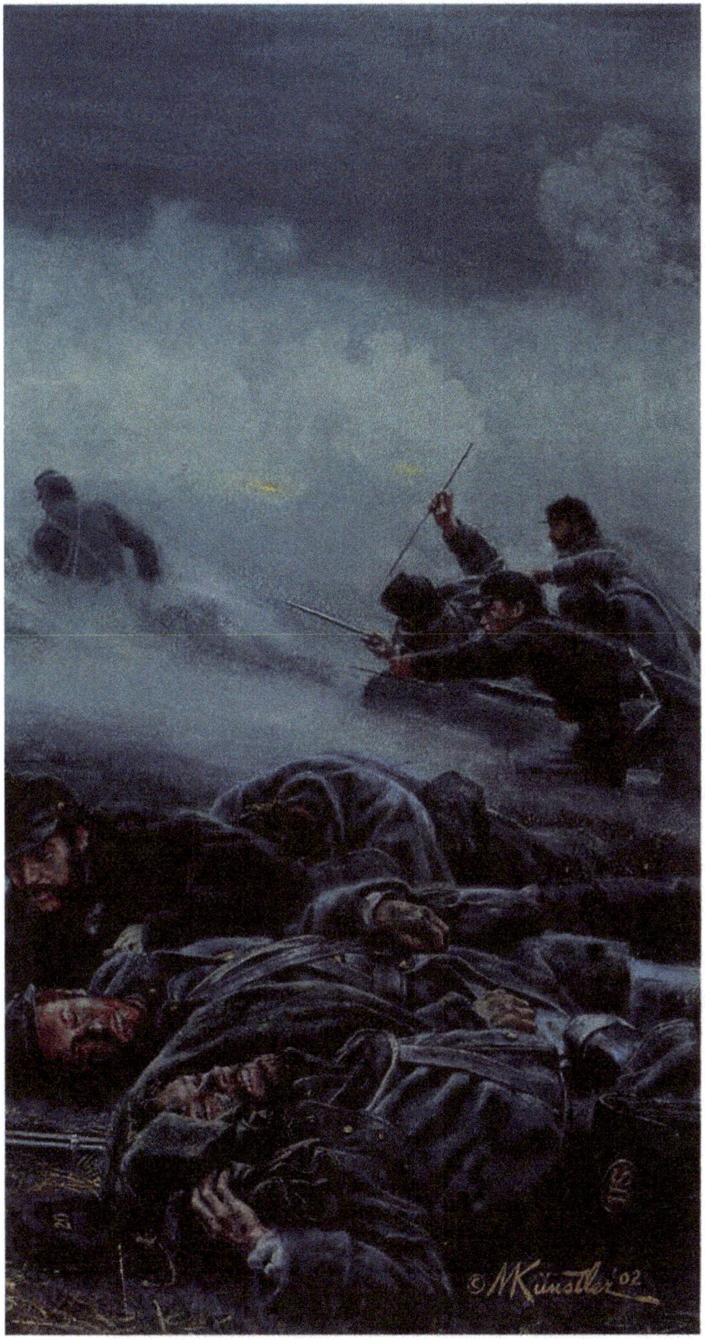

COURAGE IN BLUE

CHAMBERLAIN AT FREDERICKSBURG
DECEMBER 13, 1862

2002, oil, 14¼ x 23⅛

IN THIS companion piece to the previous painting, *Valor in Gray*, I wanted to show the determination of the attacking Federals against the insuperable odds they faced before the stone wall that protected their enemy. At least twelve separate charges had been mounted against the Confederates on Marye's Heights, and all of them had been costly failures. While not an example of brilliant tactical planning by Ambrose E. Burnside or his field commanders, the resolve of the Union troops on these slopes was an unforgettable display of courage

79

during some of the most one-sided fighting of the war. Federal casualties were horrific. In the end, the Southerners lost approximately one thousand men; the Northerners counted at least eight thousand.

After the final charge faltered just yards away from the stone wall, the Twentieth Maine was forced to hug the ground. This untested regiment had not hesitated in the face of the withering fire unleashed upon them by the Confederate defenders. Their discipline and drilling had propelled them up this slope far beyond any point that could be expected of veteran troops. And now the men from Maine pushed their way over the bodies of their fallen comrades and crawled forward to this position in order to relieve a regiment that had been shredded on this ground.

Orders came to the regimental commanders to hold their positions: the attack would be renewed with the rising sun. In the meantime, the men scattered across the slope exchanged fire with the men behind the wall until all that could be seen in the falling darkness were their muzzle flashes. When the firing slackened, the Maine men lay in the mud and shivered as the temperature dropped. There they stayed in the bitter cold all night and all the next day, lying amid the corpses of their comrades.

Chamberlain slept little that night. The moans and calls of the injured filled the air, but his efforts to find the ones who were calling to him proved futile. In the darkness, it was almost impossible to discern the living from the dead. Chamberlain found three motionless forms and pulled them around him as a makeshift shelter.

Near midnight, Chamberlain and his adjutant surveyed their position and scouted the area. They tended the wounded with what they had, offering sips

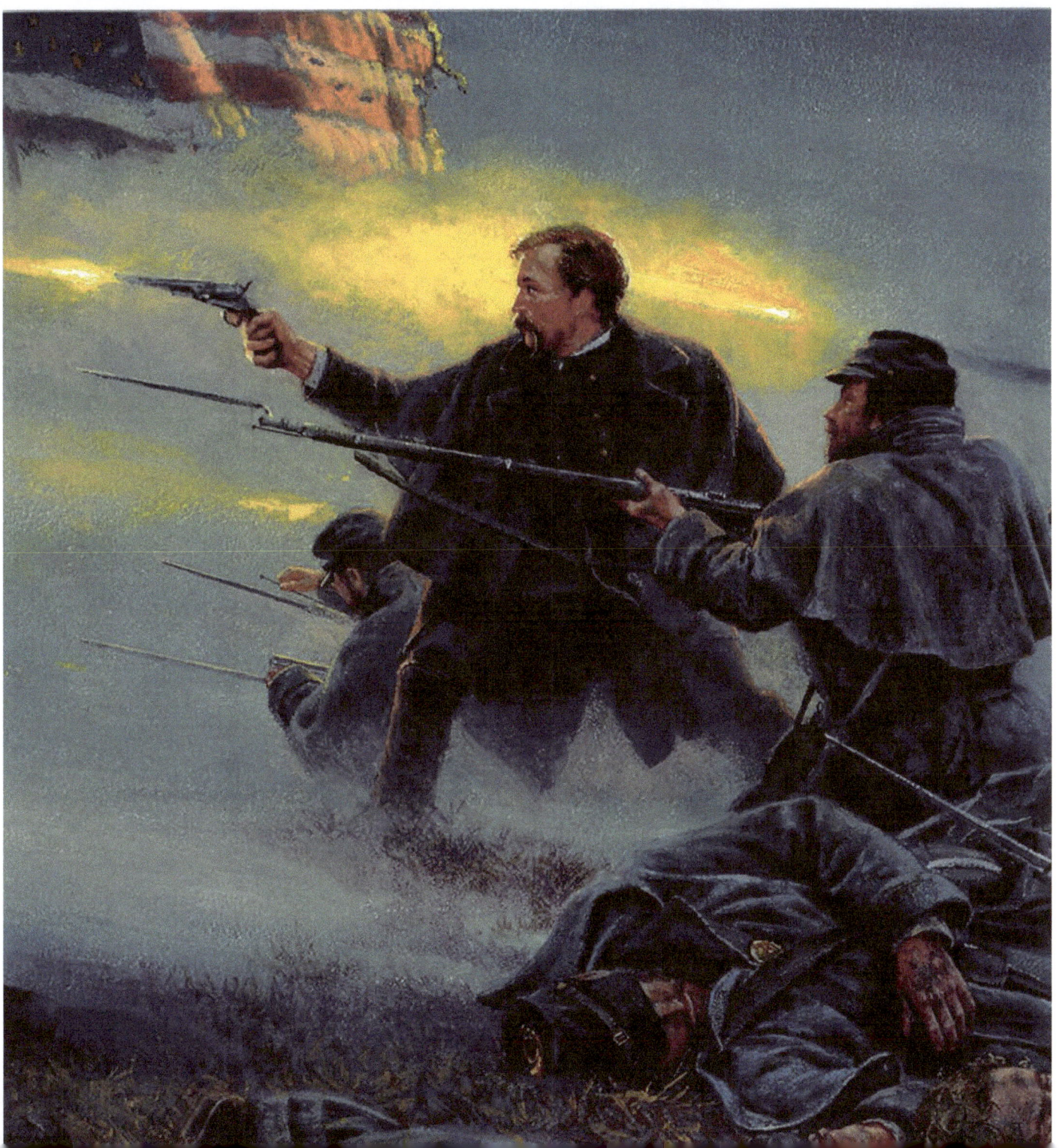

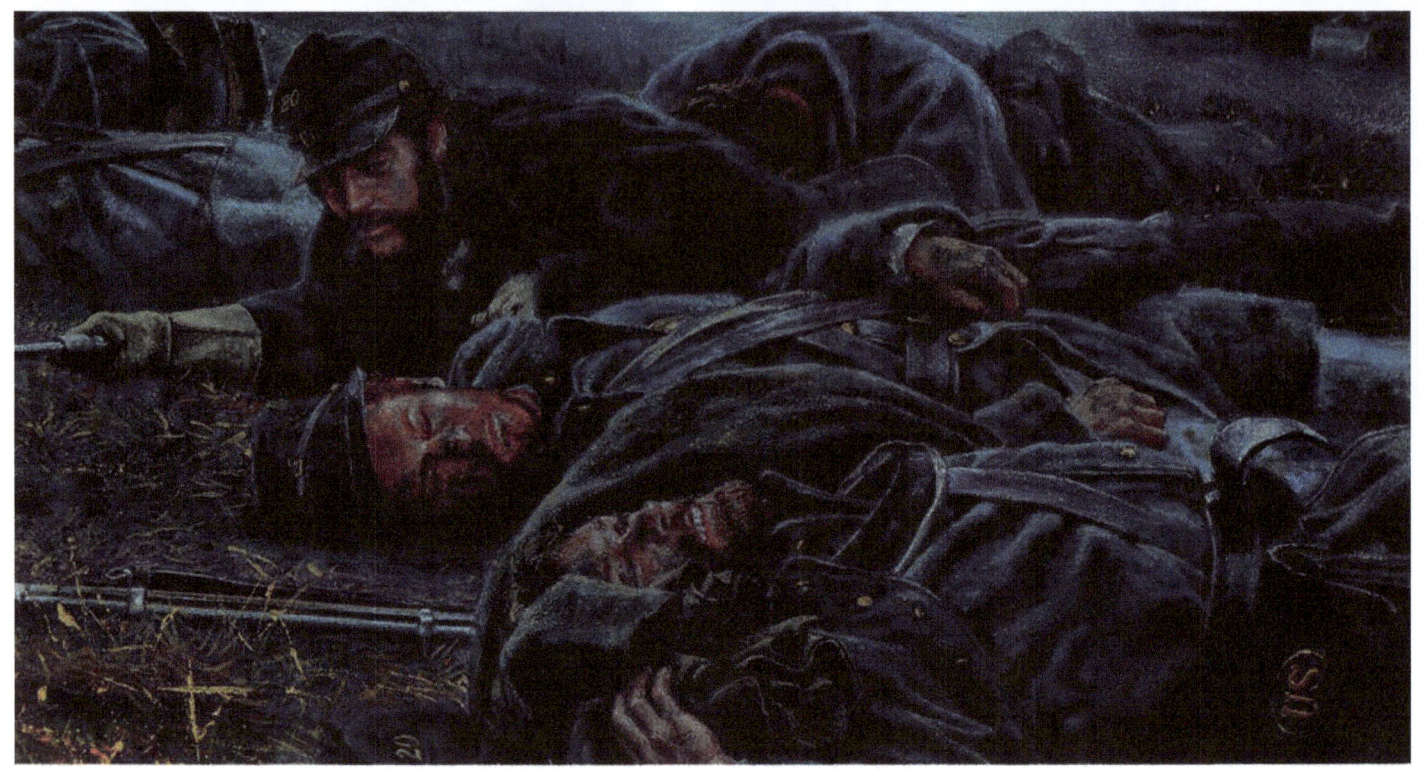

of water and binding wounds with whatever they could improvise for bandages. But the more they tried to help, the more it seemed they couldn't help enough. Chamberlain was greatly relieved when stretcher-bearers appeared and began to move the wounded back to town.

The morning, however, brought no assault. The Federals on the slope and the Confederates behind the wall traded shots, but the fighting was not renewed. Finally, on the afternoon of the next day, Chamberlain and the Twentieth Maine were withdrawn.

It was a harrowing and heartrending exposure to the worst of war for Chamberlain and his men. Still, they had proven their mettle. The courage they displayed at Fredericksburg would become one of the war's most memorable and heroic sagas. The measure of their courage would be recorded after the war by James Longstreet, who had watched their valiant assaults from atop the heights: "A series of braver, more desperate charges than those hurled against our troops . . . was never known."

In this painting, I have tried to capture the climax of the charge by the Twentieth Maine on Marye's Heights. The composition leans slightly to the left to suggest the forward movement of the assault. I've used the bright muzzle flashes of the regiment's rifles to make Chamberlain and the Union flag the focal point of the painting.

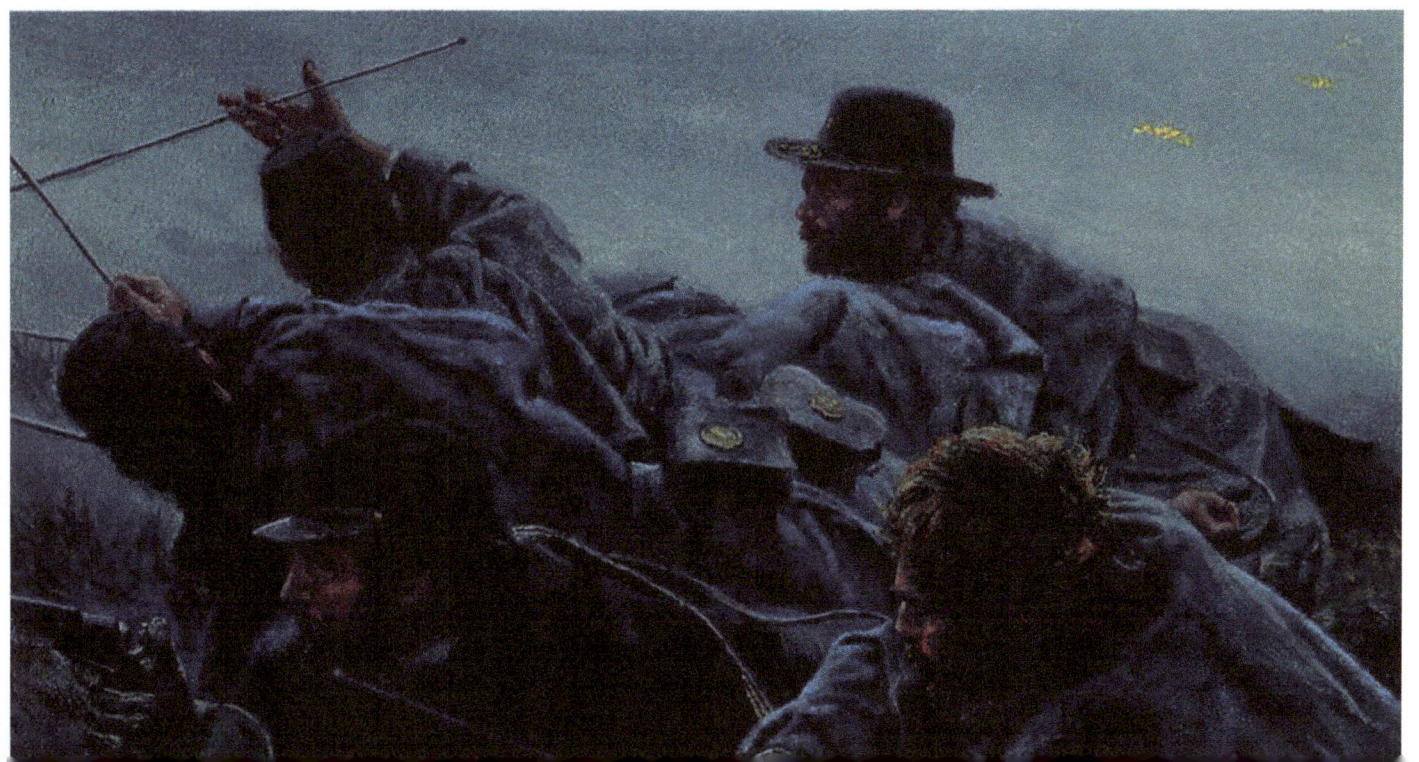

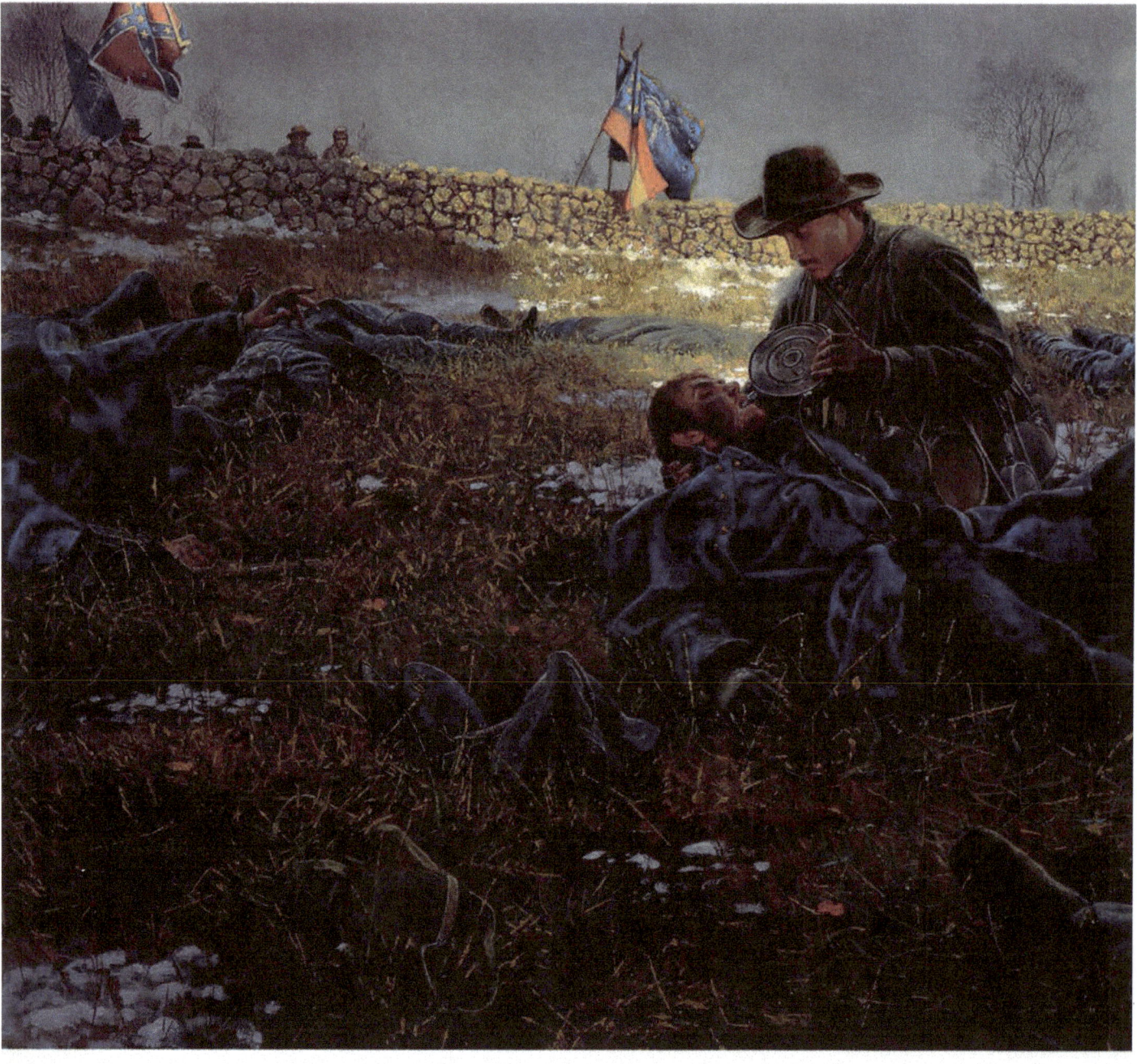

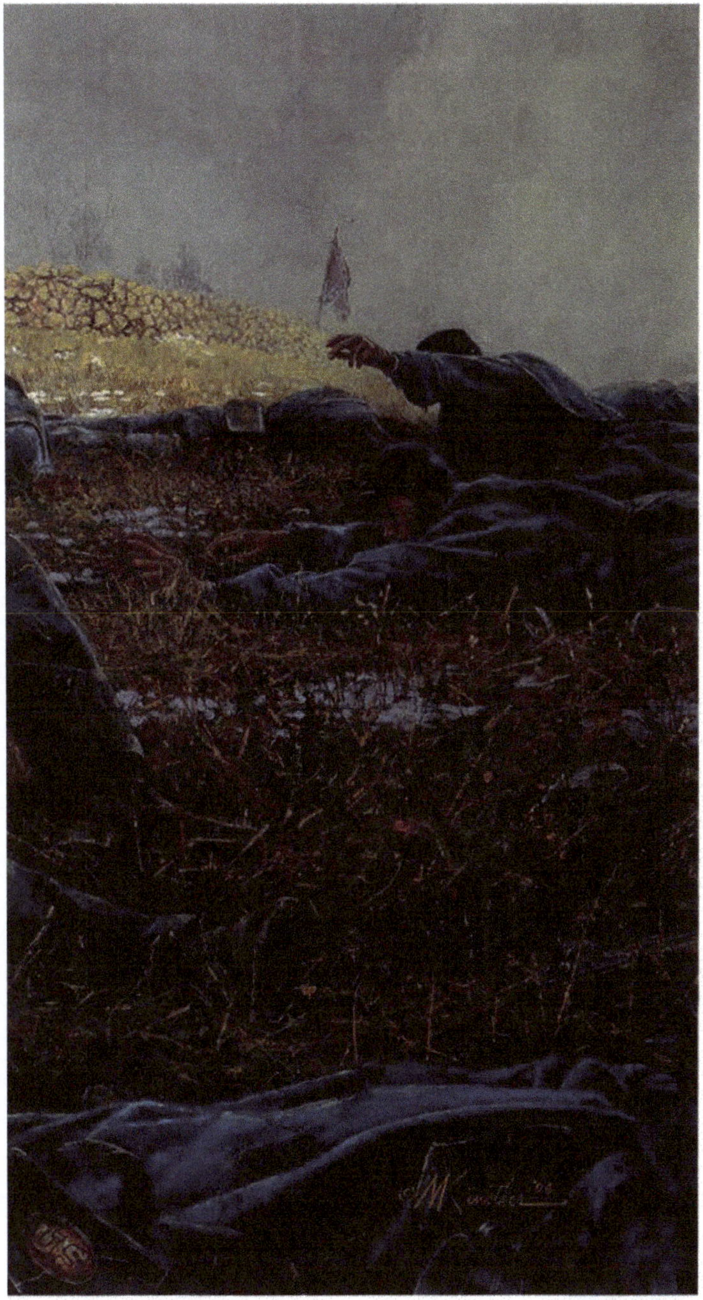

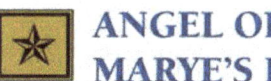

ANGEL OF MARYE'S HEIGHTS

SGT. RICHARD KIRKLAND,
FREDERICKSBURG, VIRGINIA
DECEMBER 14, 1862

2004, oil, 22 x 36

On December 14, both armies waited for the other to attack. During the lull, the wounded Union soldiers spread out on the slope in front of the stone wall pleaded for assistance. Finally, nineteen-year-old Sgt. Richard Kirkland of the Second South Carolina Volunteers received permission from General Kershaw to take some water to them, along with a warning that he risked being shot by Federals farther down the slope who might not grasp the humanitarian act. Kirkland went anyway and spent hours ministering to the men stranded on the surrounding ground.

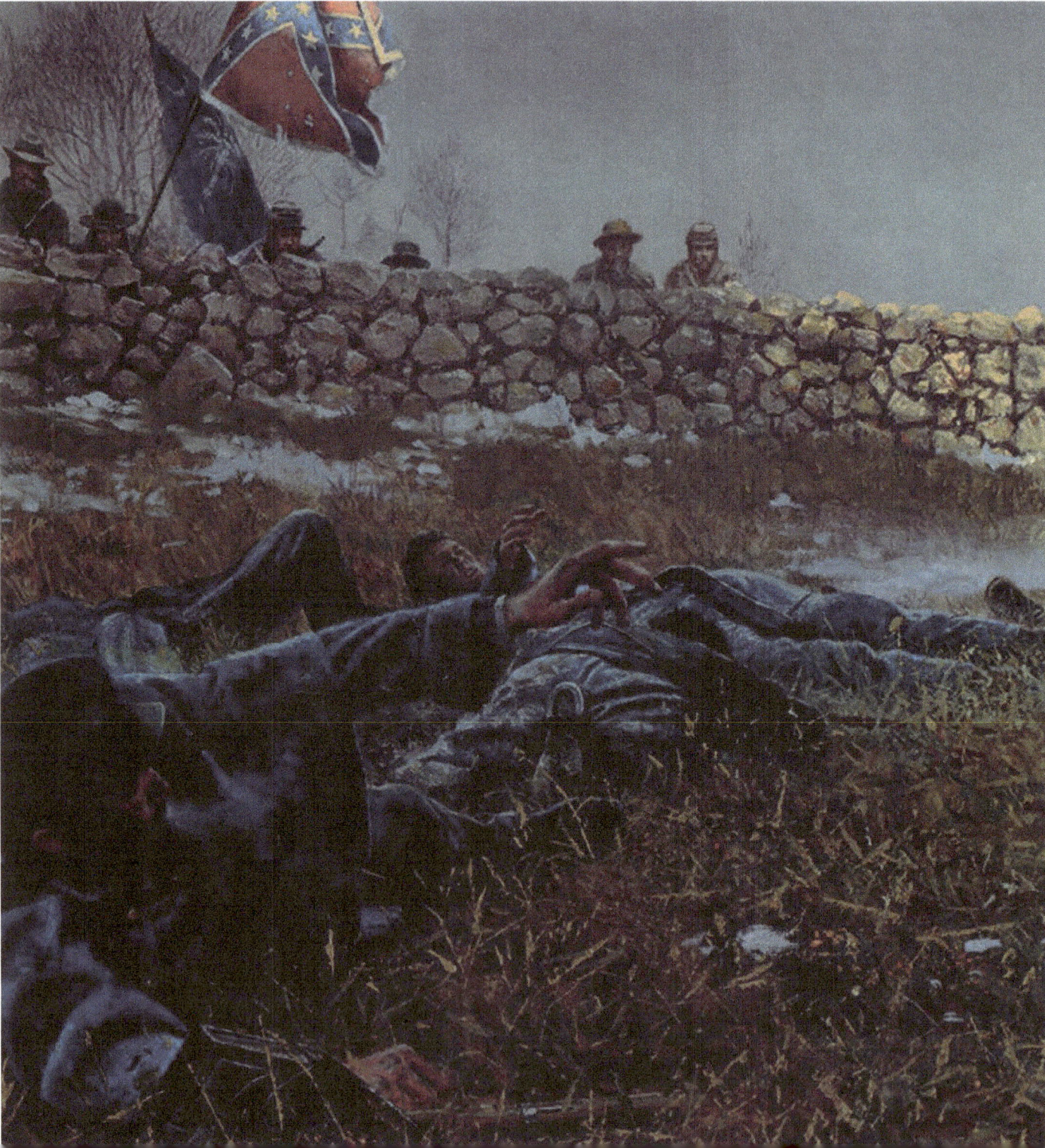

I focused on such details as the time of day this remarkable action occurred, weather conditions, and how the fallen Federals were equipped. I also needed to depict the appropriate flags. Once these details were implemented in the painting, I utilized reflections of early morning sunlight on patches of snow to focus the viewer's eye on this compassionate Southern Samaritan. I used the perspective lines of the stone wall converging at the right of the picture to silhouette a hand reaching out for water, and I used early morning fog to lighten the area behind the hand. The sunlight spreading down the stone wall illustrates the time of day and the weather conditions and allowed me to dramatically position the central focus on the courageous Kirkland, who less than a year later was killed at the September 1863 battle of Chickamauga.

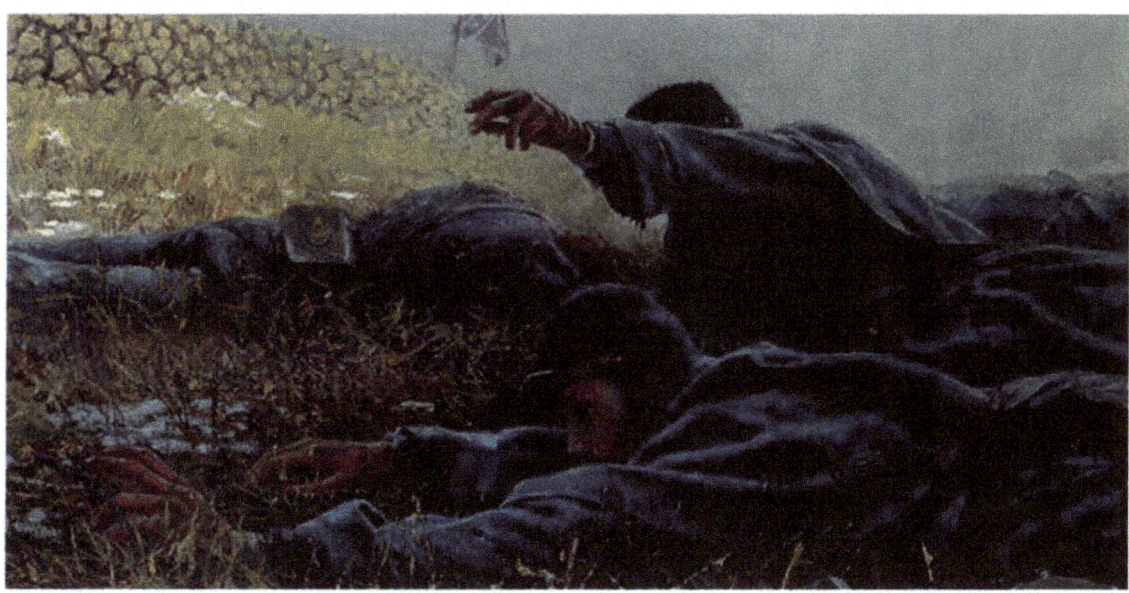

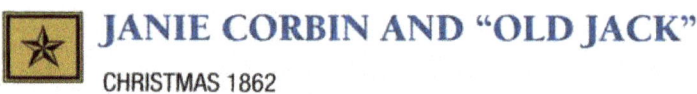

JANIE CORBIN AND "OLD JACK"

CHRISTMAS 1862

2002, oil, 10⅞ x 9⅛

$\mathbf{F}$OR A fleeting time in the winter of 1862–63, Thomas J. Jackson's inner heart was revealed to men who had only known the warrior. After the battle of Fredericksburg, Jackson established his headquarters at nearby Moss Neck plantation. The estate was owned by Richard and Roberta Corbin, whose young daughter, Janie, was known for her friendly, delightful personality. The general and the child developed an endearing friendship, encouraged perhaps either by the fact that Jackson had a newly born daughter he had not yet seen or by the barren conditions of Jackson's own childhood.

Jackson willingly put aside his duties whenever Janie appeared at his headquarters. He laughed and played with the child to the surprise of his officers and troops who knew only his formal, professional demeanor. The stern disciplinarian would romp and play piggyback and other games with Janie. During one of these playtimes, he removed the gold braiding from his forage cap to give her as a tie for her hair.

Christmas trees were becoming popular at this time, and I thought it would make a perfect background for the painting. The ornaments of the day are authentically rendered, and I believe the Christmas setting underscores the obvious love that Jackson had for this sweet little girl.

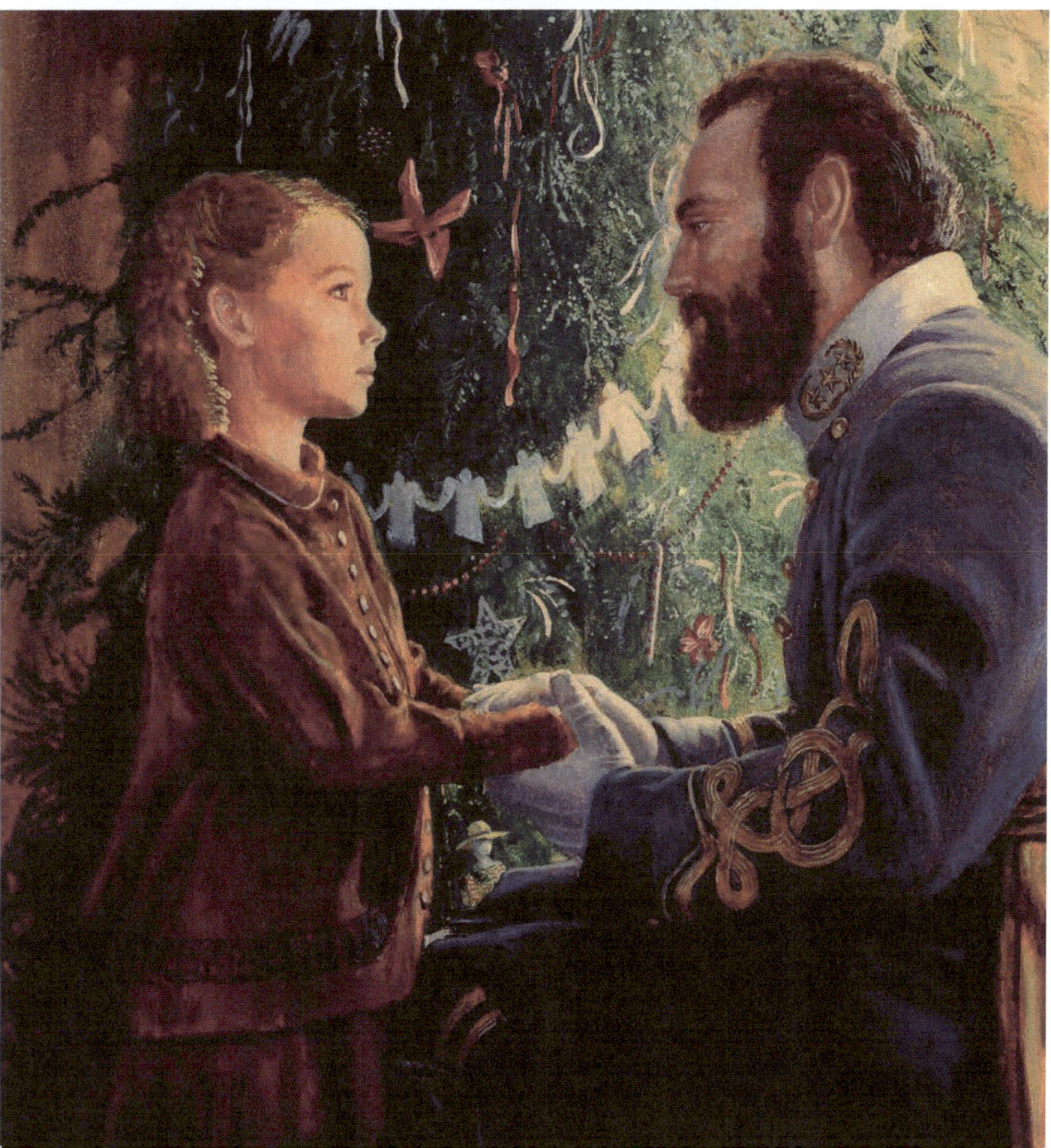

SOUTHERN STARS

KERNSTOWN, VIRGINIA

WINTER 1862

1994, oil, 28 x 40

Between the battles of Fredericksburg and Chancellorsville, a religious revival swept through the ranks of the Army of Northern Virginia. Army chaplains estimated that as many as one-quarter of the troops were affected. Prayer meetings and open-air worship services multiplied.

I addressed this element of faith in an evening snow scene with a group of horsemen riding by a church just as services ended. The congregation is visible, but the church is the dominant backdrop to the scene. I based the building on the Opequon Presbyterian Church in Kernstown, near historic Winchester.

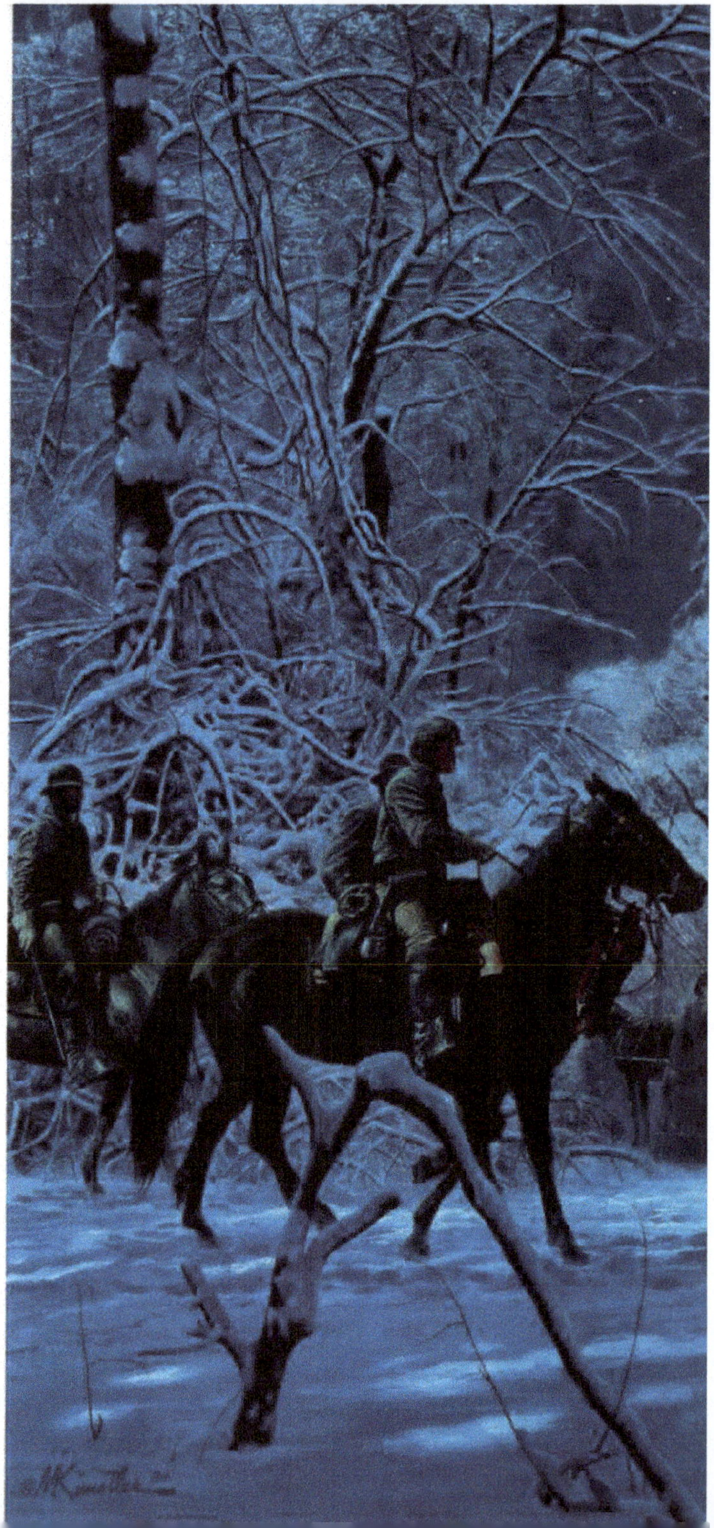

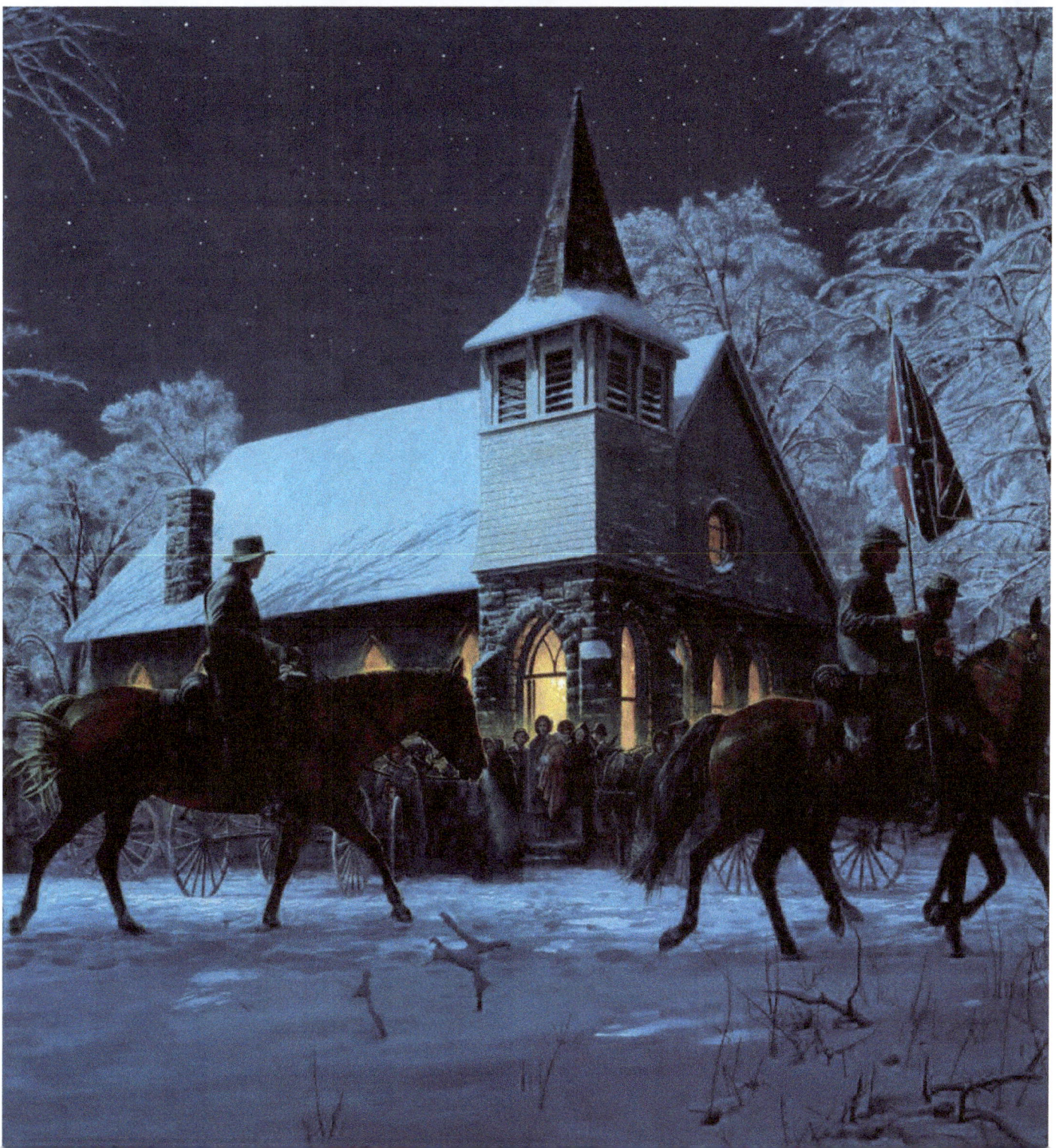

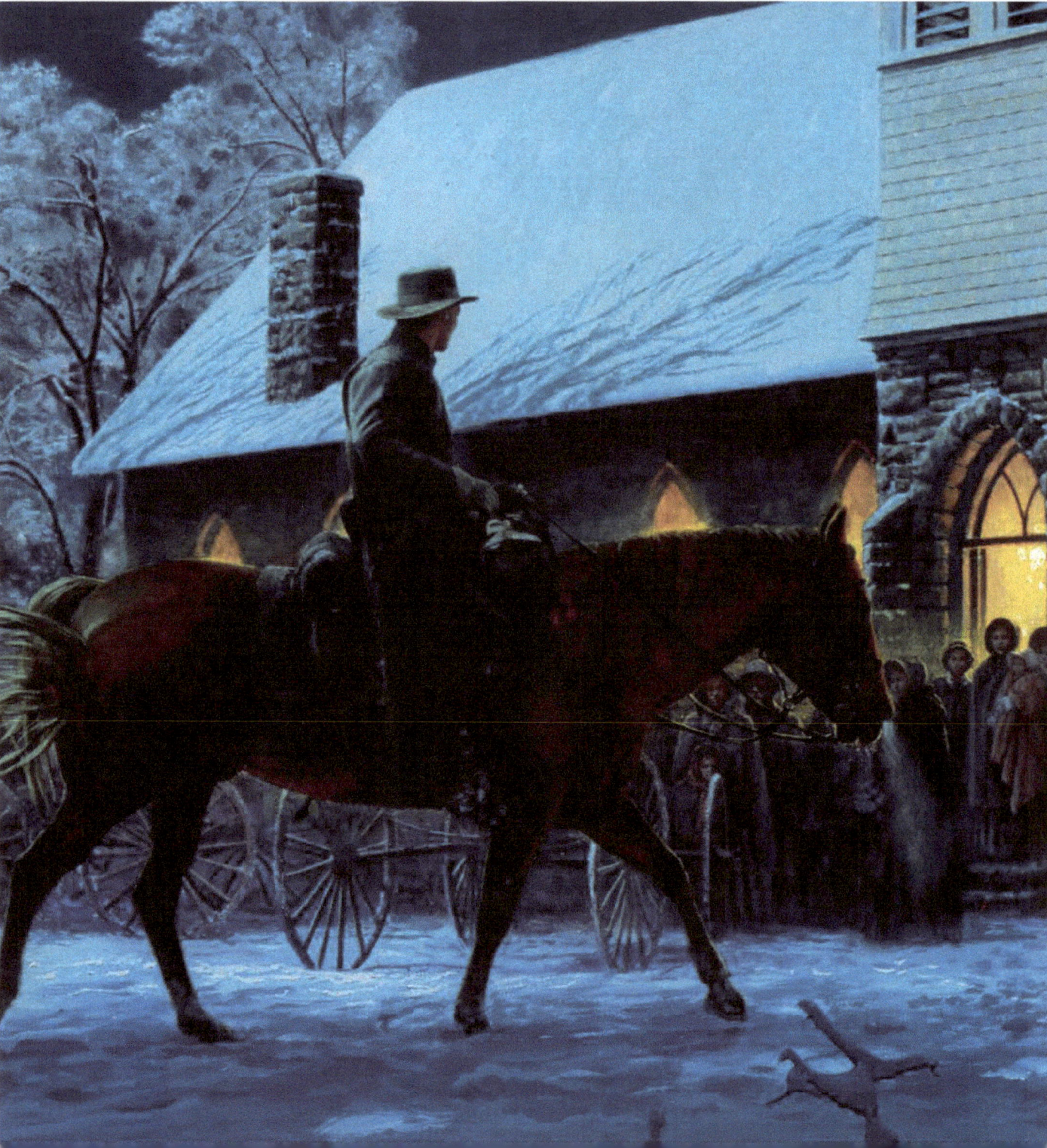

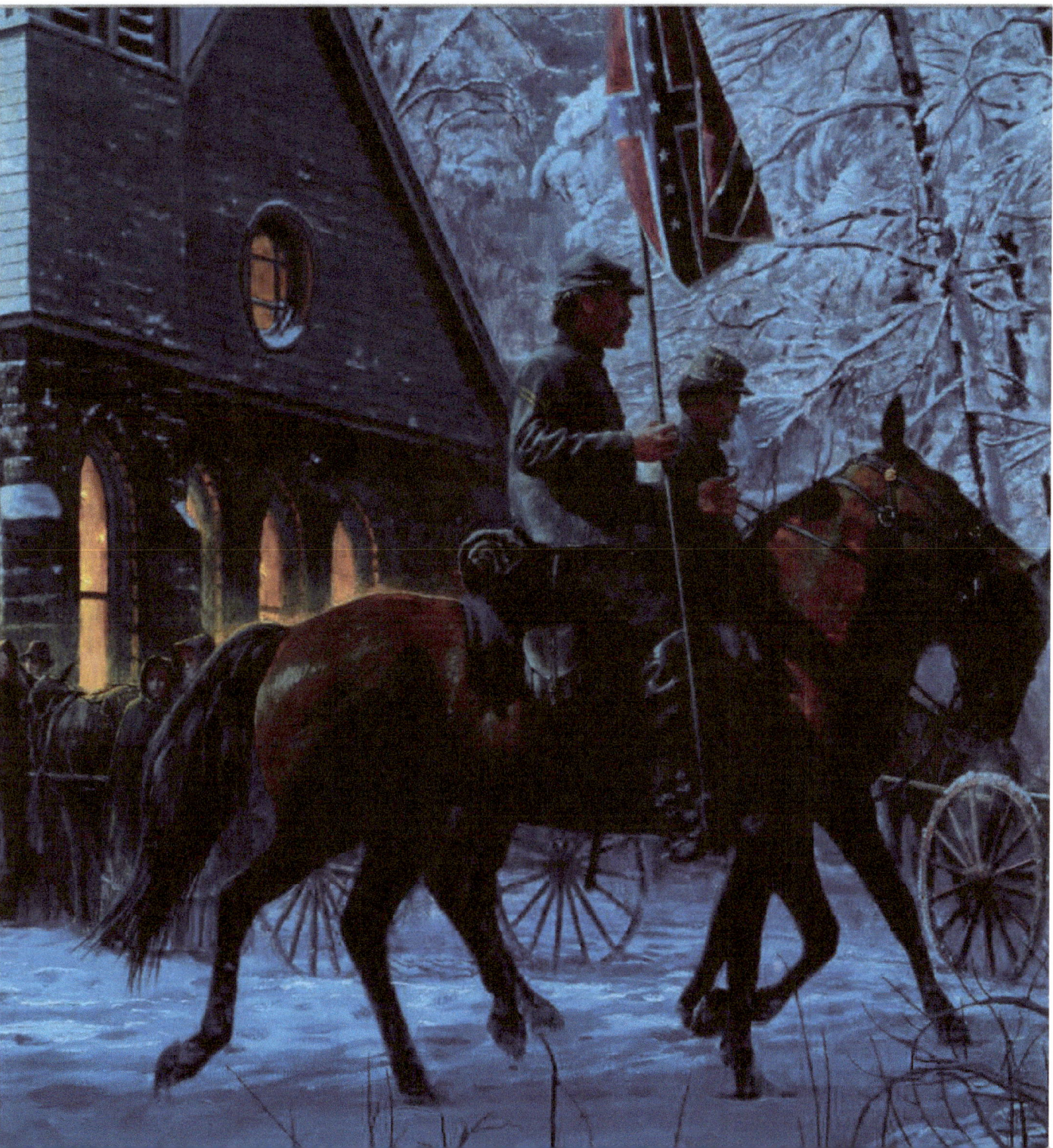

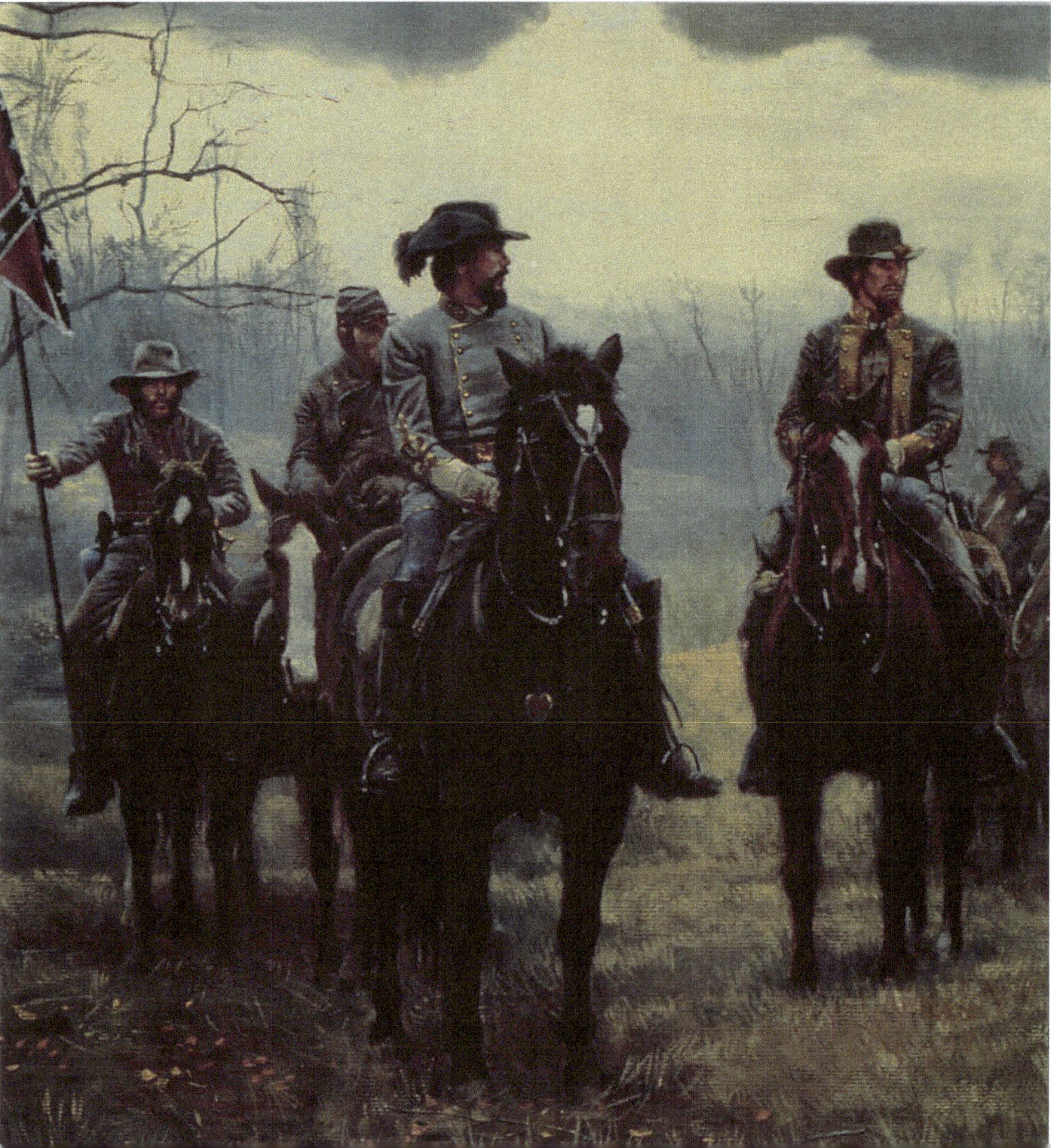

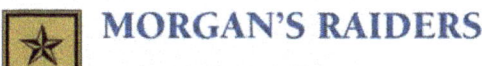

MORGAN'S RAIDERS

ALEXANDRIA, TENNESSEE
DECEMBER 21, 1862

1982, oil, 25 x 40

detail, left

Iɴ ᴛʜᴇ western theater, in his camp near Alexandria, Tennessee, Confederate Brig. Gen. John Hunt Morgan inspected his troops the day before he led them on a ride deep into Union-occupied Kentucky. Morgan's fame was rapidly growing in the South, and commanders such as Braxton Bragg held him in high regard. Jefferson Davis was visiting the army, but he was overshadowed by the events of the review. Still, the Confederate president was intrigued by the dashing thirty-seven-year-old Morgan.

The objective of the raid was to destroy the main supply line between Union Gen. William S. Rosecrans's Army of the Cumberland in Tennessee and his supply base at Louisville. Despite encountering driving rain and sleet, Morgan succeeded in capturing supplies and small garrisons. The raiders burned a railroad bridge near Elizabethtown, a vital link in the supply line, and completely halted the flow of supplies to Rosecrans's men. With his mission accomplished, Morgan returned to Tennessee, and his troopers toasted the success of their Christmas raid.

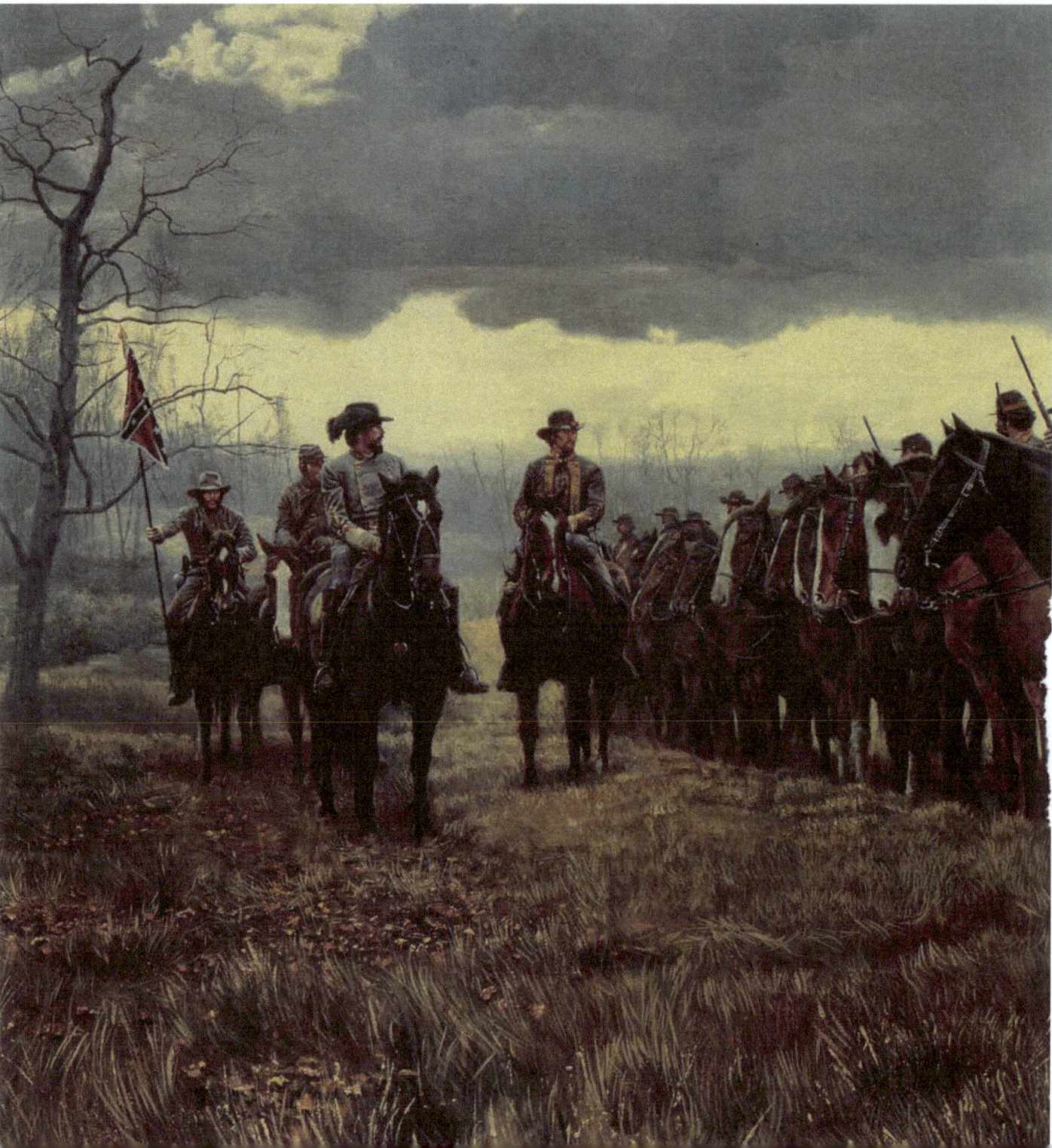

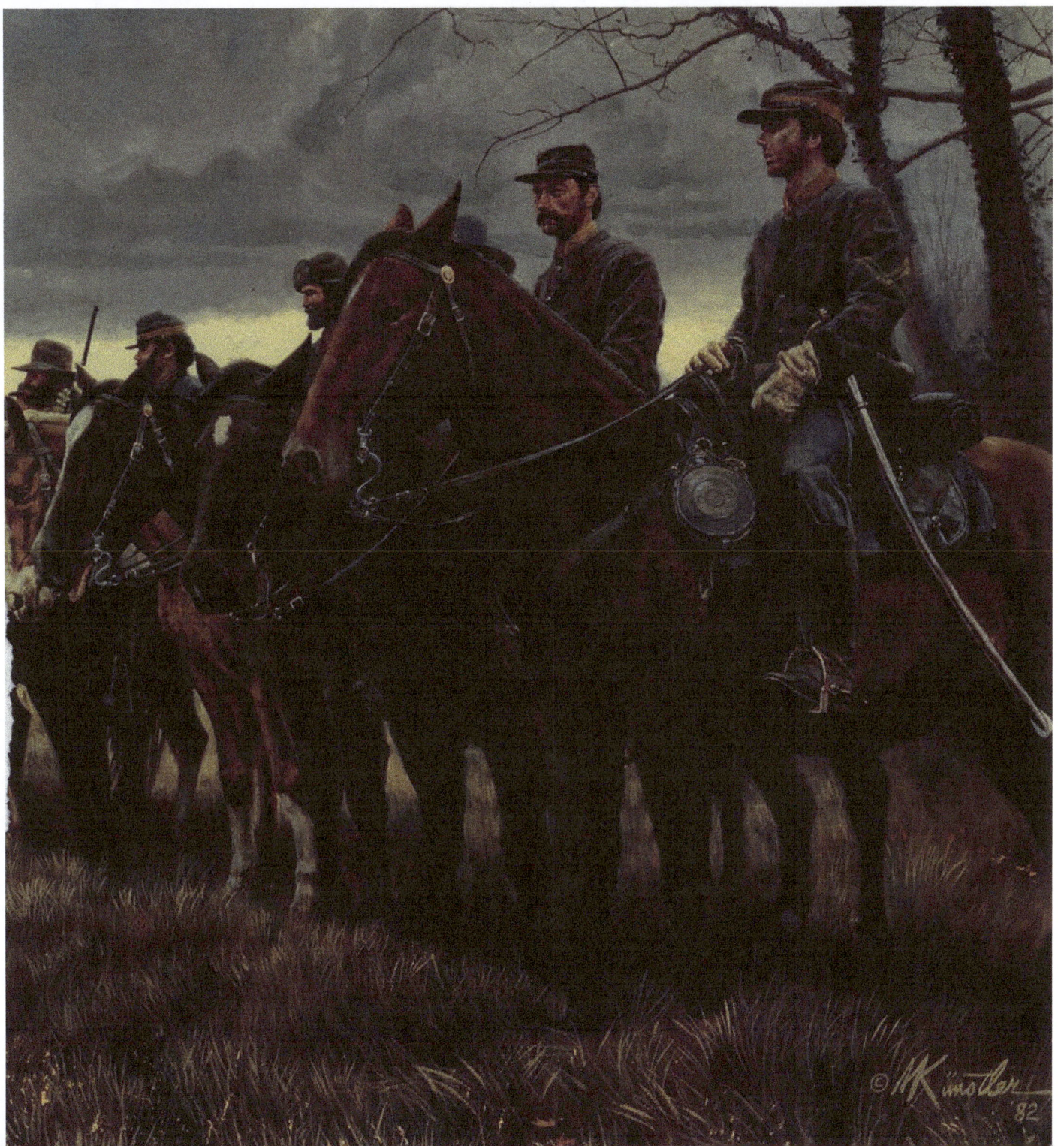

By the President of the United States of America:

A Proclamation.

Whereas,
September,
eight
war
con
to

"against the United States; and the fact that
State, or the people thereof, shall on that day
"good faith, represented in the Congress of the
"States by members chosen thereto at elec
"herein a majority of the qualified voters
"State shall have participated, shall, in the
"of strong countervailing testimony, be deem
"clusive evidence that such State, and the
"thereof, are not then in rebellion against
"United States."

Now, therefore, I, Abraha
Lincoln, President of the United States, b
the power in one vested as Commande
of the Army and Navy of the Uni
States in time of actual armed rebellion a
authority and government of the United
and as a fit and necessary war measure
pressing said rebellion, do, on this first d
January, in the year of our Lord one tho
eight hundred and sixty three, and in acc
with my purpose so to do publicly procla
for the full period of one hundred days, fo
day first above mentioned, order and
the States and parts of States where
be thereof respectively, are this day i
against the United States, the g

©M Künstler '04

EMANCIPATION PROCLAMATION

ABRAHAM LINCOLN
JANUARY 1, 1863

2004, mixed media, 12 x 12

ON NEW YEAR'S DAY 1863, Abraham Lincoln signed the Emancipation Proclamation and freed all the slaves in the states then in rebellion against the Union. He later said, "If my name ever goes into history it will be for this act, and my whole soul is in it." With the stroke of his pen, he redefined the war as being against and for slavery as opposed to the more abstract restoration or dissolution of the Union.

I had already painted a historical recreation of the Emancipation Proclamation and wanted to commemorate the event a second time. I wanted to do a portrait of Lincoln. Since I had already painted some portraits of him already, I decided to paint him in profile on a reproduction of the Emancipation Proclamation.

The other painting depicts the signing of the document (see page 101). A great deal of information,

PAGE 101 >

THE EMANCIPATION PROCLAMATION

JANUARY 1, 1863

1987, oil, 30 x 30

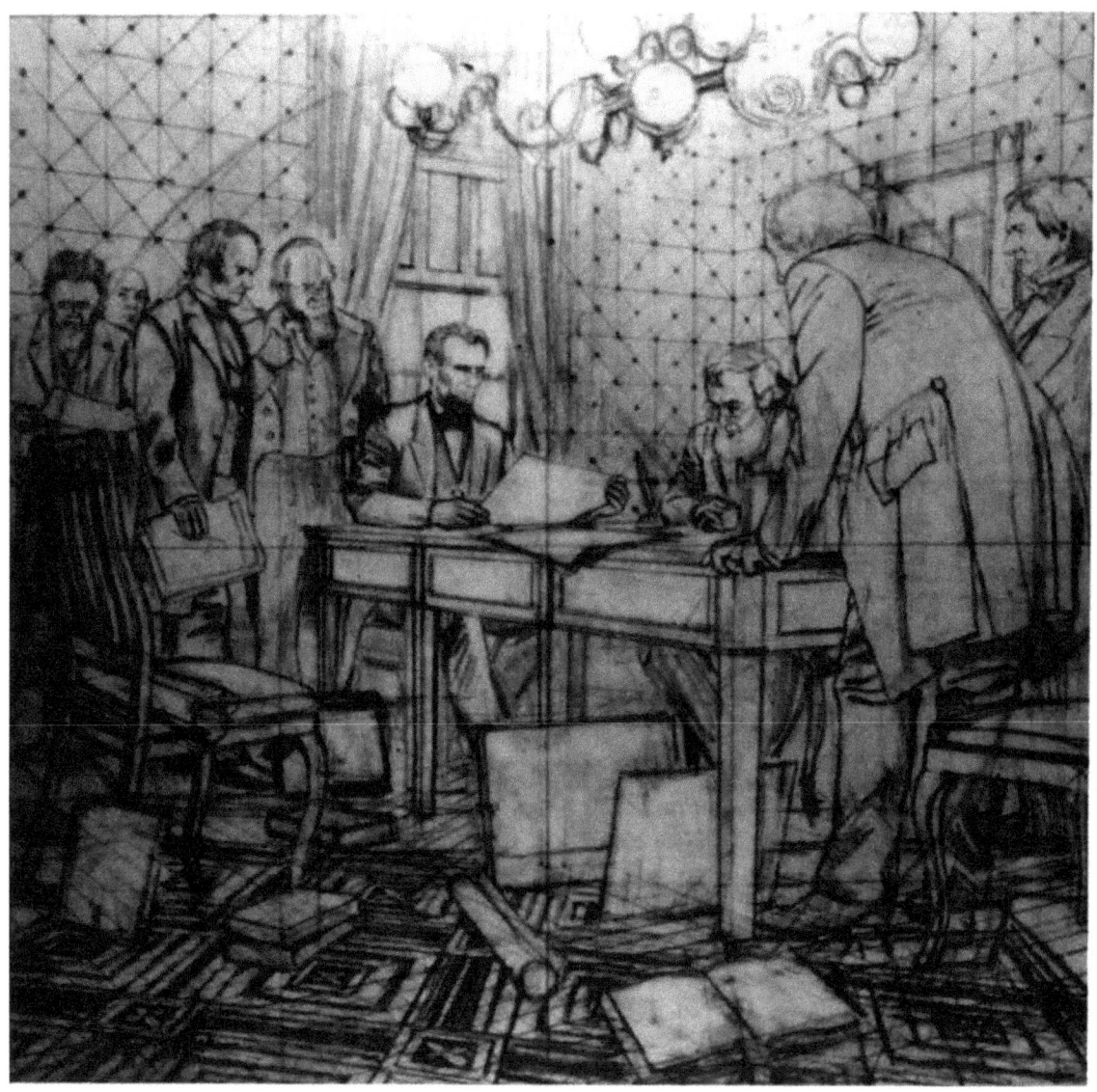

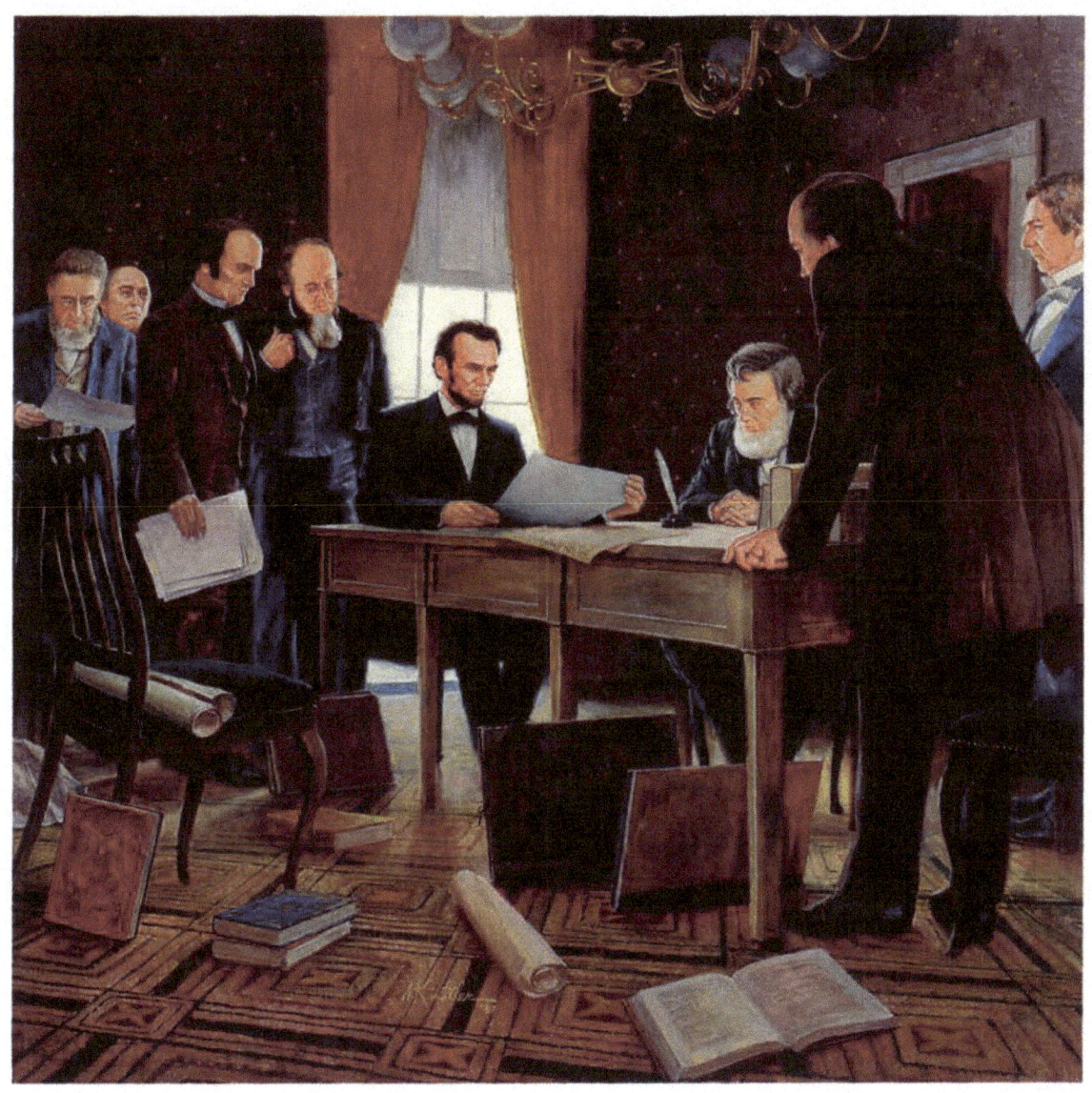

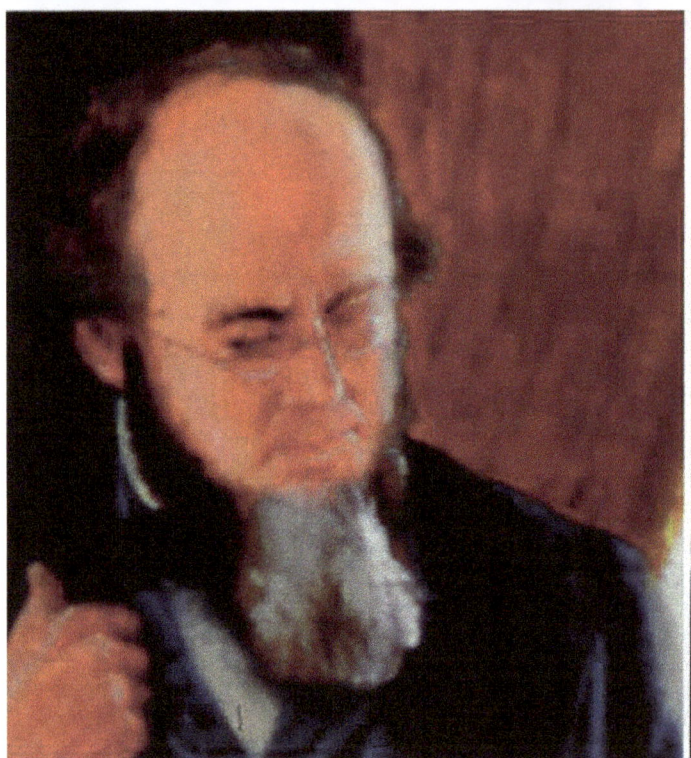
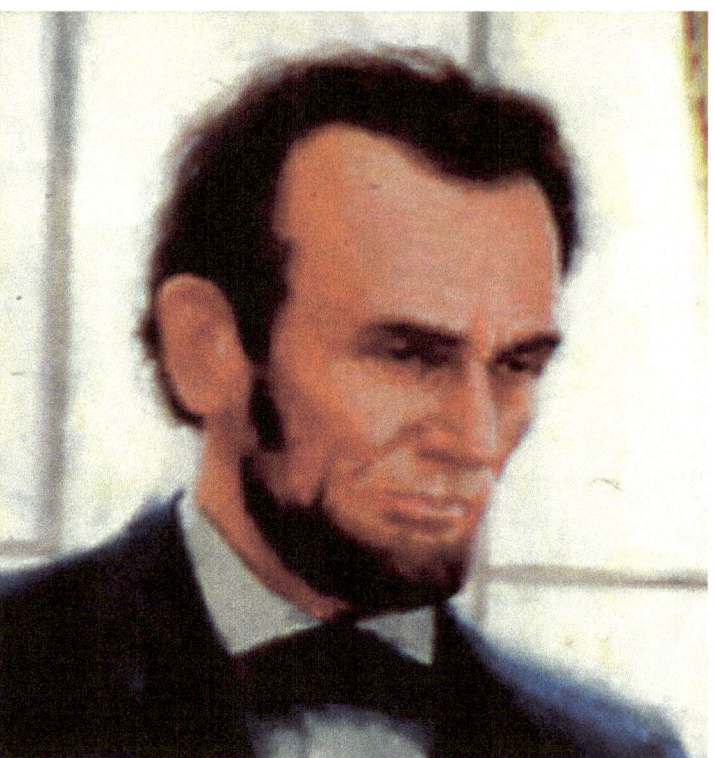

both written and pictorial, is available on this subject. Most of my visual information came from artist Francis B. Carpenter, a contemporary of Lincoln, whose famous painting The Emancipation Proclamation hangs in the Capitol in Washington, D.C. Carpenter had almost unlimited access to the White House and even convinced Lincoln and his cabinet to pose. A photographer also took pictures of the president and the secretaries, and the artist made numerous sketches of the room. While I gained very little from his finished painting, Carpenter's sketch pad was a treasure trove of detail.

This project posed several unusual problems for me. My predicament was that while I easily learned the patterns and colors of the rug, wallpaper, and drapes, putting this information into perspective for my painting was tedious

102

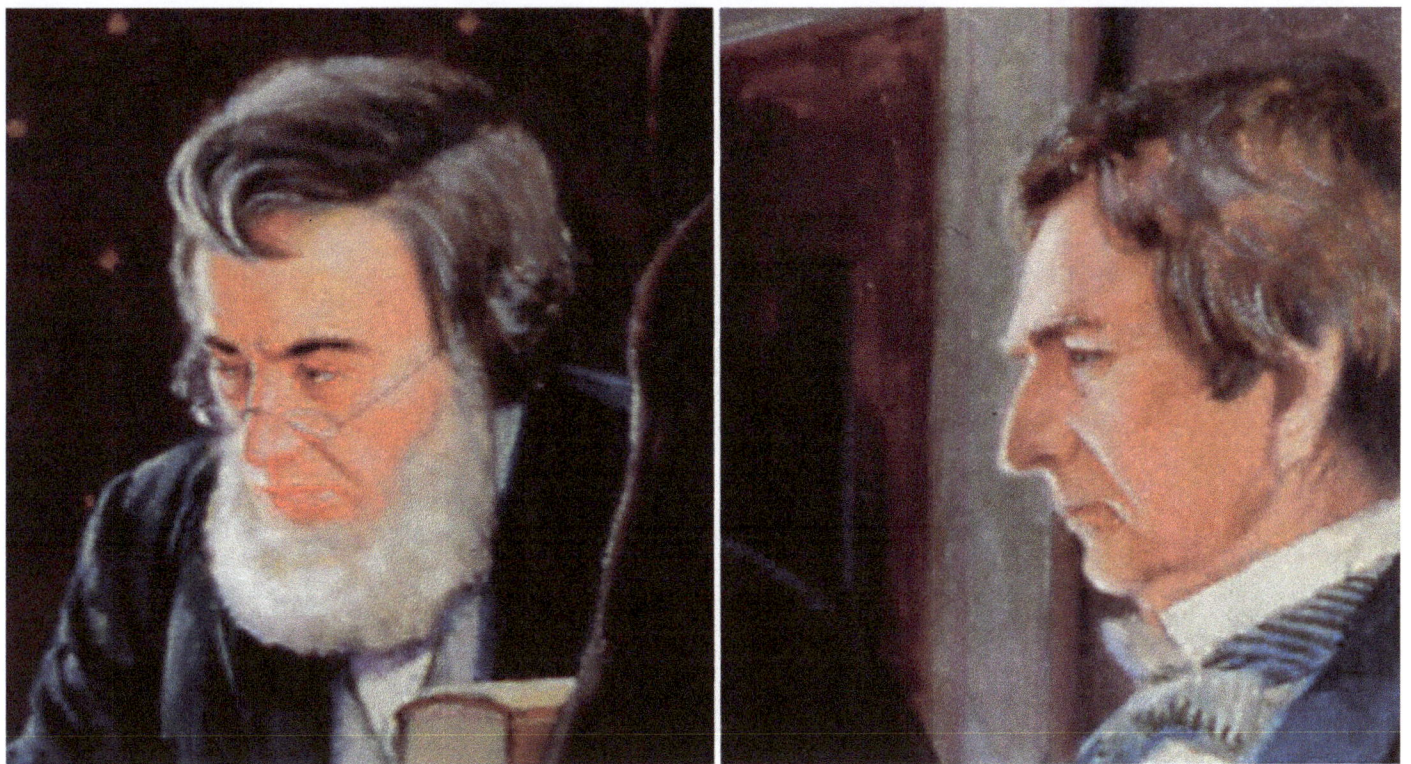

and laborious. Since I had seen Carpenter's finished picture, I tried not to duplicate his vantage point, making my task that much harder.

After the usual number of thumbnail and preliminary sketches, I began a detailed line drawing, which I used to solve these problems, particularly that of perspective. The pencil drawing (page 100) alone took more than eight days. The likenesses were relatively easy since there are many photographs of Lincoln and his cabinet. The chairs in the painting are still in the White House today, having been found and restored to the mansion by First Lady Lou Hoover. The lighting fixture is based on Carpenter's sketches.

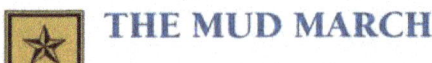

THE MUD MARCH

FREDERICKSBURG, VIRGINIA, JANUARY 21, 1863   2005, oil, 27 x 60

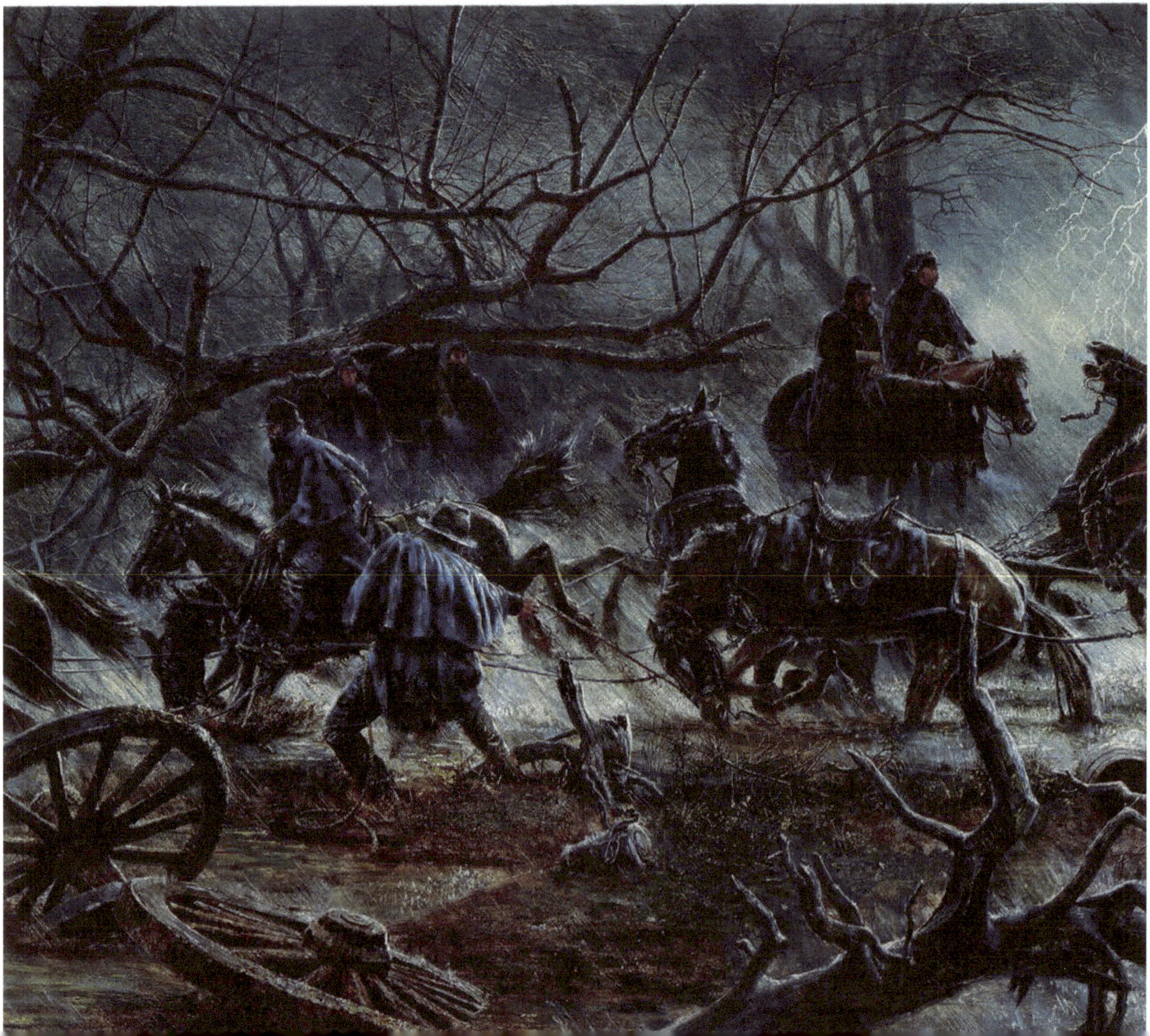

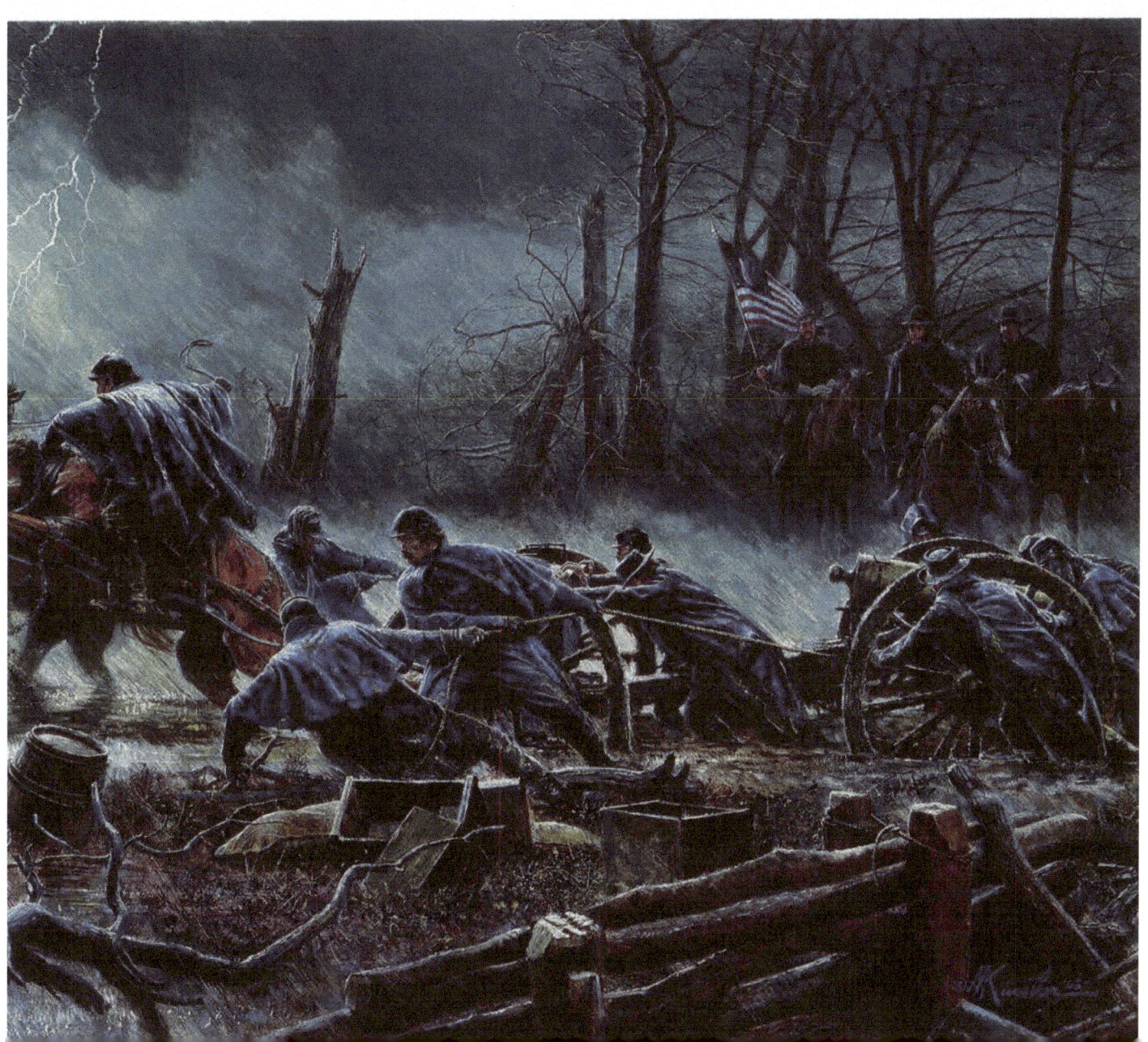

AFTER THE defeat at Fredericksburg, the Army of the Potomac returned to its camps on the northern bank of the Rappahannock. Anxious to redress the disaster, Ambrose E. Burnside proposed to cross the river upstream and circle around and behind Lee. The plan might have worked, but political intrigues delayed the operation, set to begin on December 30, until January 20. By then the weather turned and extinguished any chance of success.

Before the first day's march had concluded, a winter storm began to brew. The rain turned to torrents, and the roads became rivers of mud. Wagons sank to their axles, and field guns became so mired that 12-horse teams and 150 men hauling on ropes could not extricate them. Animals died of exhaustion, and men wore themselves out wrestling with the equipment. Across the river, Confederates mocked the struggling soldiers, posting signs such as "Burnside's Army Stuck in the Mud."

The storm passed four days later, but the Union army was spent. The operation was canceled and soon ingloriously labeled the "Mud March." Burnside was reassigned, and Joseph Hooker was named the new commander of the Army of the Potomac.

In 2002, Larry Silver of Silver Companies in Fredericksburg asked me if I might be interested in doing a painting of the famous Mud March. At first I wasn't interested in a failed military movement. Then I read Frank O'Reilly's *The Fredericksburg Campaign,* which deals in depth with the Mud March, and I became intrigued with the topic both as an expression of the willpower of men in the field and also as a work of historical art.

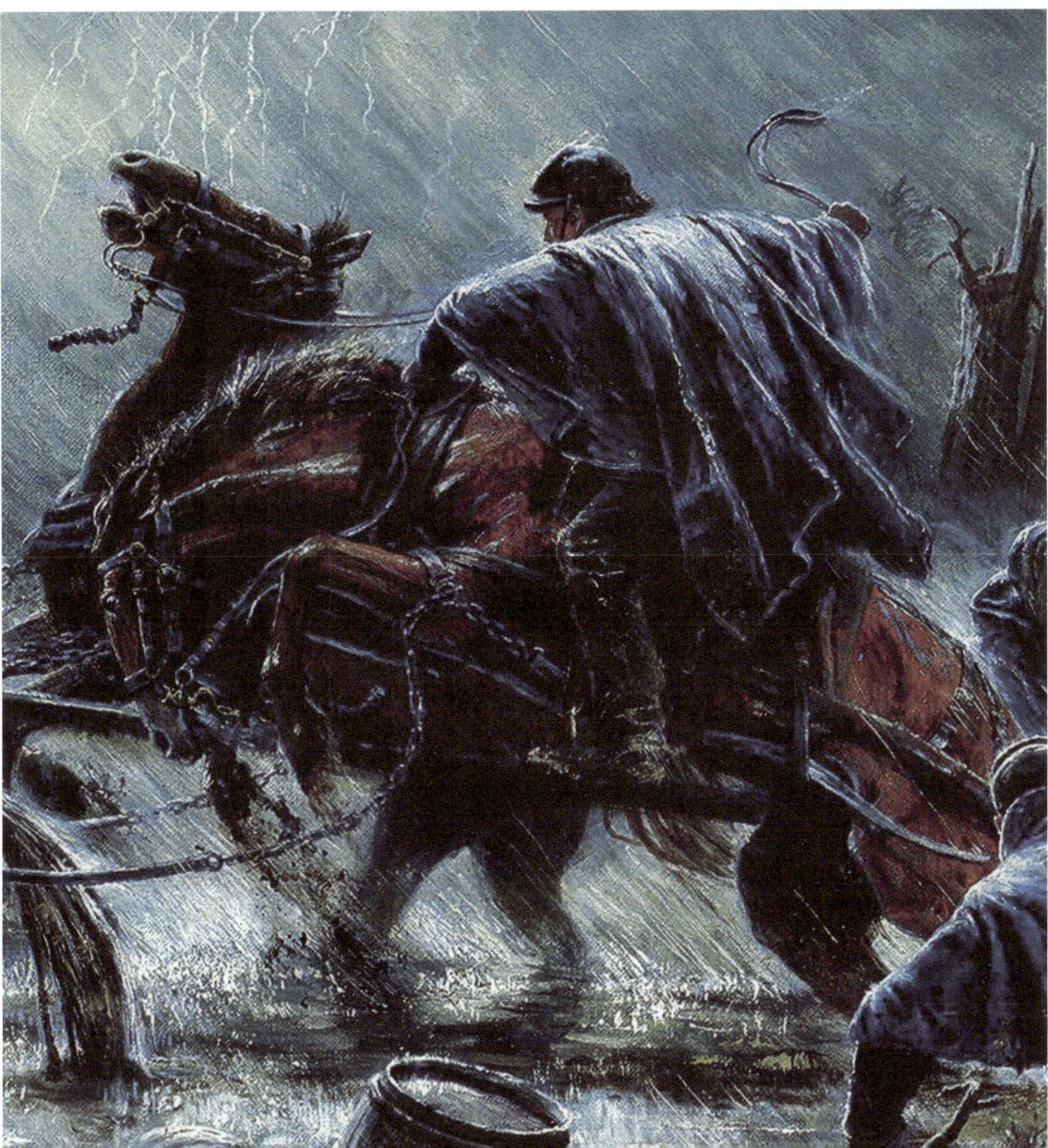

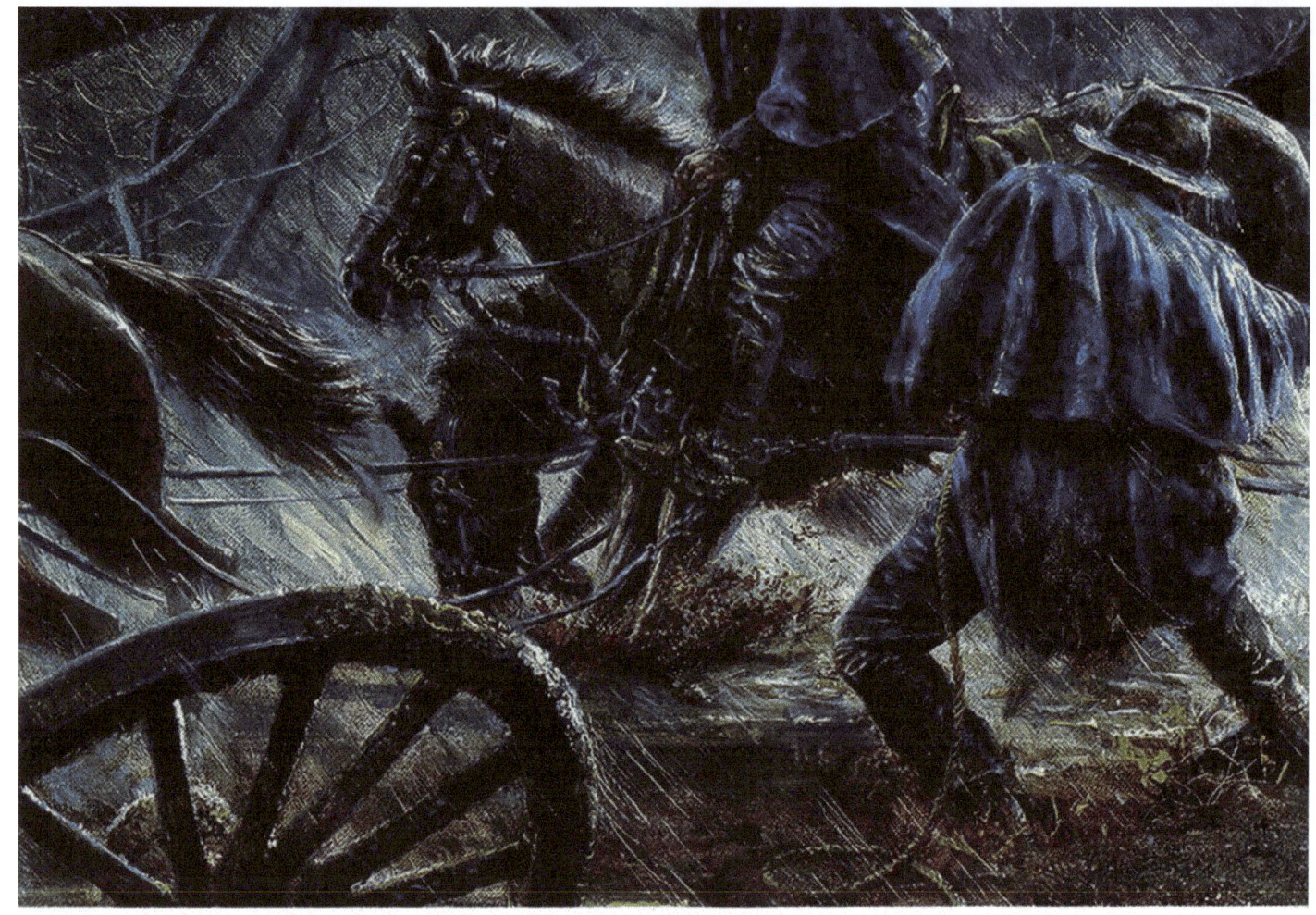

The idea of a painting showing the struggle of man and animal against nature had tremendous potential for drama. I traveled the muddy roads on which the Army of the Potomac had marched so futilely, and I was struck by the incredible hardships these soldiers endured. I was also impressed by the power of the storm and the conditions it created: troops struggling against the elements; cannon, caissons, and pontoon bridges bogged in the mud; and teams of horses fighting through the mire. Everyone and everything was

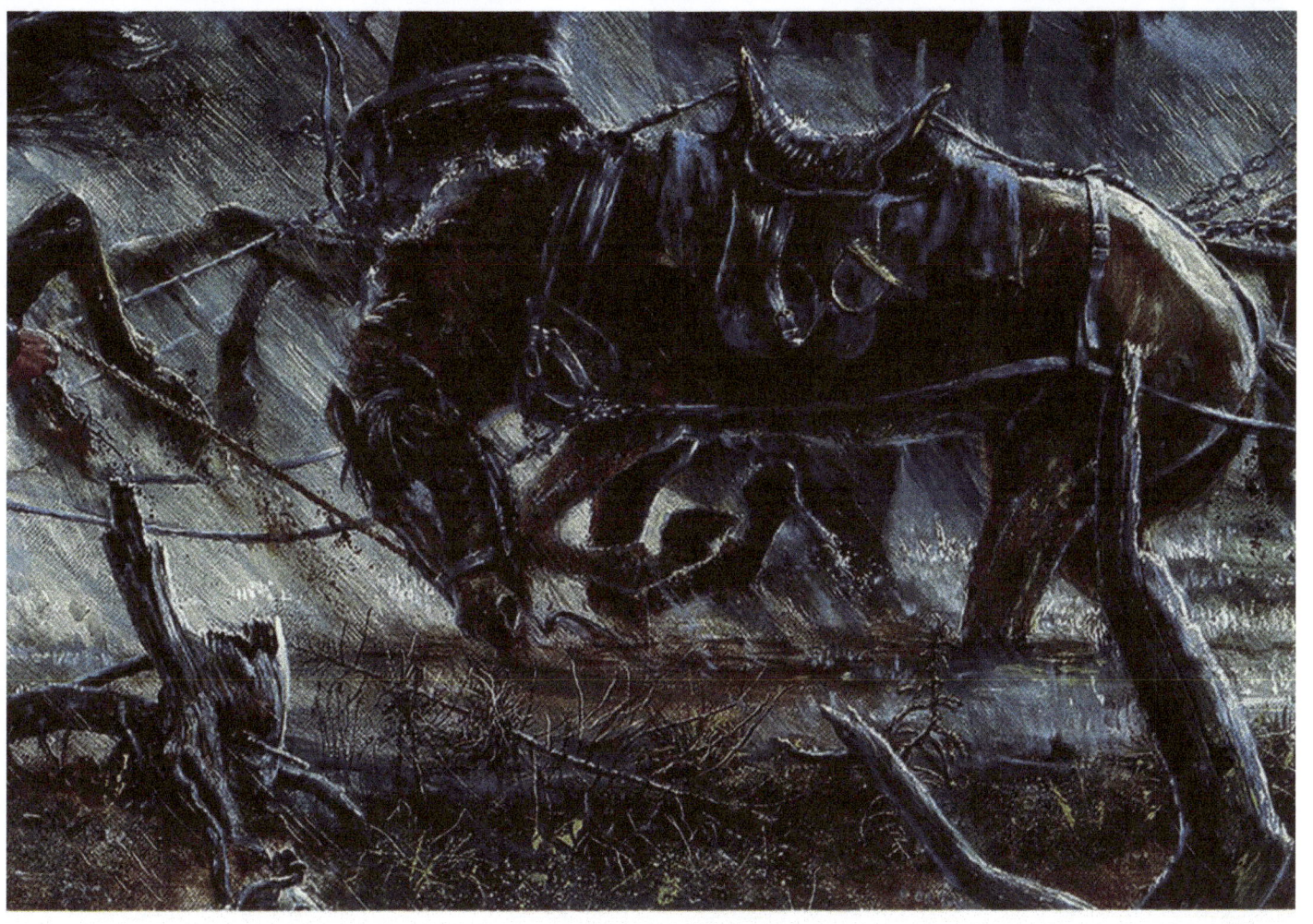

dripping wet and dirty, and lightning flashes added even more drama to the struggle.

In the painting, Joshua L. Chamberlain and his brother Tom, both of the Twentieth Maine, observe the exertions of the troops from the side of the road in the center background. Burnside is set in the background, on the right side of the painting, with members of his staff and his official head-quarters flag.

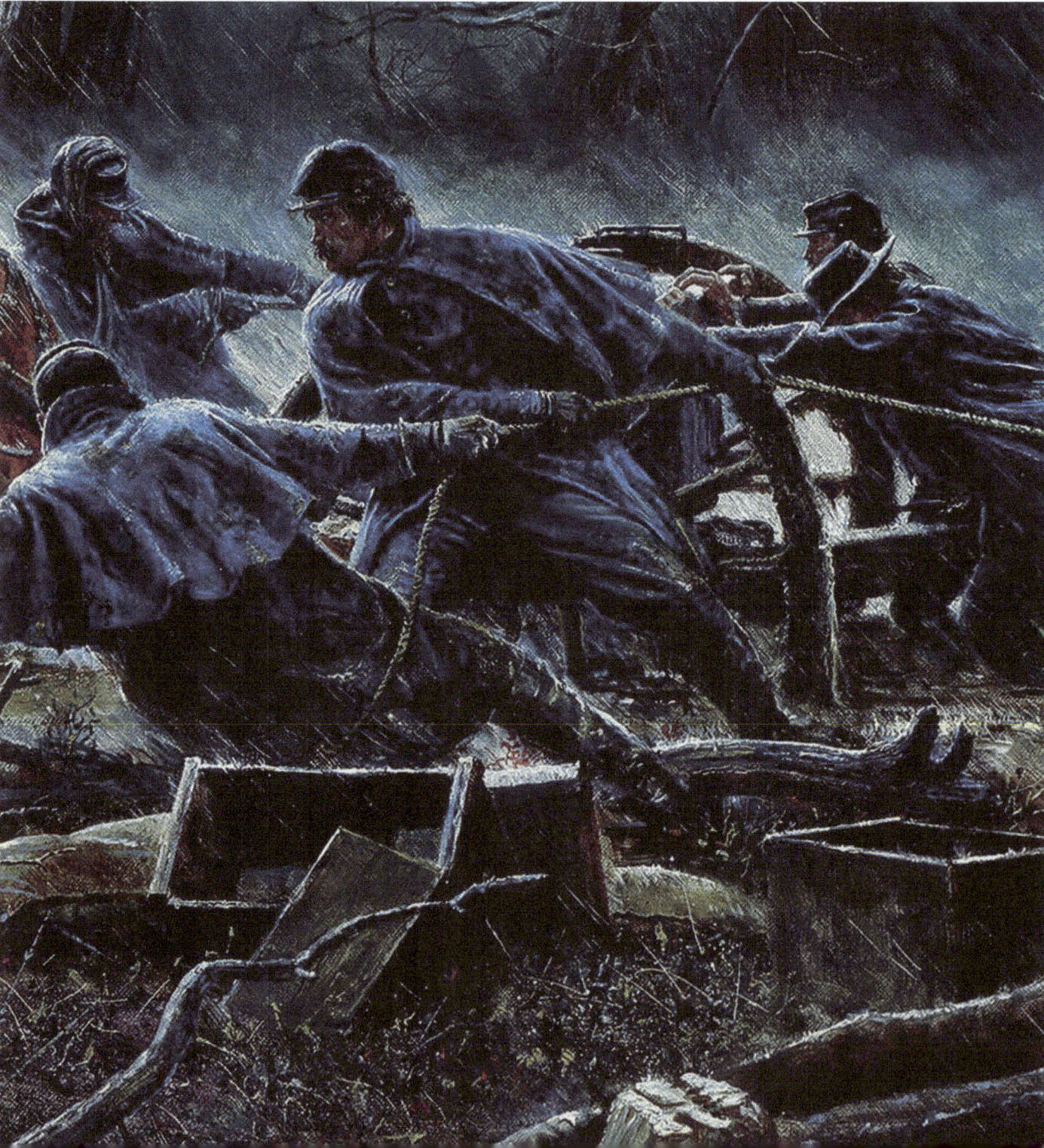

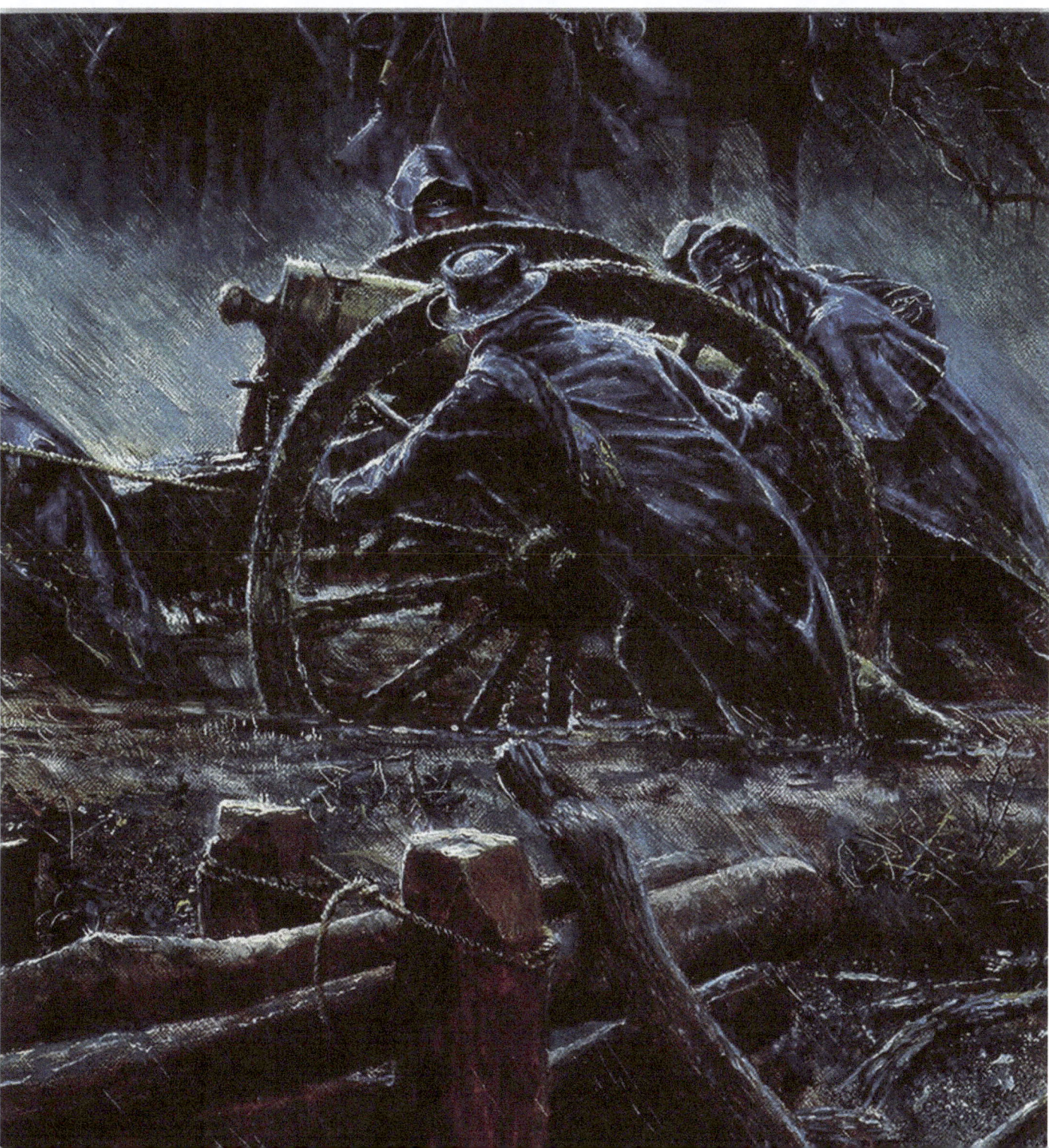

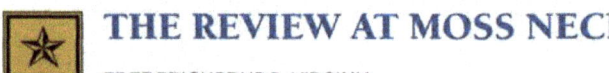

THE REVIEW AT MOSS NECK

FREDERICKSBURG, VIRGINIA

JANUARY 20, 1863

1995, oil, 24 x 42

detail, right

To SET the scene for this painting, we have to go back to the frigid night of December 16, 1862. Thomas J. Jackson was exhausted, cold, and hungry. He was close to Moss Neck Manor, a formerly imposing estate now reflecting the deprivations of war. When Jackson could bear the cold no longer, he and his staff sought shelter in the house. Roberta Corbin was more than happy to accommodate the legendary general, but in the morning, Jackson insisted that his headquarters tents be set near the stables, a distance away from the house.

For the next three months, Moss Neck served as winter quarters for Jackson's corps. The sixteen-hundred-acre estate was eleven miles downriver from Fredericksburg and two miles from the Rappahannock. The Corbin family had been in the area for two centuries and was among the most prominent in Virginia. During the war, Richard Corbin served in the Ninth Virginia Cavalry, leaving his wife and five-year-old daughter alone in the house with his sister. A cold complicated by an earache moved Jackson from his tent to a small wood-frame office building a short distance from the house.

There was no winter campaign, so Jackson's time was focused on writing battle reports. He received numerous visitors and frequently hosted his

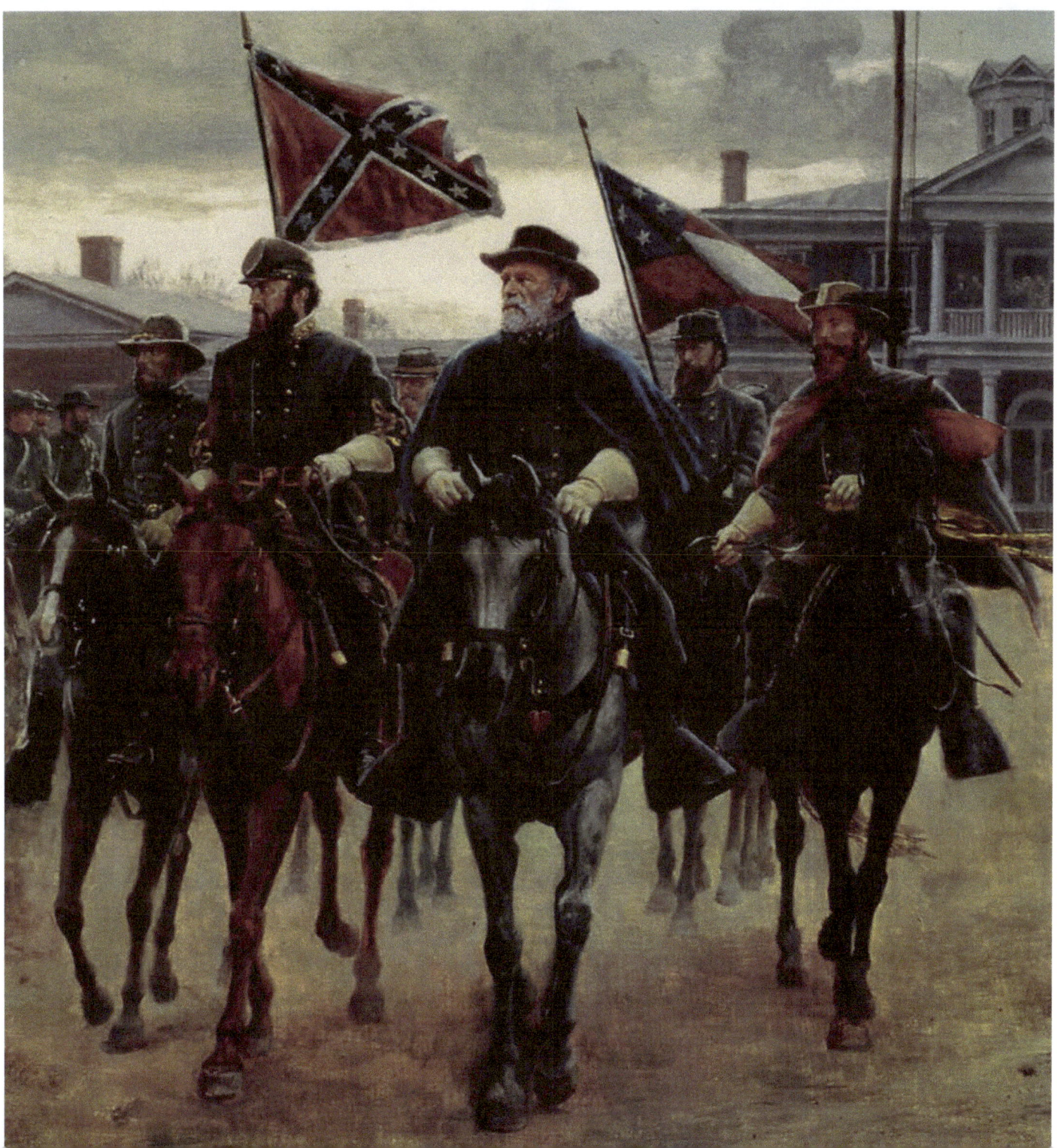

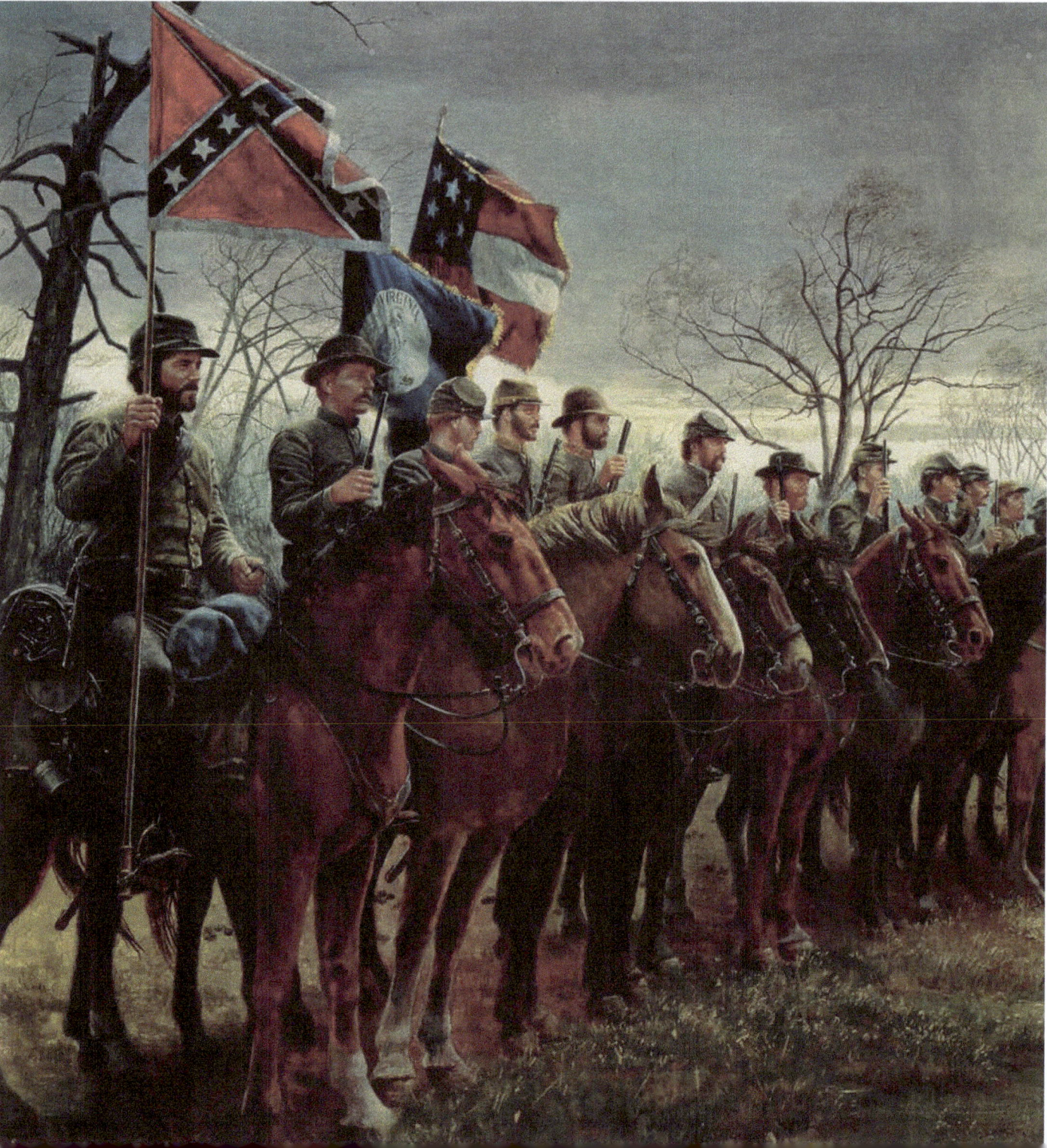

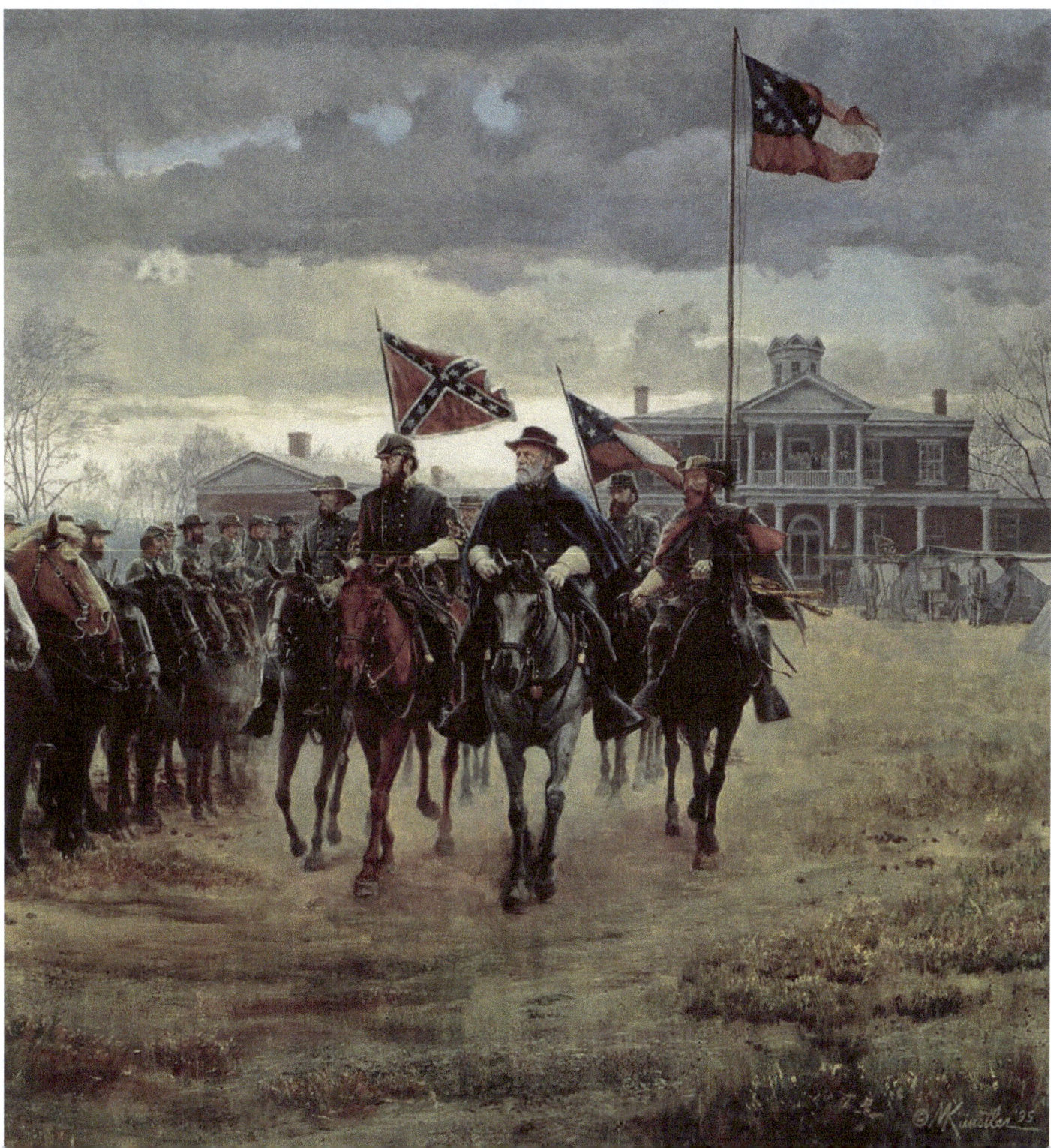

fellow commanders. During this time, Jackson fell under the spell of five-year-old Janie (see page 88).

I came across a reference in Henry Kyd Douglas's *I Rode with Stonewall* in which he mentions that Jackson and Lee reviewed Stuart's troops at Moss Neck on January 20, 1863. I consulted James I. Robertson Jr., the foremost authority on Jackson, about the review. Not only did he verify the event, but he cross-referenced it with other primary sources, placing Lee's son "Rooney" and James Longstreet there as well. With Professor Robertson's help, I was able to obtain photographs of the Moss Neck mansion the way it looked at the time. It still exists and has changed little in appearance since the war.

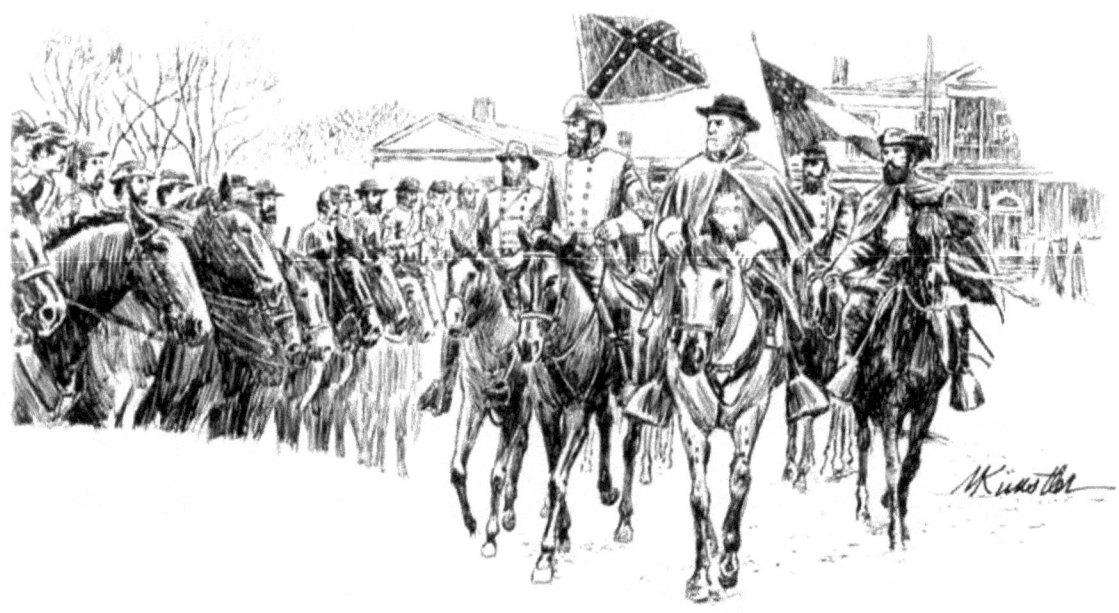

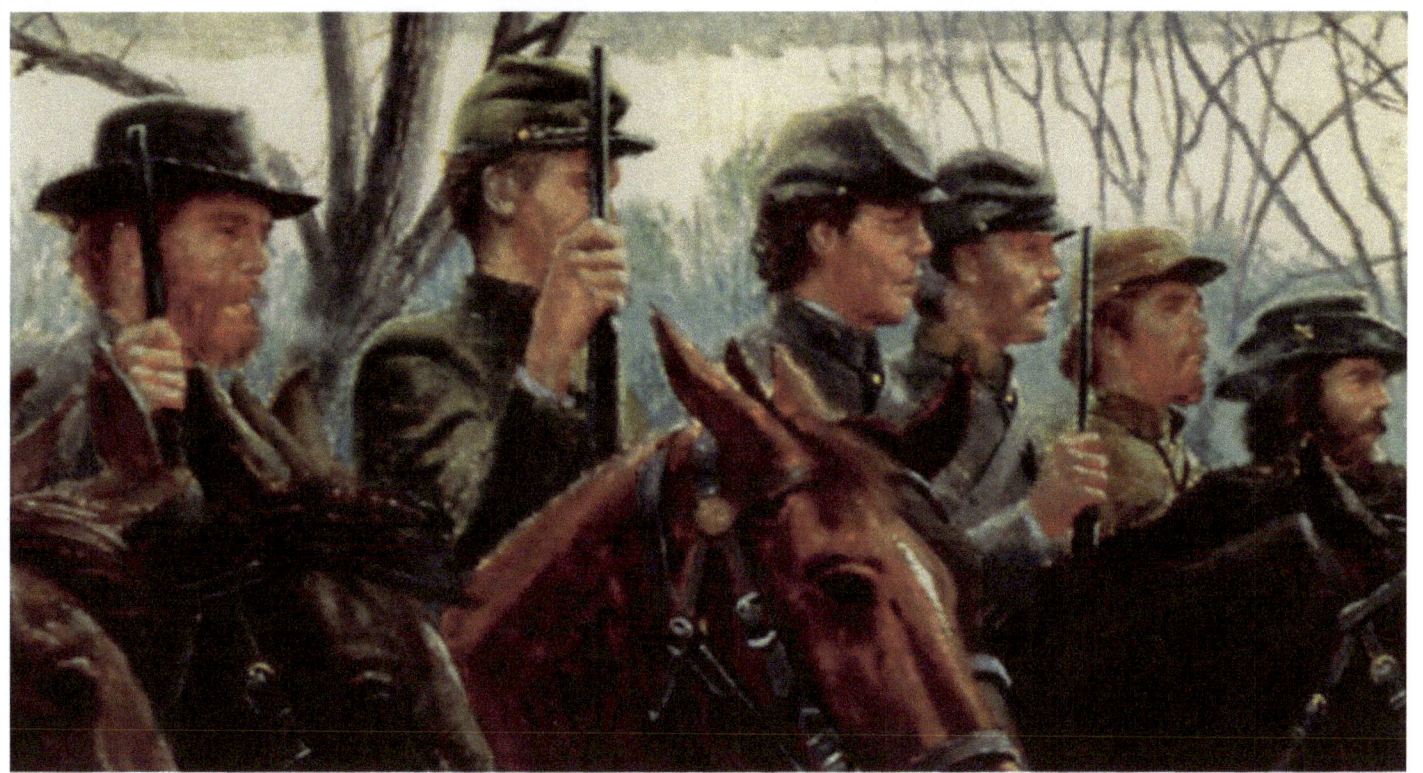

The review was of Rooney Lee's regiment. We see them lined up on the left with the battle flag, the Virginia state flag, the First National flag of the Confederacy, and a variety of firearms from carbines to sawed-off shotguns.

The inspection party shows Lee in a blue cape, flanked on the left by Jackson, directly under the battle flag, and on the far left by Rooney Lee, who is closest to his troops. On the right, in the red-lined cape, with a plume in his hat, is Jeb Stuart. Directly behind him is Longstreet.

Jackson's "office" was a wood-frame building behind the cavalry. His headquarters' tents can be seen in the right background. Naturally, any civilians around, including the Corbin family, would have taken advantage of the good vantage point on the upper porch to enjoy the exciting event. The resulting painting conveys a memorable moment of peaceful pageantry.

CONFEDERATE SUNSET

FREDERICKSBURG, VIRGINIA
FEBRUARY 1863

1995, oil, 26 x 38

THE WINTER of 1862–63 was a period of winter camps and entrenchment. It would also be the last time that the trio of Lee, Jackson, and Longstreet would be together.

For his part, James Longstreet was maneuvering for a change of command, preferring an appointment to the western theater, because he saw there "opportunities for all kinds of moves to great advantages." To Lee, he proposed "that one army corps [Jackson's] could hold the line of the Rappahannock while the other [his]

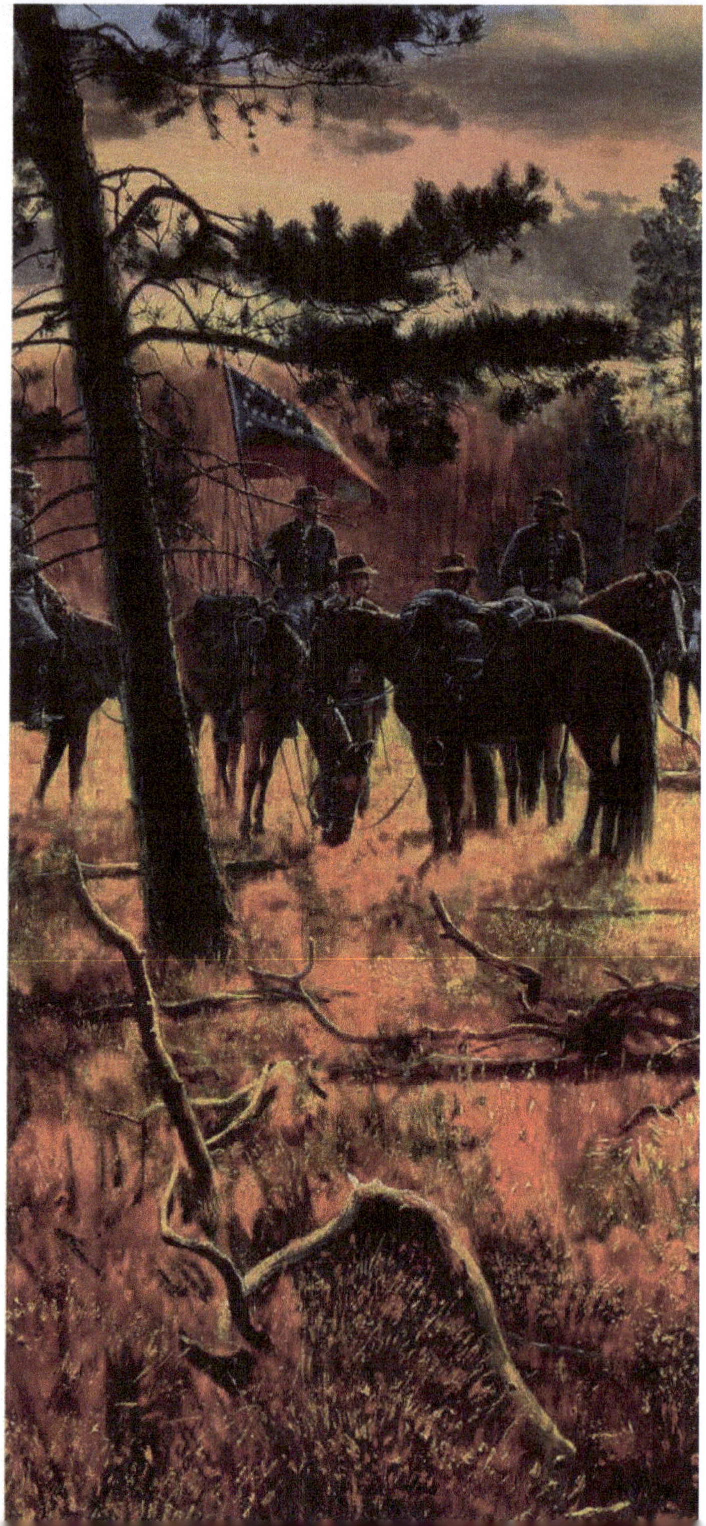

118

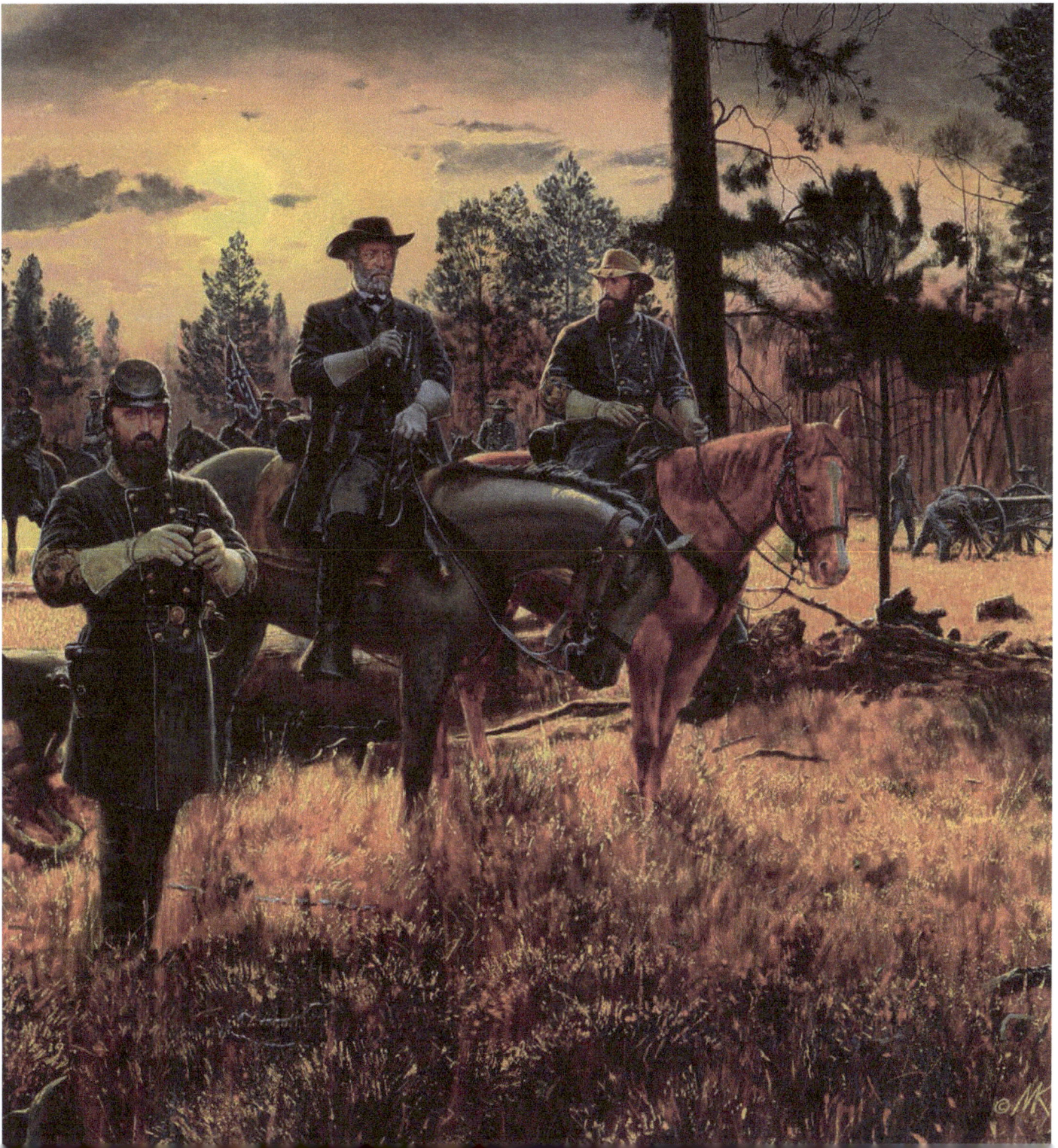

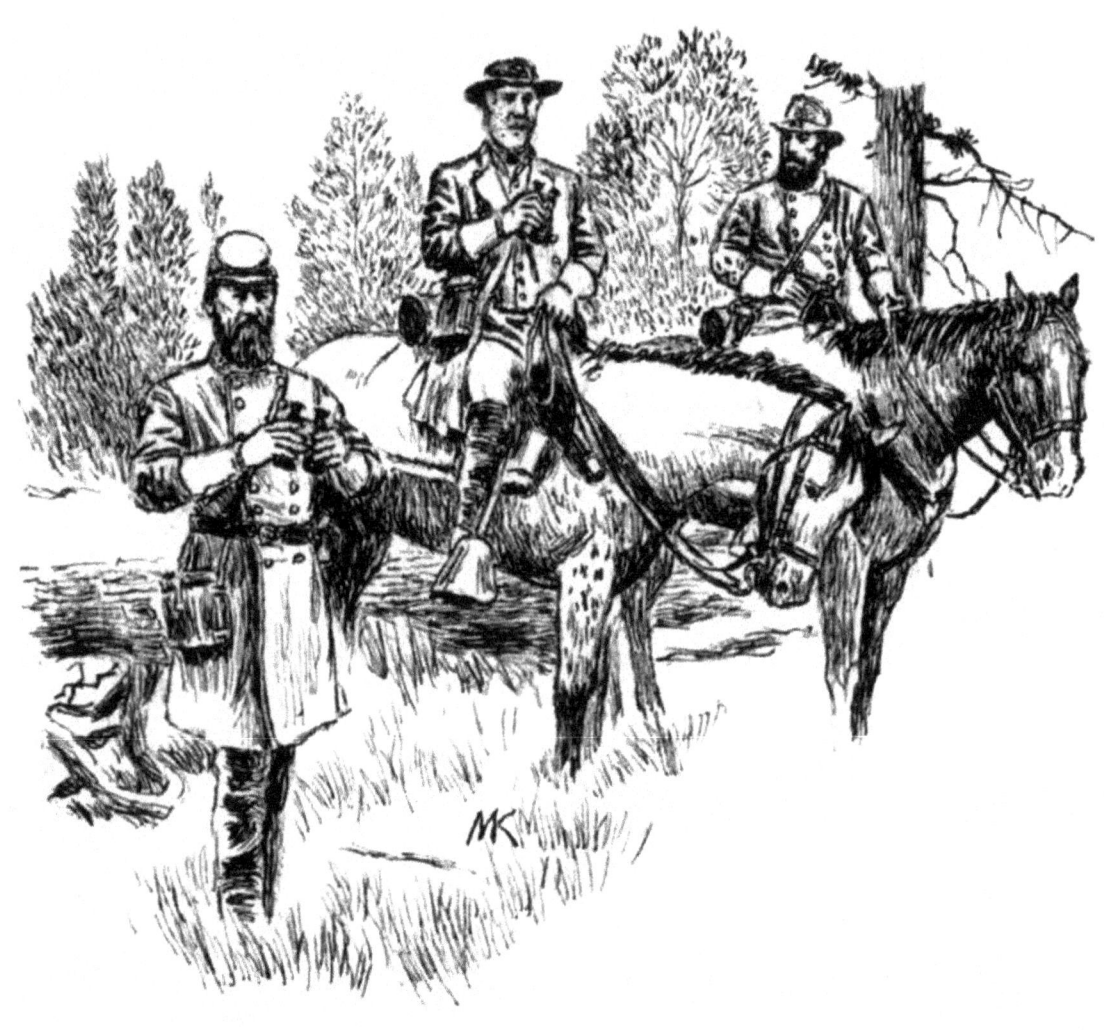

was operating elsewhere." Longstreet hoped his corps would be sent to Tennessee to bolster the army there that had failed at Murfreesboro and lost Middle Tennessee. Lee rejected the plan but soon dispatched two of Longstreet's divisions to Richmond to address Federal activity in southeastern Virginia and North Carolina.

In mid-February, Union troop movements induced Lee to send Longstreet to Richmond, where he was appointed to command the Department of Virginia and North Carolina, roughly the area between Richmond and Wilmington. In this capacity, Longstreet balanced his responsibilities in a way that thwarted Federal probing efforts and gathered supplies from the untouched counties of his department. Together Lee and Longstreet devised a campaign against the Union base in Suffolk in order to further supply the army. In essence, it was a foraging expedition under the guise of a siege, and Longstreet pursued it until Joseph Hooker, the new commander of the Army of the Potomac, launched the spring offensive that became the battle of Chancellorsville.

Lee, Jackson, and Longstreet are the Confederate commanders who fascinate me the most. Robert E. Lee was a military commander like no other at the time. He valued and depended upon Thomas J. Jackson, whom he praised as "his right arm." And after Jackson, none could compare with Lee's "Old War Horse"—James Longstreet.

I decided to paint this Southern trio at sunset. I had not done a sunset in any of my prior Civil War work, so the idea was not only appropriate but personally appealing. James I. Robertson Jr. informed me that the three commanders were together many times on staff reconnaissances in early

1863. I chose to place the painting in early February, shortly before Longstreet departed for detached duty.

The terrain is typical of the woodlands near Fredericksburg. The hardwood forest has not leafed out yet and adds a distant, somber tone to the background. Near the Confederate front line, the three observe the distant enemy from a broom-straw clearing amid a sparse stand of pines. There's a golden glow to the setting, which I think is appropriate for the scene. Although they could not know it at the time, these three exceptional commanders were in the sunset of their time together.

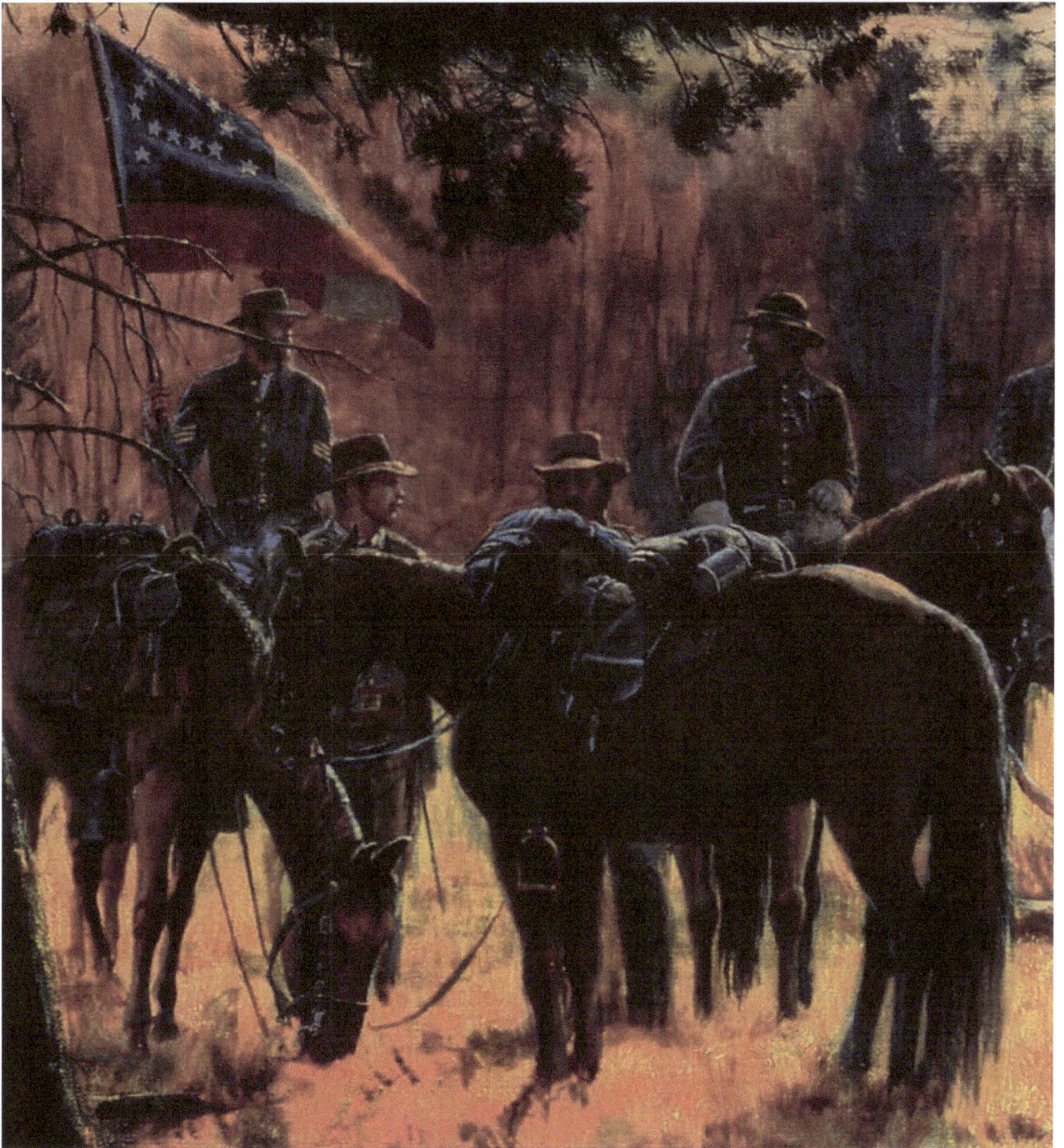

BRIEF ENCOUNTER

MIDDLEBURG, VIRGINIA
FEBRUARY 1863
2005, oil, 28 x 38

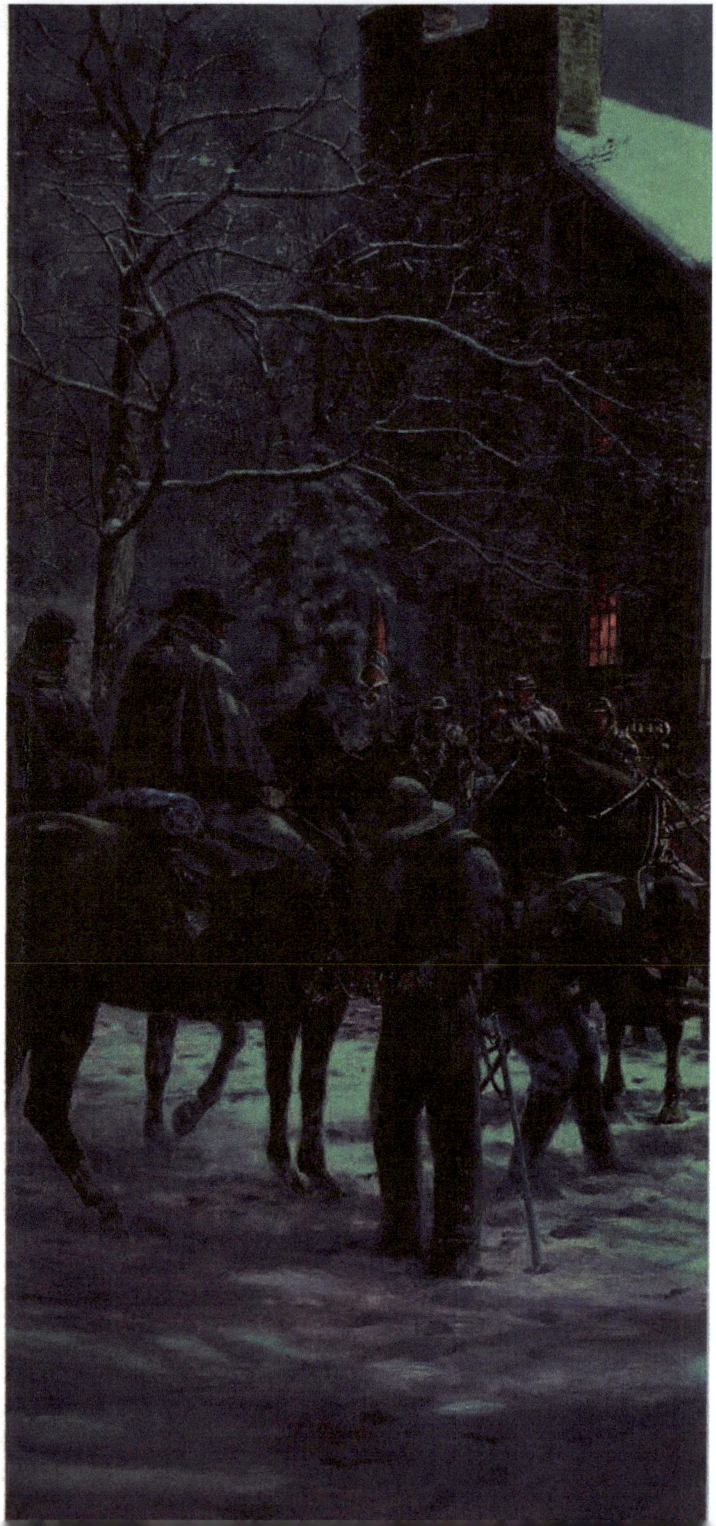

VIRGINIA'S PIEDMONT is beautiful in every season, and one of the most picturesque areas in the Piedmont is Middleburg, which is where I have set *Brief Encounter.* The scene is outside the Red Fox Inn, which was known as the Beveridge House during the war. The building dates to the 1700s and is an interesting-looking structure that captures the spirit of the region.

There are four dormers on the roof now; during the 1860s there were two. The porches were different then too, but the distinctive twin

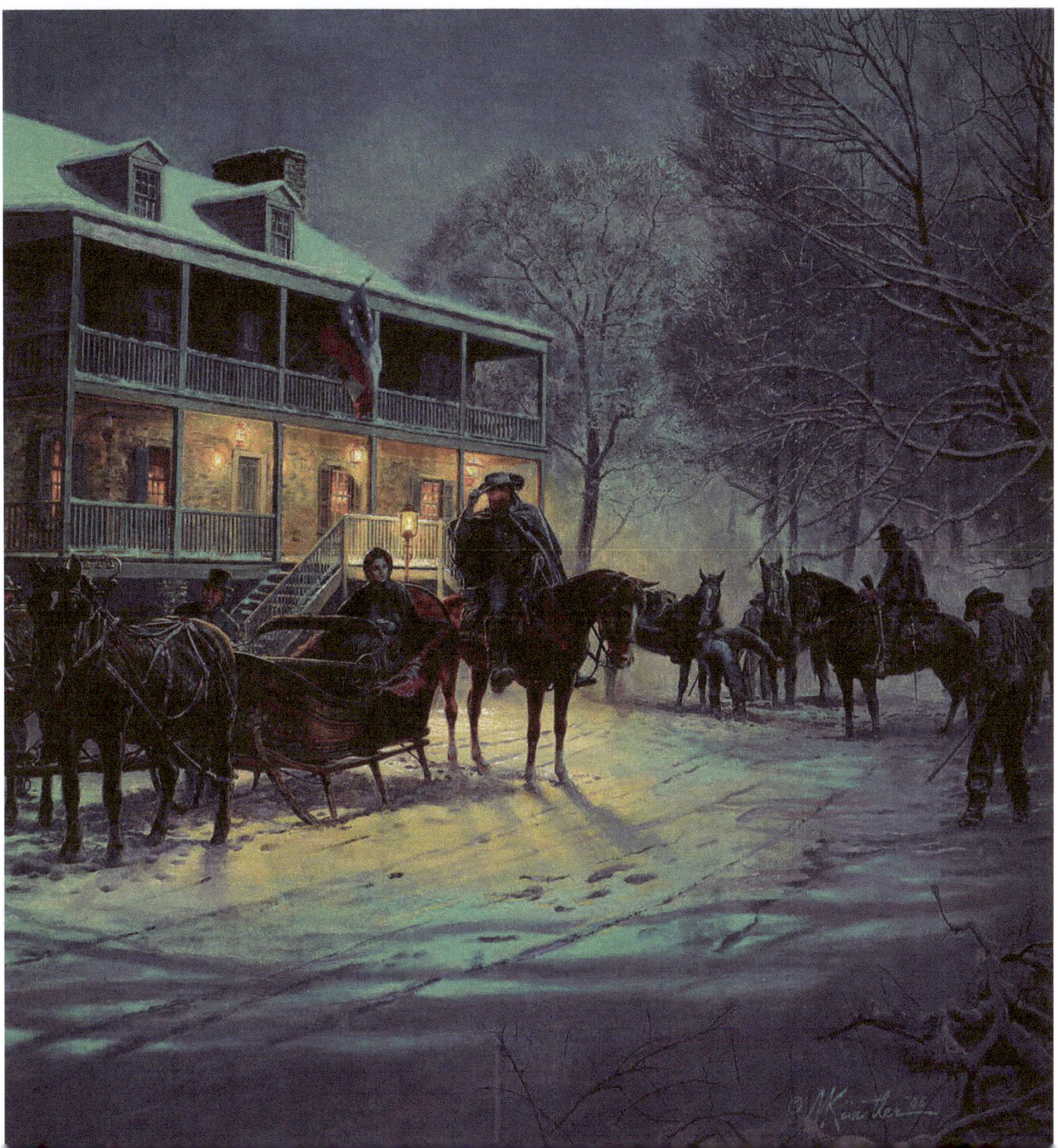

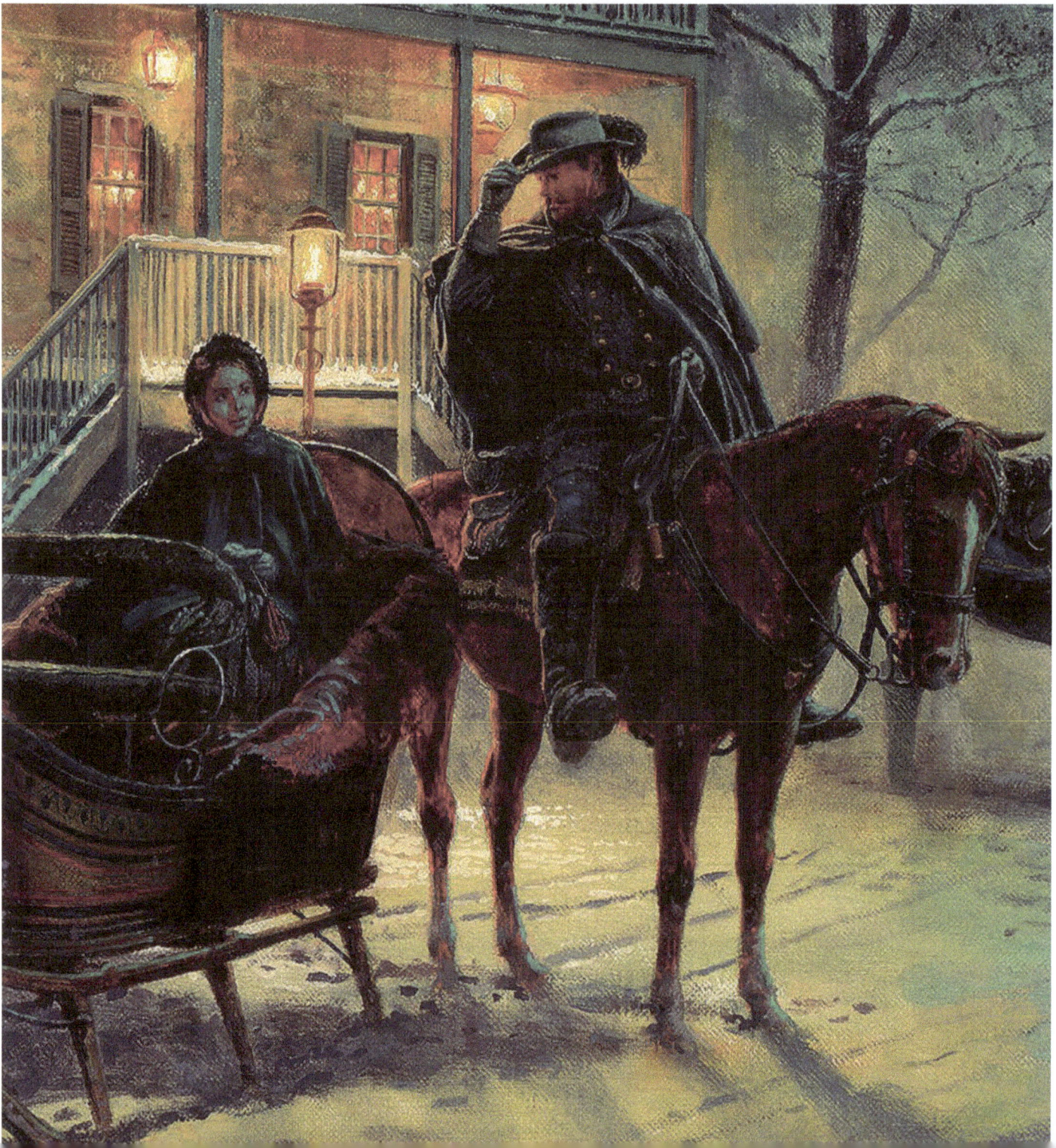

chimneys on the west side of the building are unchanged, as is the unusual window alignment on the second floor.

I decided to use this historic setting to represent how the fortunes of war led to so many partings and so many fleeting encounters. I painted the main figures small, as if dwarfed by events. I utilized the lamplight from the inn to silhouette the figures and then emphasized the warm light by making the scene a cool-color moonlit night.

Historian James I. Robertson Jr. was my source for weather conditions. Joshua Ruff and the staff at the Long Island Museum of American Art, History and Carriages were of great help to me on the sleigh and the harnesses.

The cavalry squadron is depicted in a brief calm moment. The soldiers are checking their weapons and equipment. One trooper is checking the harness on the team of horses. Others wait patiently to move out.

The center of interest is an officer tipping his hat to a young woman. Is he saying good-bye to his wife or to a sweetheart? Or is it a chance encounter that offers hope for the future? Viewers can ponder so many scenarios. Either way, it's a leave-taking in the midst of war, and there may be no return. It might be a last good-bye—every soldier knew that. One of the keenest hardships of soldier life was separation from loved ones. Left behind when a soldier went to war were sweethearts or wives and children, along with parents, brothers, sisters, and others who were dear to one's heart. Ever present was the knowledge that reunion might never occur.

The demands of life in the field were a welcome distraction from the pain of separation, but for most soldiers, the anguish returned in the quiet moments. "I assure you that I am lonely and sad," wrote a soldier to his wife. "I cannot sleep

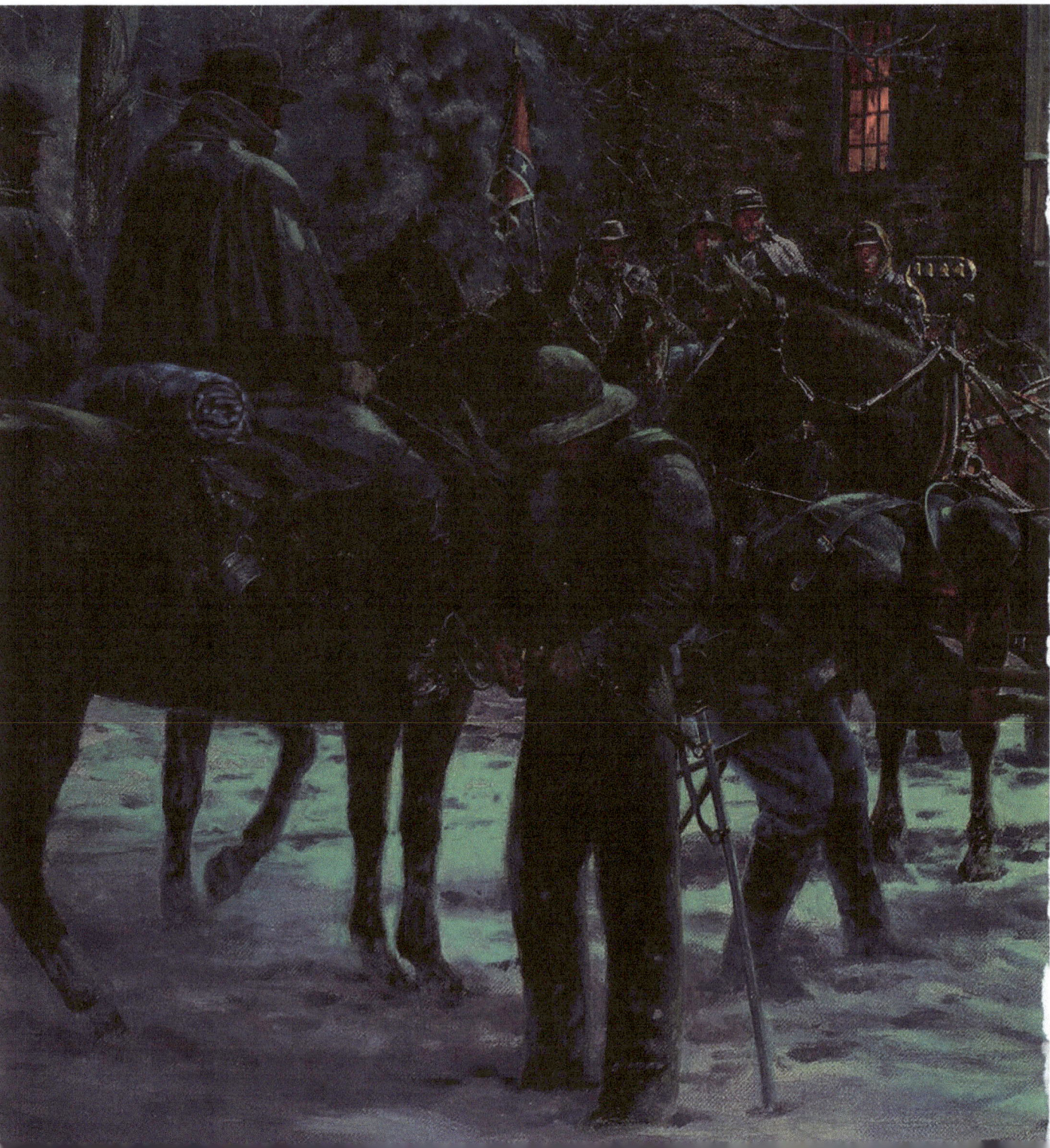

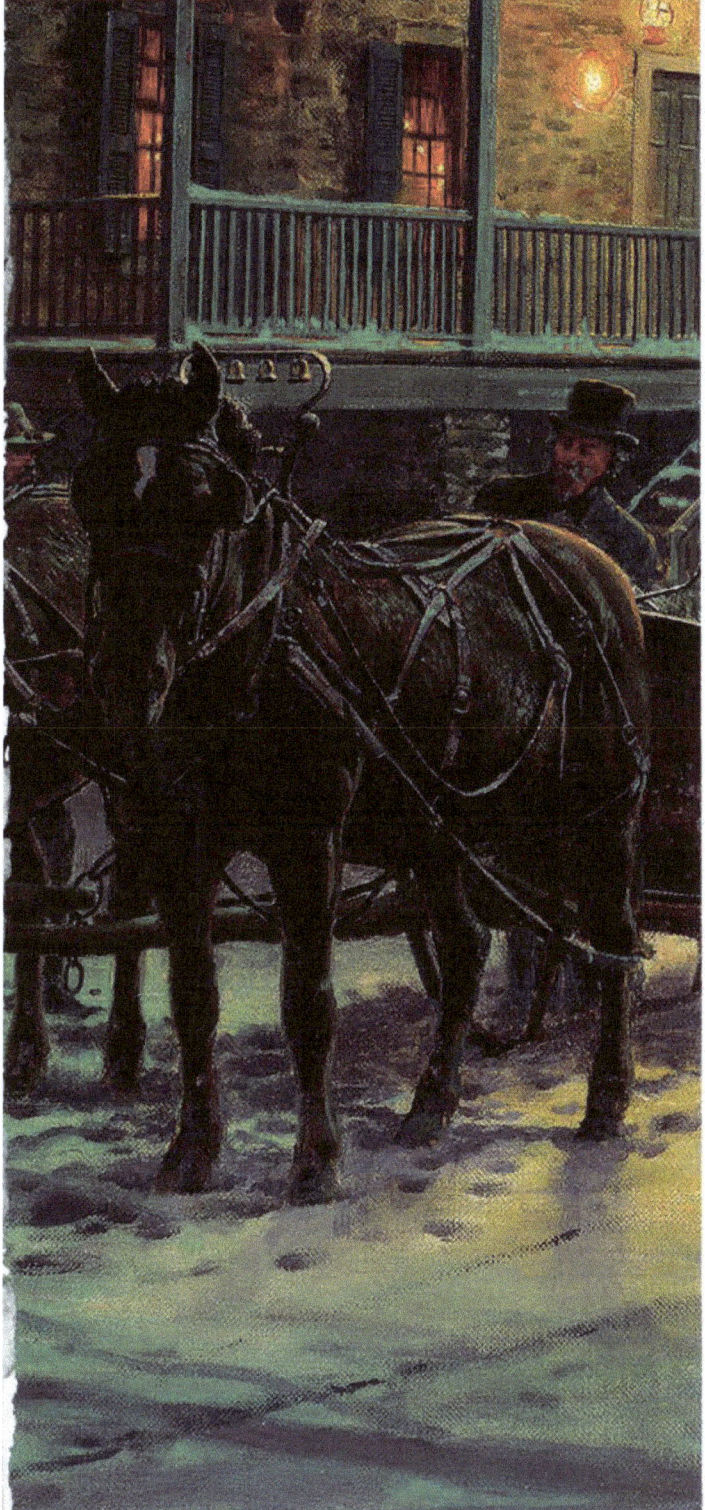

but little at night. I roll from side to side on the damp ground and think of you my dear wife and children." Wrote another: "Well, son, I often think of you. . . . Study your books so you can write to me. Let me know what the old mare is doing; how all the cows, hogs and corn and potatoes and everything is doing—whether you have any apples, peaches or waterm[e]lons."

The promise of homecoming was cherished above all. "Oh how earnestly I pray that death may not intervene to prevent our meeting with my darling children around our own hearth," wrote a Confederate major to his wife. "Now, my dear wife I do not want you to grieve and fret because I am going to the front. May the God of Heaven bless you and my dear children is my sincere prayer." But for 620,000 Americans in blue and gray, such homecomings never came.

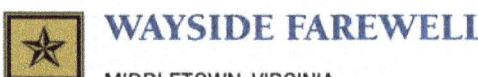

WAYSIDE FAREWELL

MIDDLETOWN, VIRGINIA
FEBRUARY 3, 1863

1996, oil, 28 x 46

detail, right

MIDDLETOWN, VIRGINIA, provided the setting for this painting. The town was named for its location between Winchester and Woodstock and saw little fighting during the war until the battle of Cedar Creek in 1864. Jackson maneuvered nearby during his 1862 Shenandoah campaign. Confederate cavalry was active here, so the sight of horsemen in the town was not unusual. Later, the town would fall into the area that came to be known as Mosby's Confederacy.

Wayside Farewell depicts a moment that thousands of couples experienced during the war: a lingering tearful good-bye complicated by the question of when—and whether—the two would see each other again. The scene is of a Confederate cavalry officer and his wife. The setting is the Valley Pike in front of Larrick's Hotel—known now as the Wayside Inn. The couple had been overnight guests and are saying good-bye in the predawn darkness while the officer's troops wait nearby. An attendant holds a team of horses

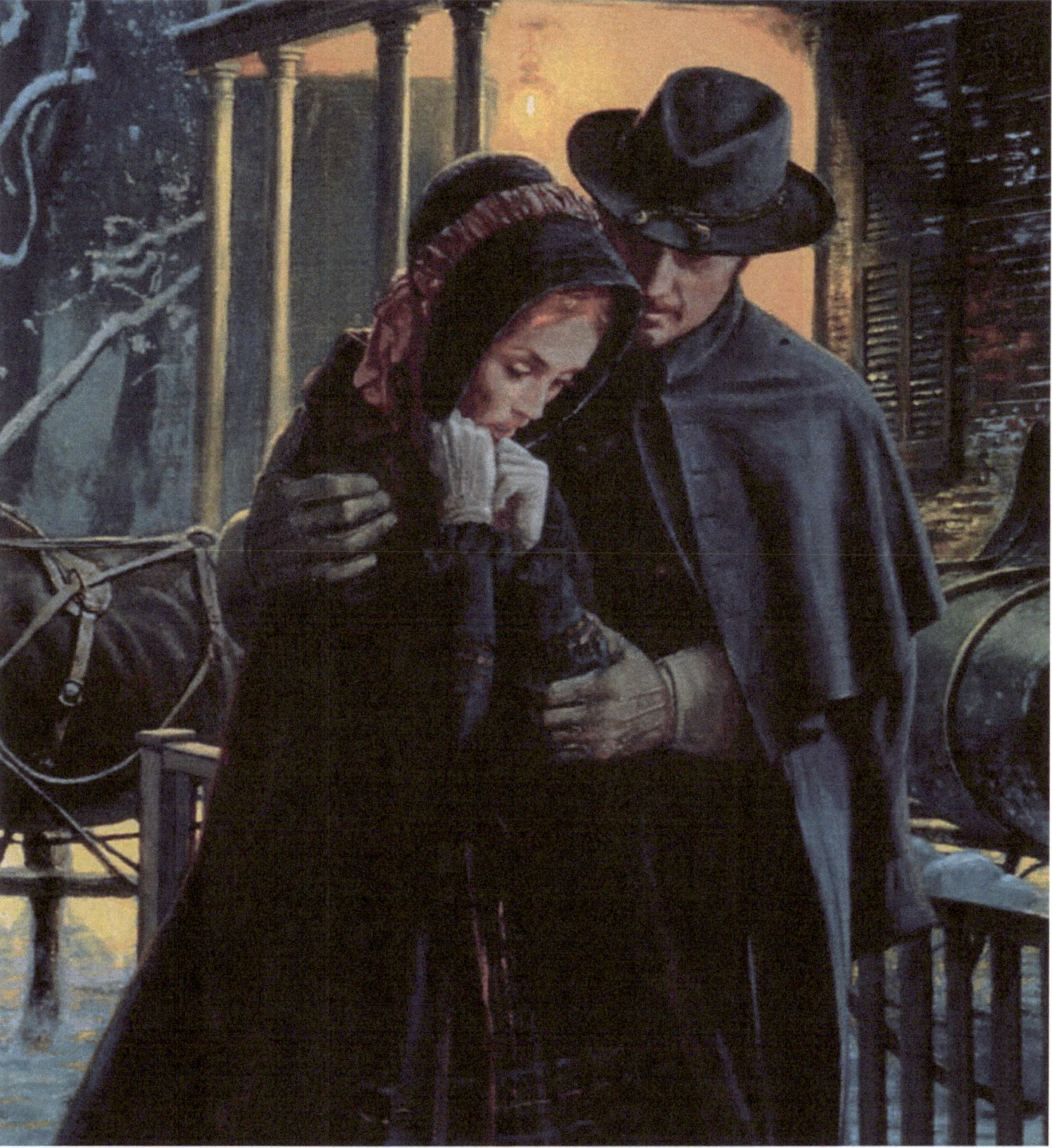

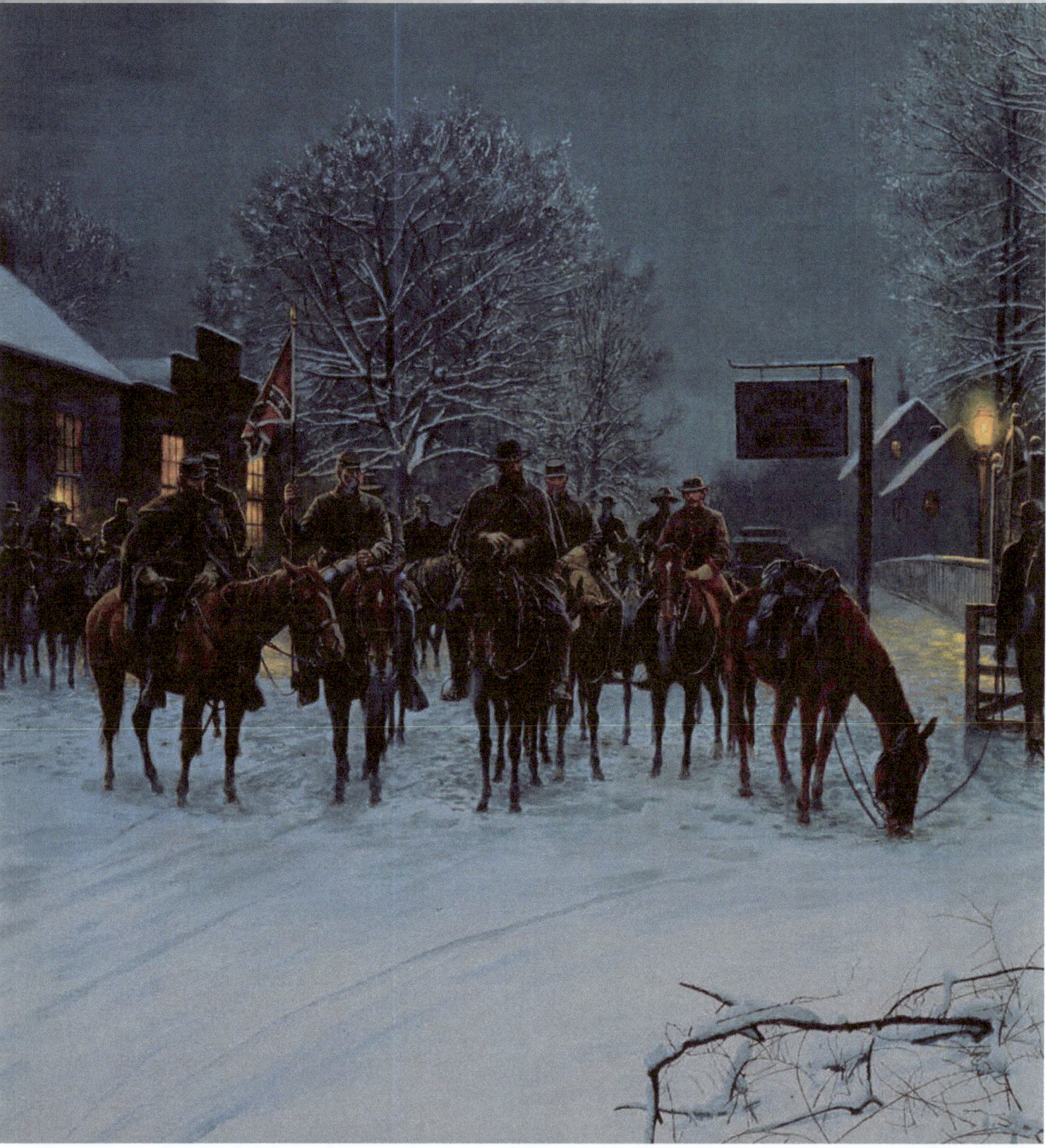

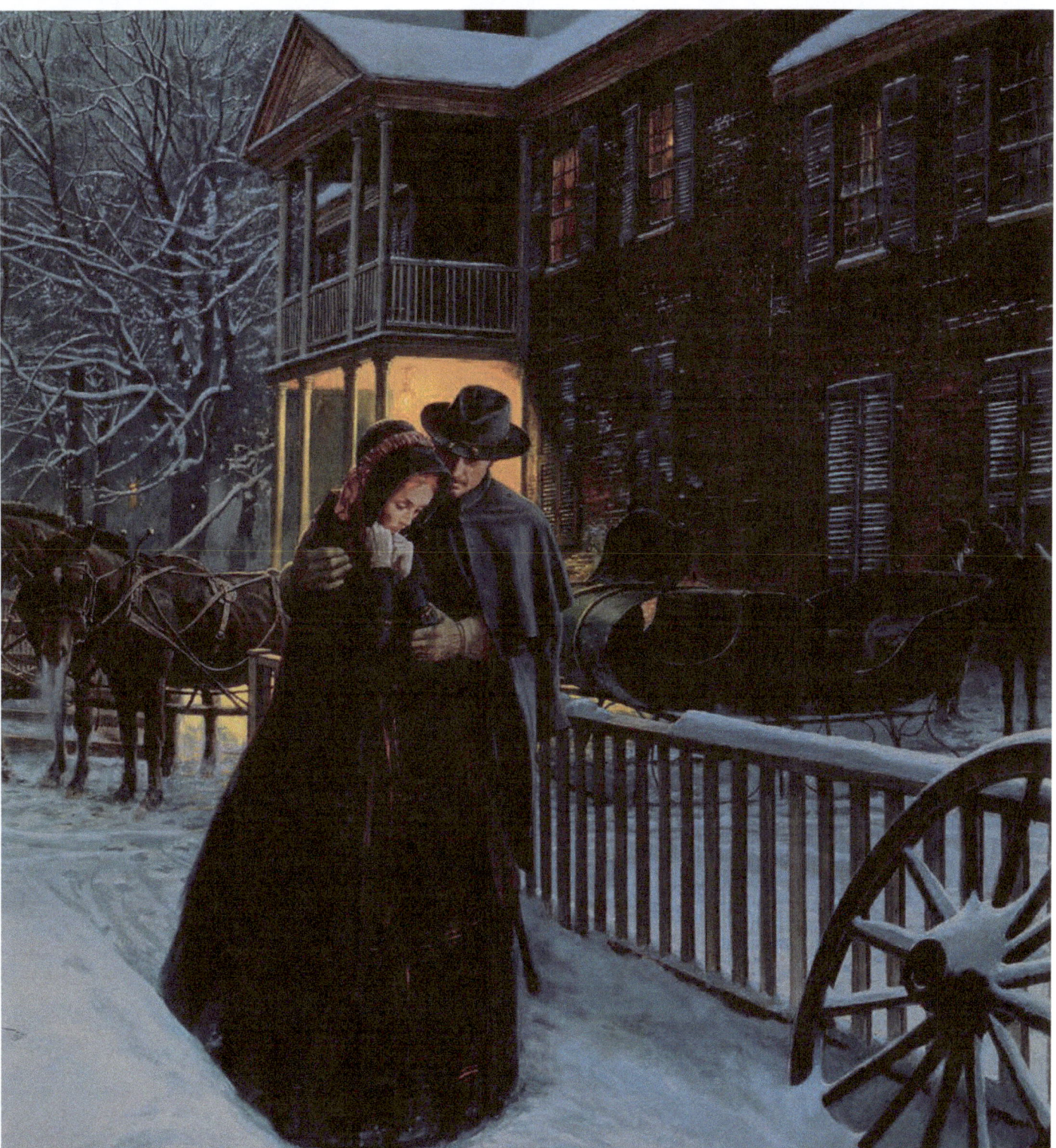

hitched to a sleigh, which will take the young woman home when her husband and his men return to war. It is a moving scene that occurred frequently during the war.

I have enjoyed so many visits to the Shenandoah Valley and the Winchester area that I consider the region to be my "hometown" in the South. Middletown's Wayside Inn is one of my favorite places partly because it is a unique

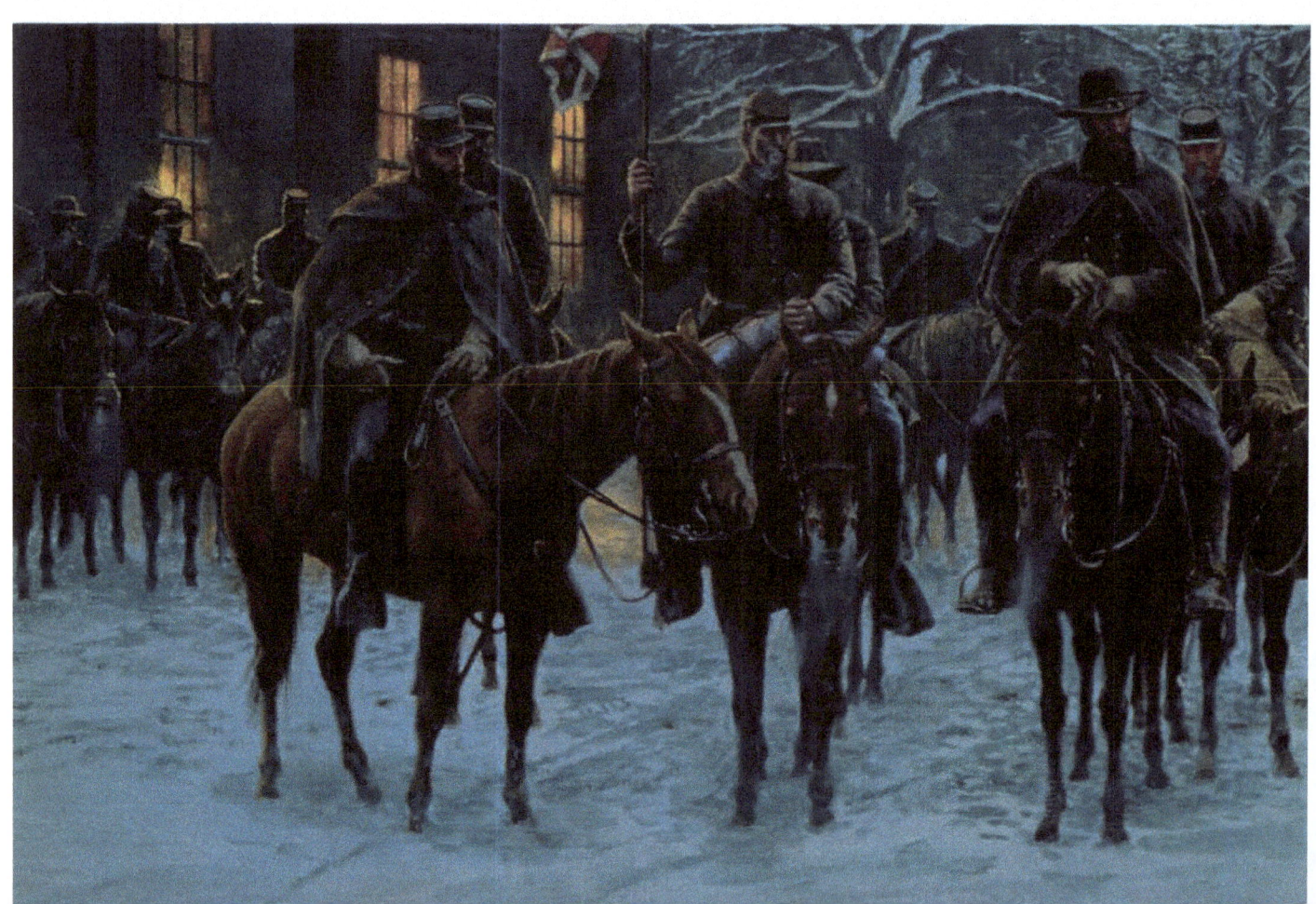

structure. I have painted the building as I believe it appeared in the 1860s. In the extreme left background are the Sperry house and store, and in the center background is Richard's Tavern. The sign, lamppost, and gate of the hotel are based on wartime sketches by James E. Taylor. And I learned that a four-inch snowfall covered the region on February 3, 1863, which is the time in which I placed the painting.

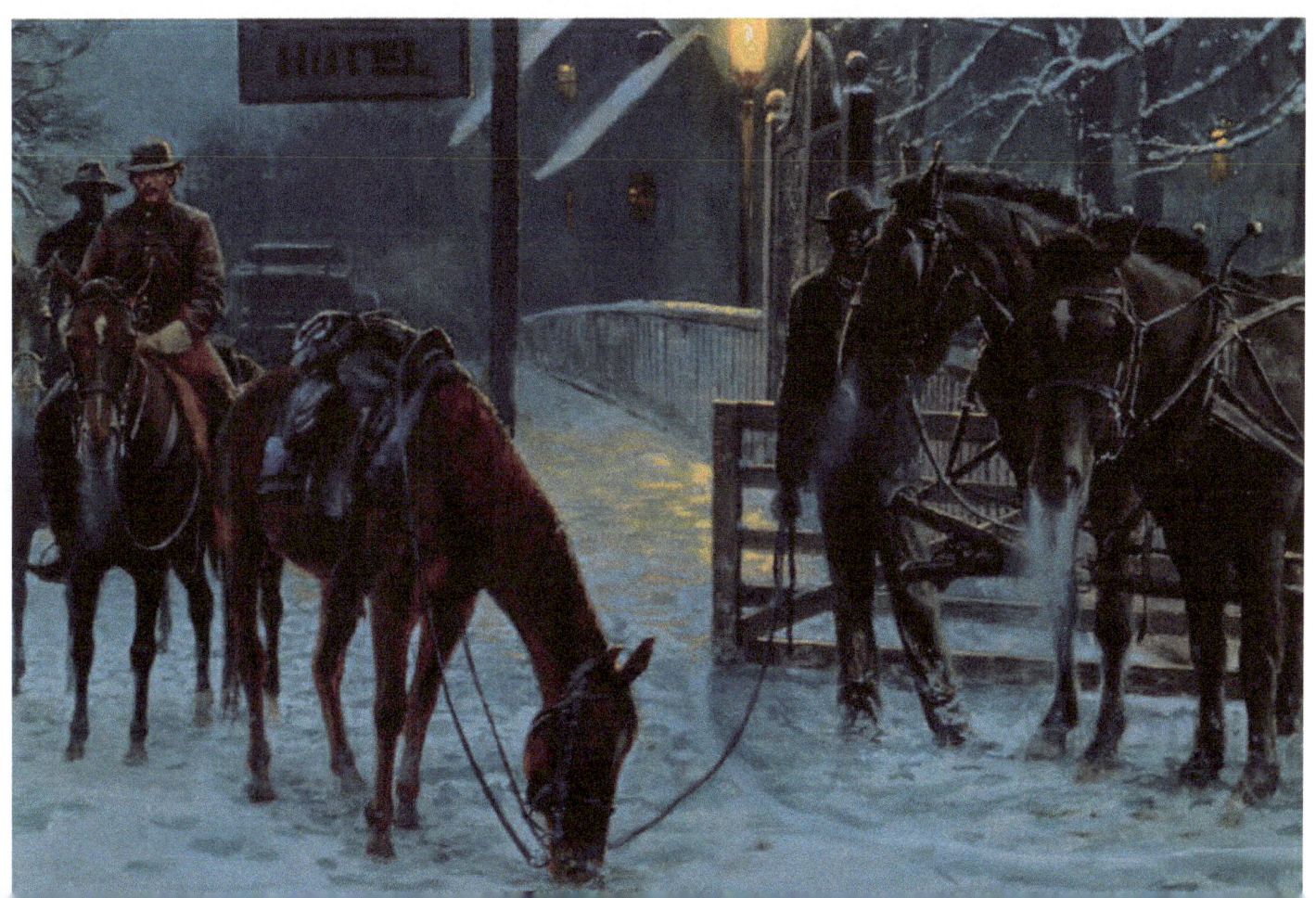

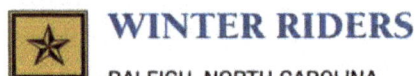

WINTER RIDERS

RALEIGH, NORTH CAROLINA
FEBRUARY 5, 1863

1995, oil, 28 x 46

detail, right

THIS PAINTING originated in 1992 with an invitation from the North Carolina Museum of History in Raleigh to host a one-man exhibition of my art. I was honored and wanted to do a unique painting that symbolized North Carolina's role in the war. Choosing an appropriate subject was difficult. I had already painted the state's most famous engagement—the battle of Fort Fisher—in *The Gunner and the Colonel,* and I had also painted the heroic charge of the Twenty-sixth North Carolina at Gettysburg in *The High Water Mark.*

Finally, after several visits to Raleigh, the concept for *Winter Riders* came into focus. Featuring Confederate troops and civilians, it represents the Tarheel State's greatest contribution to the Confederate war effort: its people. The painting also allowed me to focus on a snow scene and a night theme set near the North Carolina capitol, which is appropriately near the site of the museum.

With the help of Raymond Beck, the capitol historian, I learned what shops were on Fayetteville Street during the war, which added color as well

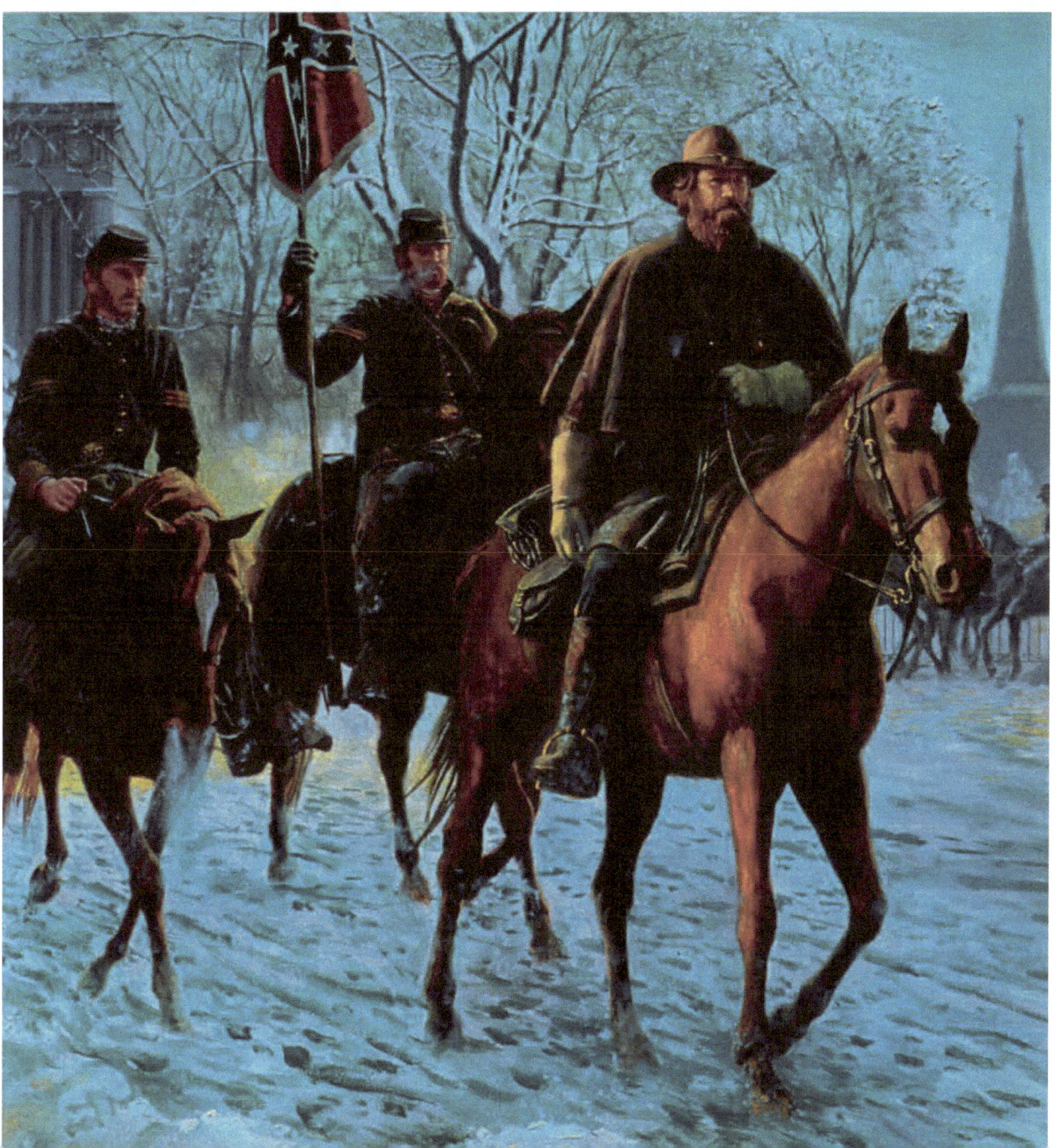

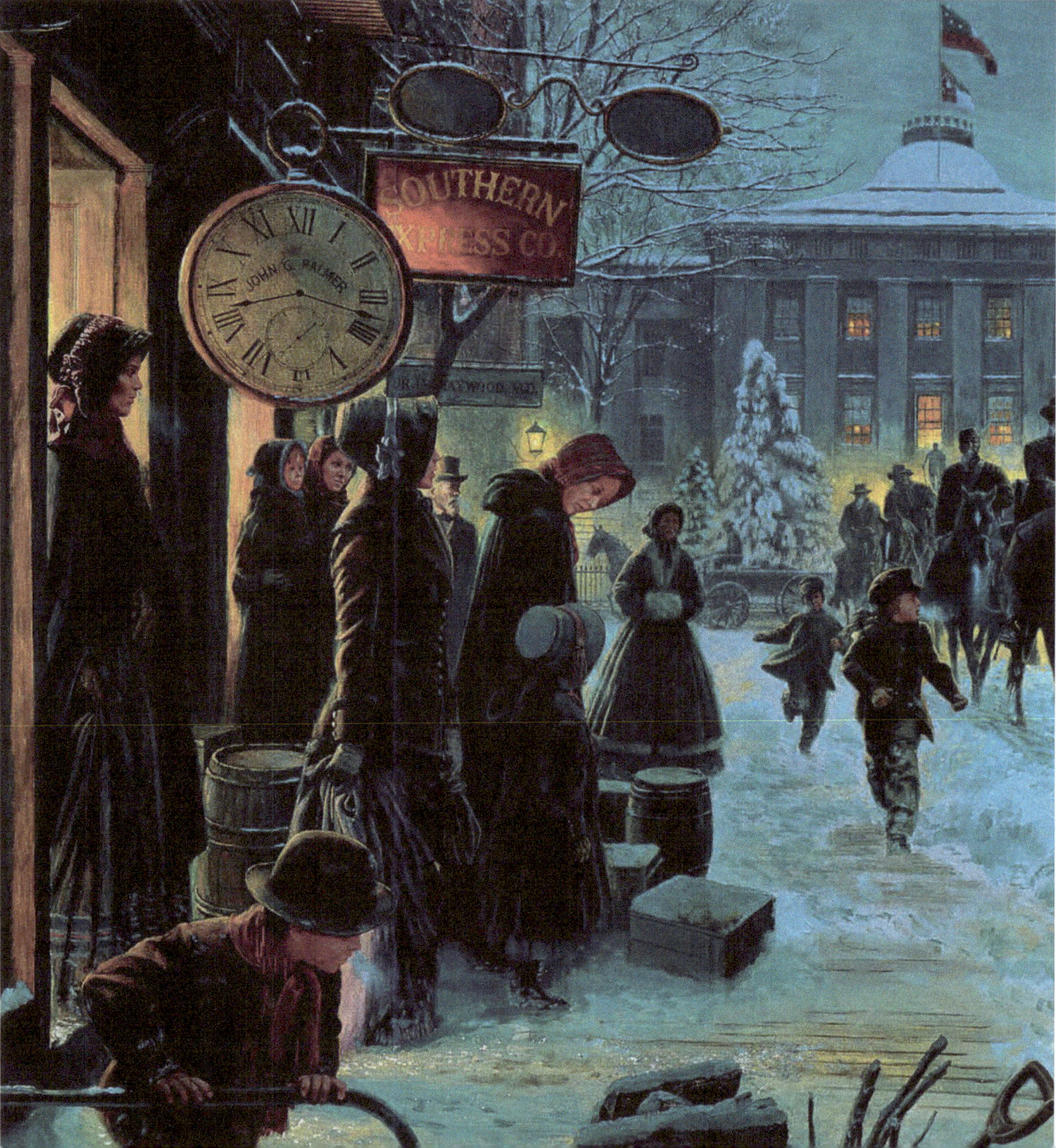

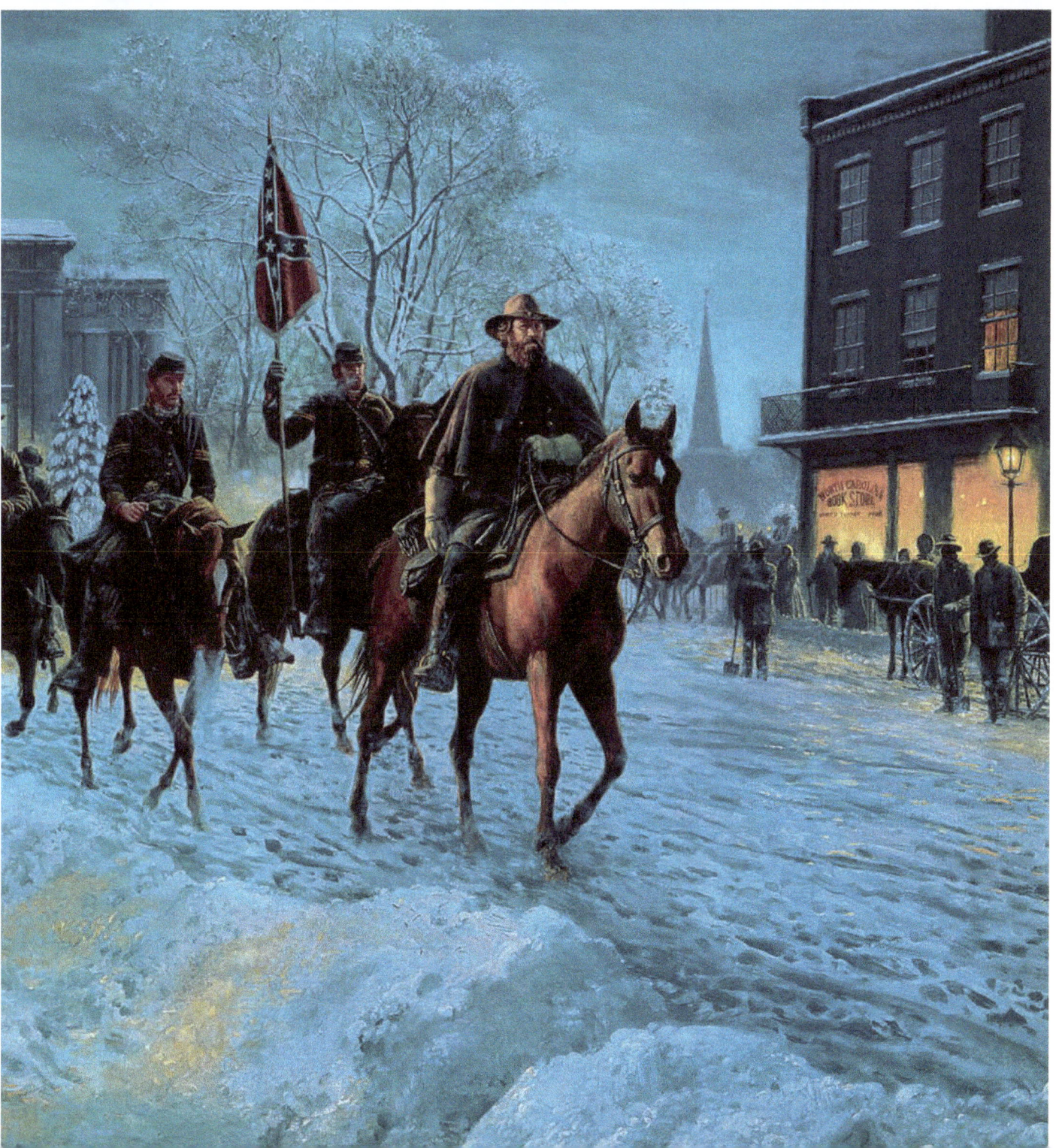

as authenticity to the painting. The owner of the jewelry store, for instance, was silversmith John C. Palmer, whose handiwork is part of the museum's collection. The capitol and Christ Episcopal Church have changed little in appearance since the war. In front of the south facade of the capitol is sculptor Jean-Antoine Houdon's statue of George Washington, which still stands in the same spot today. The iron fence, glimpsed just to the left of the horse and wagon, encircled the capitol building in the 1860s and today can be seen surrounding Raleigh's City Cemetery. I learned that the capital was blanketed with snow on February 5, 1863, so that was the date I picked to paint this scene.

The state museum's military curator, Tom Belton, provided research on uniforms, equipment, and accoutrements. The painting reflects the careful research of knowledgeable North Carolina historians. Even the location of the street lamps and the lighting in the capitol windows are accurate.

Flying atop the capitol dome is the First National flag of the Confederacy and the North Carolina state flag. The battle flag carried by North Carolina cavalry gave me the opportunity to show all three flags in the same painting.

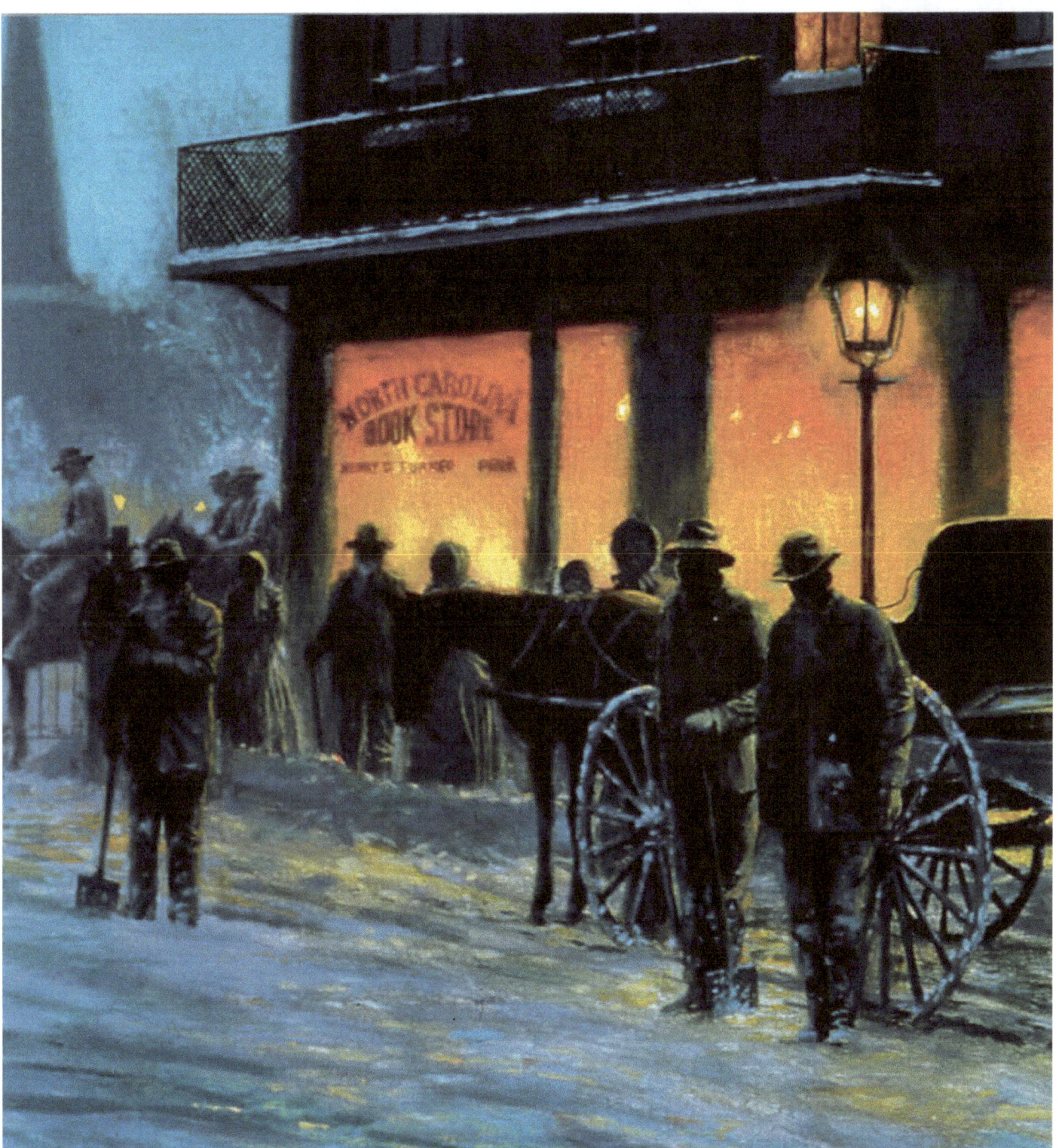

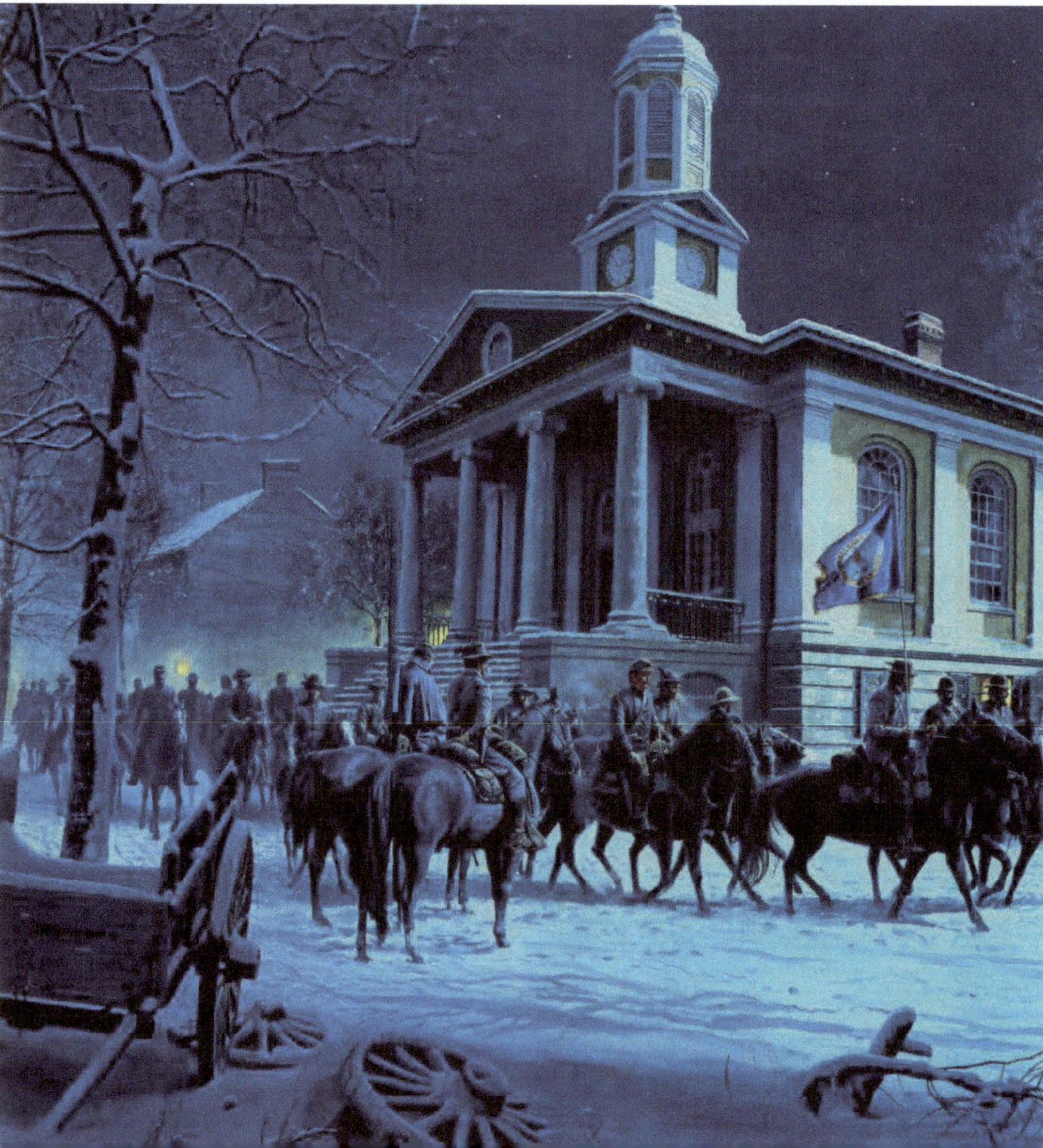

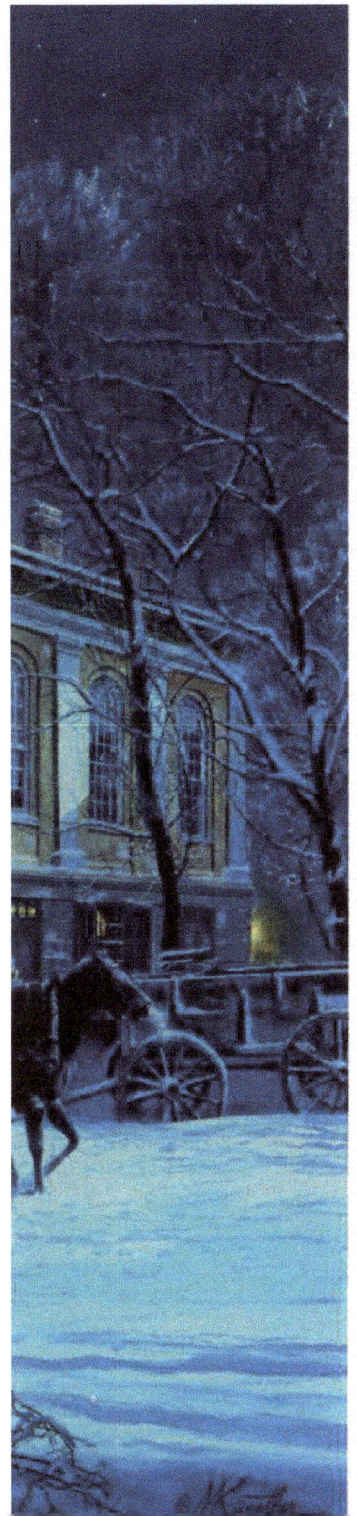

BRAVEST OF THE BRAVE

BLACK HORSE CAVALRY, WARRENTON, VIRGINIA
FEBRUARY 22, 1863

1999, oil, 30 x 34

THE BLACK Horse Cavalry was formed prior to the war, in 1859, as an independent volunteer cavalry company in Warrenton, the county seat of Fauquier County. The unit mustered into the Confederate army in May 1861 and was later designated Company H of the Fourth Virginia Cavalry. At the battle of First Manassas, the Black Horse played a decisive role that established the name and reputation of the unit as fierce fighters and extraordinary horsemen.

When I toured Warrenton, I was struck by the charm and beauty of the courthouse. The more I studied the building, the more it demanded to be the backdrop for this painting.

The most dramatic way in which I could show off the black horses was to pose them against a white background, which led me to the idea of snow and bright moonlight. This would also set off the white and yellow of the courthouse. I titled the painting after the forthcoming book by Lynn Hopewell, an expert on the Black Horse.

143

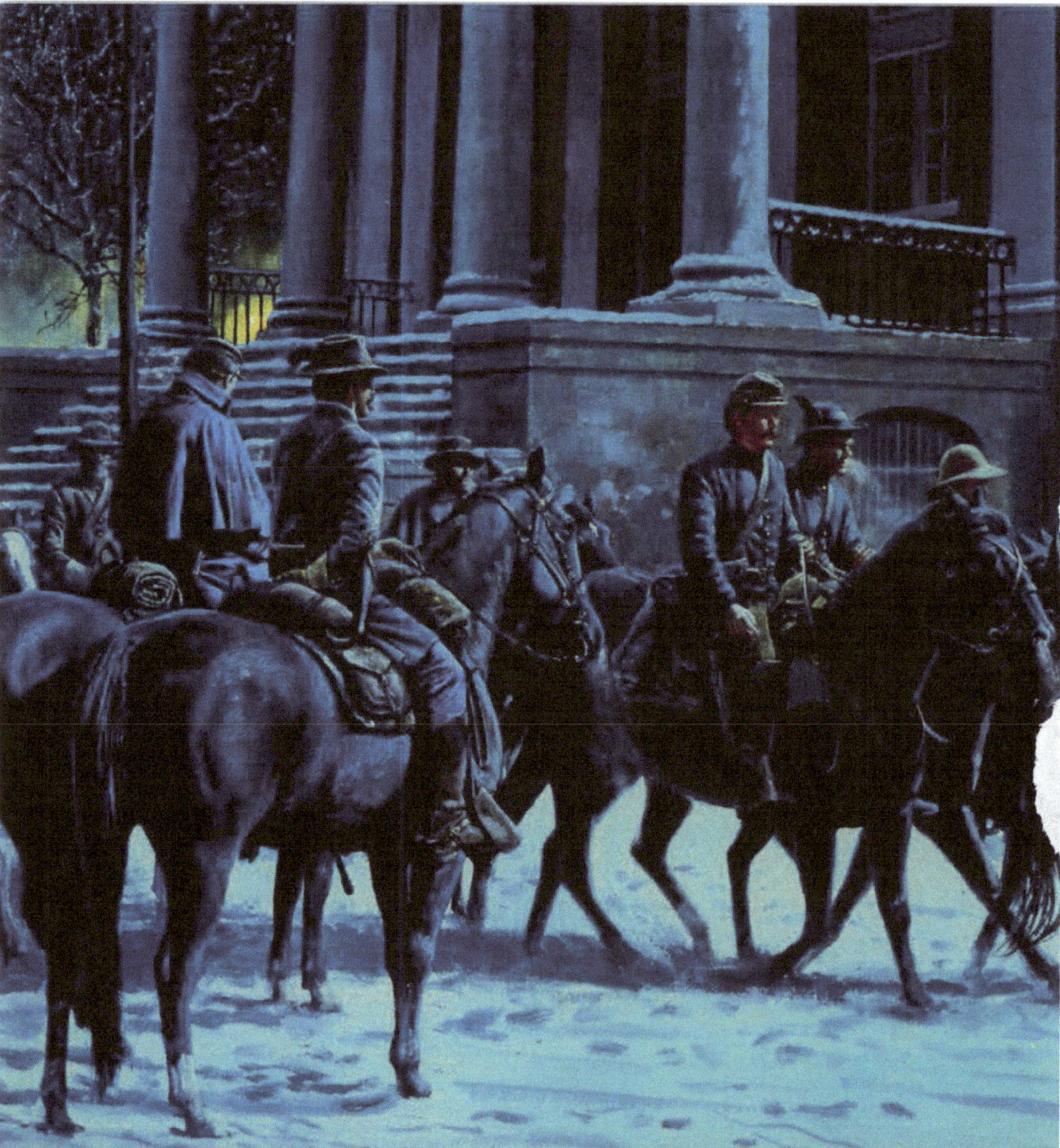

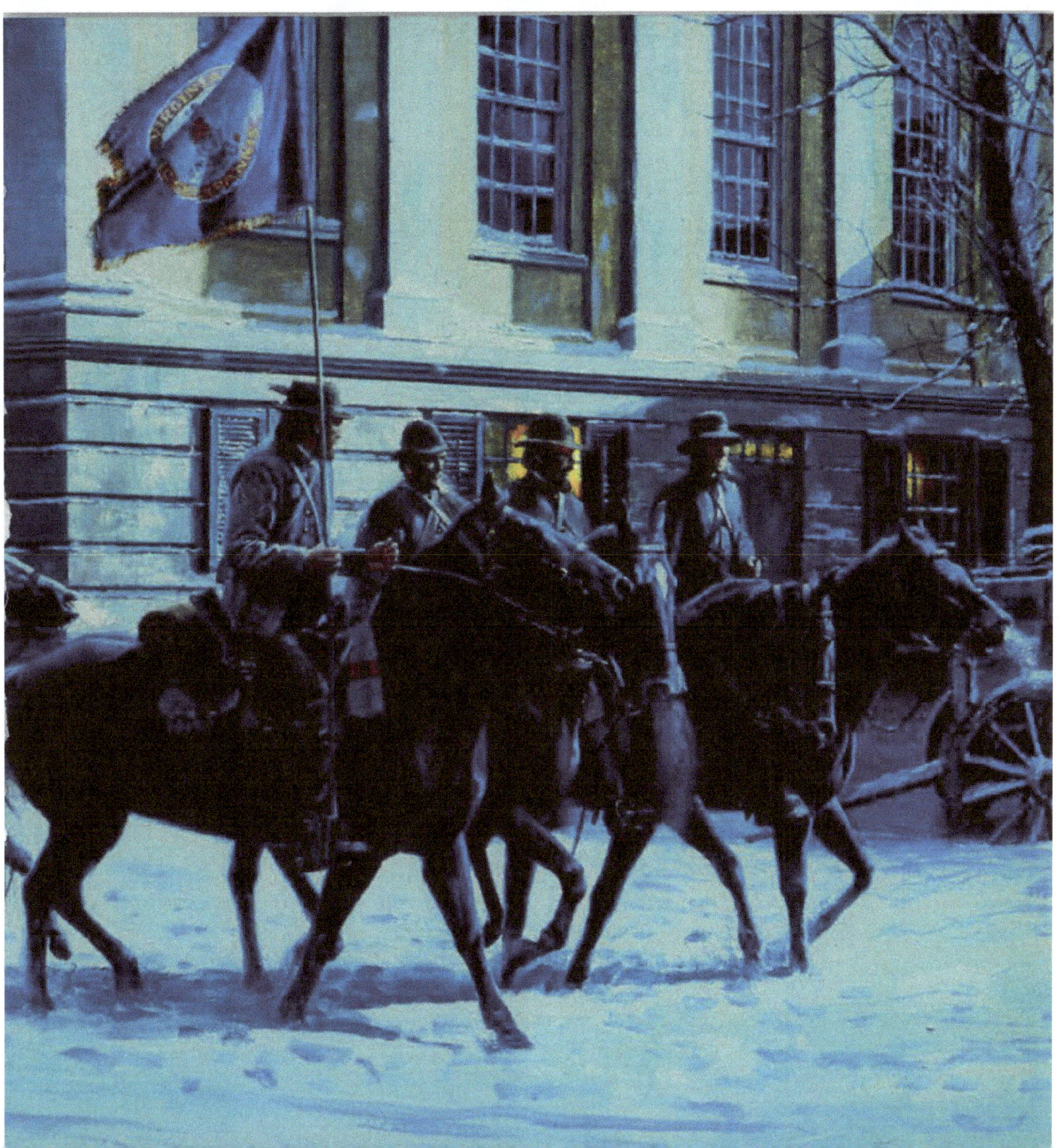

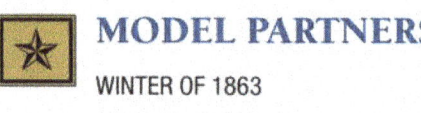

MODEL PARTNERSHIP

WINTER OF 1863

1996, oil, 24 x 32

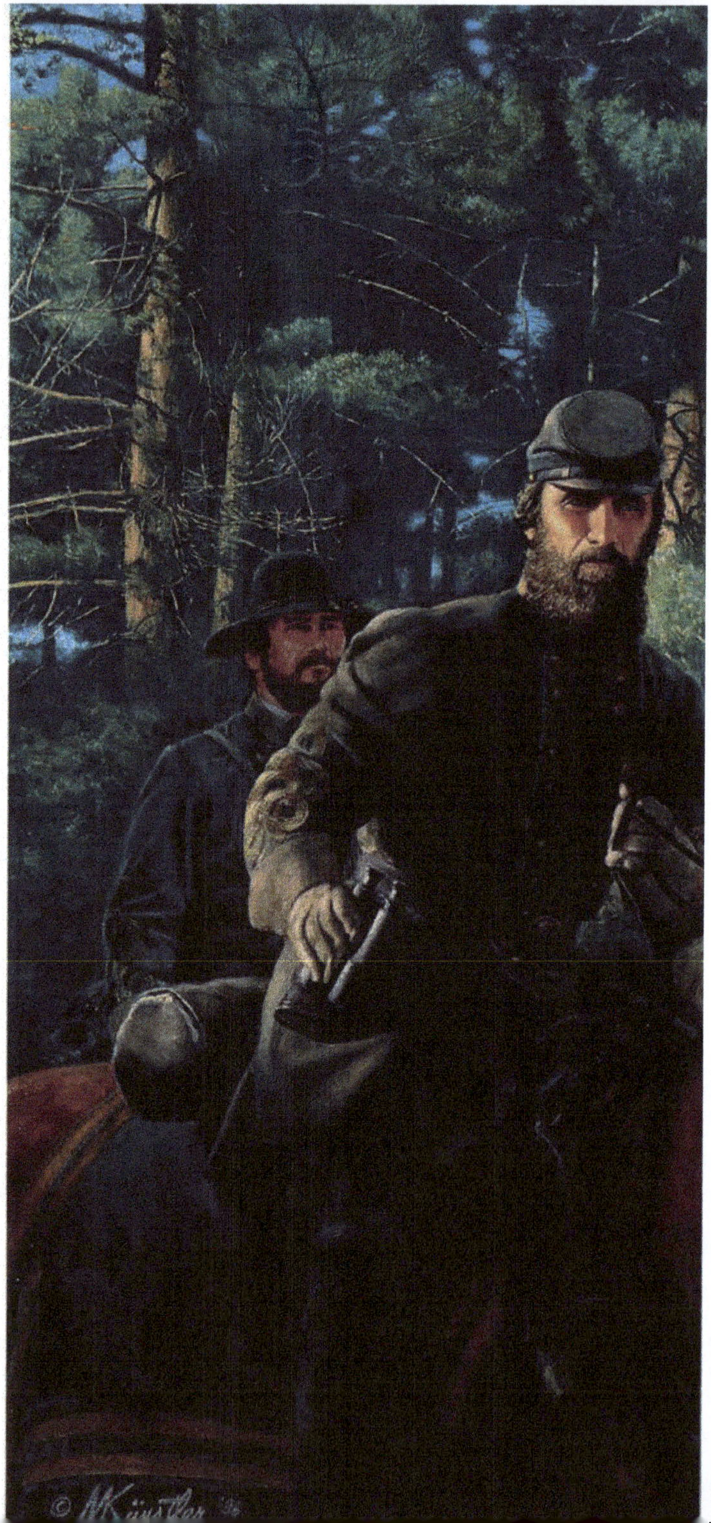

Lee and Jackson were Virginians, West Pointers, Mexican War heroes, and accomplished soldiers. Working in concert for only a year, they shaped the conflict as no two commanders had ever done before. Yet theirs was a strange partnership of the aristocrat and the ordinary. They were of different generations and vastly different cultures. Their greatness, though, emerged from their similarities. Equally bold in conception and in fierceness of execution, neither general hesitated to take risks for the larger goal of ultimate victory. Each

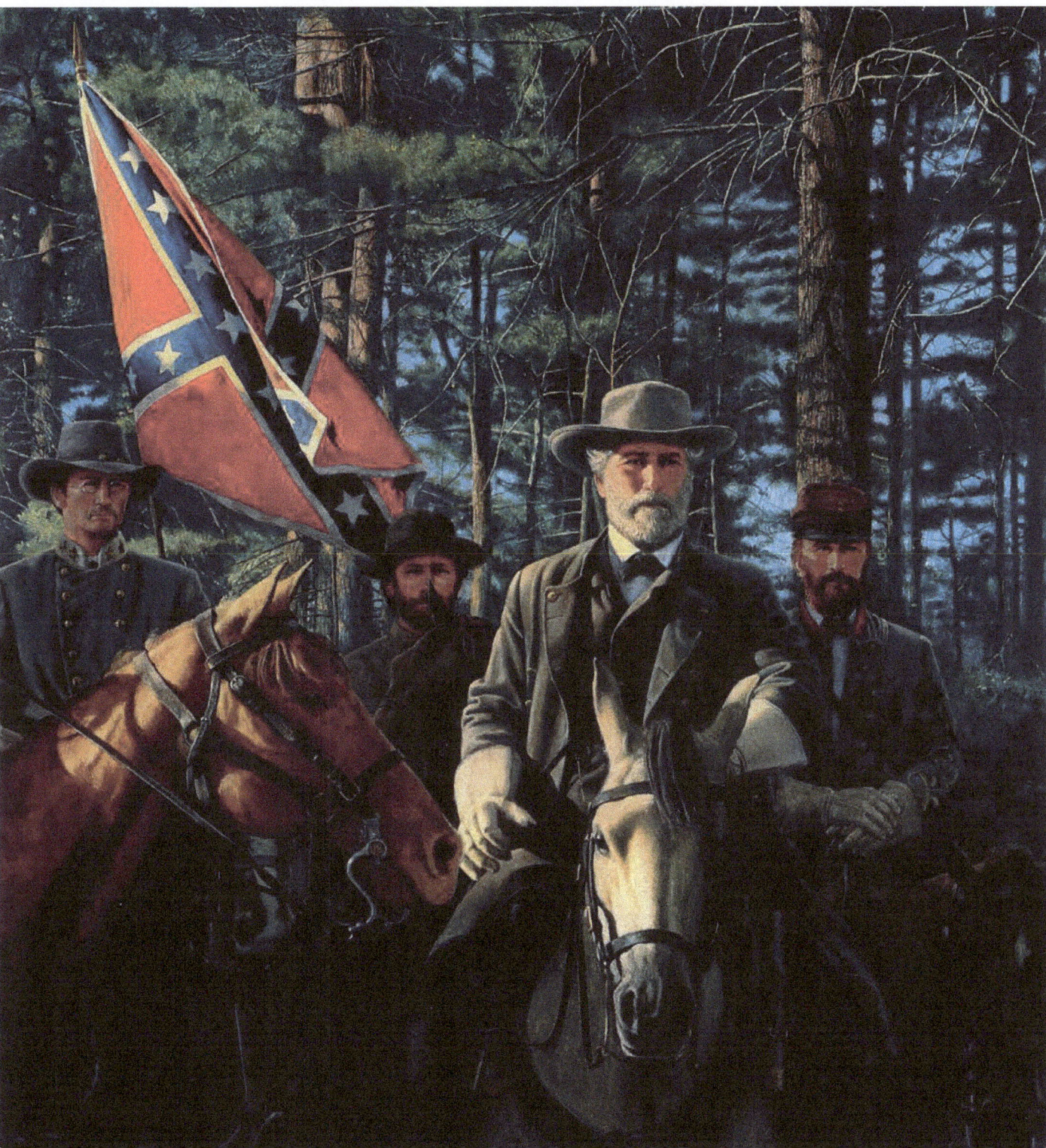

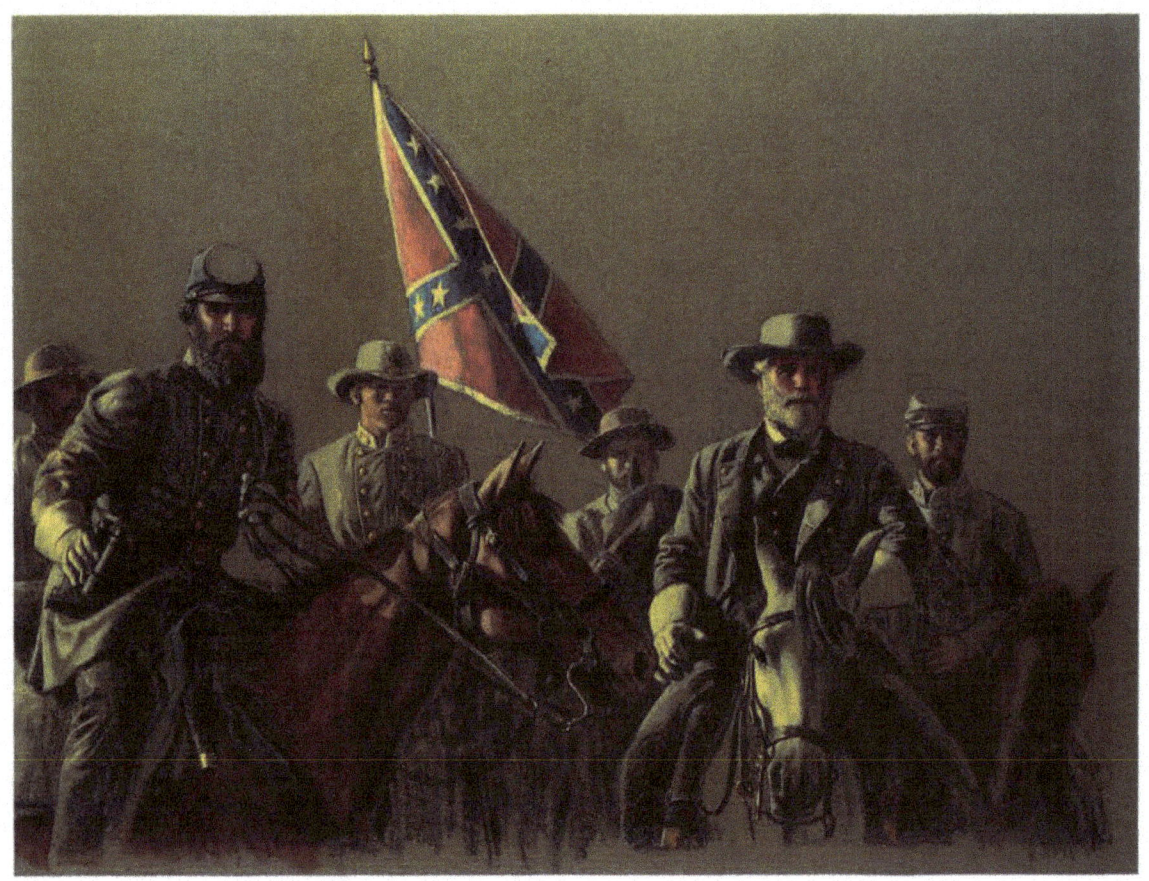

MODEL PARTNERSHIP

STUDY

1995, mixed media, 16 x 22

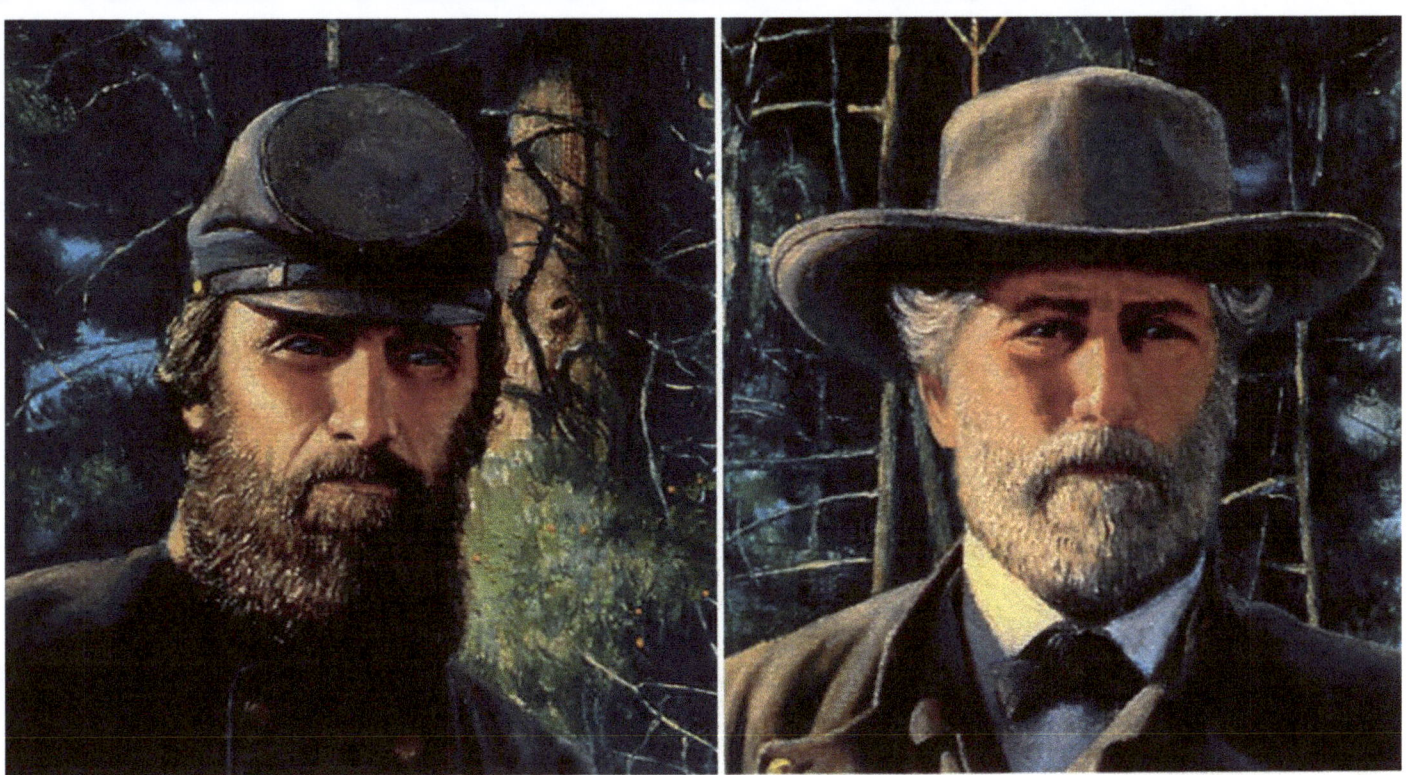

possessed the same selfless devotion to his country and its fight for independence. Each had the same abiding faith in God's blessing on that country.

For this painting, I wanted to show Jackson and Lee up close and facing the viewer. The last time I painted them in such an intimate setting was years earlier in "... *And the Generals Were Brought to Tears.*" There, I featured them in profile. Here, I wanted them boldly facing forward, as if facing the future with the courage and earnestness for which they were so well known. And I wanted them close together to emphasize the closeness of their working relationship.

I placed the two generals in a late-afternoon sun in order to give them a warm glow. The sunlight highlights both faces and the flag. The staff officers, like supporting characters in a great drama, remain appropriately in shadow.

THE FAIRFAX RAID

JOHN S. MOSBY
MARCH 9, 1863
1996, oil, 26 x 40

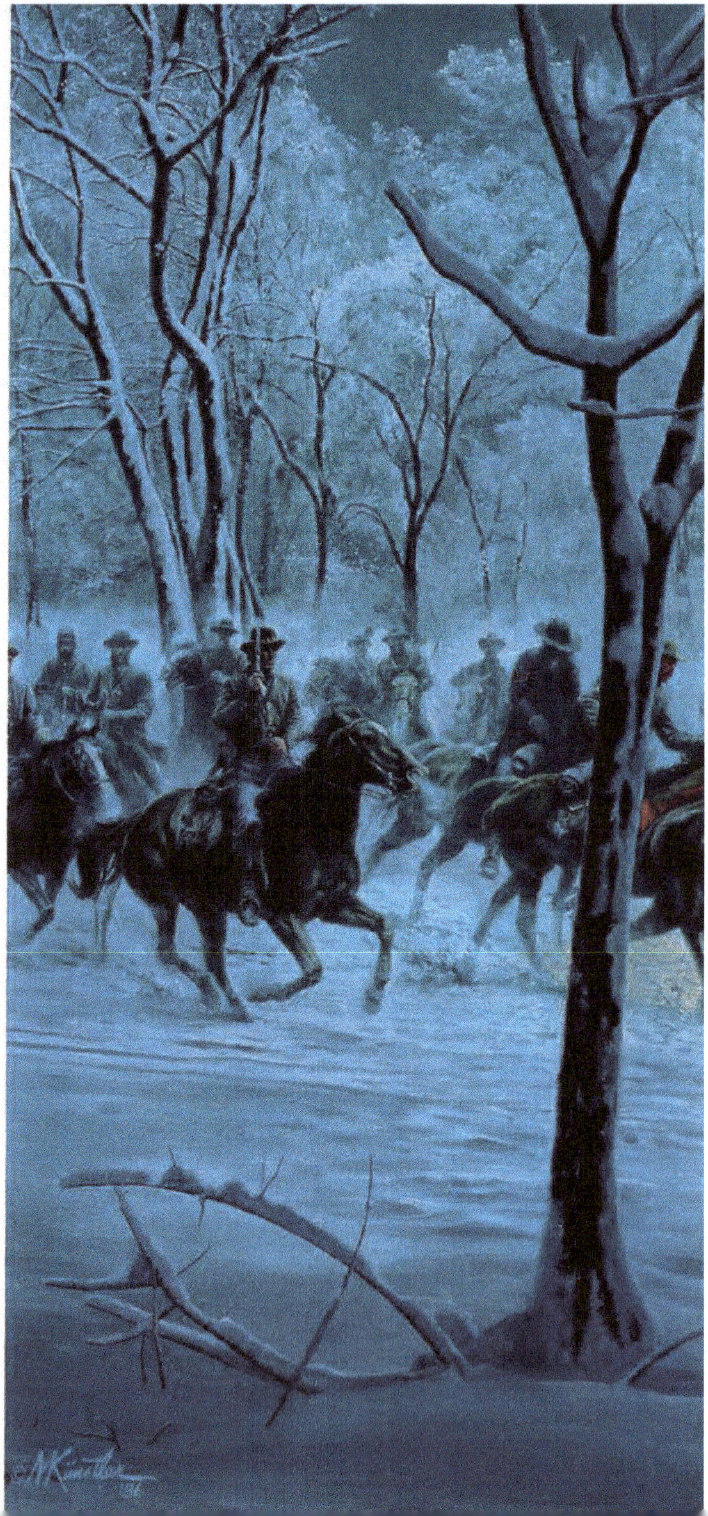

As soon as I began to paint the Civil War, I wanted to portray John S. Mosby. Naturally, the image that sprang to mind was his legendary Fairfax raid, the most daring exploit of his astounding career.

In January 1863, Jeb Stuart authorized Mosby to form a company of partisan rangers to operate in northern Virginia. Mosby subsequently led several raids in the Washington area. He took offense when he heard that a British soldier of fortune, Union Col. Sir Percy Wyndham, had described Mosby as a horse thief. So at 2:00 a.m.

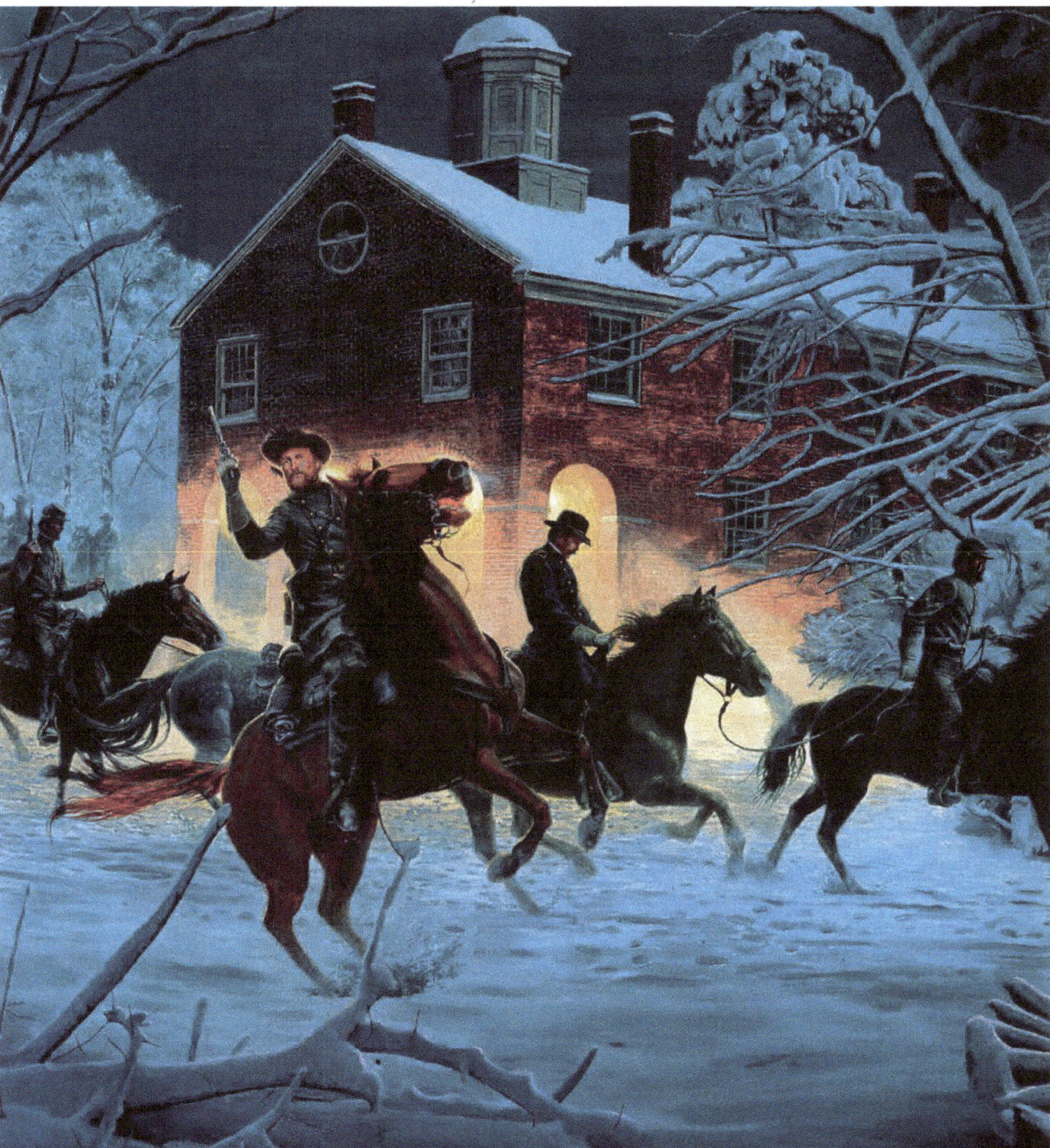

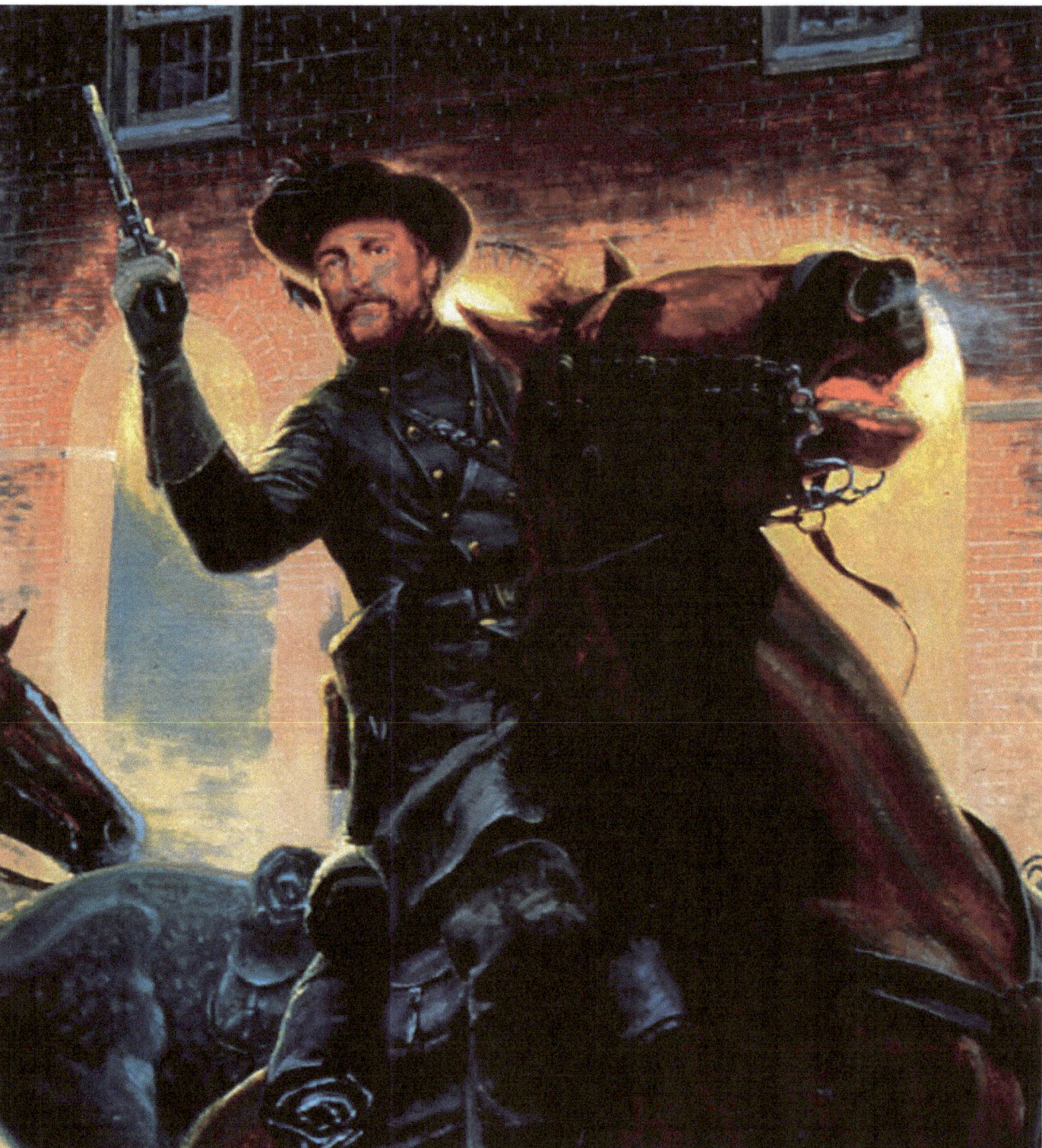

on March 9, 1863, Mosby and twenty-nine of his men raided Wyndham's headquarters in Fairfax. But when the Southerners arrived, they found that Wyndham was away. So they seized Brig. Gen. Edwin H. Stoughton from his bed and also captured two captains, thirty enlisted men, and fifty-eight horses. All without firing a shot.

I always like doing paintings with something in them that still exists today, so that people can take my image to the site and compare the two. That the old historic Fairfax courthouse still exists added to my interest in doing the painting. I worked closely with Brian Conley, a historian at the Virginia Room at the Fairfax County Public Library. He obtained period photographs of the building, maps, and other materials and told me which parts of the present building had been added since the war. The view of the courthouse from the angle I chose presented a much more rural look than most people might have supposed, with no other buildings in sight.

I featured Mosby in the center of the painting, silhouetted by the light from the courthouse. He wears a captain's uniform, although he was a lieutenant at the time of the raid. A photograph exists of Mosby in this uniform with writing in his own hand stating "the uniform is the one I wore on March 8th, 1863 on the night of General Stoughton's capture."

To help tell the story of the capture, I deliberately have Stoughton and his captor, William Hunter, who leads the general's horse, on the right side of the painting and the rest of the figures and horses on the left. With the light also behind them reflecting brightly on the snow to show the reins clearly, the eye moves instinctively to that area of the picture. I also placed Stoughton on a light-colored horse and Hunter on a dark one to emphasize

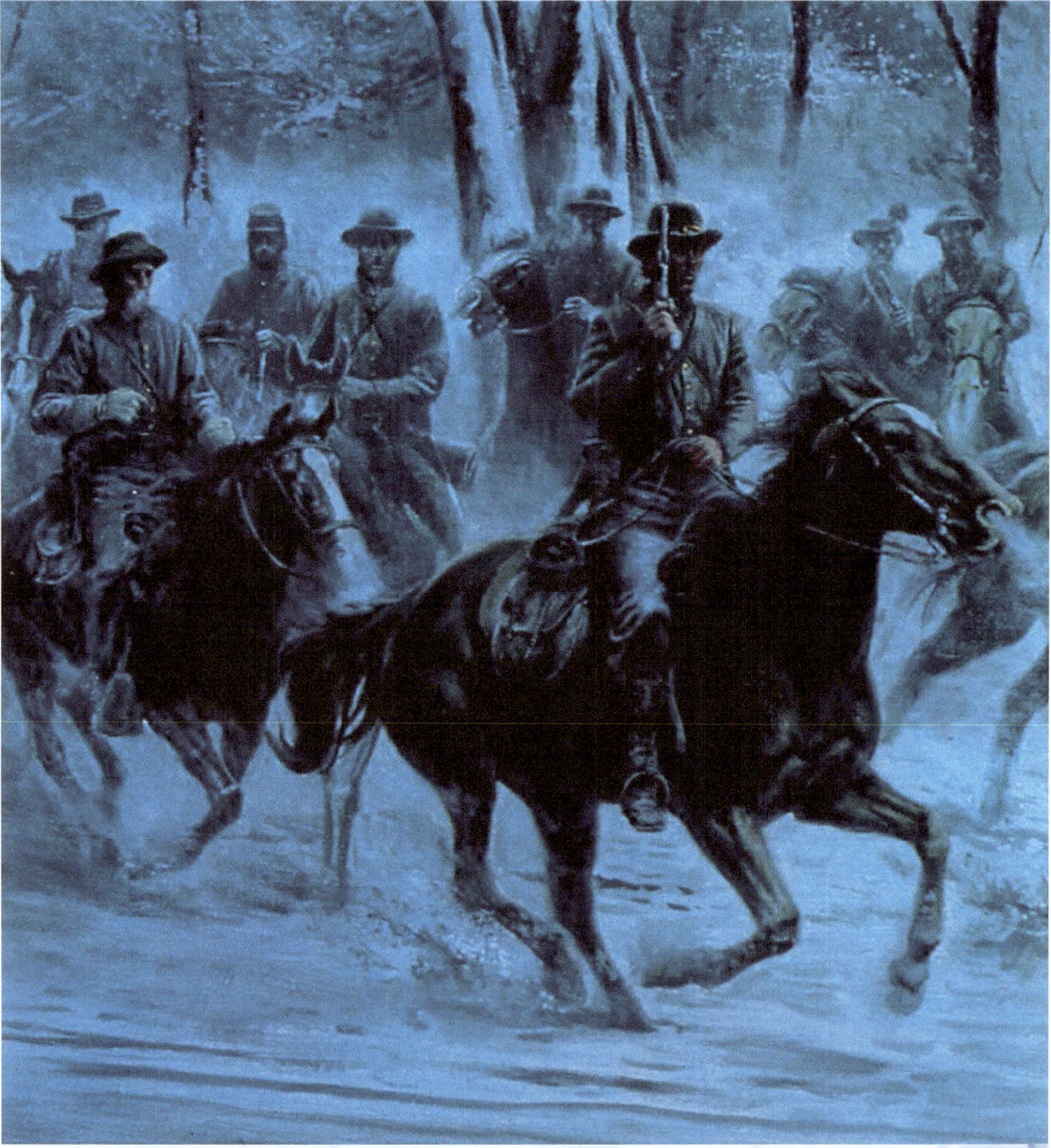

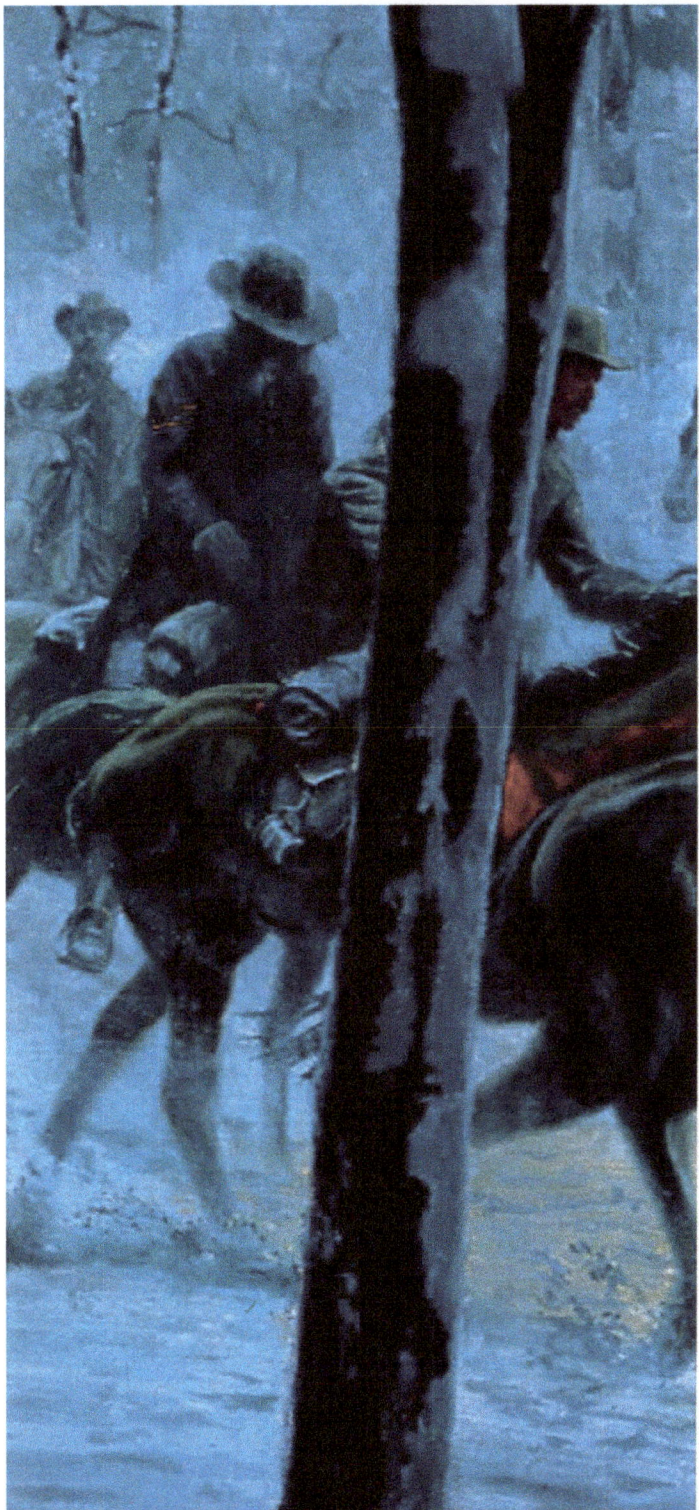

the dark blue and gray uniforms. The differences would have been very difficult to see at night.

Added to this is that the raid took place at 2:00 a.m. in the snow. My night snow scenes seem to be very popular, so I don't shy away from portraying events such as this because of the time and setting.

Apparently, few bemoaned the capture of Stoughton. Someone allegedly overheard President Lincoln say that "he did not so much mind the loss of a brigadier general, for he could make another in five minutes; 'but those horses cost $125 apiece.'" The general was a guest of the Confederate government in Libby Prison for a month and then exchanged. He was never given another command.

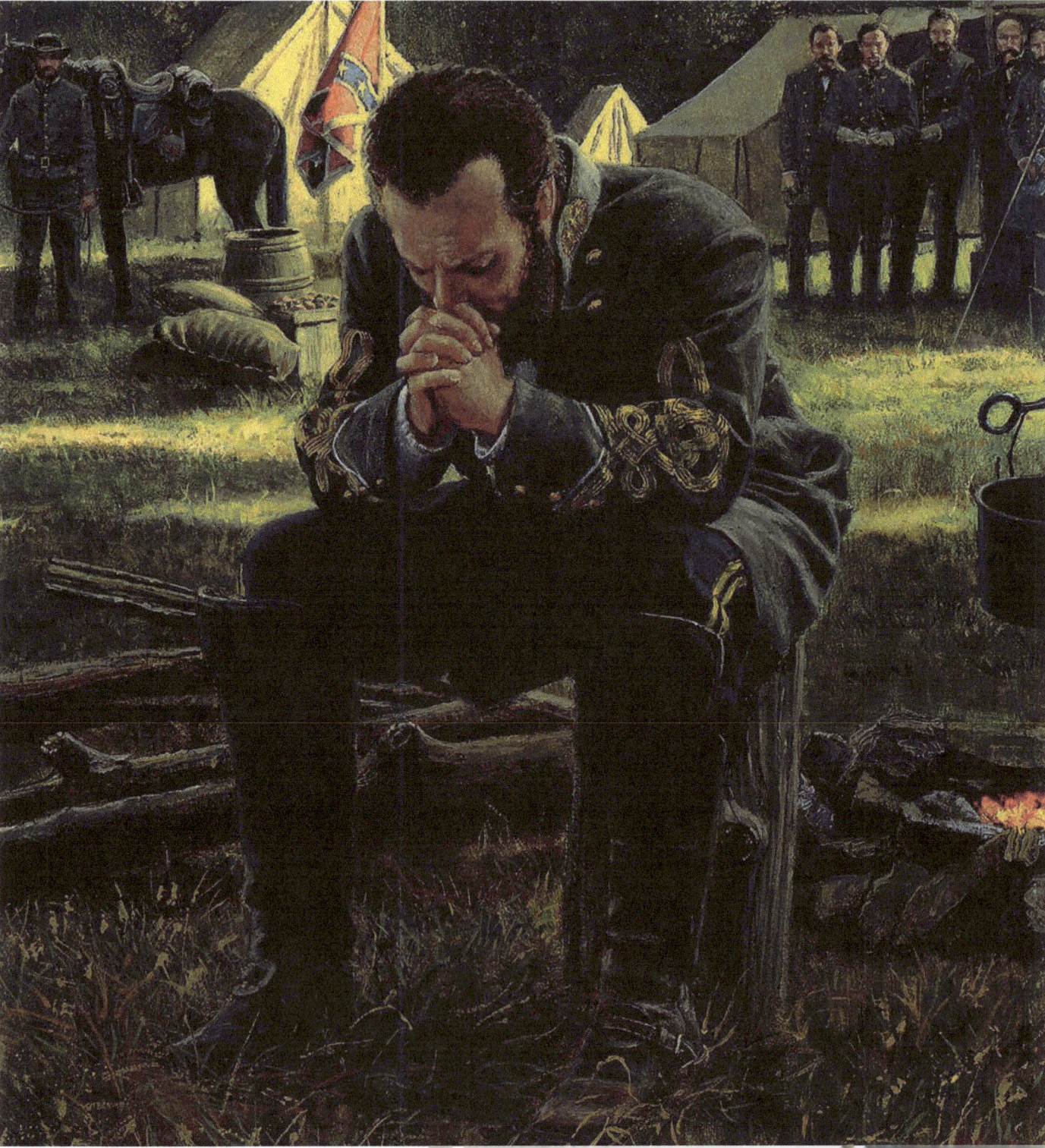

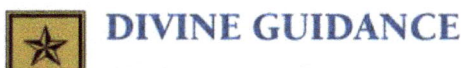

DIVINE GUIDANCE

STONEWALL JACKSON

MARCH 17, 1863

2002, oil, 10¾ x 9¼

WITH THE approach of spring, Jackson moved his headquarters from Moss Neck to nearby Hamilton's Crossing in preparation for the upcoming offensive. When he bade farewell to the Corbin family on March 16, he learned that five-year-old Janie had contracted scarlet fever, but Roberta Corbin assured him that her prognosis was good. A day later, however, Jackson was informed that Janie had died. He burst into tears and then knelt in prayer.

An aide wondered aloud why this legendary warrior could cry over a child's life after witnessing dry-eyed all the deaths his army had sustained during two years of combat. A colleague answered, "I think he is weeping for them all."

The news reached Jackson in the early morning, so I painted the long shadows of early daylight and placed the general in shade. The lightest part of the painting is the bright sunlight on the tent and flag. Thus the focus is immediately on Jackson and the flag.

In the dark times of his life, Jackson always resorted to his faith. Although he was stern at times, he was also a man of deeply felt emotions, genuine kindness, and remarkable tenderness. This is the side of Jackson that I see as he wept and prayed at the news of Janie Corbin's death.

"... AND THE TWO GENERALS WERE BROUGHT TO TEARS"

JACKSON AND LEE
FREDERICKSBURG, VIRGINIA
SPRING 1863

1992, oil, 24 x 20

T HE RELIGIOUS revival alluded to on page 90 had begun in the lower Shenandoah Valley after Lee's army had returned from Maryland in September 1862. It was not unusual that men who had faced imminent death might now find their religious sensitivities awakened.

While reading Douglas Southall Freeman's biography of Lee, I came across a description of Lee and Jackson at a religious revival meeting during the winter of 1862–63. On an estate known as Belvoir, just south of Fredericksburg, the two generals attended a prayer meeting. They sat side by side on a log and "were moved to tears one Sunday by the affecting eloquence with which Reverend B. T. Lacy described the homes from which the army had been drawn."

To show both generals in such a poignant moment was an opportunity for an extraordinary painting. There were always children at the winter camps, and I decided this was also an opportunity to portray the great men in the company of children.

Both men were devout. So this portrayal of two of the war's most notable heroes is in sharp contrast to the fighting men usually portrayed on canvas.

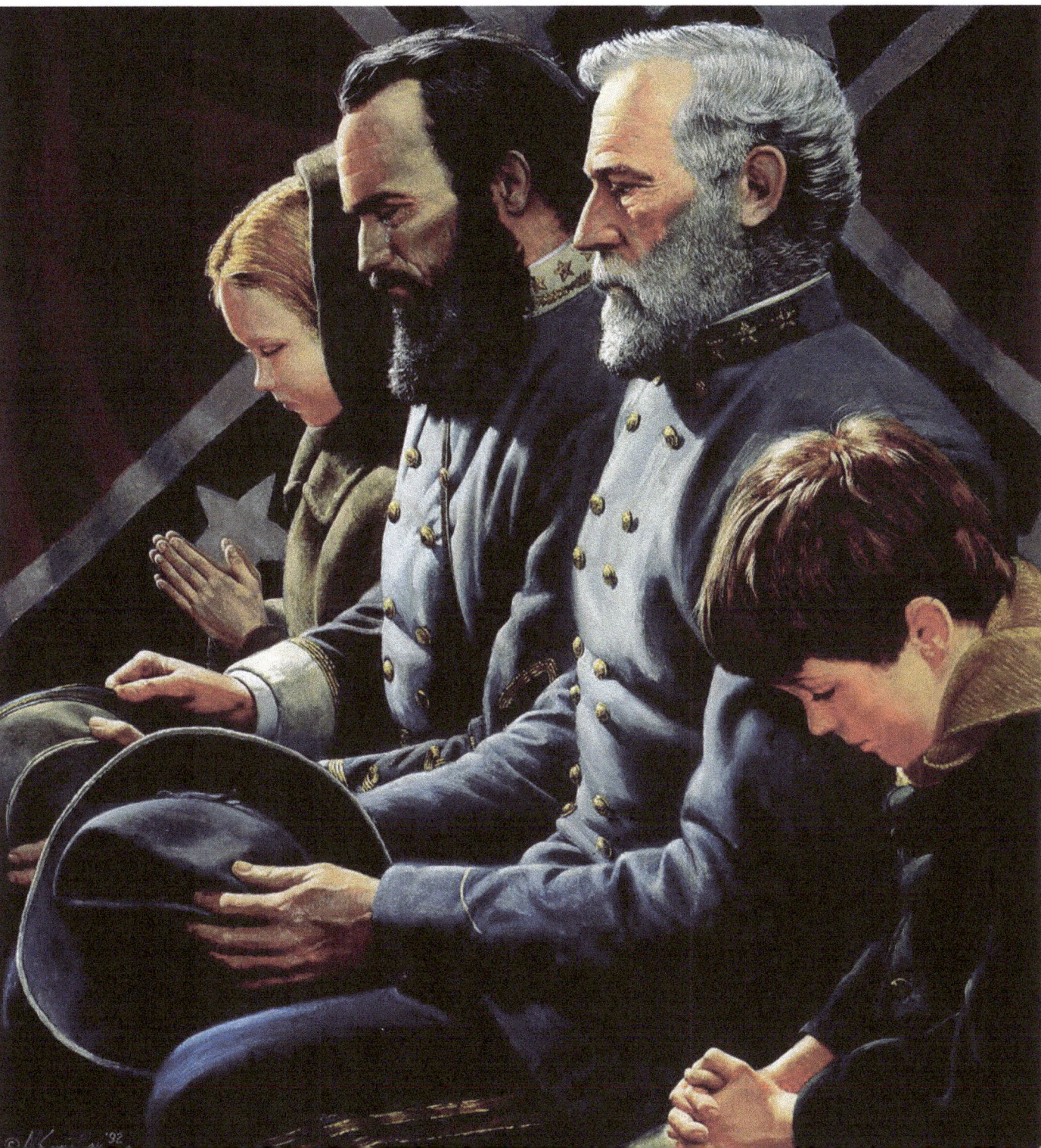

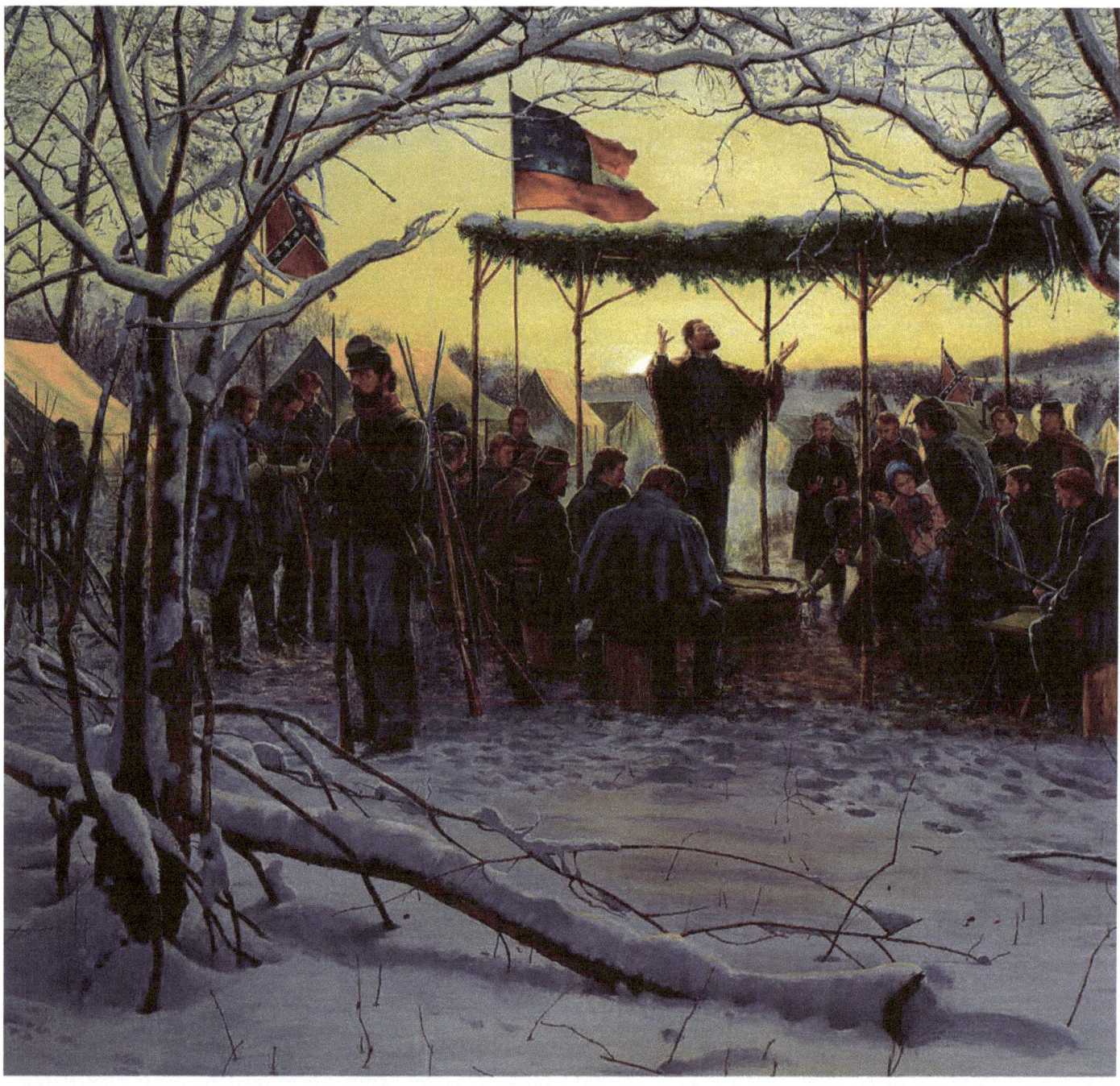

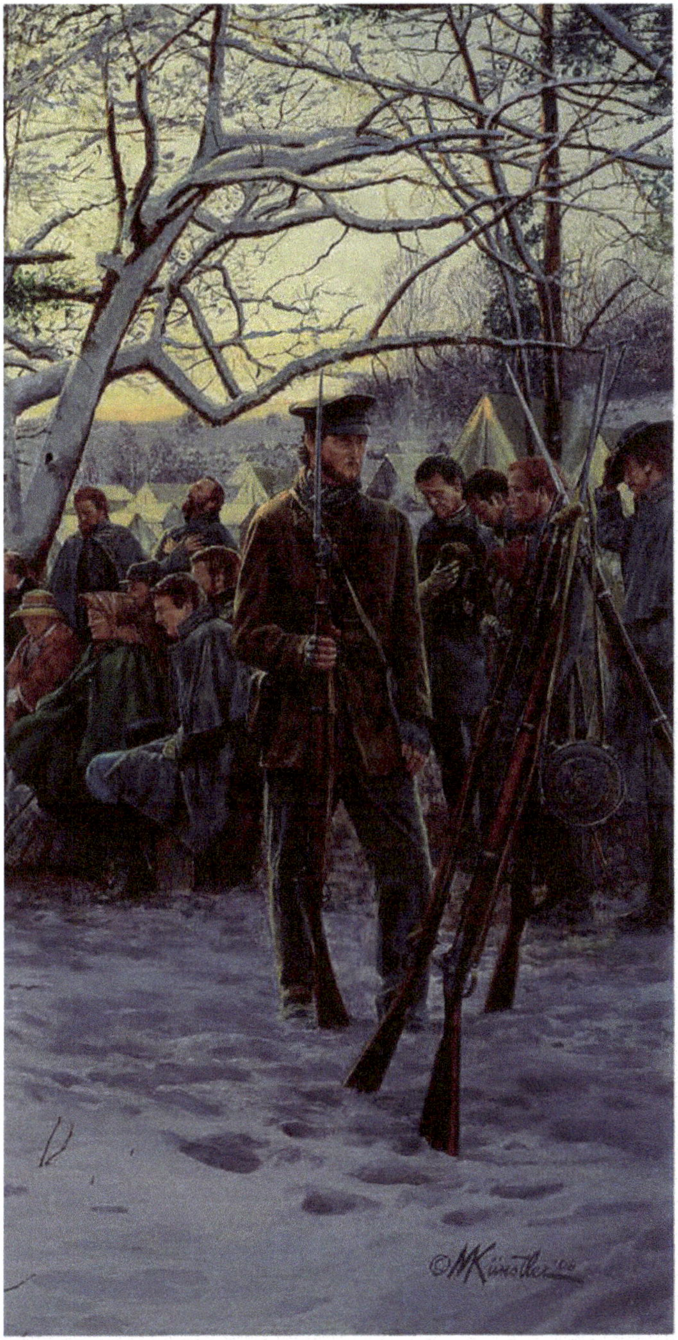

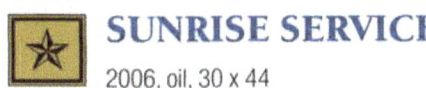

SUNRISE SERVICE

2006, oil, 30 x 44

DESPITE A hefty measure of shirkers, scoundrels, and skeptics, the ranks of Civil War armies were thoroughly leavened with believers. Nineteenth-century American society was firmly founded on the Judeo-Christian worldview and a biblical faith was openly expressed in the ranks, even in official military reports.

While his corps was in winter quarters after the battle of Fredericksburg, Jackson determined to improve the spiritual character of his army by installing the Reverend B. Tucker Lacy as corps chaplain. Then several

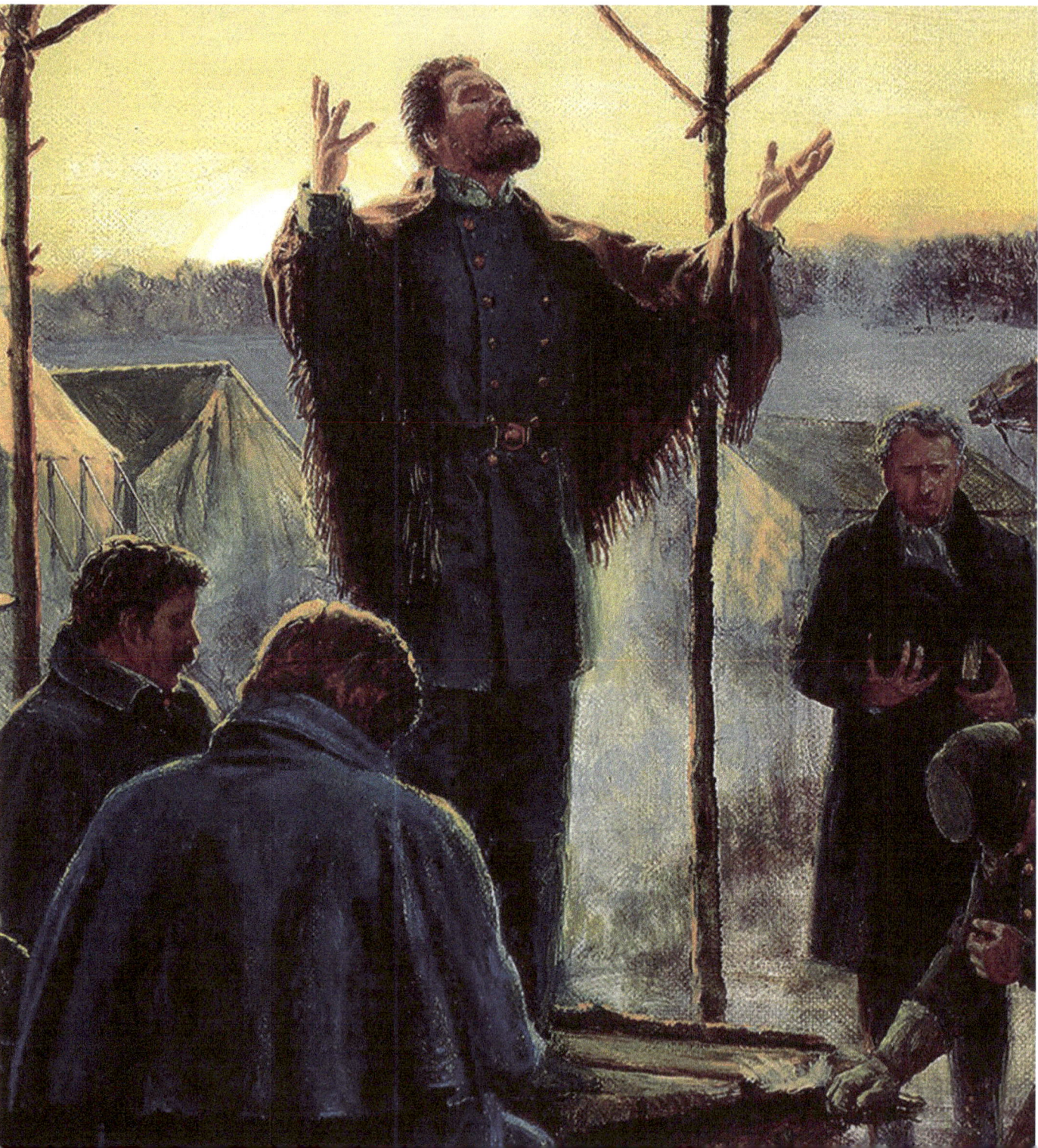

log chapels were built to encourage the troops to develop daily habits of prayer, Bible study, meditation, and worship. Chaplains were enlisted from across the region with both long-term and short-term commitments and no denominational bias.

"I derive great comfort from the precious promises of Our Lord & Savior," wrote a Southern infantryman in 1862, sentiments repeated in countless soldier letters. "May God give me faith to sustain me under every trial." In a letter written in the same year, a Northern cavalryman agreed: "I am trying to become a more devoted Christian, a better Man—and the best Soldier I am capable of becoming."

More than a quarter million copies of a gospel tract called *Parting Words* were distributed among the Southern armies, and the U.S. Christian Commission donated more than a half million Bibles to Northern troops in one year.

In 1862 and 1863, the armies of the Confederacy were transformed by a revival akin to the colonial-era Great Awakening. It produced tens of thousands of new Christians, spurred a wave of campground worship services, and launched countless prayer meetings.

In the Army of Tennessee, an average of forty soldiers a night professed newfound faith in Jesus Christ as Lord and Savior in a single two-week period. On the Virginia front, a joint baptism organized by Southern soldiers on the Rapidan River attracted a group of Northern troops to the opposite bank. Spontaneously, men from both sides joined in a hymn singing at the water's edge. From the front lines to the backwaters of the war, soldiers North and South regularly paused from the ways of war to open the Sabbath with a sunrise worship service—expressing a common faith amid an uncommon conflict.

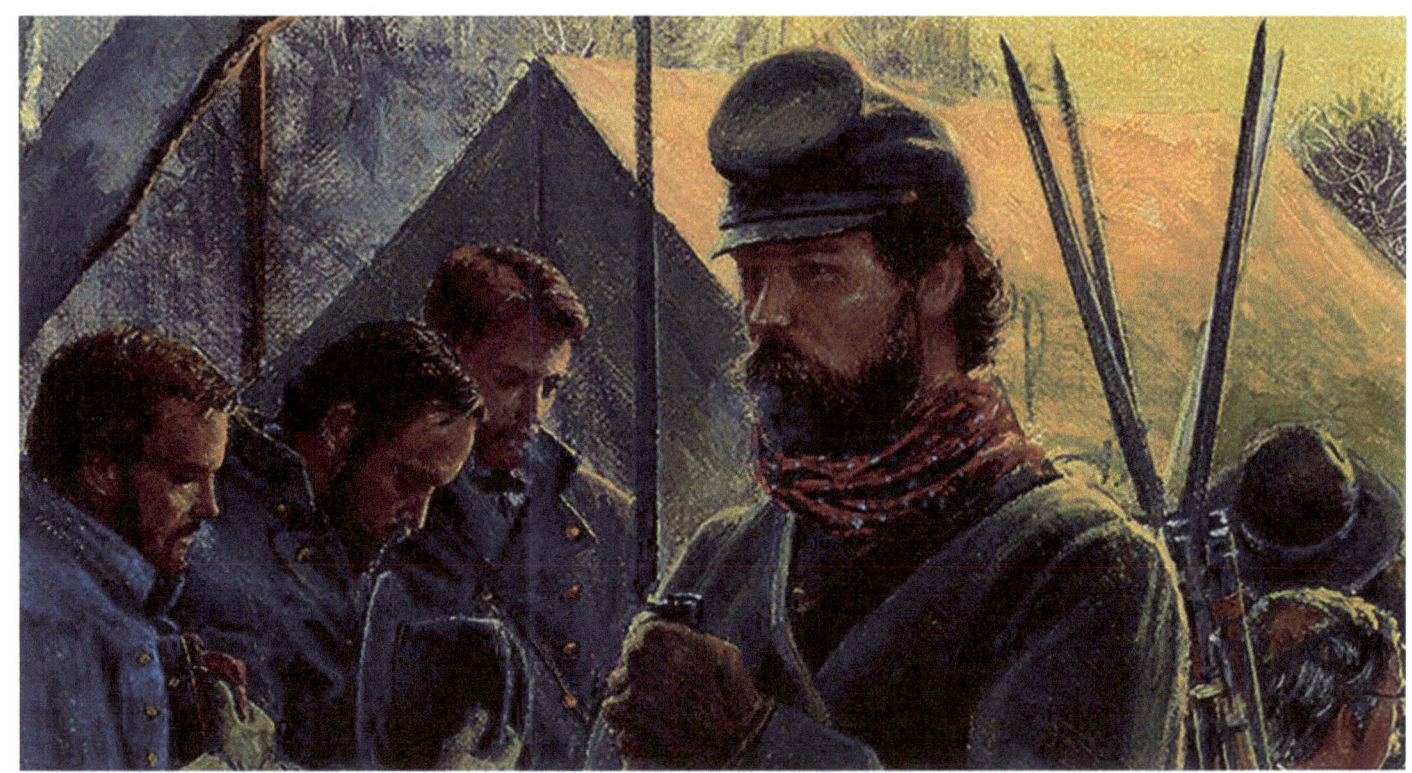

The more I study and paint events from the war, the more I ask myself, "How did they bear it?" Of course the answer for so many can be found in their faith. One cannot study these soldiers and their families and not be impressed with the depth and dedication of their devotion.

A countryside draped in a mantle of snow is, of course, a spectacular setting for any painting. Add to that the gorgeous tones of a winter sunrise, and a memorable stage is set for a painting. I incorporated many personal elements of nineteenth-century American outdoor worship services, the different characters and poses that would have been seen at such events, for example, the typical praying poses of the "hat over heart" and the "crossed arms."

The focal point of the painting is the Southern chaplain, and I painted his dark figure against the lightest background. This design element, using the greatest contrast, brings the eye of the viewer straight to the chaplain and immediately tells the story I want to convey. Another design element, using tree branches as pointers, brings the eye to the focal point as well. For color accents, I have shown the First National flag and the battle flag, both of which came into use in the Army of Northern Virginia in the winter of 1861–62. During winter camping, some officers were visited by their wives, and this gave me the opportunity to include women and an infant in the painting.

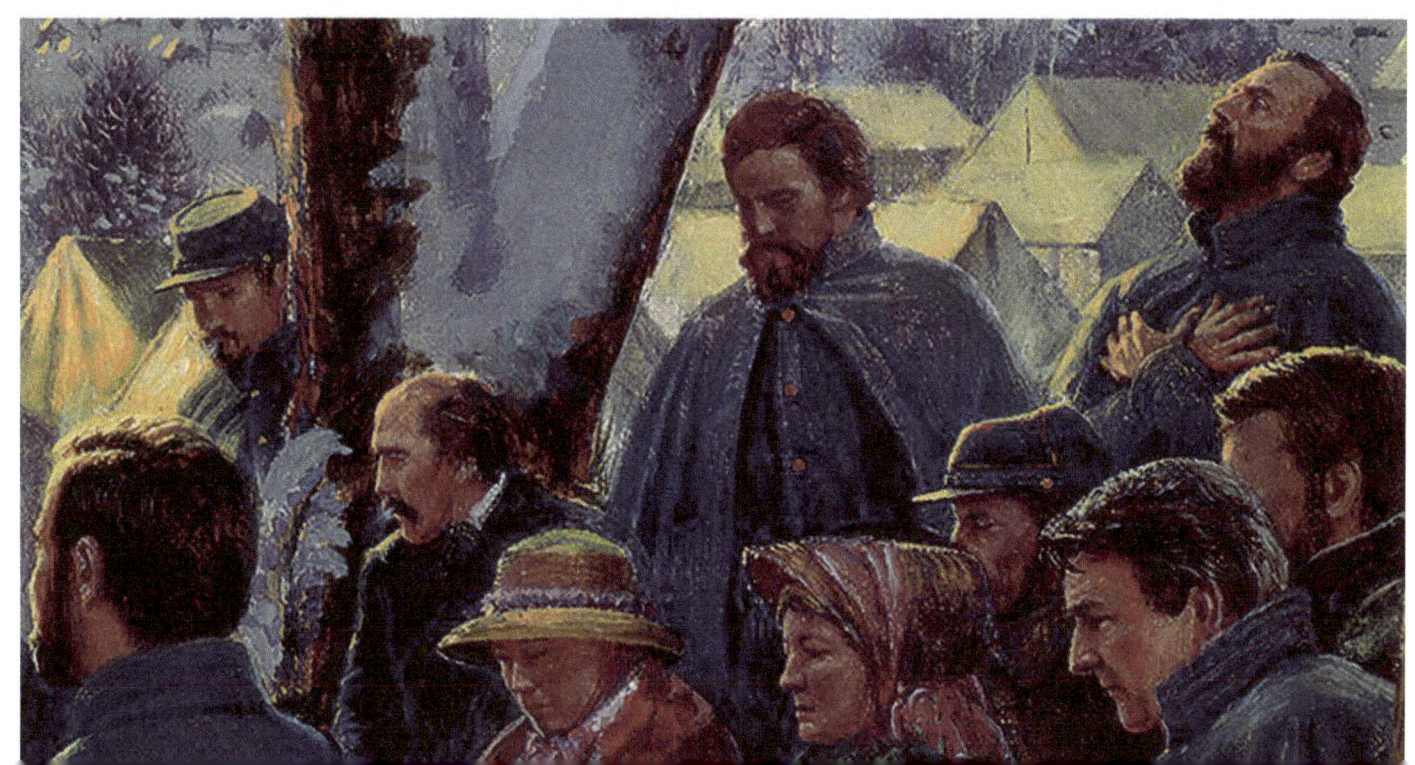

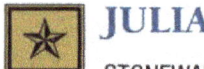

JULIA

STONEWALL JACKSON AND FAMILY
GUINEY'S STATION, VIRGINIA
APRIL 20, 1863
1998, oil, 32 x 32

ONE OF the most wonderful moments in Thomas J. Jackson's life occurred on April 20, 1863, when he saw his daughter, Julia, for the first time. The child was five months old; she had been conceived in Winchester, where Jackson sojourned during the winter of 1861–62 with his wife, Anna. Julia had been born the following November, while Jackson was in the Fredericksburg area. The general refused to visit Anna and the new baby during the winter inactivity, feeling he could not abandon his troops even for a short time. By April, he decided that it was safe enough for his family to visit him at the front.

Guiney's Station was the railhead for Fredericksburg, and it was there that Anna and Julia arrived. It was the first time Jackson had seen his wife in more than a year. The day was dreary and rainy, but the general's spirits were bright. He met his wife and daughter in the railroad car. Anna recalled, "His face was all sunshine and gladness; and, after greeting his wife, it was a picture, indeed, to see his look of perfect delight and admiration as his eyes fell upon the baby!"

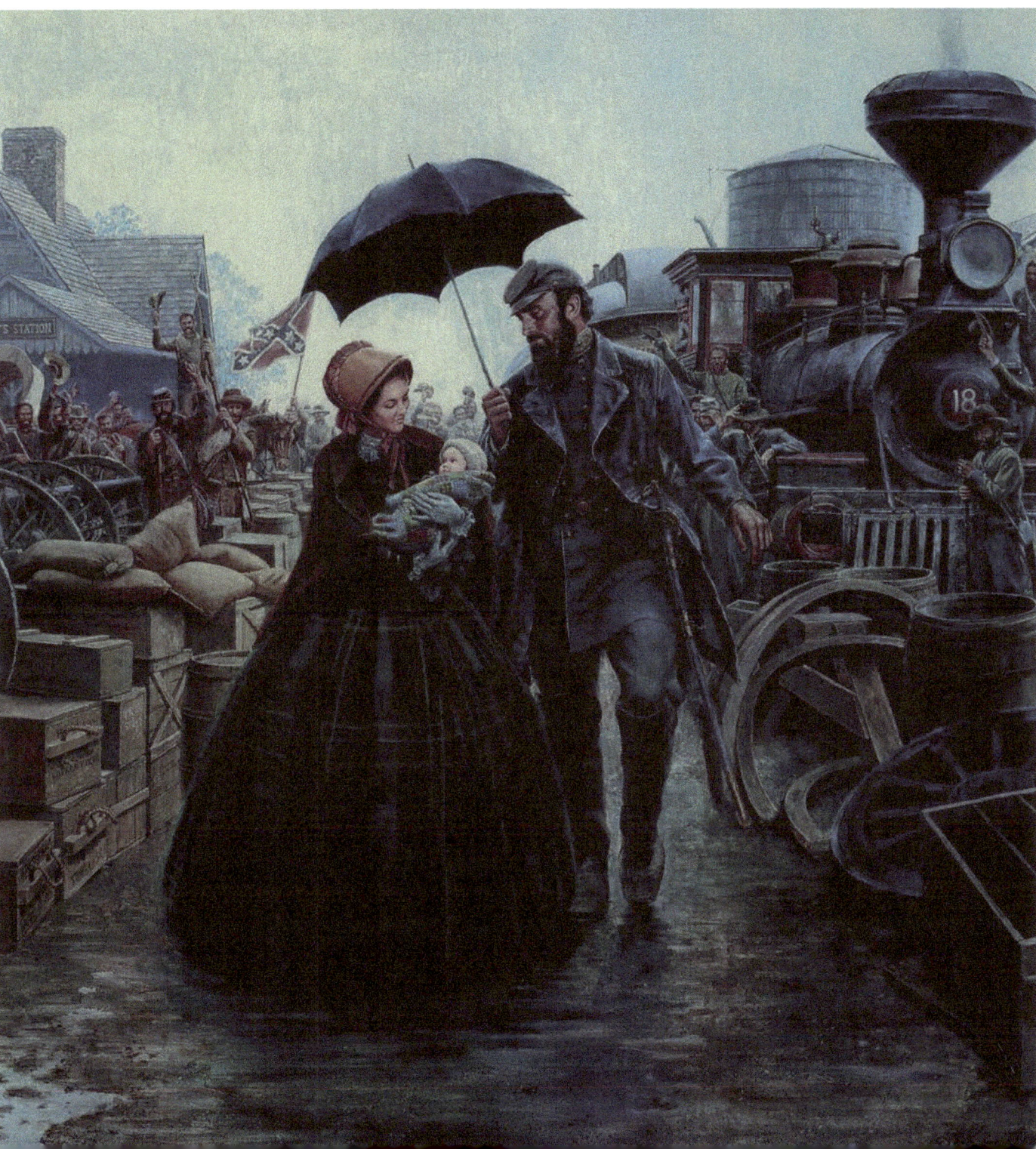

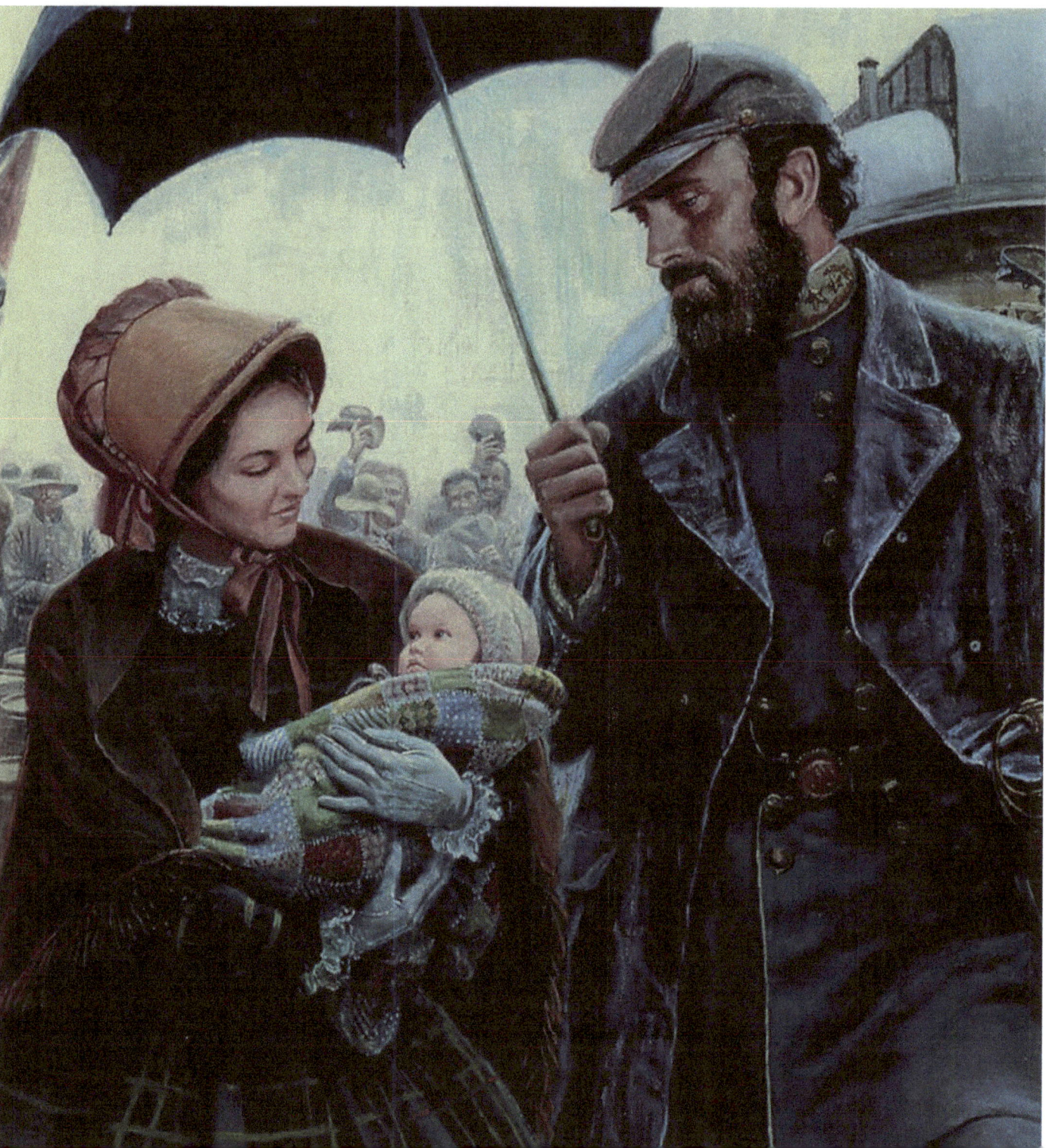

Troops clustered around the depot cheered wildly for the family as they descended from the coach and departed in a carriage. Jackson had shied away from holding the baby because of his wet raincoat, "but as [they] drove in a carriage to Mr. Yerby's, his face reflected all the happiness and delight that were in his heart." Once they reached the accommodations the general had secured at the Thomas Yerby estate known as Belvoir, Anna noted that her husband "speedily divested himself of his overcoat, and, taking the baby in his arms, he caressed her with the tenderest affection, and held her long and lovingly."

During the family's time together, many observed that Julia resembled her father. Jackson always disagreed, saying that she was too pretty for that.

Of her time with her husband, Anna recalled: "I never saw him look *so well*. He seemed to be in excellent health & looked *handsomer* than I had ever seen him, & then he was so full of happiness at having us with him & seeing & caressing his sweet babe, that I thought we had never been so blest & so happy in our lives."

Jackson still adhered to his schedule at his headquarters office and would join his family in the afternoon. Visits by officers, old friends, and prominent citizens somewhat limited the Jacksons' time together. But regardless of who was around, Anna recalled that Jackson always held his daughter. She noted, "When [Julia] slept in the day, he would often kneel over her cradle, and gaze upon her little face with the most rapt admiration, and he said he felt almost as if she were an angel, in her innocence and purity."

Adoration did not lead to a break down in discipline, however. When Julia cried for seemingly no reason, Jackson would set her in her crib and stand

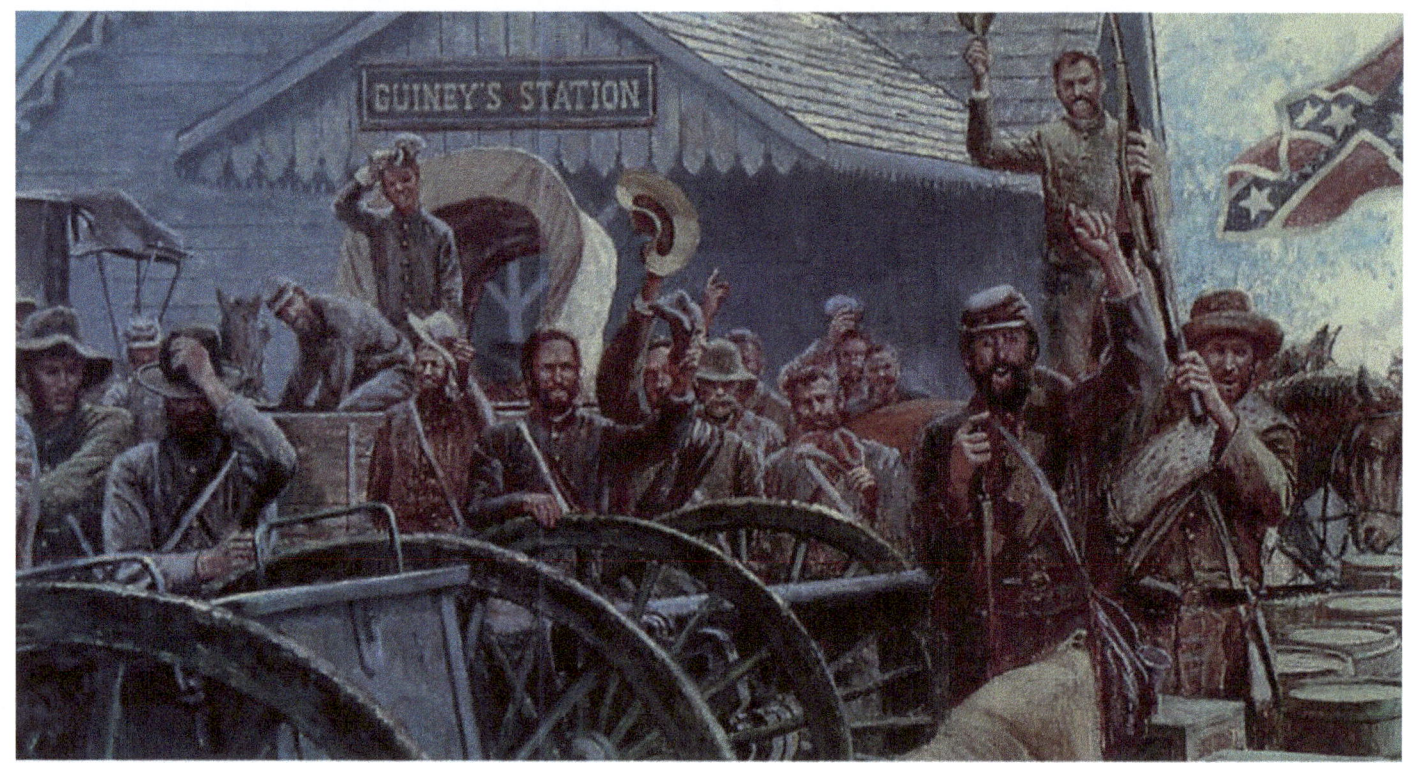

over her, Anna observed, "with as much coolness and determination as if he were directing a battle; and he was true to the name *Stonewall* even in disciplining a baby!" After Julia had ceased to cry, Jackson would pick her up. If she should again cry, he returned her to the crib. Soon thereafter she ceased to fuss around him.

On the fourth day of their time together, Jackson arranged for Julia's baptism in the parlor of Belvoir. Corps chaplain B. Tucker Lacy conducted the ceremony. The child was christened Julia Laura in honor of the general's mother and sister.

That Sunday the general and his wife attended the corps worship service together. More than a thousand soldiers—including Robert E. Lee, Jubal Early, and Joseph B. Kershaw—gathered that morning.

In the early morning hours of April 29, a courier arrived with news that the Army of the Potomac was moving to cross the Rappahannock. Immediately, Jackson had Anna pack to return to Richmond while he attended to matters at headquarters. He would send someone to escort her on the train. In the end, that turned out to be Chaplain Lacy. The last Anna saw of her husband, he was disappearing into the woods.

As a tribute to the Jackson family, I chose to use a square composition: the shape of the battle flag used by the general's troops. The perspective lines form a St. Andrew's cross. Baby Julia is at the center, with her adoring parents gazing down at her. In some ways it is a sequel to my painting *Until We Meet Again.*

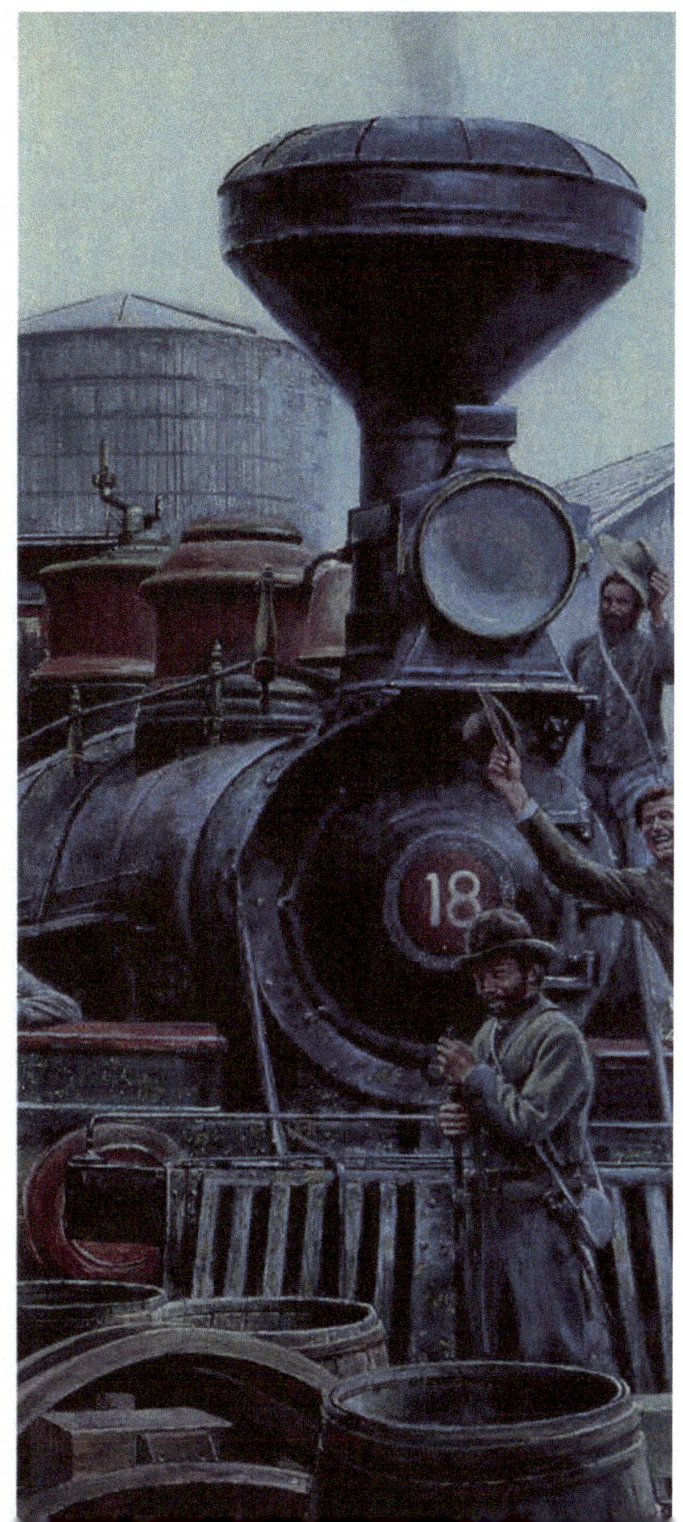

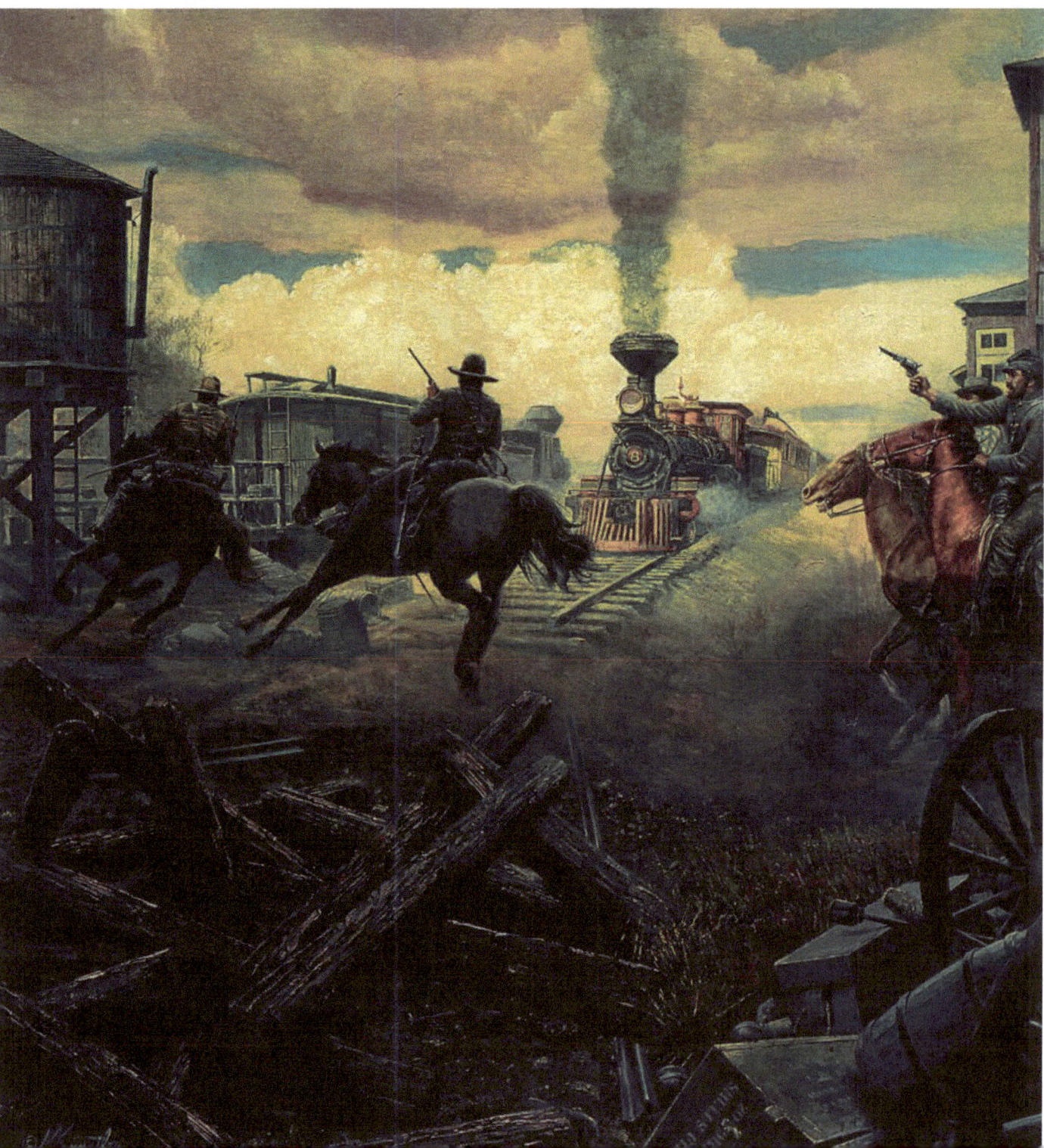

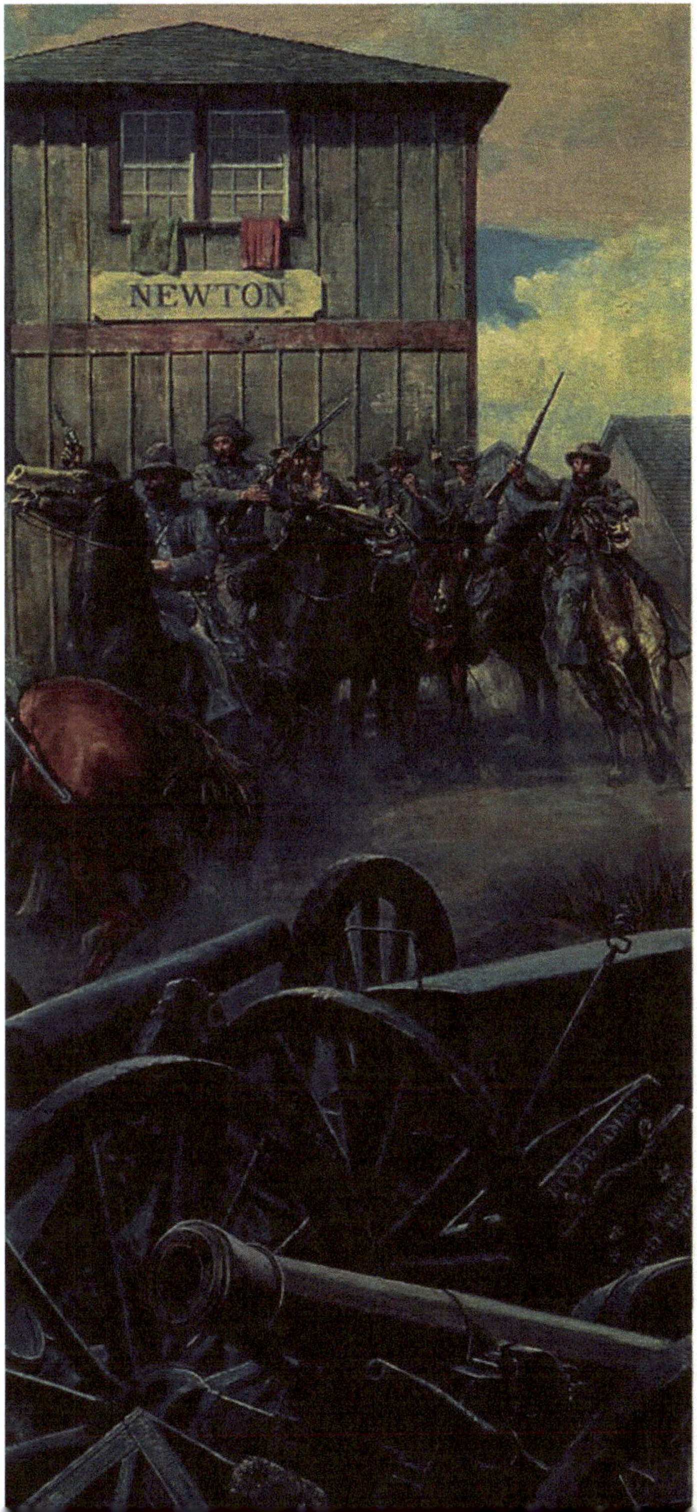

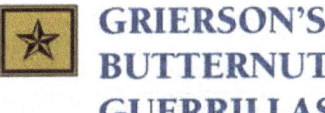

GRIERSON'S BUTTERNUT GUERRILLAS

NEWTON STATION, MISSISSIPPI
APRIL 24, 1863
1991, oil, 28 x 38

EARLY ON the morning of April 24, 1863, a gray-clad band quietly rode into Newton Station, Mississippi. No one suspected the havoc they would wreak. They were the Butternut Guerrillas, Union soldiers dressed as Confederates, and the advance party of Col. Benjamin Grierson's raiding force of seventeen hundred men. At Newton, the guerrillas captured one train and then pounced upon another, destroying vital supplies meant for Vicksburg. Then they raced to the Union lines at Baton Rouge, Louisiana. U. S. Grant described the raid as one of the most brilliant cavalry exploits of the war.

173

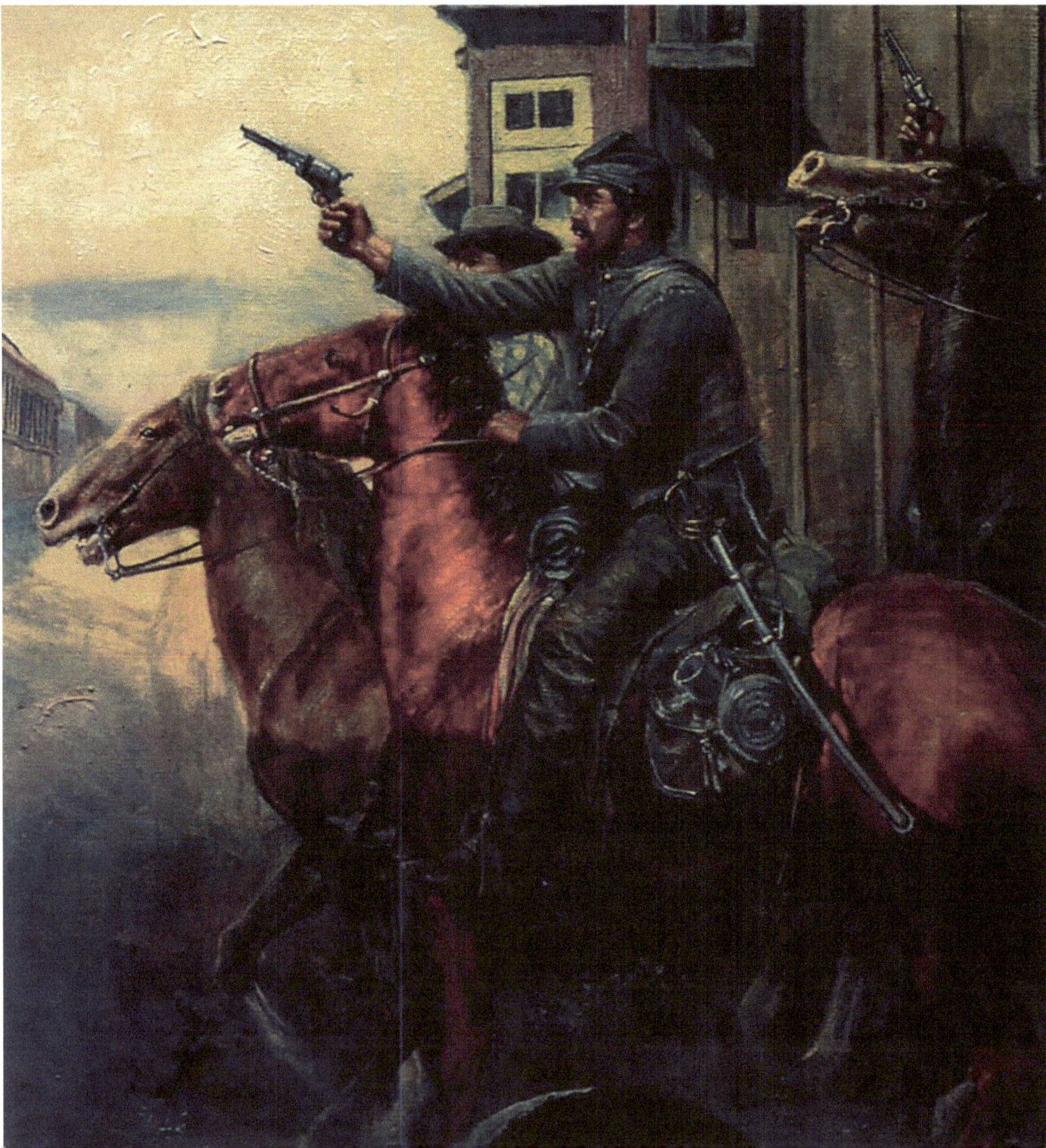

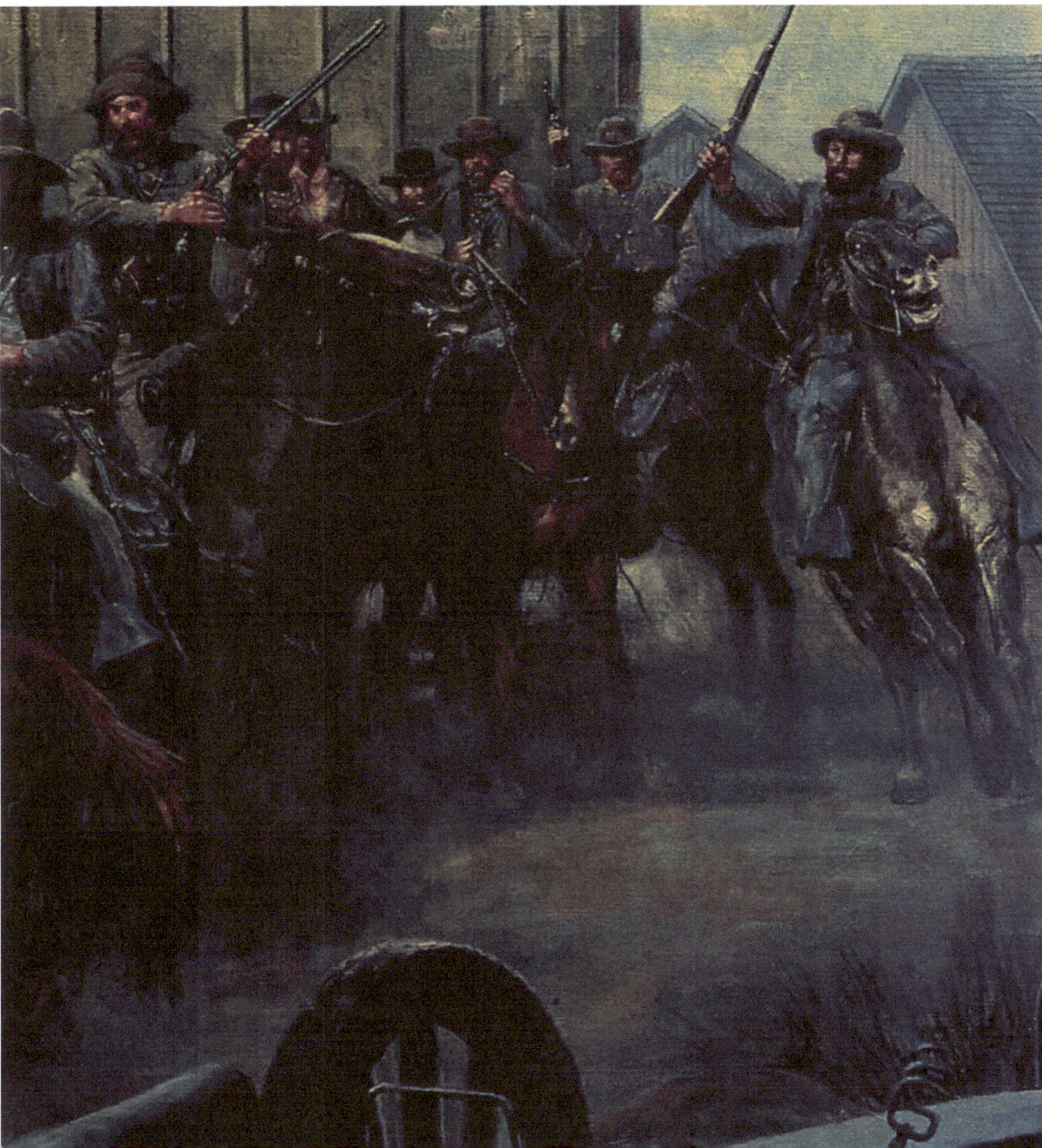

THE LAST COUNCIL

JACKSON, LEE, AND STUART AT
CHANCELLORSVILLE
MAY 1, 1863

1990, oil, 28 x 36

THIS IS one of my earliest Civil War paintings and one of my first depictions of Lee and Jackson together. At the time, I was reading James M. McPherson's *Battle Cry of Freedom* and came across his account of Jeb Stuart's arrival at Lee's headquarters on the night of May 1, 1863, with the startling news that the Union right flank was "in the air," that is, not anchored by a natural barrier. A painting of Stuart's meeting with Lee and Jackson would allow me to show not two but three Confederate greats on the same canvas. And as far as I knew, this scene had never been portrayed before.

Lee had been playing a guessing game ever since he learned that Joseph Hooker had put the Army of the Potomac in motion.

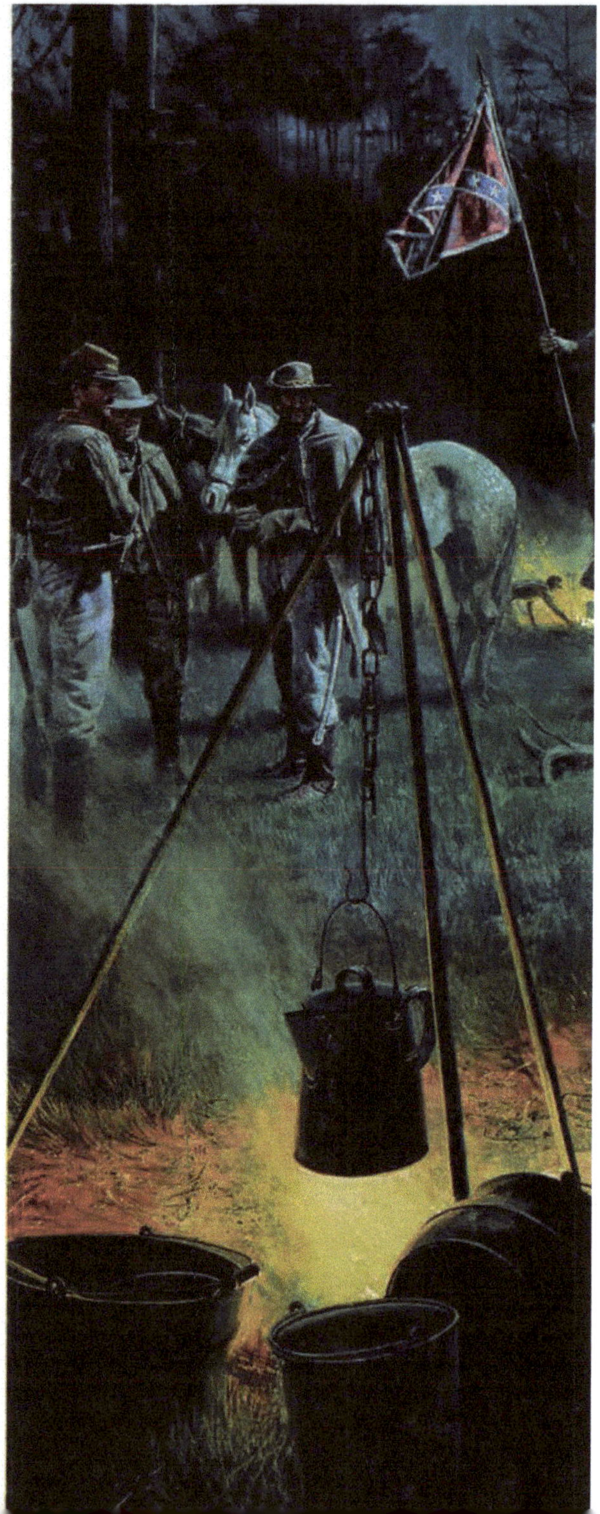

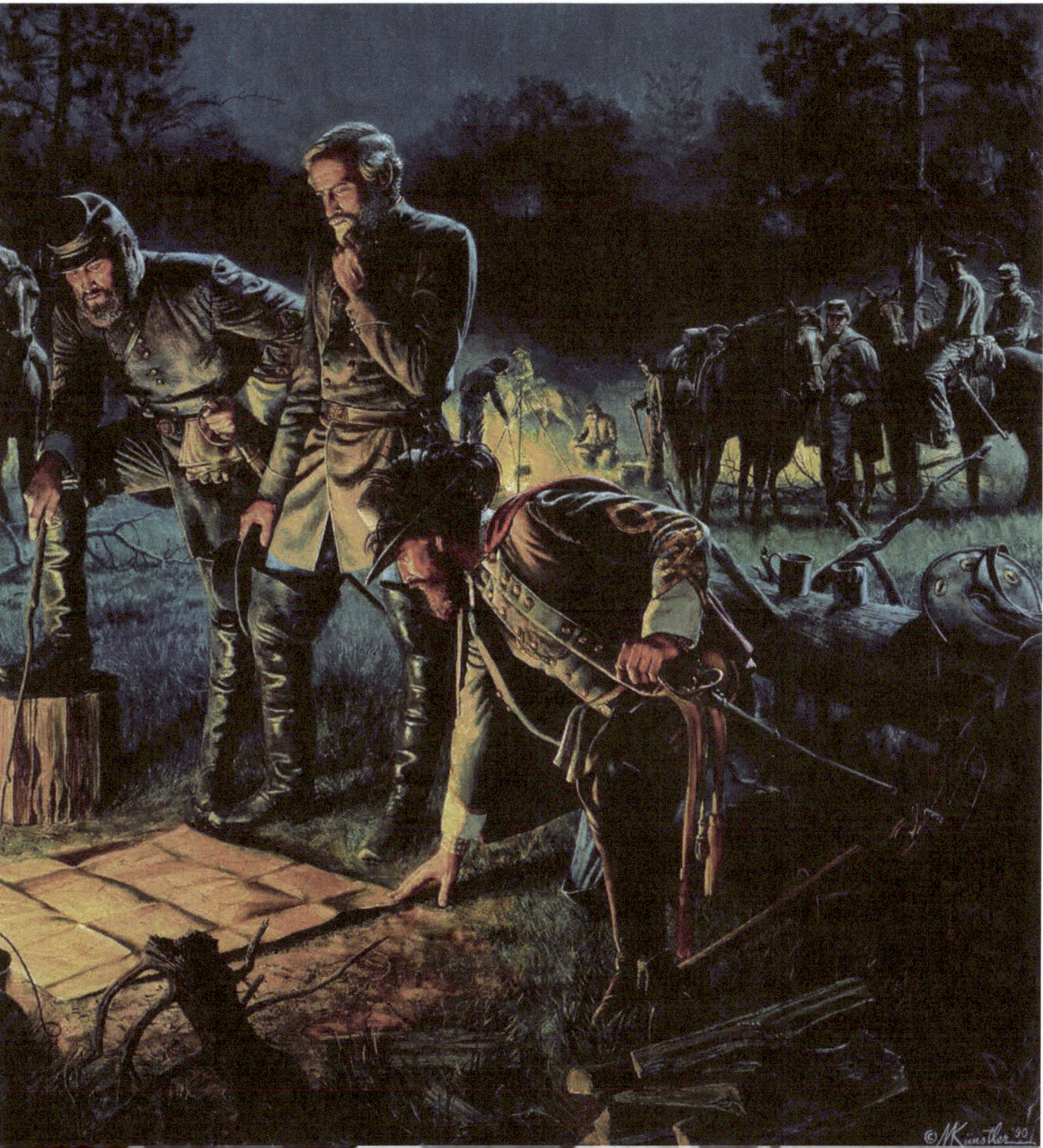

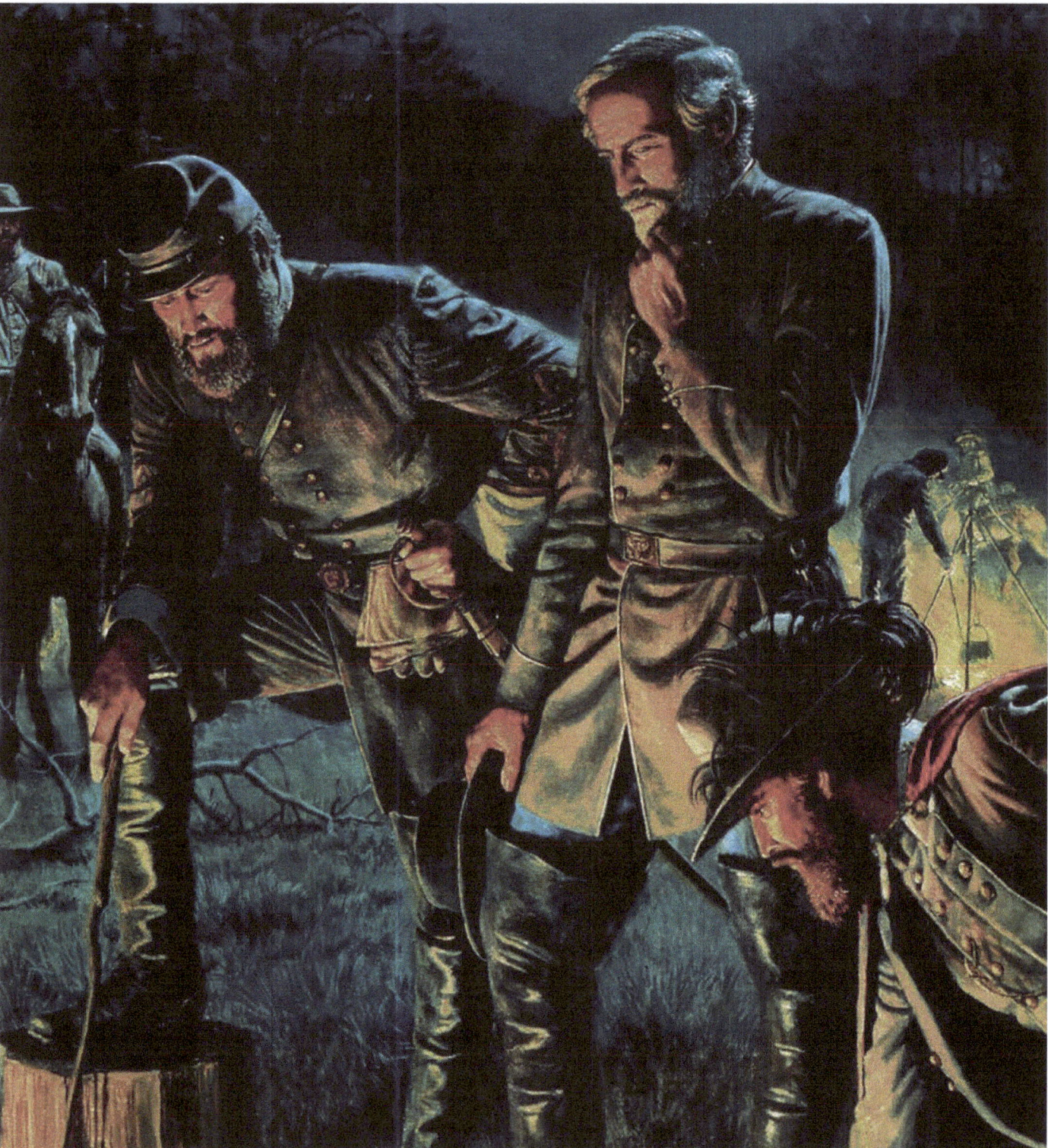

After shifting most of his divisions to the west, Lee dispatched Stuart's cavalry to scout out the Union army. He left a small force in the trenches overlooking Fredericksburg. Subsequently, Jackson's corps probed along the wide Union front. Suddenly, Hooker's army halted and dug in around a crossroads known as Chancellorsville, fourteen miles west of Fredericksburg.

As the sun set on May 1, Lee was puzzled as to why Hooker had concentrated his forces around the Chancellor house (for that was all that stood at the crossroads) and switched to a defensive posture. The Union commander had at least seventy thousand men and had been advancing against little resistance. What Lee did not know was that Hooker had no cavalry; he had sent his horsemen on a mission he hoped would divert Stuart's cavalry. Stuart had responded, but not with his whole force. Jackson's attacks, meanwhile, had put three Union corps on the defensive. Thus Hooker was not thinking about how to win but rather how not to lose.

When Jackson approached Lee that night, they assessed Hooker's position and saw that his left flank and center were not vulnerable to attack. Still, Lee sent his chief of engineers along with Jackson's to assess the Union front.

Then Stuart arrived with news that Lee's nephew—Fitz Lee—had been successfully scouting to the west of the main thoroughfare and found that Hooker's right flank was open. Immediately Lee began weighing the practicality of a sweeping westward movement of Jackson's corps around the Union right. He then dispatched Stuart to scout the roads in that area of the Wilderness.

The two engineers returned with news that the Union center was heavily entrenched and protected by thick woods and massed artillery. Lee saw that a

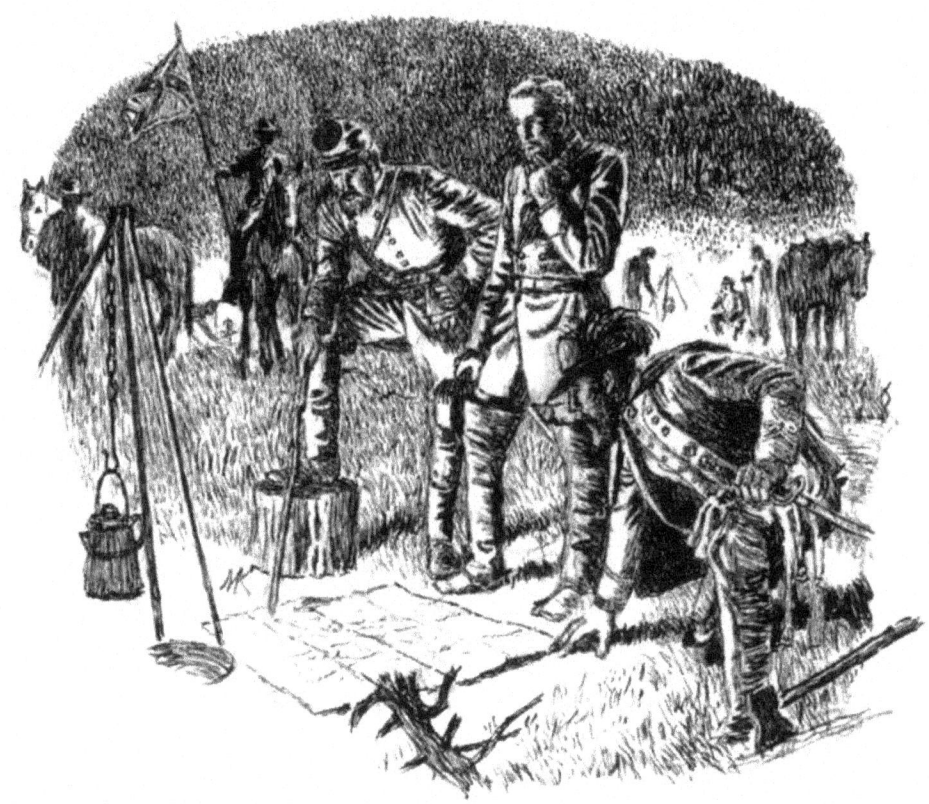

two-pronged attack against a seemingly demoralized enemy was his only chance for success. Jackson would attack from the west; Lee would attack from the southeast; Hooker would be trapped with his back against the river.

Jackson announced, "My troops will move at four o'clock." And he left Lee and found a place to lie down and sleep for a couple of hours.

In my painting of Stuart's appearance at Lee's headquarters, the lighting proved difficult. My goal was to make it dramatic. The warm firelight contrasts with the cool moonlight. Because of Jackson's reputation as a strategist, I have him pointing out the attack plan, which would require Lee to divide his force and remain with only fifteen thousand men to confront Hooker's main force while Jackson marched around the Union flank with more than twenty-eight thousand men. As he contemplates this high-risk strategy, Lee is the center of interest. The cavalry in the rear is part of Stuart's entourage.

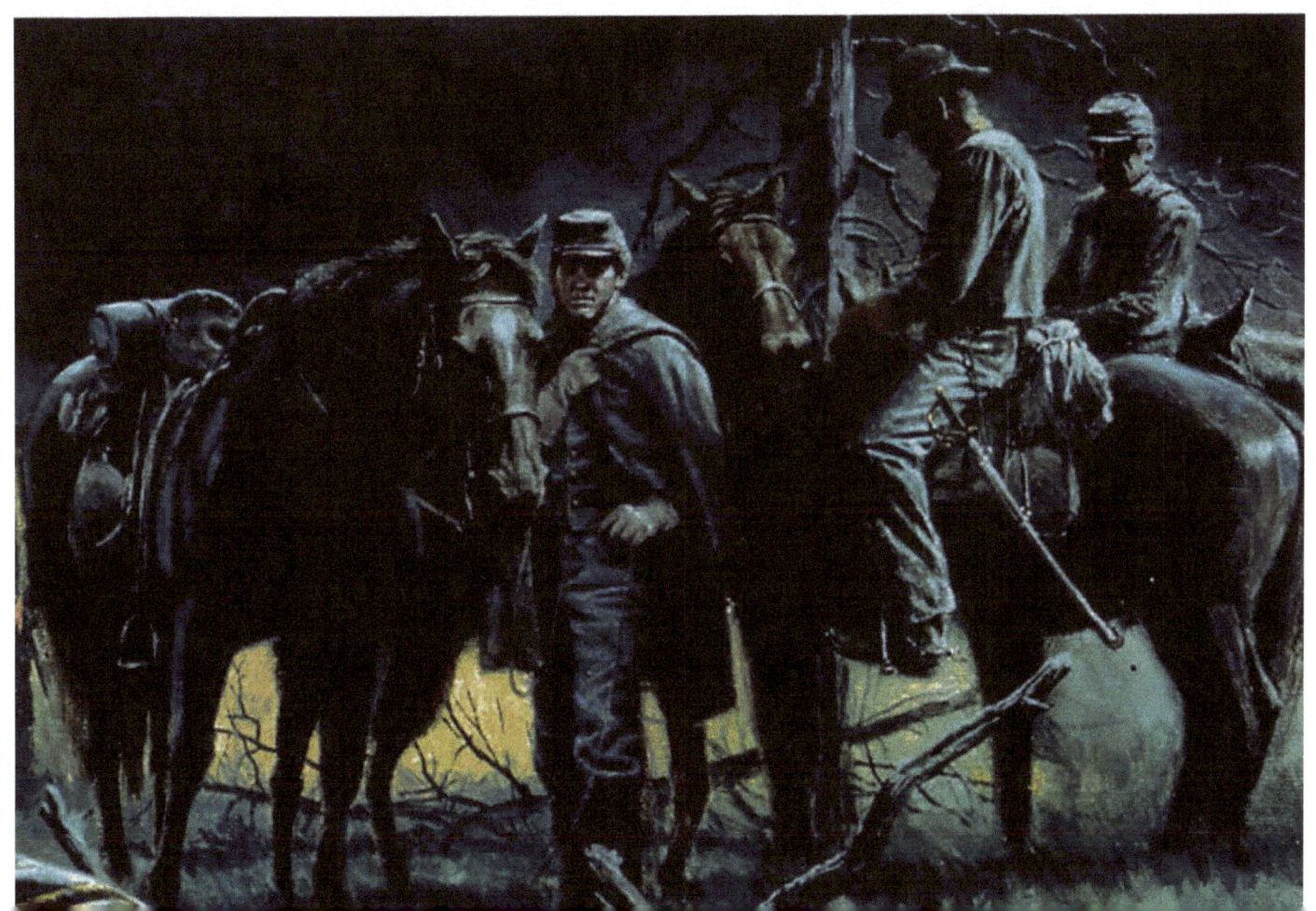

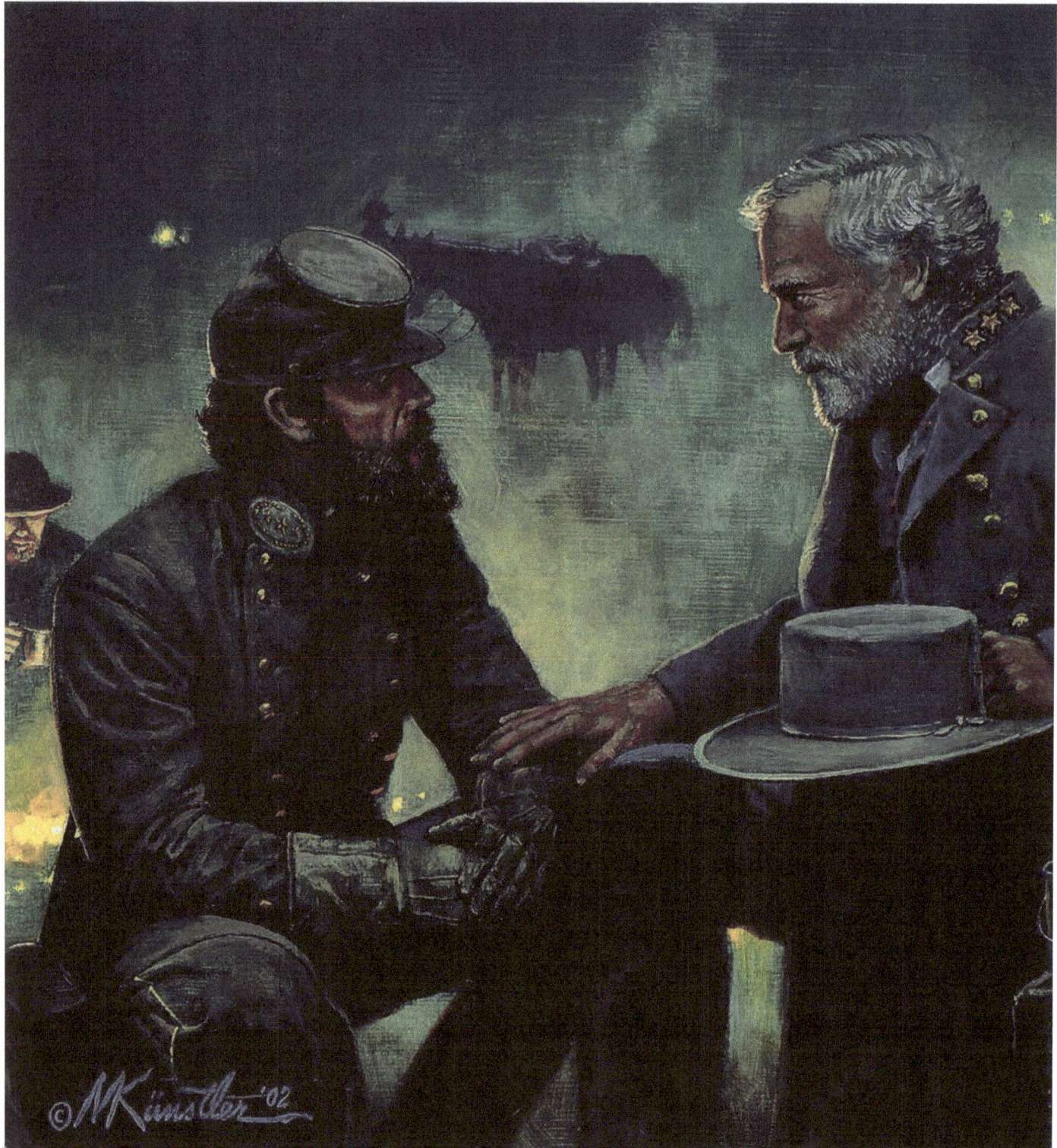

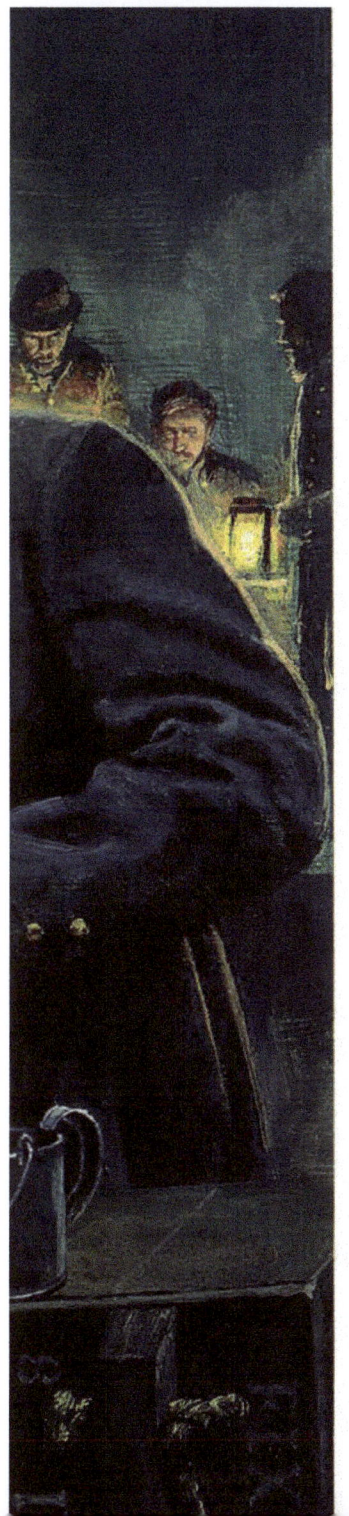

TACTICS AND STRATEGY

JACKSON AND LEE AT CHANCELLORSVILLE
MAY 2, 1863

2002, oil, 10 x 11½

JACKSON AWAKENED, wandered toward a campfire, and sat down on a discarded cracker box. A short time later, Chaplain B. Tucker Lacy, who was well acquainted with the area around Chancellorsville, joined him. The two talked about the roads the corps might use for the movement to Hooker's right flank. Lacy and mapmaker Jedediah Hotchkiss then left in search of information about the roads. When they returned to camp around 3:30 a.m., they found Lee and Jackson in anxious conversation over the plans for the day.

This is the moment I tried to capture here. The bond between the two men went beyond the shared mentality of two military geniuses. Theirs was a father-son relationship. A close-up painting is appropriate to convey this kind of depth and devotion. And the timing of the conversation enabled me to paint a dramatically lit night scene that places a strong focus on the two generals in earnest dialogue.

THE LAST MEETING

CHANCELLORSVILLE, VIRGINIA

MAY 2, 1863

1994, oil, 28 x 40

ORDERS WERE issued, and Jackson's corps prepared for the upcoming twelve-mile march. The sun rose around 5:00 a.m., and there was a slight chill in the air. Jackson wore his black raincoat. His lead elements began to move out around 7:30 a.m., and Jackson rode to the front with his staff. Lee emerged from a thicket and stood by the roadway. Jackson left his staff and rode to him. The two men talked for a few minutes. At one point Jackson pointed to the west and Lee nodded. Then Jackson turned Little Sorrel back and rejoined his staff and corps. It was the last time Lee and Jackson would see each other.

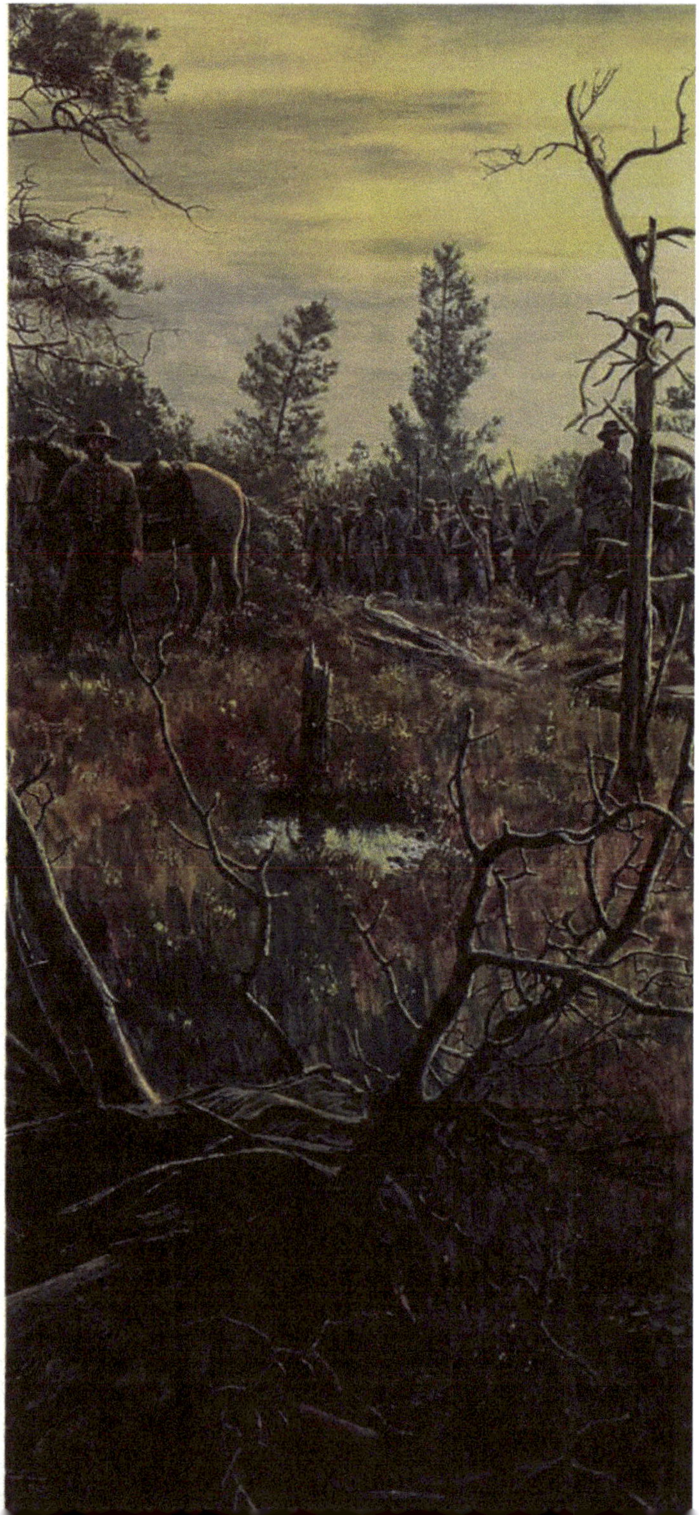

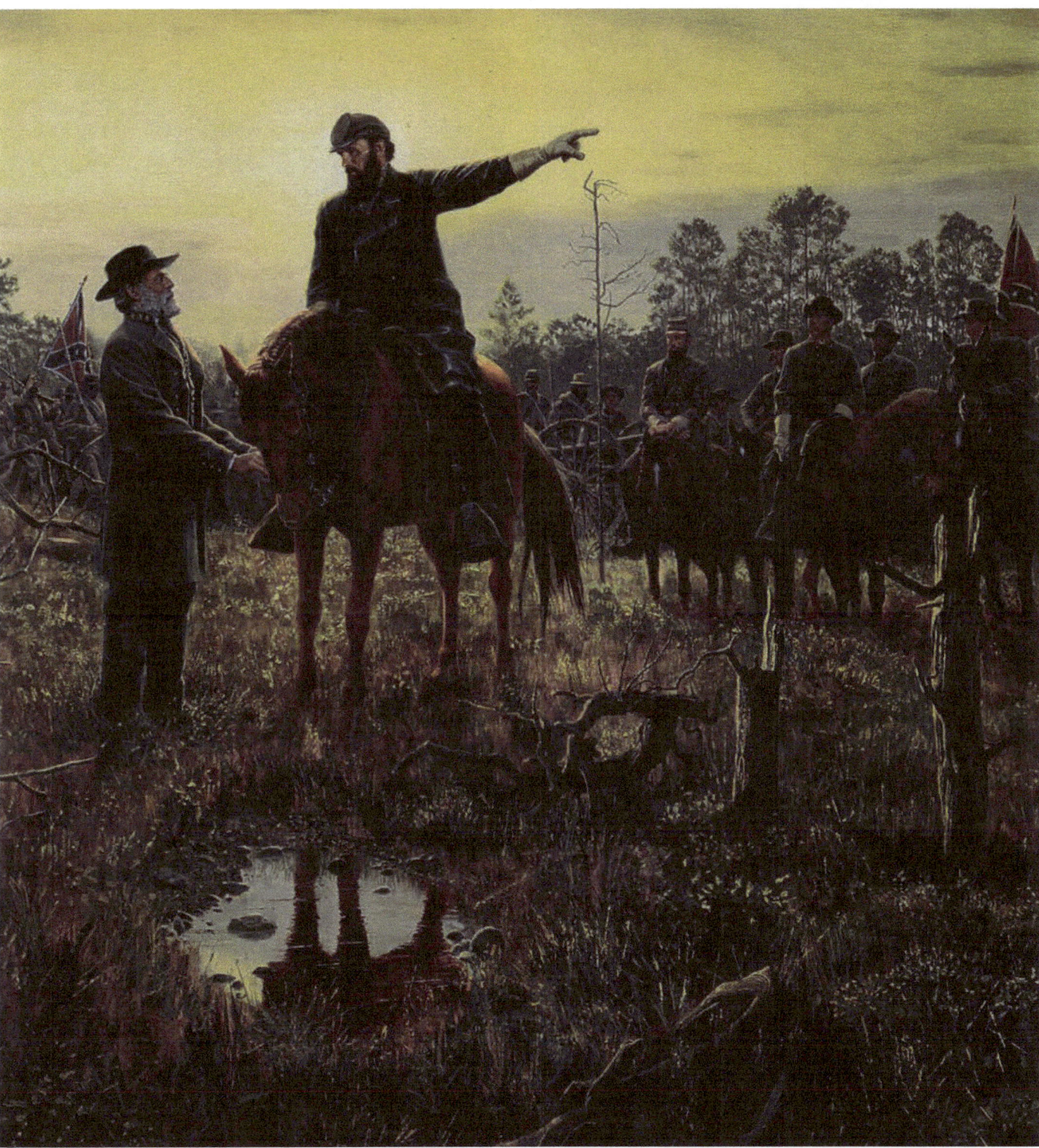

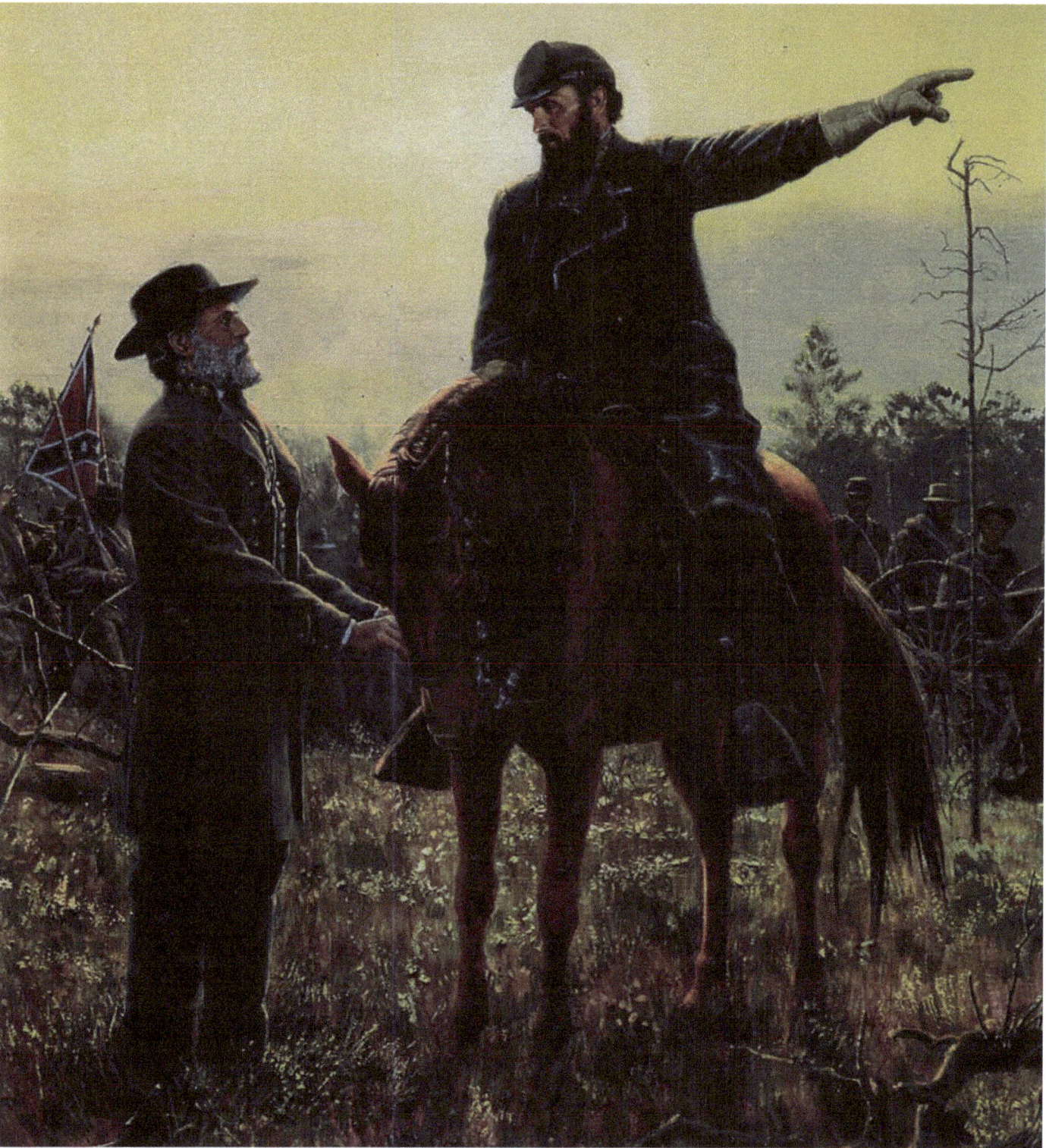

I waited a long time to paint this last meeting between Lee and Jackson. My research indicated that the moment was vastly different from the iconic image conveyed by the 1869 Everett B. D. F. Julio painting entitled *The Last Meeting*. Even though the artist obviously intended his painting to be romantic, it became so well known that many had some form of the image in mind whenever they thought about this last encounter between Lee and Jackson.

The dead trees, old stumps, and broken branches in the painting are typical of the Wilderness at that time. They also convey the somber mood of two soldiers meeting prior to an all-or-nothing venture.

Lee and Jackson conferred on the north side of the road, which gave me an opportunity to look farther to the east, to obtain a dramatic lighting effect by having Jackson silhouetted against the dawn sky. The puddles are a reminder that it had rained the night before. Jackson's raincoat is based on the one he wore that day, which is displayed currently at the Virginia Military Institute. Jackson's staff, in the right background, waits for their commander. Shown, left to right, are Capt. Jedediah Hotchkiss, Dr. Hunter McGuire, Lt. Col. Alexander H. Pendleton, Maj. Wells J. Hawks, Capt. James Power Smith, and Maj. Henry Kyd Douglas. In the left background are Traveller and some of Lee's staff.

Painting history as it really occurred is the great challenge for a historical artist. It was exciting to break new ground with this painting by showing the last meeting as it really happened.

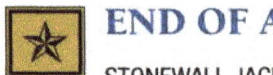

END OF A LEGEND

STONEWALL JACKSON, CHANCELLORSVILLE, VIRGINIA
MAY 2, 1863

1995, gouache, 16 x 26¼

detail, right

JACKSON'S SUDDEN appearance on the right flank of Hooker's army shortly after 5:00 p.m. transformed a Federal corps into a confused rabble that fled and fell back into the center of the Union line. The Confederates swept over all resistance. Nightfall darkened the field with thirty thousand men still locked in combat. But Jackson was not content with his success or concerned about the darkness and the dense woods. Sometime around 9:30 p.m. he rode forward to reconnoiter. After pinpointing the improvised Union position, he rode back toward his own lines. As his party came rapidly through the woods from the direction of the enemy, troops in one of Jackson's own brigades understandably mistook the riders for Federal cavalry. A volley of rifle fire blazed in the faces of the horsemen some twenty yards away.

Three bullets struck Jackson. One pierced his left forearm, another struck a bone in his upper left arm, and the third penetrated his right hand.

For the first time, Little Sorrel bolted at the sound of gunfire.

Eventually, litter-bearers bore the badly wounded general to the rear.

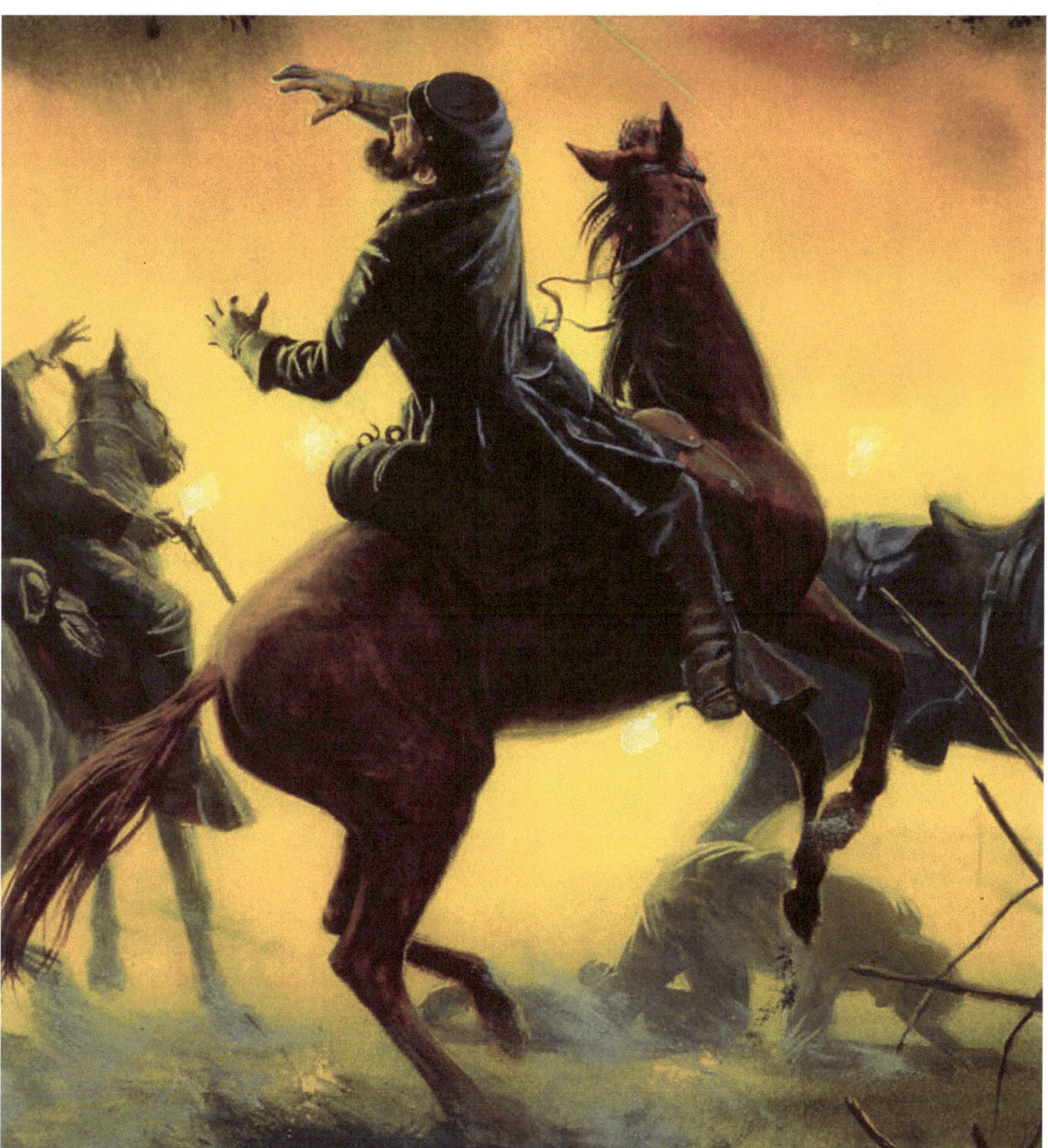

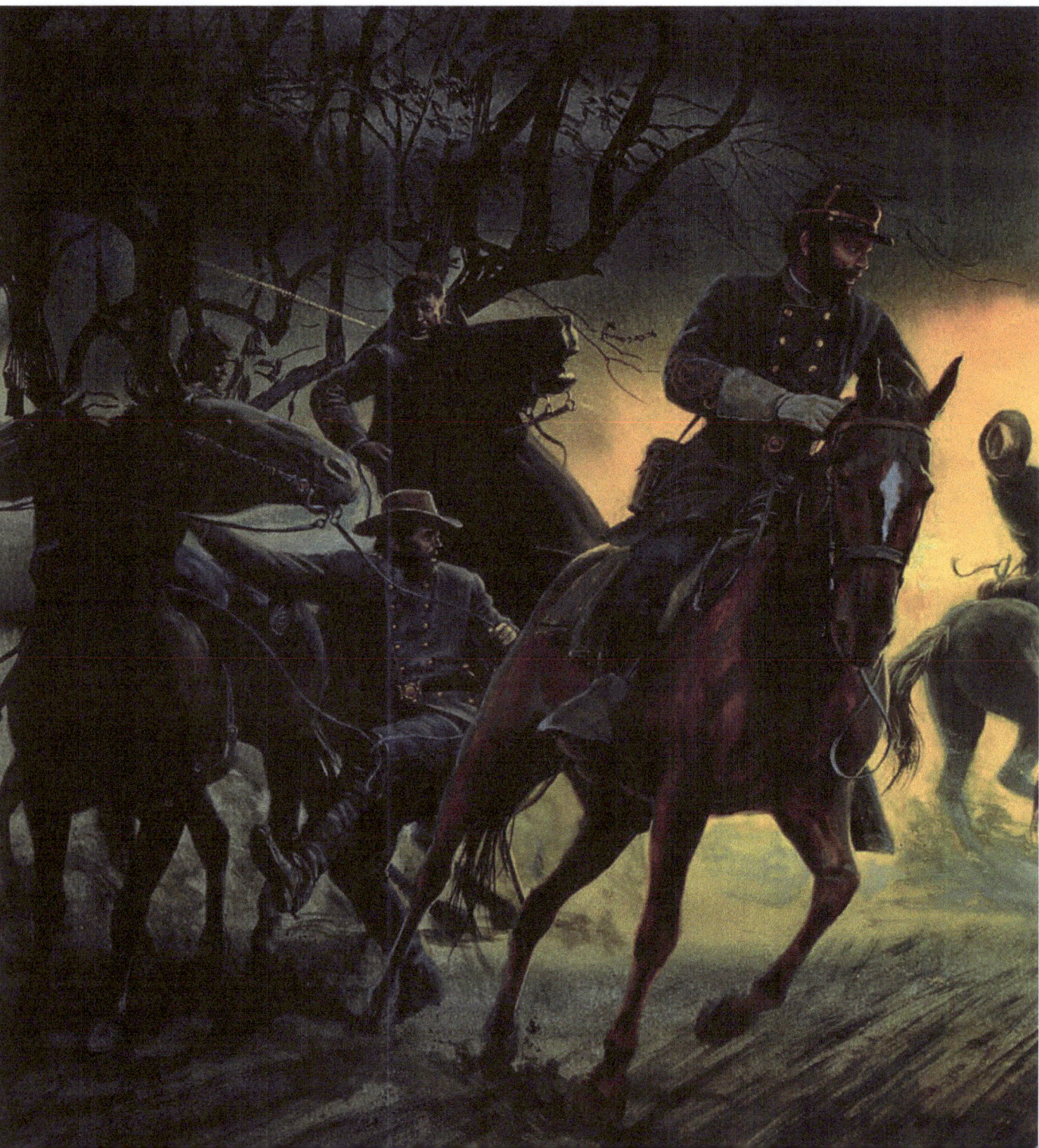

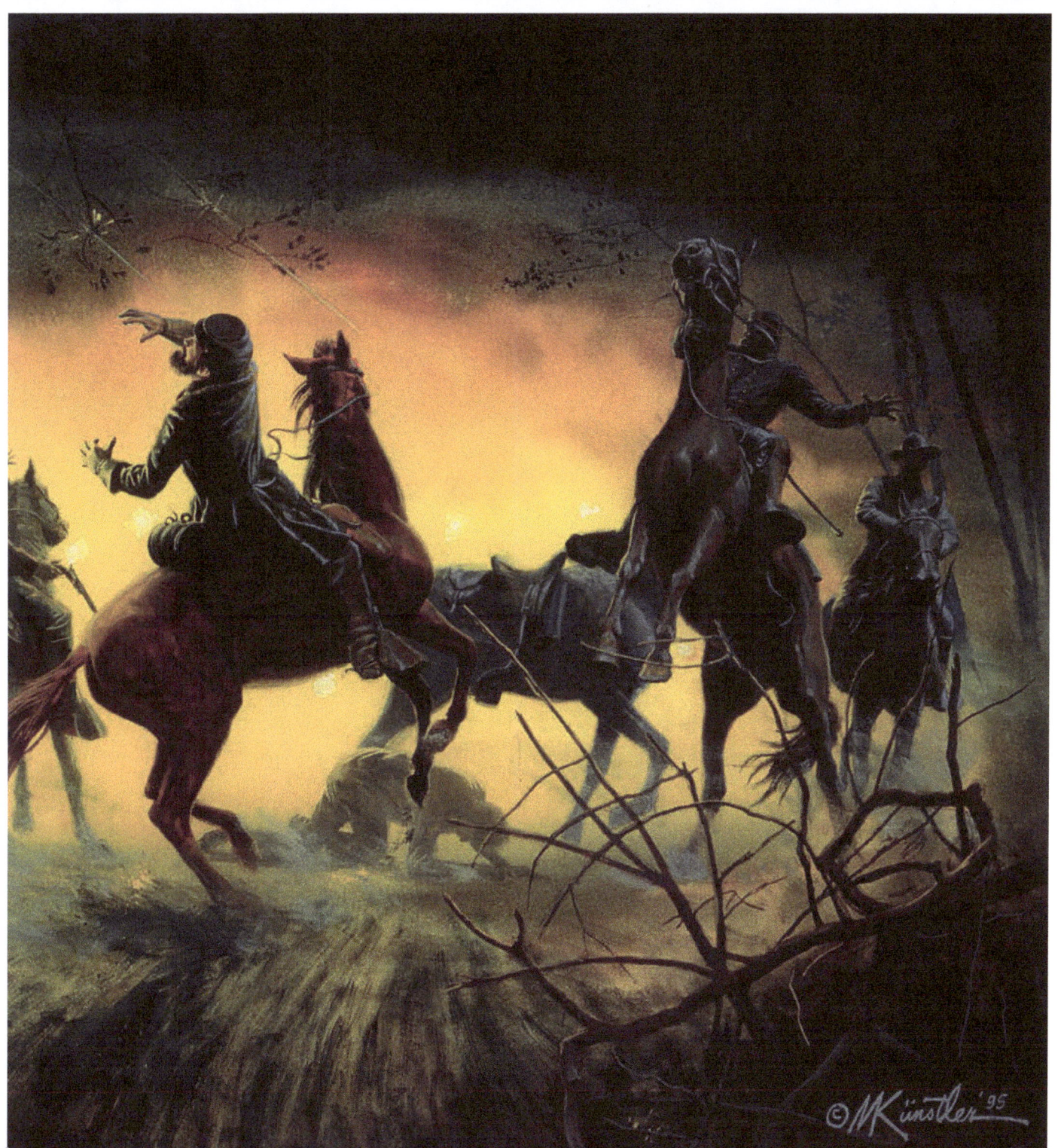

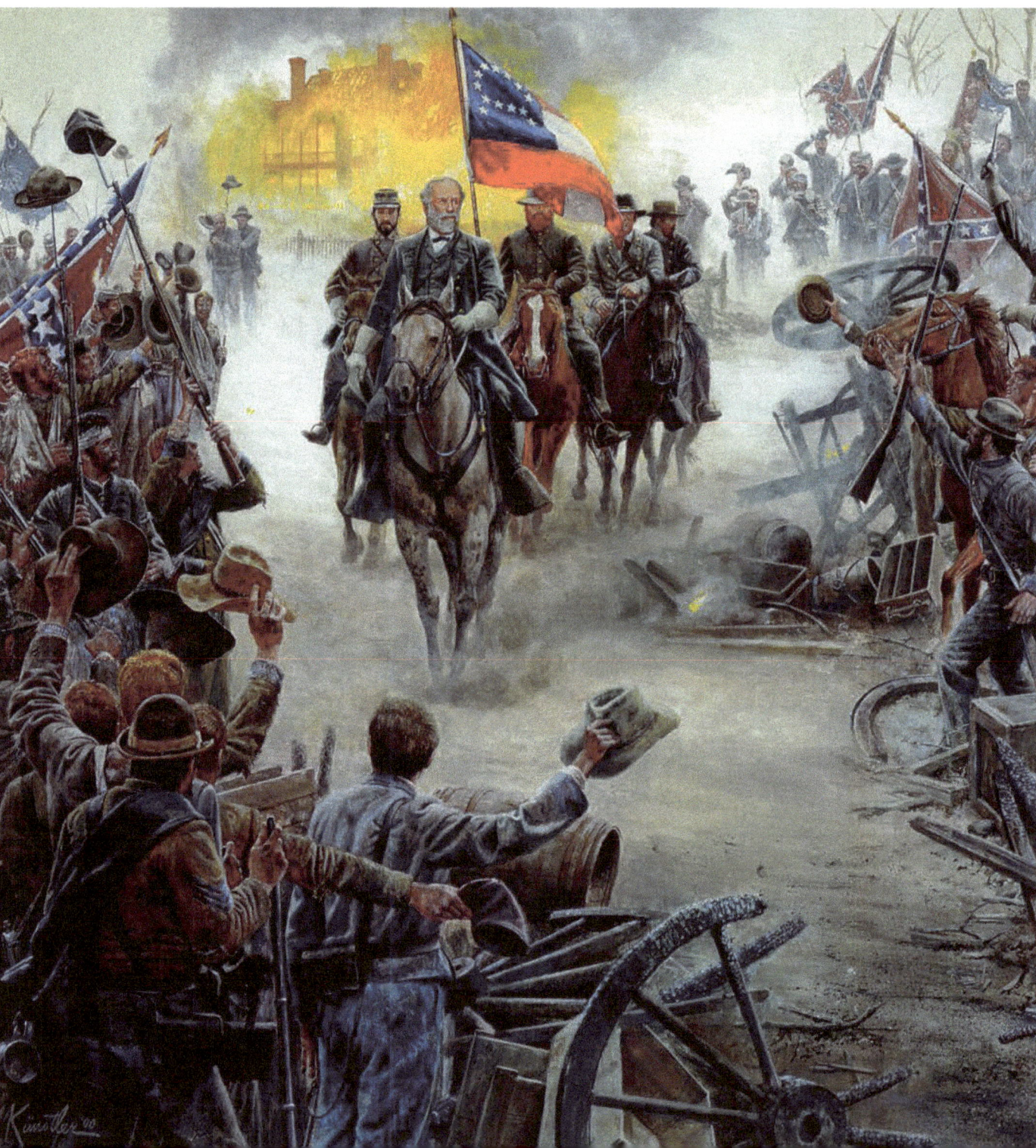

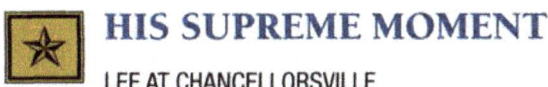

HIS SUPREME MOMENT

LEE AT CHANCELLORSVILLE
MAY 3, 1863
2000, oil, 27½ x 23

MUCH OF the battle of Chancellorsville was to be fought after the wounding of Jackson. Victory was still within Hooker's reach. But Hooker could not comprehend that forty-two thousand Confederates had "surrounded" his seemingly unbeatable army. So at dawn, May 3, he sat immobile and let the Southerners attack again. And they did: Jackson's troops (now under Jeb Stuart) from one direction, and Lee from another.

Southerners took possession of a key position within artillery range of the Chancellorsville intersection. From there they began an effective fire into the center of Hooker's line. The Federal commander was standing on the porch of the Chancellor house when a shell struck the pillar against which he was leaning. Dazed more than wounded, Hooker lost all reasoning ability.

The Federals thereupon abandoned much of the field and huddled in a new line while their general thought only of how to avoid annihilation. This constricting of the Union line allowed Lee and Stuart to rejoin forces.

Chancellorsville was now Lee's battle. It was a staggering victory but a costly one: Jackson would die a week later of complications from his

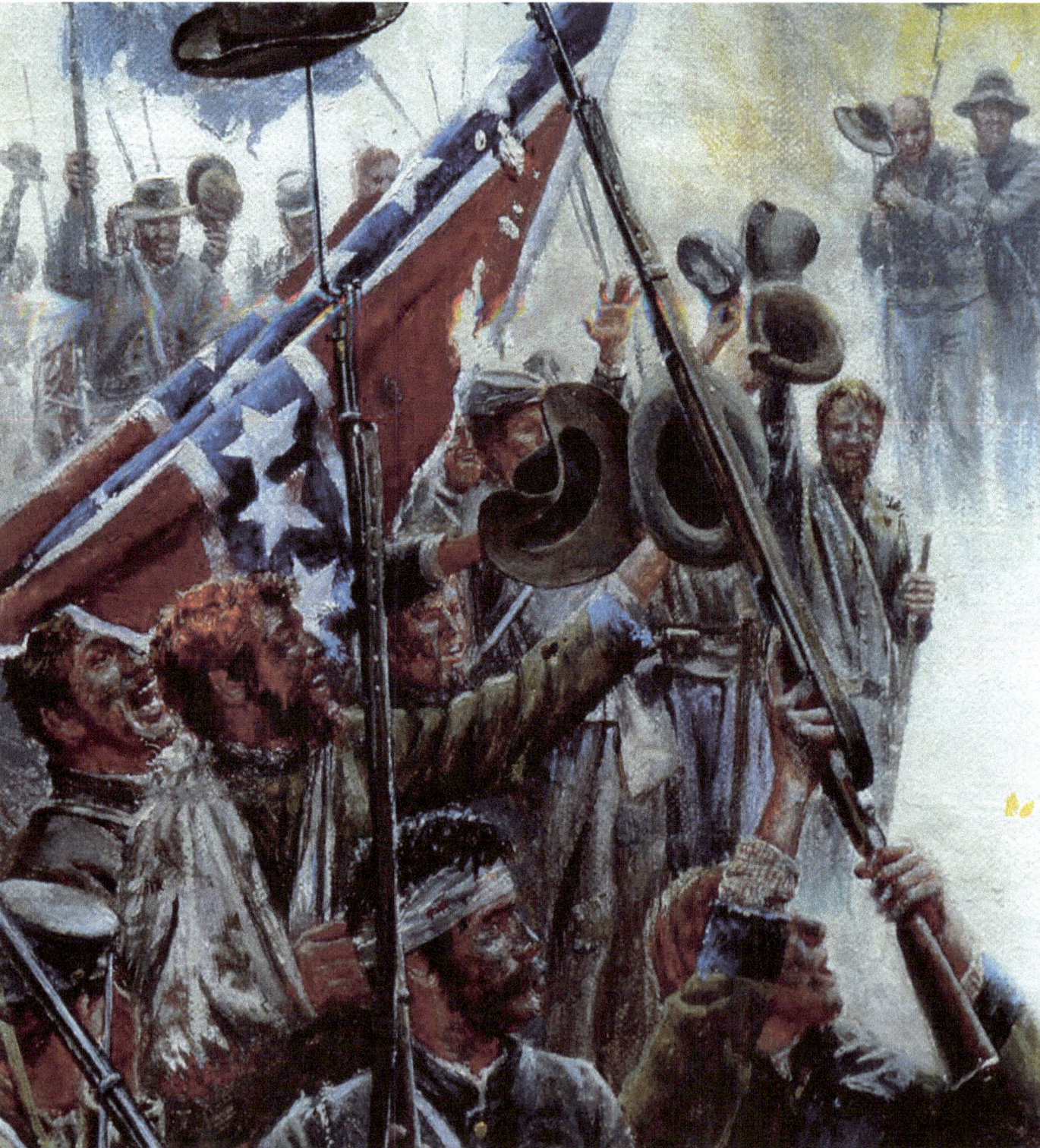

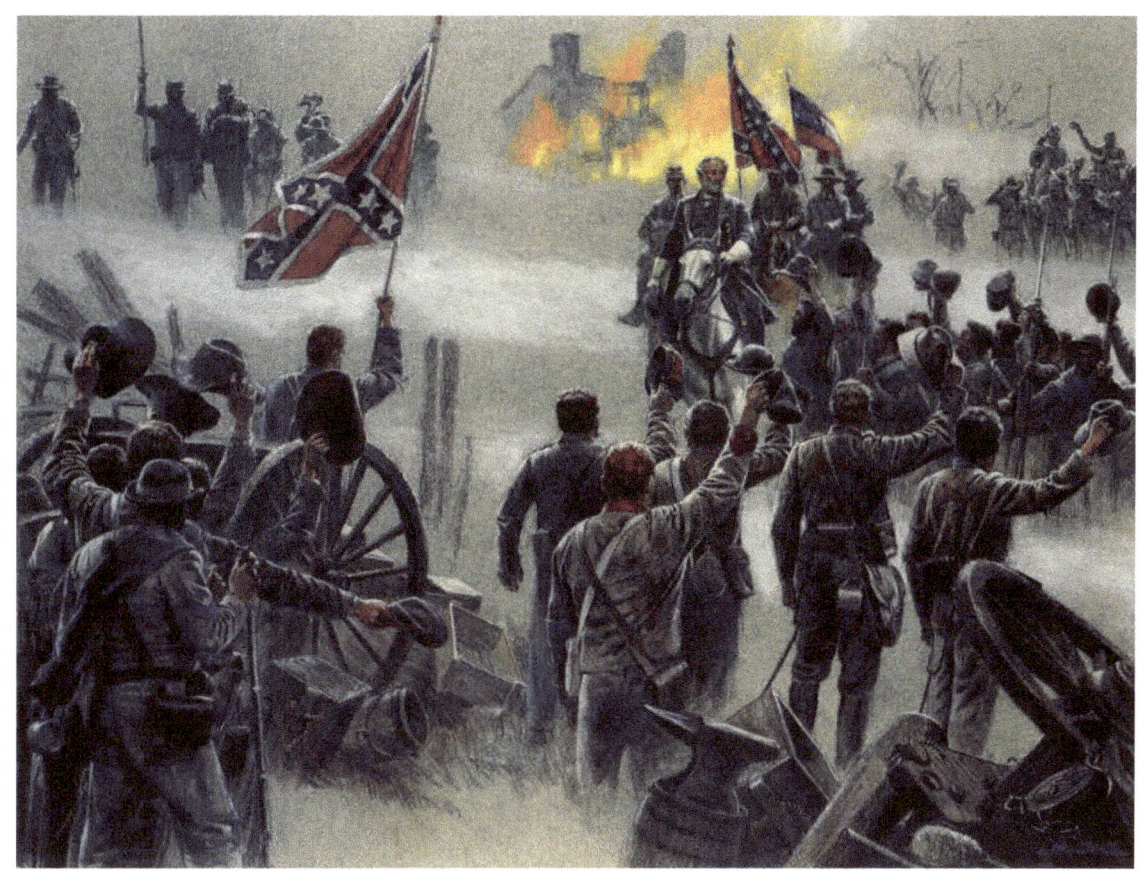

HIS SUPREME MOMENT

STUDY

1995, mixed media, 18 x 23¾

wounds. For the moment, however, the Army of Northern Virginia was again victorious.

As Lee moved among his army near the blazing Chancellor house, he was mobbed by his cheering troops. Again they had done the impossible. Again they had turned back the invader. The triumph at Chancellorsville was Lee's supreme moment.

Some paintings take years to develop. I did a painting of *His Supreme Moment* in 1995. More than five years later, I liked the subject so much that I decided to paint it again as a vertical composition. I left the right foreground without figures to lead the eye into the main center of interest: Lee. In consultation with park historian Frank O'Reilly of the Fredericksburg and Spotsylvania National Military Park, I learned that regiments from Virginia, North and South Carolina, and Georgia were at the Chancellor house at the moment Lee rode by. This gave me the opportunity to show the South Carolina flag in the left background and the North Carolina flag in the right background. In addition to the battle flag, Lee's headquarters flag also can be seen.

The Chancellor house, aflame in the background, is based on drawings of the house done before the war, which were made available to me by Janice Fry, the librarian at the Fredericksburg and Spotsylvania National Military Park.

Professor James I. Robertson Jr. describes the scene clearly in his biography of Jackson: "Lee appeared at the front. Weary Southerners—some blackened by smoke, others limping from wounds—yelled hysterically at the sight of their leader. A staff officer commented, 'I thought that it must have been from such a scene that men in ancient days rose to the dignity of the gods.'"

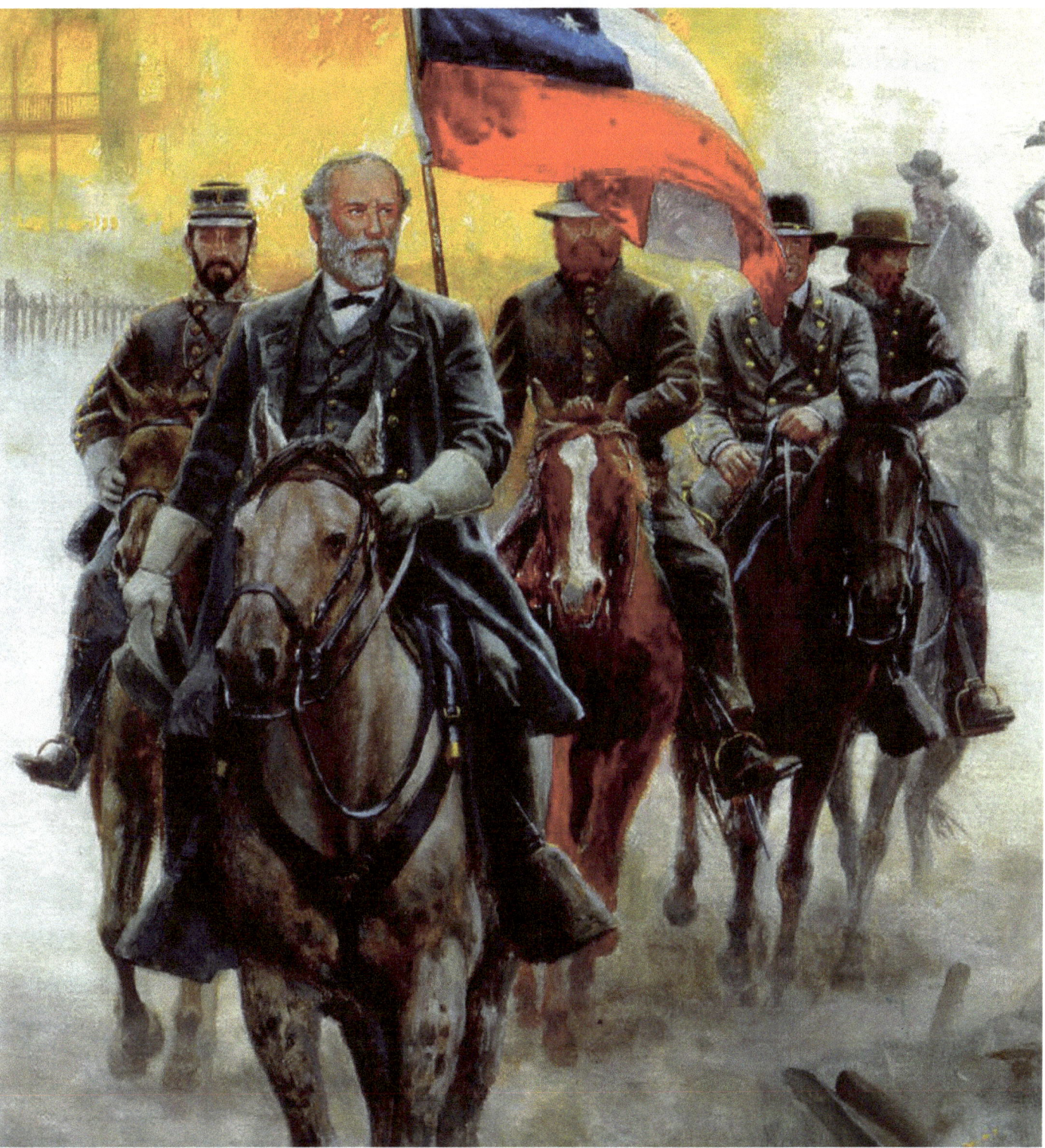

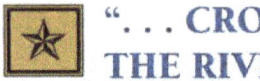

"... CROSS OVER THE RIVER"

STONEWALL JACKSON

1995, oil, 24 x 32

ᴸET US cross over the river and rest under the shade of the trees" were the last words spoken by Thomas J. "Stonewall" Jackson, and they are the inspiration for this painting.

Jackson was very devout and would pause two or three times a day to pray. This painting, which is set on the banks of a Virginia river, depicts one of those quiet moments. The autumn foliage symbolically suggests the end of Jackson's life.

This painting allowed me to do something different from what is usually expected of my historical works, and it enabled me to paint with colors I rarely use.

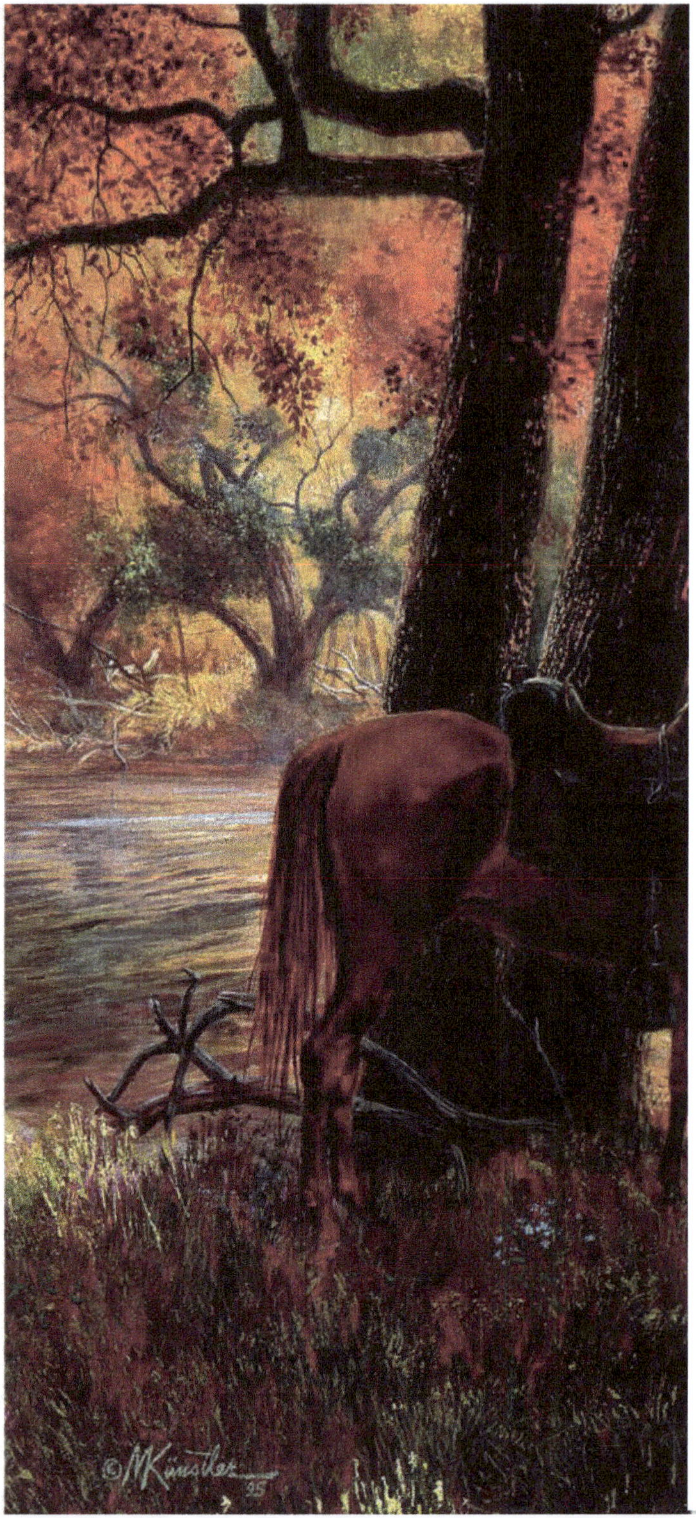

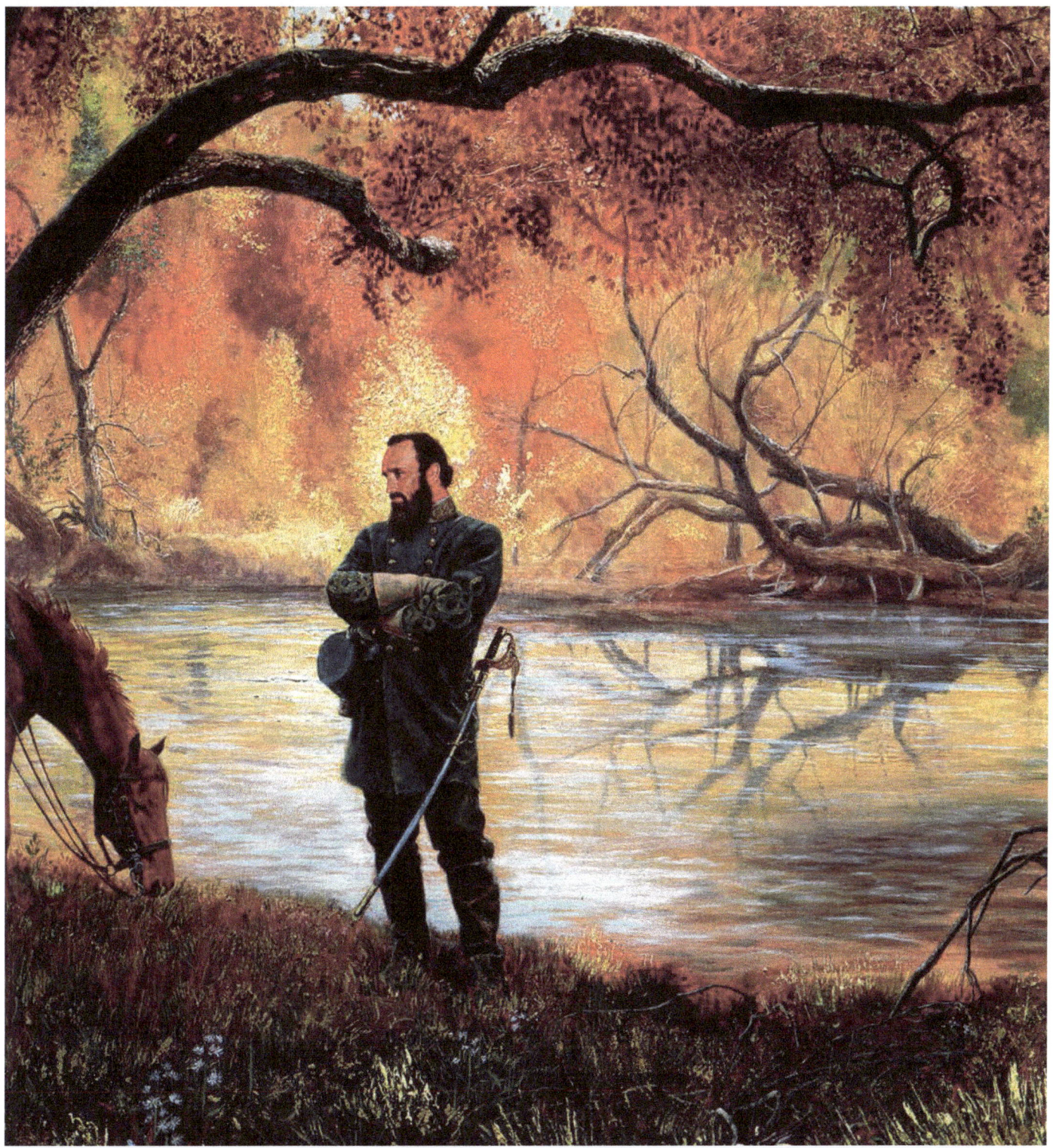

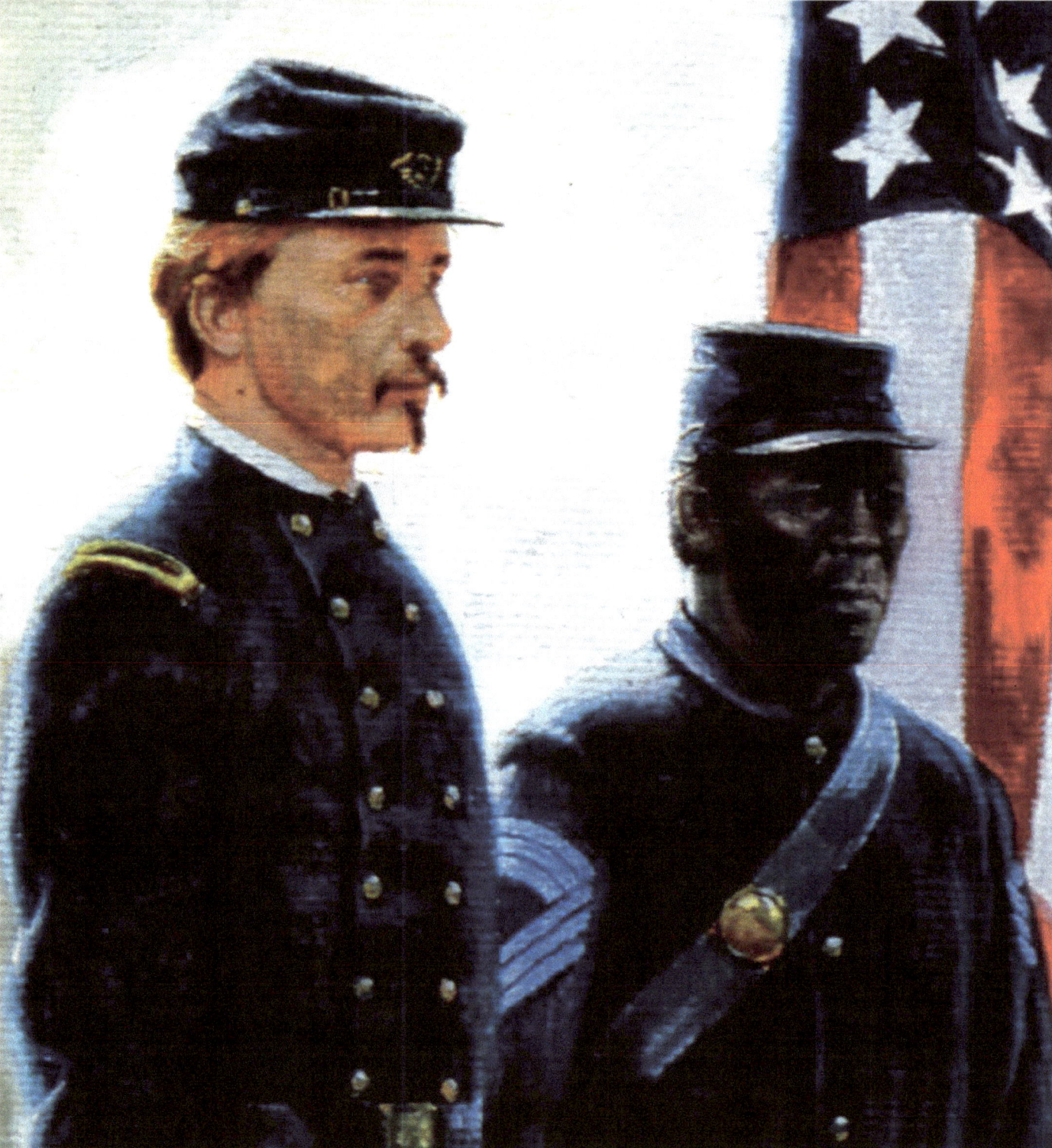

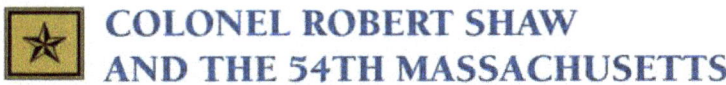

COLONEL ROBERT SHAW
AND THE 54TH MASSACHUSETTS

BOSTON, MAY 28, 1863

1991, oil, 16 x 20

detail, left

The 1989 movie *Glory* presented the story of the famous Fifty-fourth Massachusetts Infantry and inspired me to do this painting. The unit was the first all-volunteer African American regiment to be recruited in the North. It was authorized by Governor John Andrews, who envisioned it as a model regiment of former slaves and freedmen. Among the recruits were two of Frederick Douglass's sons, Charles and Lewis. The son of a prominent abolitionist family, Col. Robert Gould Shaw, was appointed to command the regiment, whose founding was controversial as not all white Northerners believed in the fighting abilities of African Americans.

The Fifty-fourth became a model of perfection and drill in camp. When the regiment completed its training and marched through Boston on May 28, 1863, to embark for the South Atlantic theater, Governor Andrews presented the colors to Shaw with these words: "I know not, Mr. Commander, when in all human history, to any given thousand men in arms there has been committed a work at once so proud, so precious, so full of hope and glory as the work committed to you. I stand as a man and a magistrate, with the rise or fall in history of the Fifty-fourth Massachusetts Regiment."

On July 18, 1863, the Fifty-fourth found fame after its brave but suicidal assault on South Carolina's Fort Wagner, an earthen fort less than two miles from Charleston's Fort Sumter. Shaw and almost half the regiment were killed during the attack. Shaw was buried in an unmarked grave with the rest of the casualties.

Following Shaw's death, Col. Edward N. Hallowell assumed command of the Fifty-fourth. The unit remained based in South Carolina for the remainder of the war and was used in operations in Georgia and Florida, most notably at the February 20, 1864, battle of Olustee, Florida.

There are several good portraits of Shaw, so his likeness was easy to capture. I based the enlisted men on many period photographs of African Americans in uniform. Since the flag of the Fifty-fourth is in the collection of the Commonwealth of Massachusetts, I was able to portray it accurately.

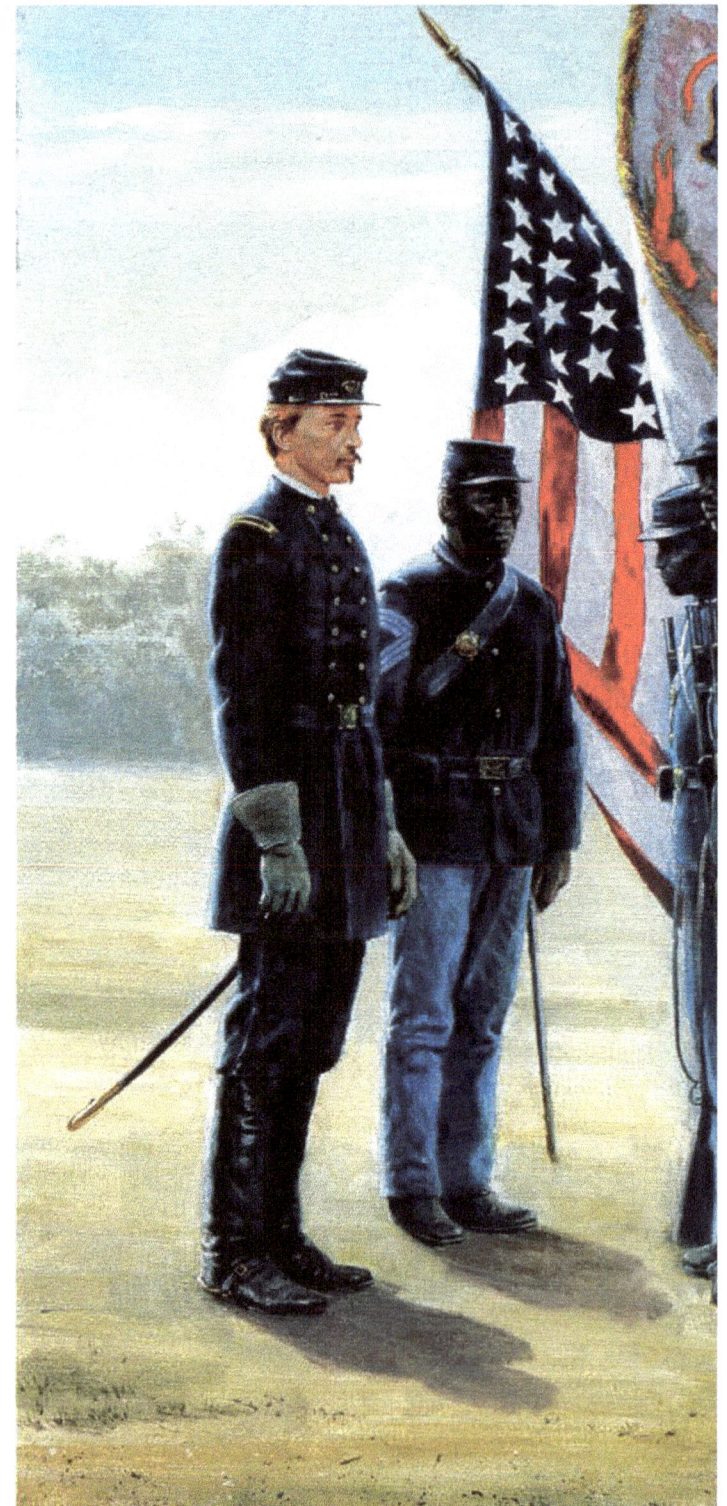

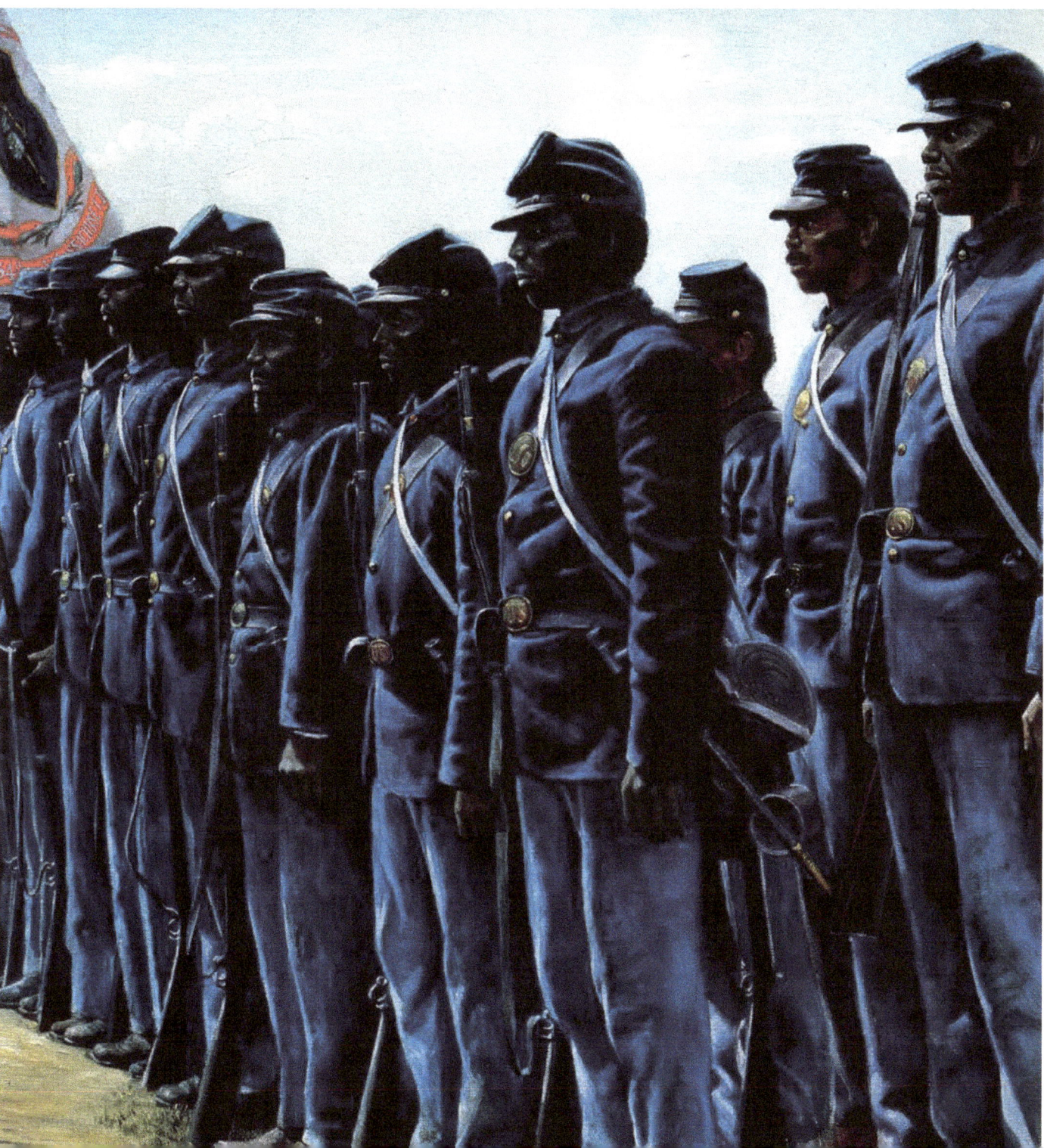

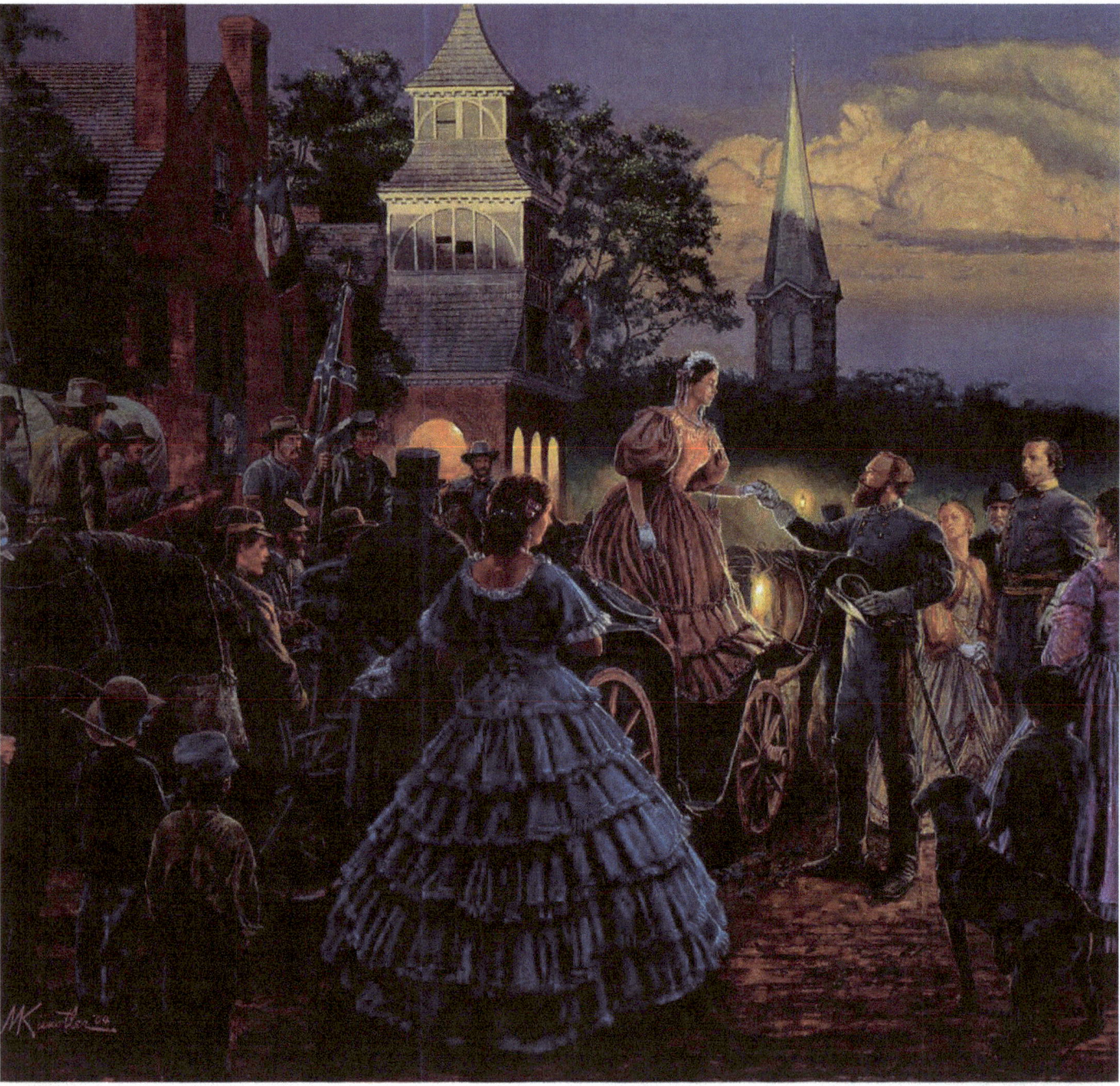

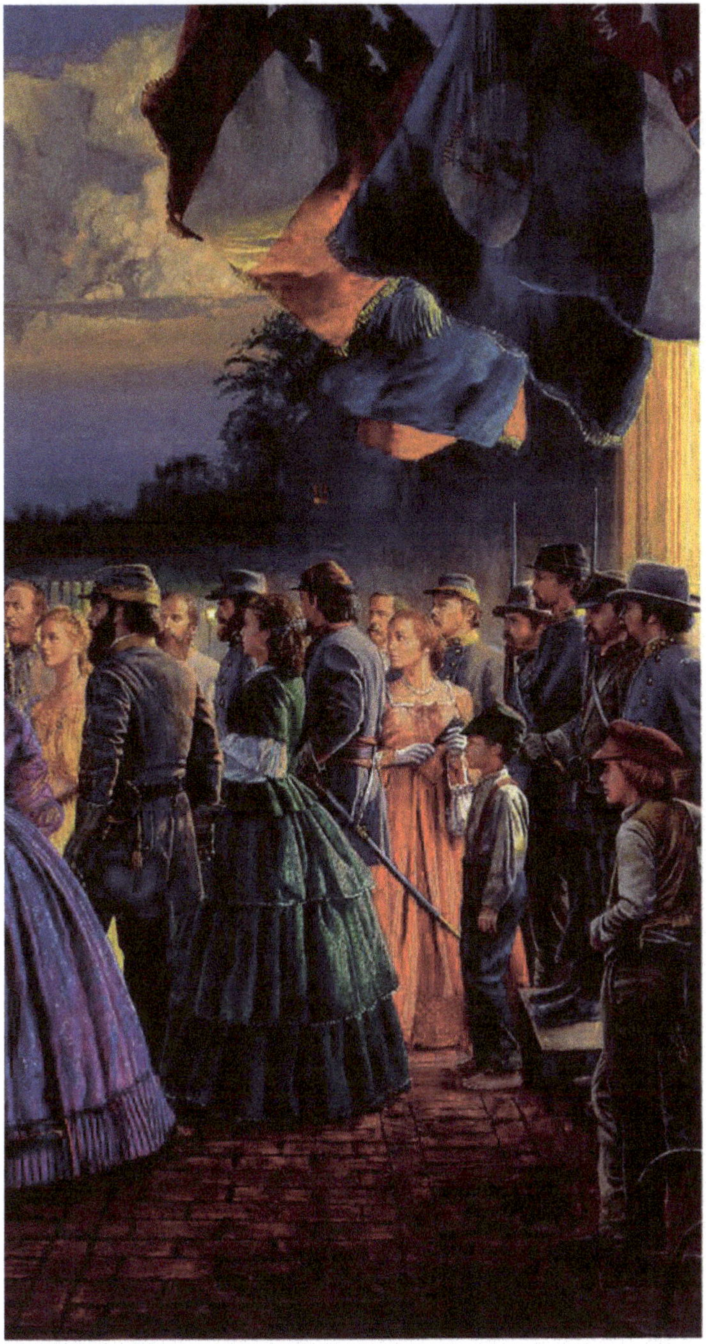

BEFORE THE BALL

GEN. J. E. B. STUART
CULPEPER, VIRGINIA
JUNE 4, 1863

2004, oil, 24 x 38

IT WAS a fleeting distraction from the hardships of war. In early June 1863, Robert E. Lee began moving his army from Fredericksburg into the campaign that would climax with the battle of Gettysburg. His cavalry, commanded by Jeb Stuart, encamped briefly near Culpeper, Virginia. The flamboyant Stuart ordered his staff to arrange a ball for officers and guests.

The town hall was commandeered as a makeshift ballroom for the occasion and was appropriately decorated. On the evening of June 4, Stuart's officers and guests began arriving. Officers wore dress uniforms adorned with gold braid, brass buttons, sash, and sword belt. Ladies came attired in the finest fashions available in the beleaguered South. Accompanying Stuart is his wife, Flora.

Selecting subjects for paintings is always a challenge. Sometimes I want to further develop a theme I have already painted. That's the case with *Before the Ball,* which captures the arrival of Stuart and his wife and other guests as they arrive for the Culpeper ball. I had depicted the ball in *Candlelight and Roses* and decided to paint a prequel.

It's a classic nineteenth-century street scene. When I visited Culpeper, I noticed its interesting courthouse. Unfortunately, the building was erected in 1870, too late for a Civil War painting. But after finding photographs of wartime Culpeper that showed the original courthouse in a different location, I was able to faithfully reconstruct the scene.

Some of the key figures from *Candlelight and Roses* also appear in *Before the Ball.* Stuart is shown helping his wife from a carriage in front of the town hall. Nearby are the general's aide Maj. Johann Heros von Borcke, along with Gens. Wade Hampton and Fitzhugh Lee and Capt. John Esten Cooke. *Before the Ball* also allowed me to paint the colorful gowns of the era as well as the various regimental colors from Georgia, North Carolina, South Carolina, and Virginia.

The view looks down Davis Street, toward the east. The 1860s courthouse is on the left, with the arches enclosing an arcade. The brick building next to the courthouse is A. P. Hill's boyhood home, still standing today. In the center is Culpeper Baptist Church. It's about 8:00 p.m., and the sunset illuminates the courthouse cupola and the church steeple, adding warm tones to the festive lights that welcome the guests.

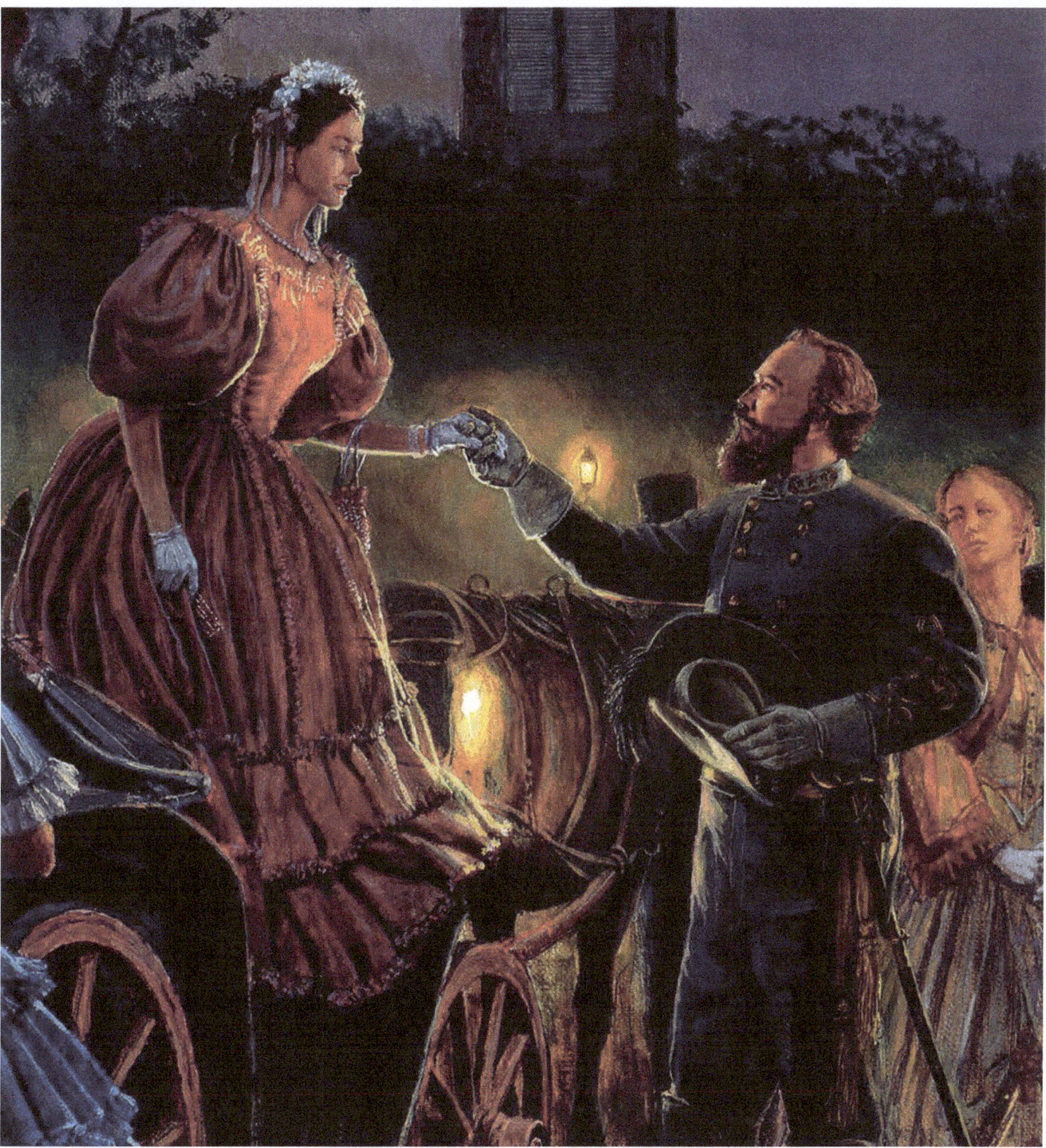

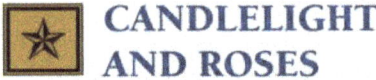

CANDLELIGHT AND ROSES

GENERAL J. E. B. STUART AT CULPEPER BALL
JUNE 4, 1863

1998, oil, 24 x 38

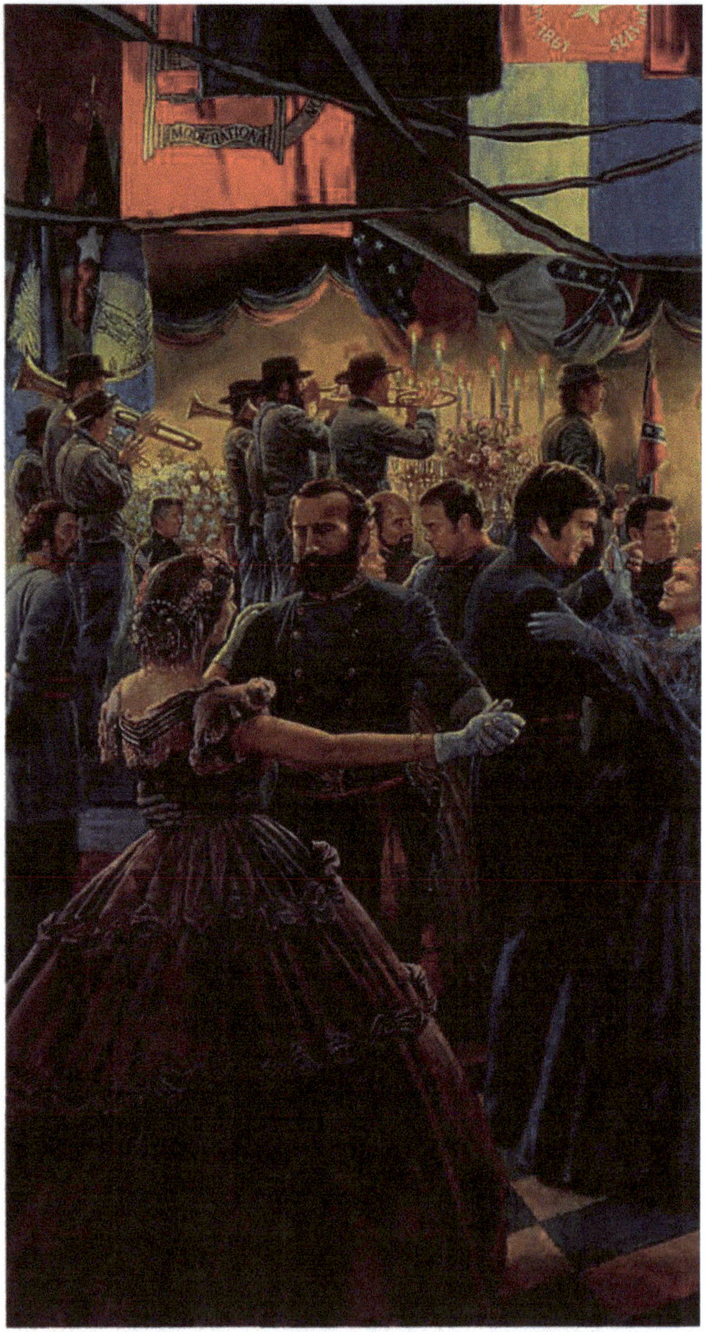

IN THIS painting of the Culpeper ball described in the previous painting, I tried to capture the glamour and pageantry and none of the dark side of the war. Stuart is the center of attention as he enters, plumed hat in hand, with his wife, Flora, on his arm. All the young women are bedazzled at the appearance of the famous general as he is greeted by John Pendleton, one of the leading town citizens. Other couples continue to dance, unaware of the arrival of the famed cavalry commander.

The decorations of flags, flowers, and bunting are described in a number of accounts and gave me a chance

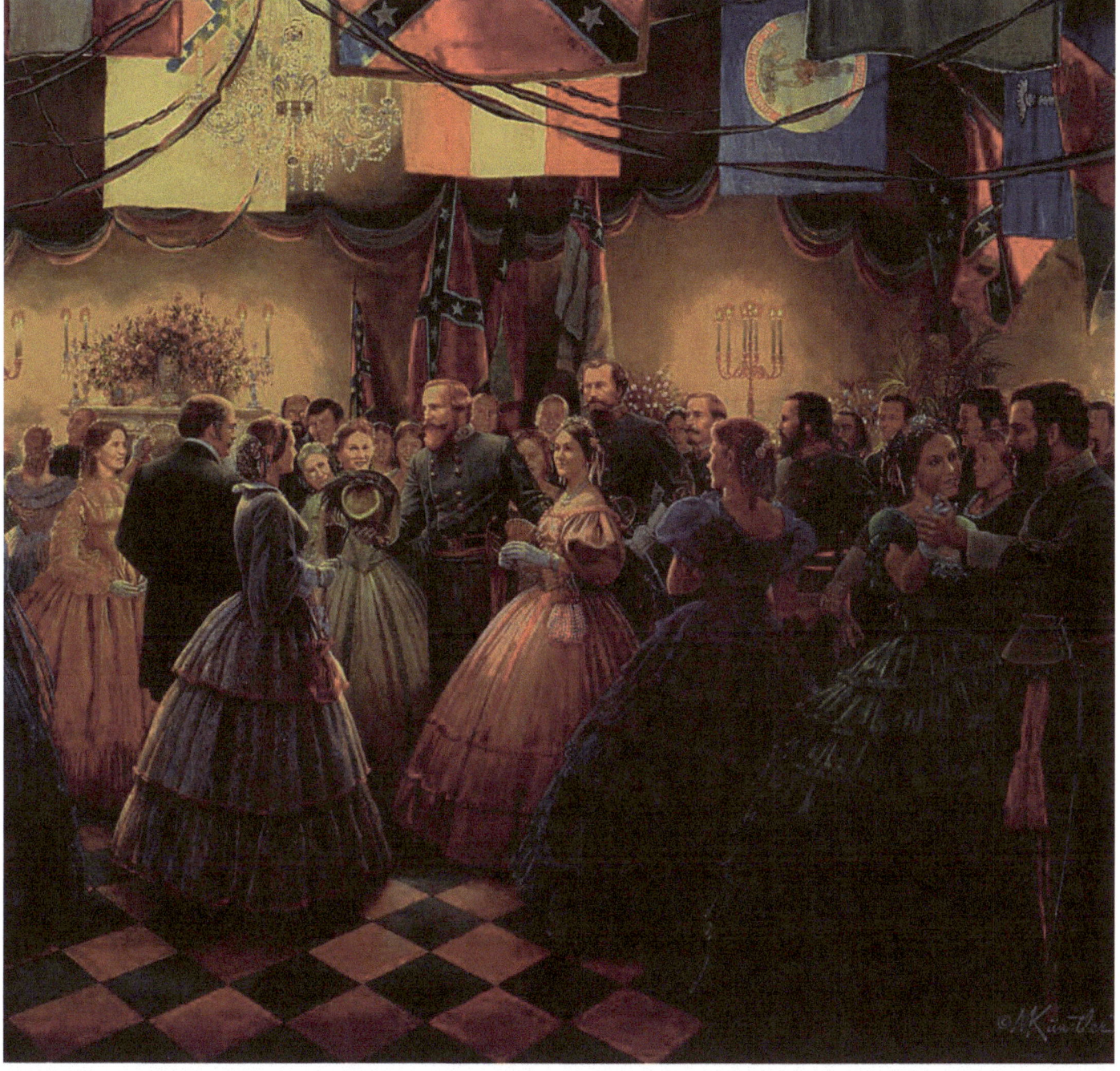

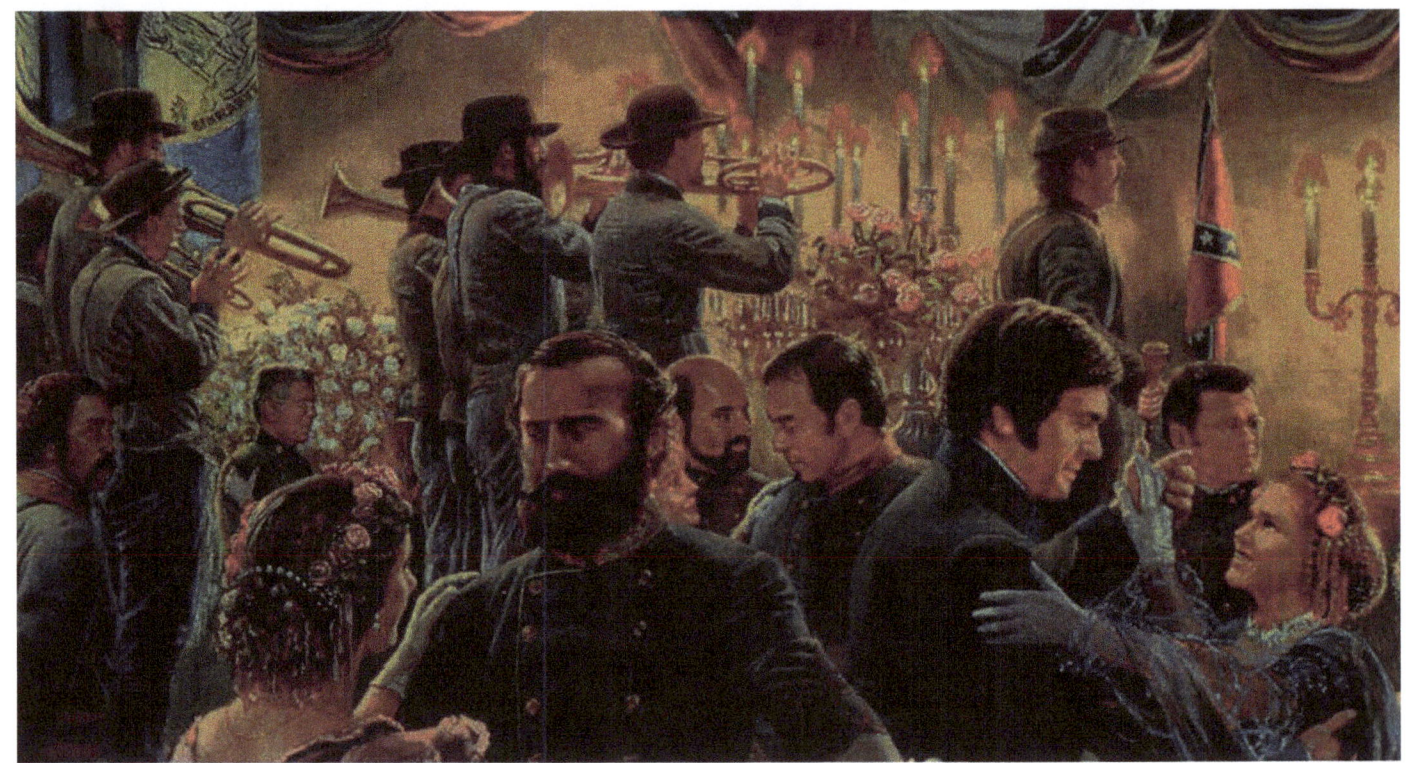

to use the bright colors of the flags and gowns in combination with the soft candlelight. The flags are from the four states comprising Stuart's division at the time: Georgia, North Carolina, South Carolina, and Virginia. Both the First and Second National flags are present; the Second National flag had been adopted on May 1, 1863, little more than a month before the ball.

On the extreme left, hands behind him, is Col. Pierce M. B. Young, commander of Cobbs Legion. Gen. Wade Hampton, in the left foreground, is dancing with a young admirer. His sword is distinctive, and I based it on a picture in an 1899 book by Edward L. Wells, who knew Hampton and served under him. We see an assortment of other officers from the infantry, artillery, and medical corps as well as cavalry. The tallest and most noticeable officer, marked by the yellow trim on his uniform, is the six-foot-four Johann Heros von Borcke, directly behind Stuart. Immediately behind von Borcke is John Esten Cooke, also of Stuart's staff. Moving farther to the right in the far background, behind the lieutenant holding one glove, is the mustachioed Capt. William Downs Farley, Stuart's most trusted scout. (Farley would be killed five days later in action near Mountain Run.) Dancing with the woman in the green gown, in the right foreground, is Gen. Fitzhugh Lee, a nephew of Robert E. Lee and another of Stuart's field commanders.

The ball would be a colorful moment of peaceful pageantry that would cast an aura of invincibility on Stuart's cavalry. Several days later, on June 9, 1863, at the battle of Brandy Station, this aura would dim, marking an end to the superiority the South had come to expect of its horsemen.

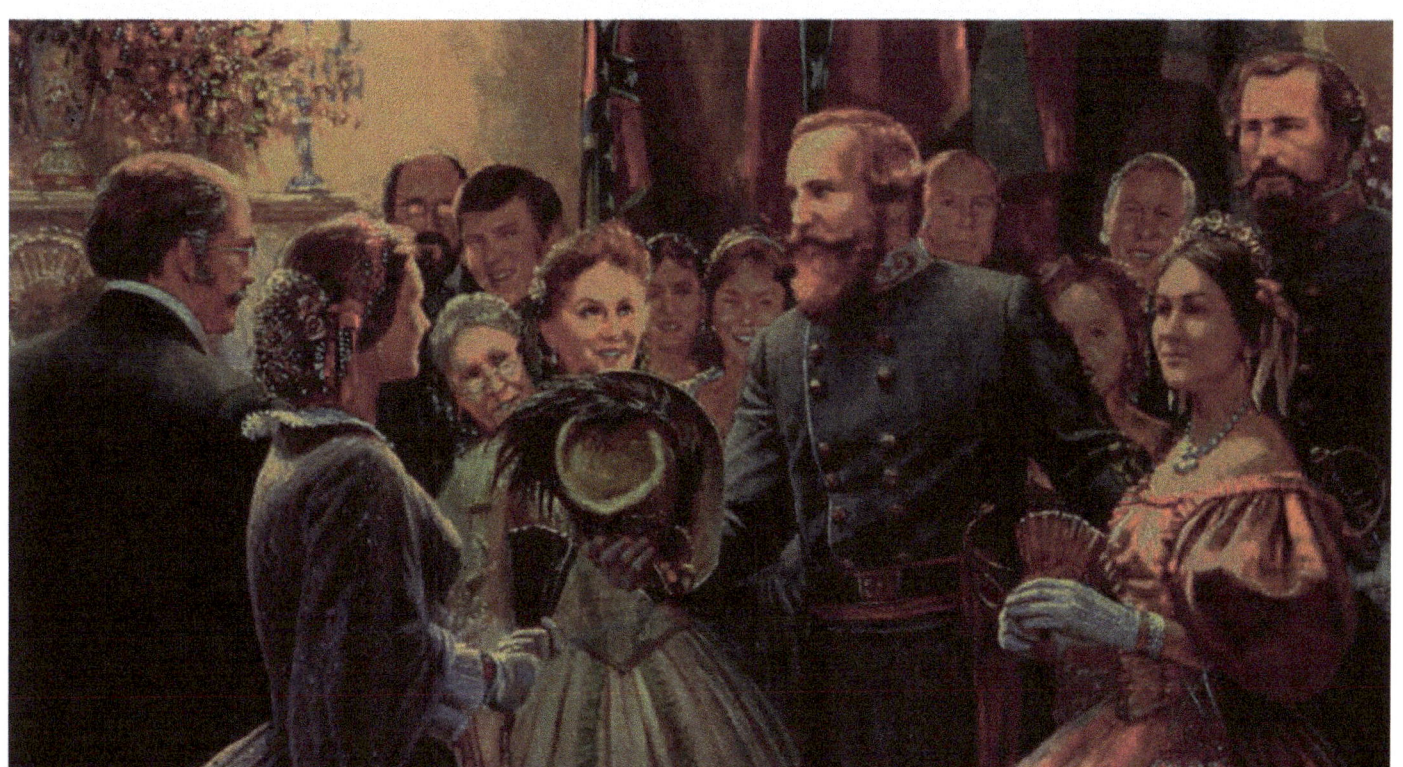

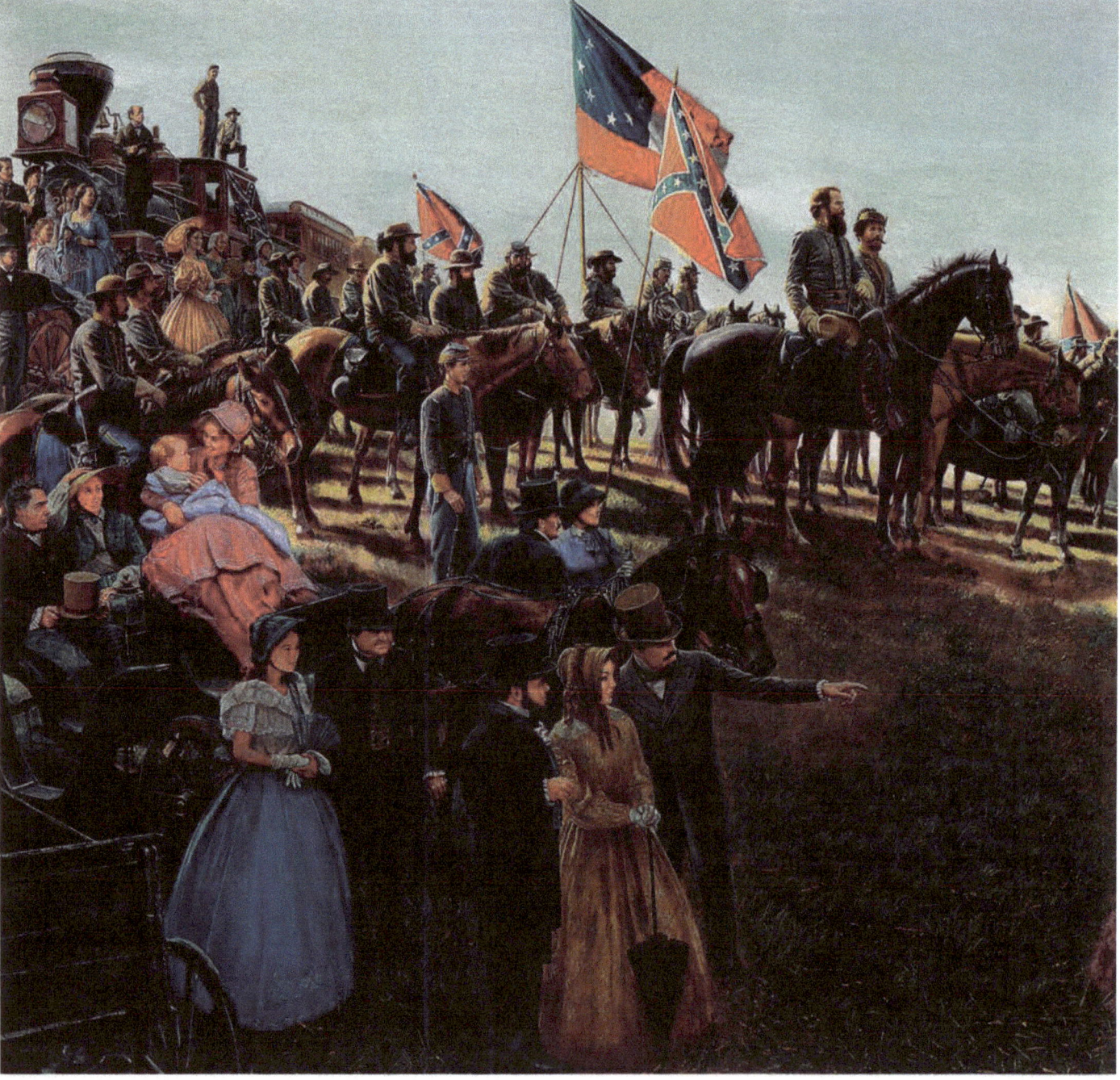

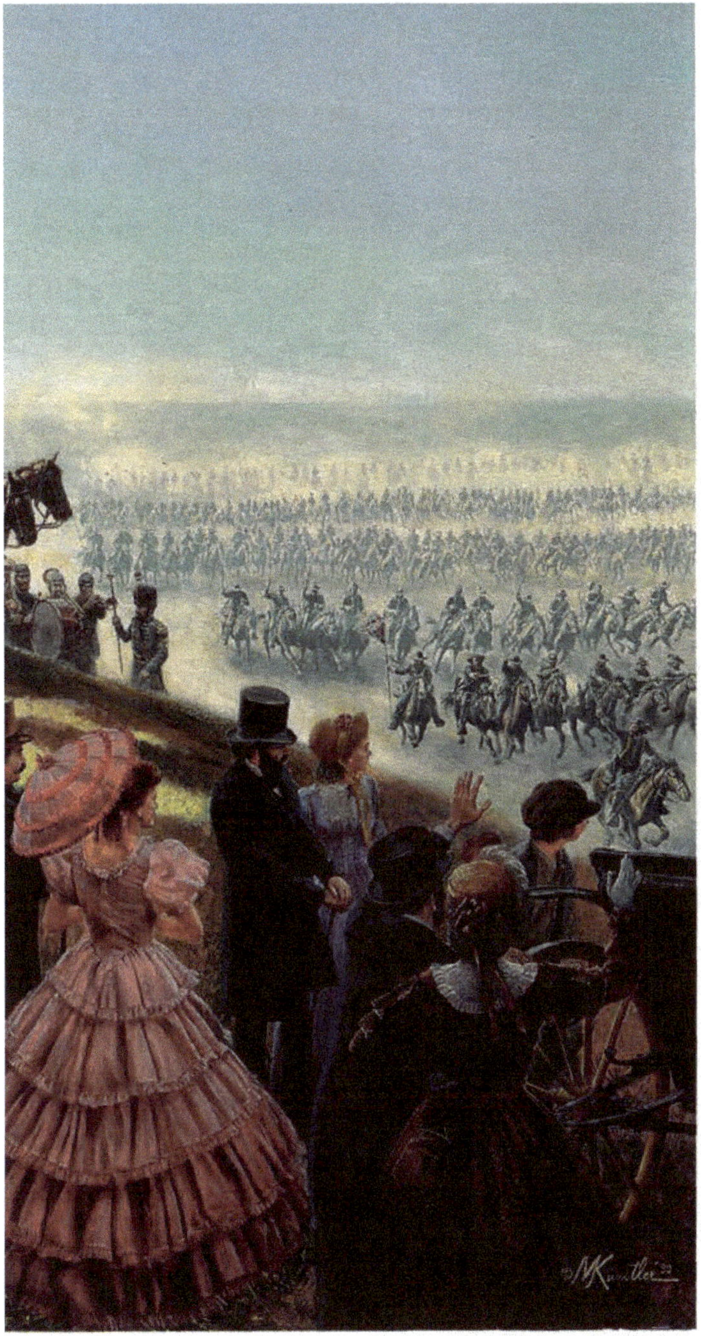

THE GRAND REVIEW

BRANDY STATION, VIRGINIA
JUNE 5, 1863
1989, oil, 28 x 44

THIS IS my first painting of the flamboyant and colorful Jeb Stuart. After I had read an account of his grand review at Brandy Station and then learned that it had never been depicted before, I knew that I wanted to bring this moment to life on my canvas.

To show off his division, Stuart planned the review of nearly ten thousand cavalrymen. Friends and dignitaries were invited to a plain about a mile southwest of Brandy Station, near a knoll and a road adjacent to the main railroad line from Culpeper

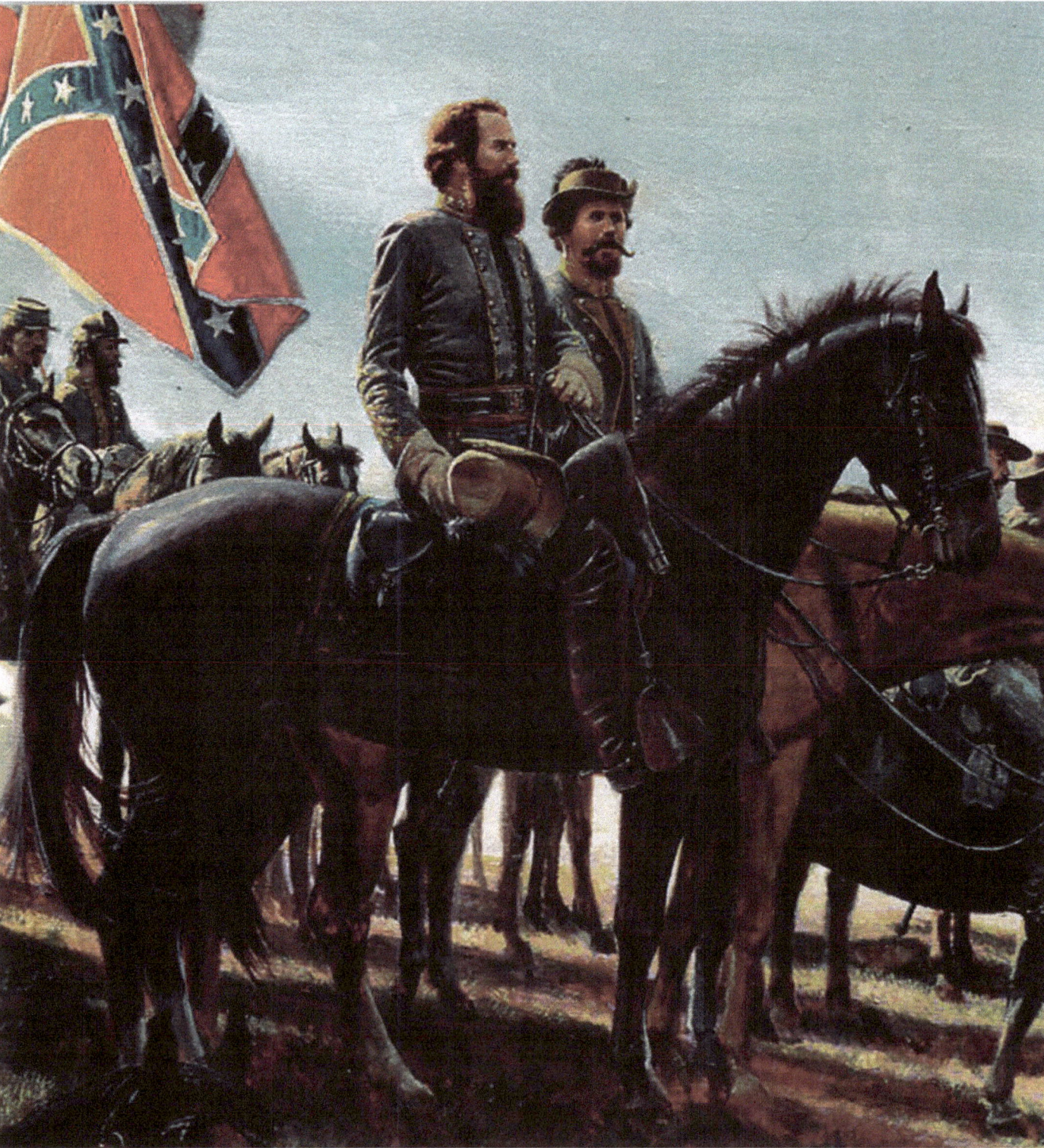

Court House. The site served as a perfect reviewing stand. The fields were wide enough to accommodate the entire division, and it was open enough for the spectators to see everything.

People arrived from Charlottesville and Richmond, and the crowd included most of the townspeople of Culpeper. The train from Richmond with Secretary of War George Wythe Randolph—as well as a large contingent of ladies—was parked on the tracks behind the reviewing area.

Based on a trip to the site and maps of the area, I reconstructed the event. Roads slice the area now and the knoll is covered with houses, but it is still easy to visualize the thousands of troopers parading on the field, which is virtually unchanged from that 1863 summer day.

The review occurred late in the afternoon, and as a grand finale, the units charged past the people assembled on and around the knoll with a final salute. The horsemen moved from west to east, with the spectators facing north. The sun in the upper left corner of the painting is in the west.

Stuart is depicted on a black charger, as eyewitnesses described him, alongside aide Heros von Borcke, who gave an excellent account of the proceedings that day in his memoirs.

Although Robert E. Lee was not present on June 5, his son, W. H. F. "Rooney" Lee was. He can be seen with plumed hat, canteen, and saddlebags directly behind the unmounted guard. The next mounted officer farther to the right and directly underneath the furling battle flag is Gen. Fitzhugh Lee, Robert E. Lee's nephew, who was described as riding "low in the saddle." Next in line is Wade Hampton, the famed South Carolinian, who later succeeded Stuart as the corps commander.

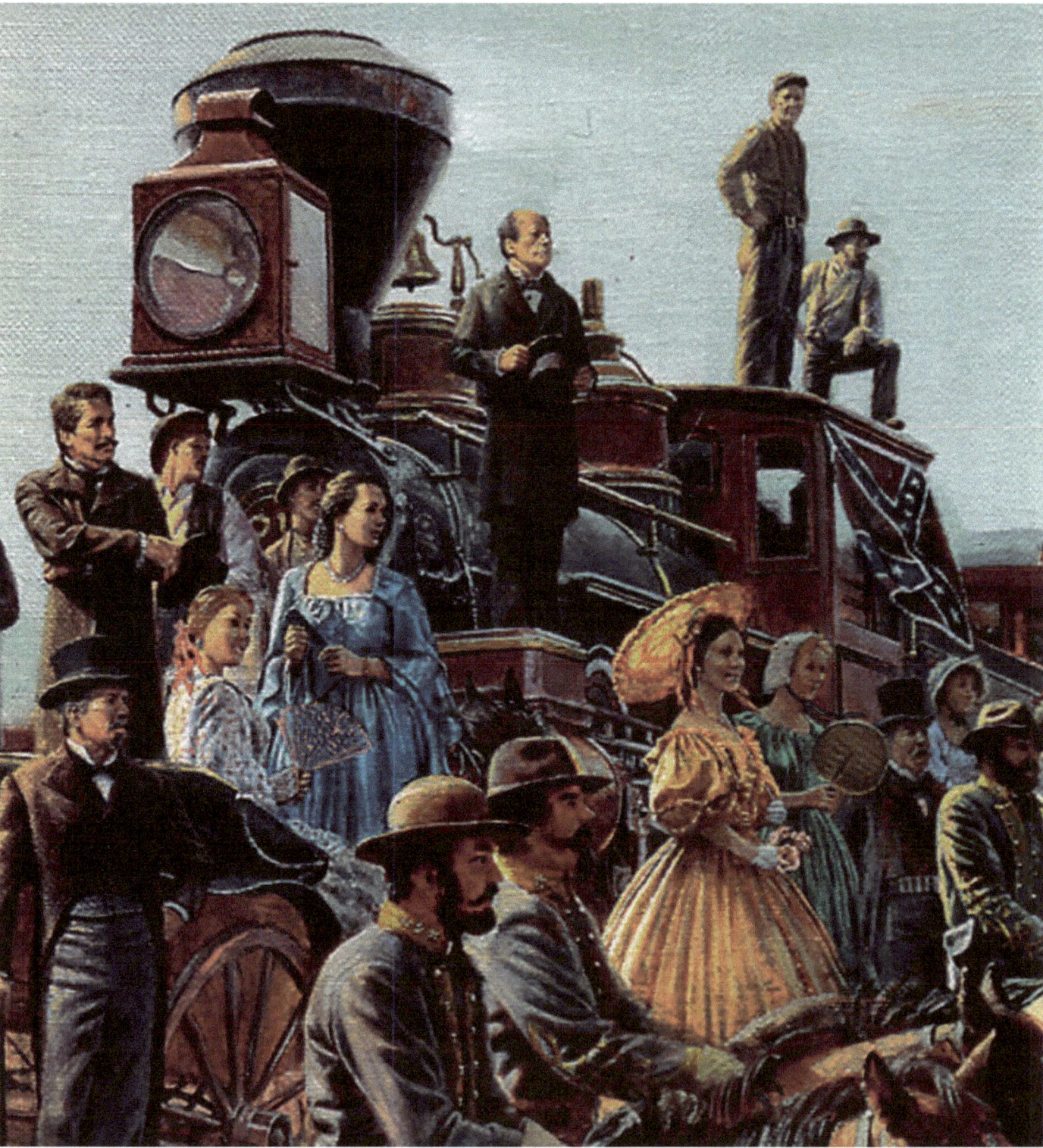

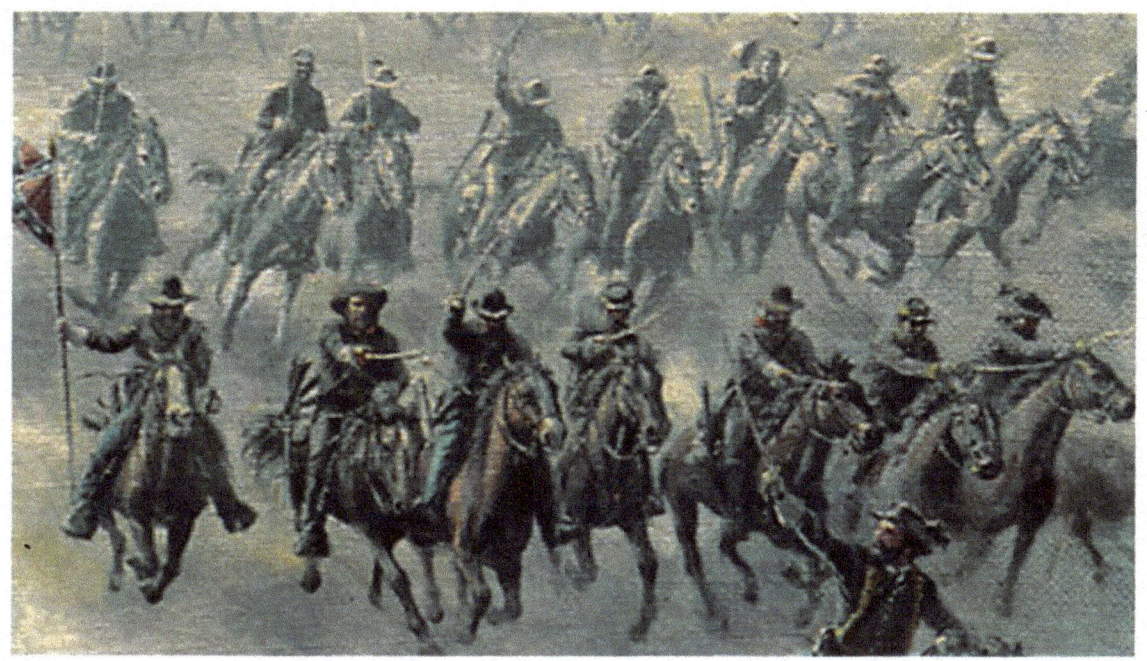

Immediately after the June 5 review, the different commands returned to their camps, and Stuart and his aides went back to Culpeper for a second evening ball and entertainment.

Perhaps von Borcke offered the best summation of the review: "One magnificent pageant, inspiring enough to make even an old woman feel fightish!"

Ironically, within days of the grand review, Stuart's cavalry was fighting on the same ground. The battle of Brandy Station was the largest cavalry engagement of the war and marked the beginning of the end of Southern dominance from the saddle.

COVERED WITH GLORY

26TH NORTH CAROLINA AT FRONT ROYAL, VIRGINIA

JUNE 20, 1863

1999, gouache, 16⅜ x 40

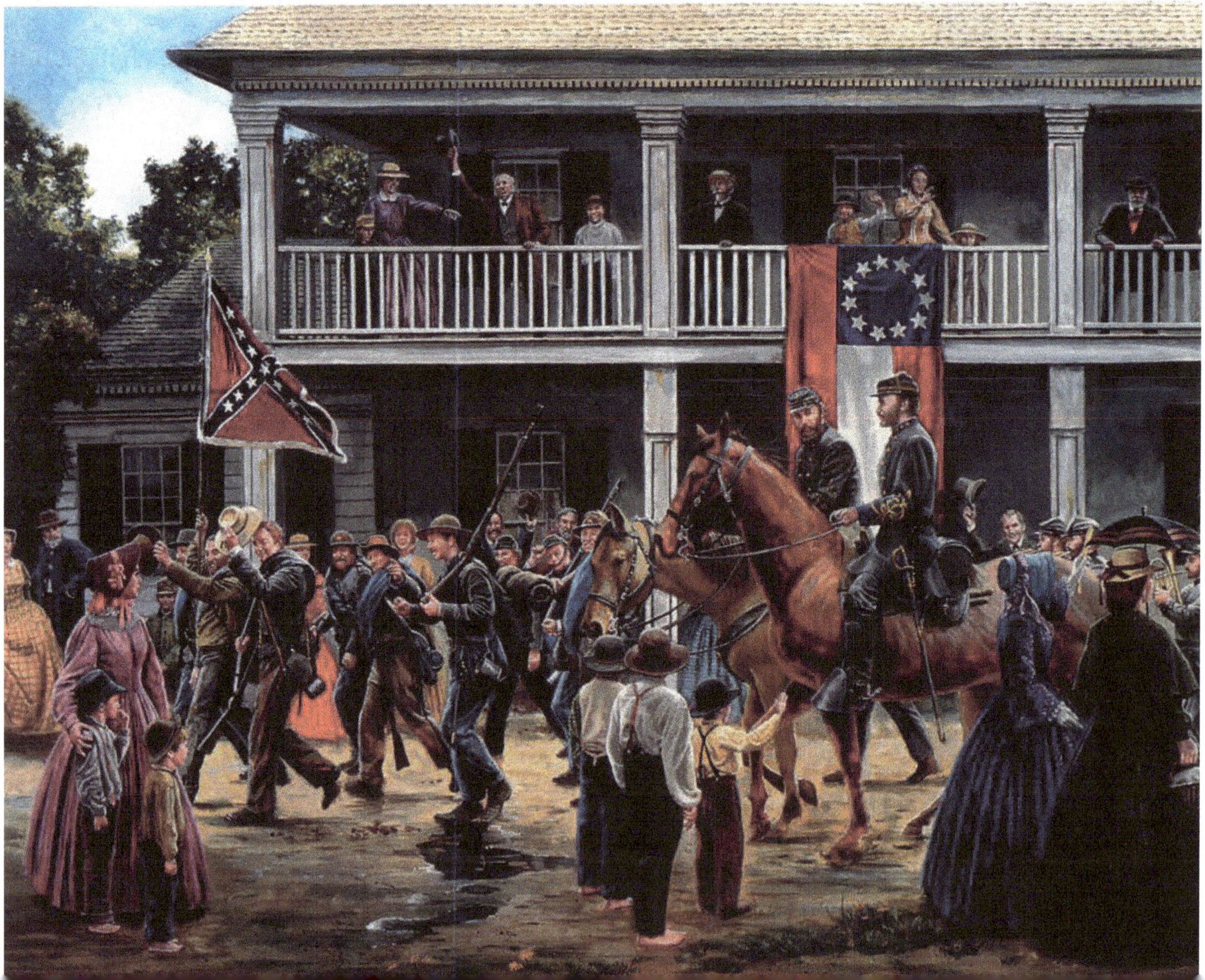

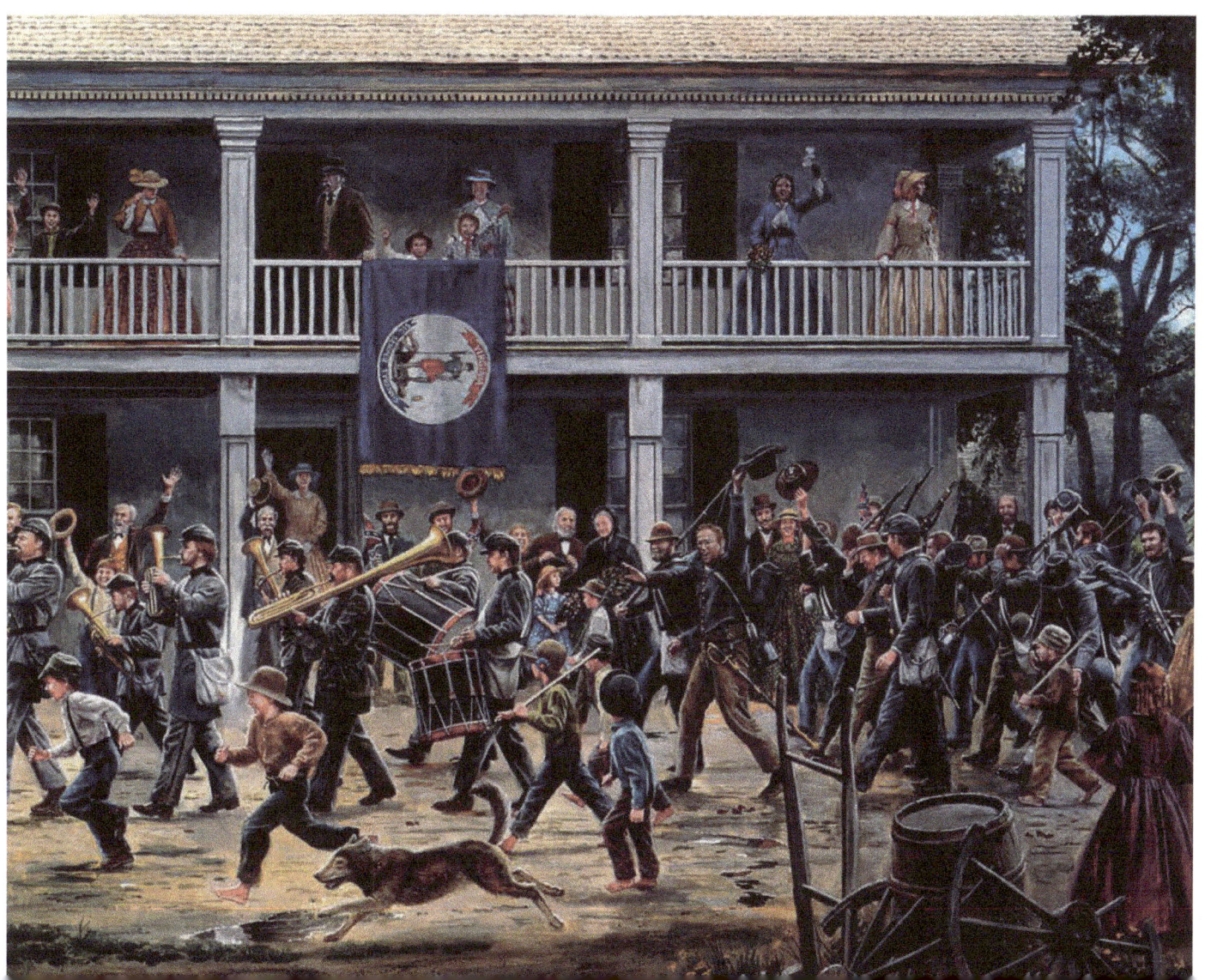

THE INSPIRATION for this painting came from my friend Rod Gragg, whose book entitled *Covered with Glory* describes the wartime exploits of the Twenty-sixth North Carolina Infantry. As he told me some of these stories, I became interested in his description of the regiment as it passed through Front Royal, Virginia, en route to Pennsylvania and the battle of Gettysburg.

The town's population—mostly women, children, and old men (the young men were in the army)—treated the Twenty-sixth North Carolina as conquering heroes. The women cheered, waving and tossing flowers, while many boys followed the troops down Chester Street and marched alongside. It had rained the previous night, which accounts for the puddles on the ground and the lack of dust.

When I visited Front Royal, I found a number of buildings that had survived the war. To me, the Samuels Apartments building on Chester Street was the most interesting. I learned from Suzanne Silek and Sam Riggs, of the Warren Rifles Confederate Memorial Museum in Front Royal, that the building had a balcony during the 1860s. Deciding that it would add interest to the painting, I featured just the building rather than the entire street.

The Twenty-sixth North Carolina regimental band was one of the most famous military bands of the war. A rare photograph of the band provided me with a lot of information: the appearance of each band member and the types of instruments that were played. In the latter case, I decided that I needed more information if I were to paint the instruments in the correct positions.

Fortunately, there are both a Twenty-sixth North Carolina Regiment and a Twenty-sixth North Carolina Band in reenactment today. I went to High

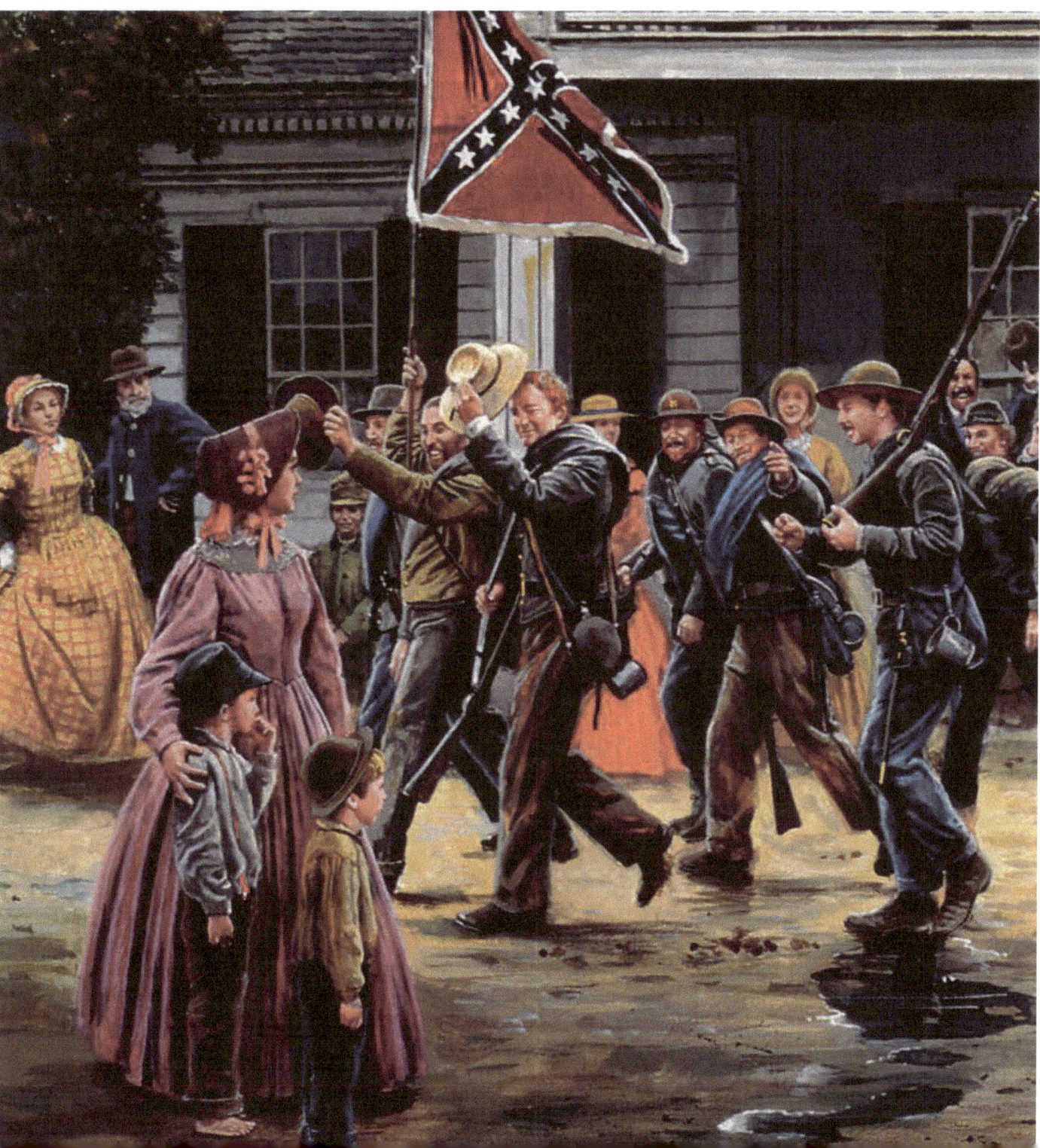

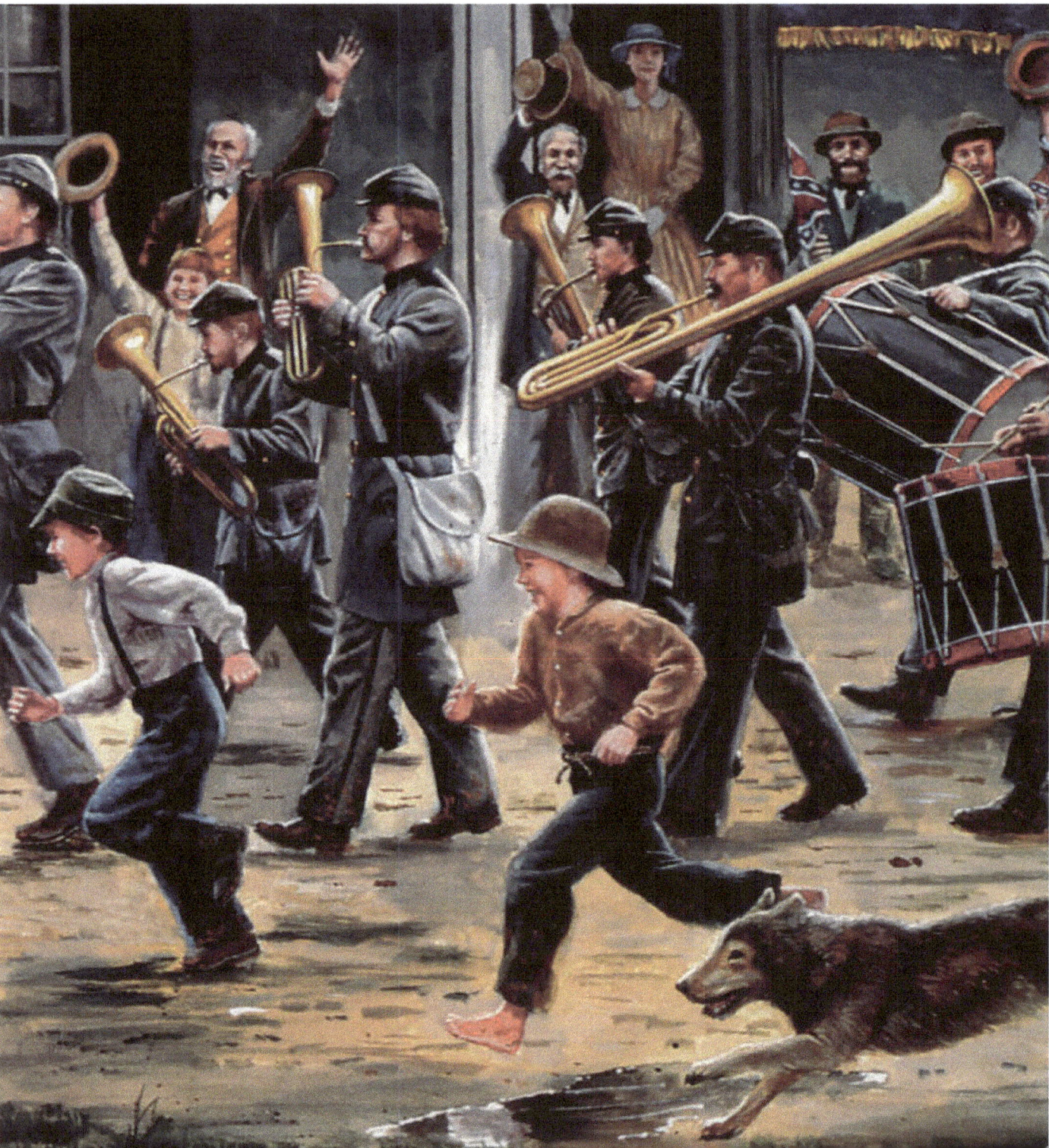

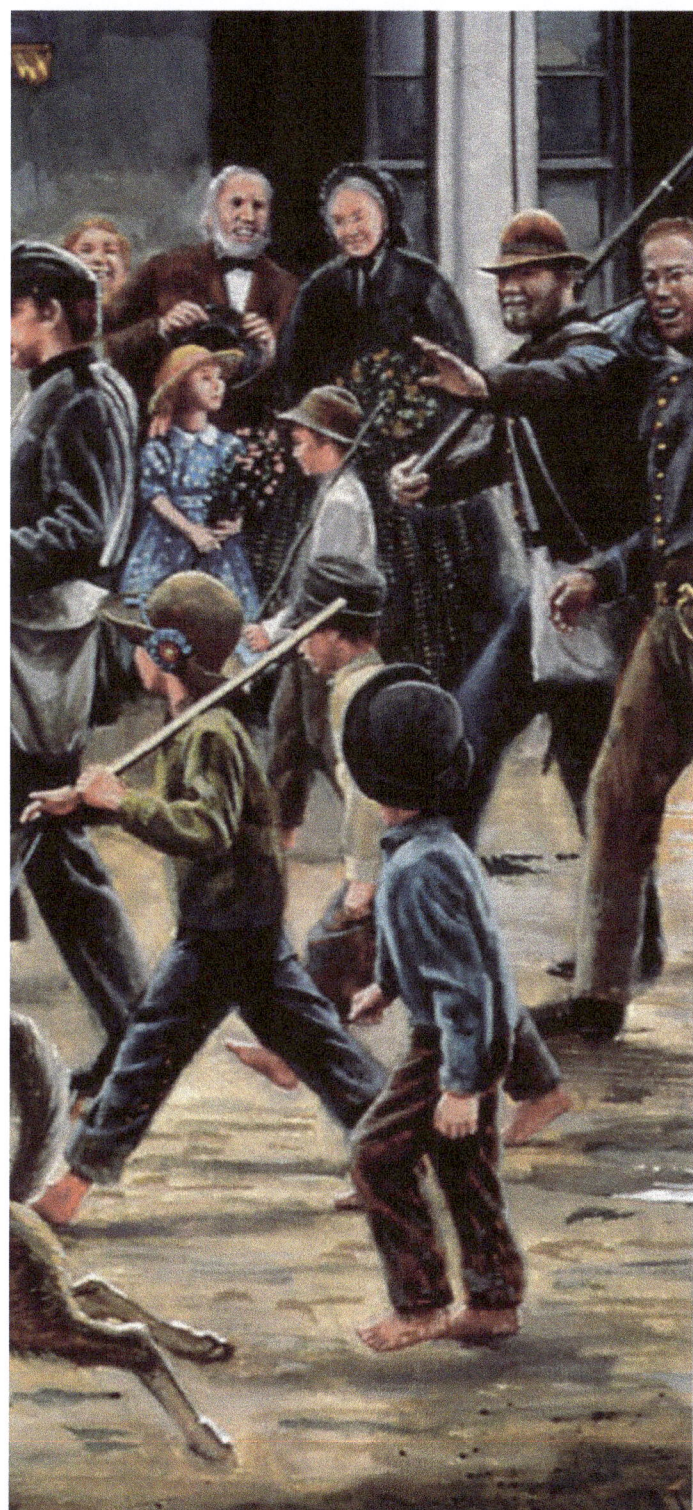

Point, North Carolina, and with the help of Jeff Stepp, the colonel of the regiment, I met several members of the regiment and the band, who all generously shared their time and expertise. I spent many hours with them, sketching, photographing, and learning more about the history of the regiment. Jackson Marshall, a historian with the State Museum of History in Raleigh and a member of the reenactment group, was very helpful in verifying and authenticating artifacts and uniforms in the painting. The spurs, swords, scabbards, and uniforms belonging to Col. Henry K. Burgwyn Jr. and Lt. Col. John R. Lane (both pictured on horseback) are in the museum's collection. With the help of various members of the museum staff, these details were all authenticated. The civilians' clothing was verified by Sheila Morris Greene, curator of textiles at the Tennessee State Museum.

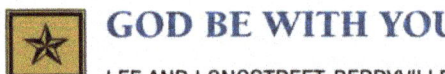

GOD BE WITH YOU

LEE AND LONGSTREET, BERRYVILLE, VIRGINIA

JUNE 21, 1863

2002, oil, 20 x 36

detail, right

IN LONG columns of gray and butternut, the Army of Northern Virginia tramped northward in late June. Victorious and confident after the spectacular success at Chancellorsville, Lee's troops were bound for Pennsylvania, where the Confederate commander hoped to fight a decisive battle that would end the unprecedented bloodshed and preserve Southern nationhood.

Lee's route of march took him and a large portion of his army through the Shenandoah Valley village of Berryville. Central landmarks in the hamlet were the county courthouse and Grace Episcopal Church. The general arrived there on Sunday morning, June 21, and took the opportunity to attend Sunday-morning services at the church. Among the officers accompanying him was James Longstreet. Throughout the army on this day, chaplains held services, and countless sons of the South paused and prayed and worshiped.

When the quiet time ended, Lee emerged from the church, gave a respectful greeting to the assembled townspeople, and parted with Longstreet. Lee left the Berryville church prepared to face a fierce and uncertain future. In a few days, the two leaders would meet again at Gettysburg, where they would wage the greatest battle of the war.

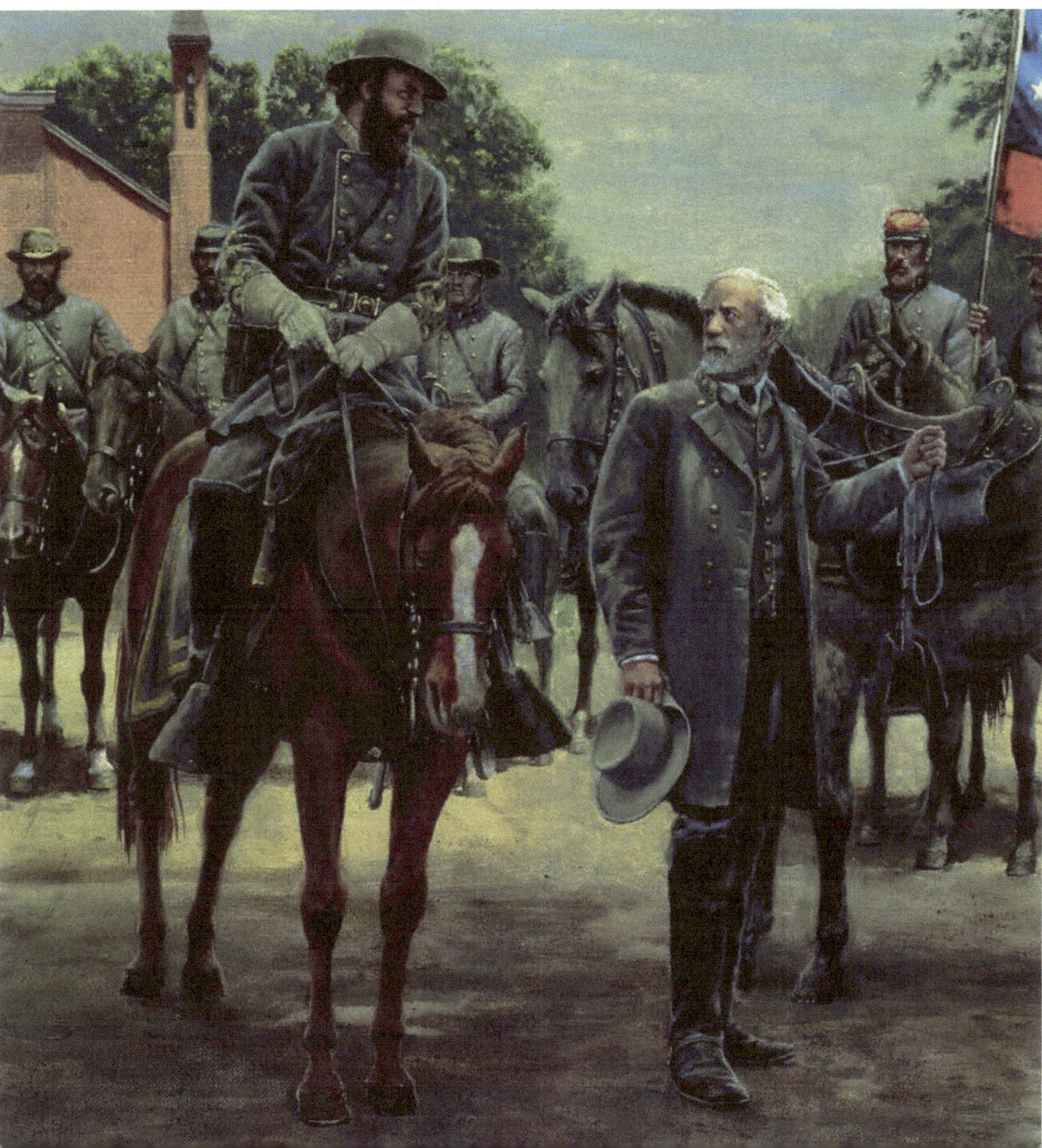

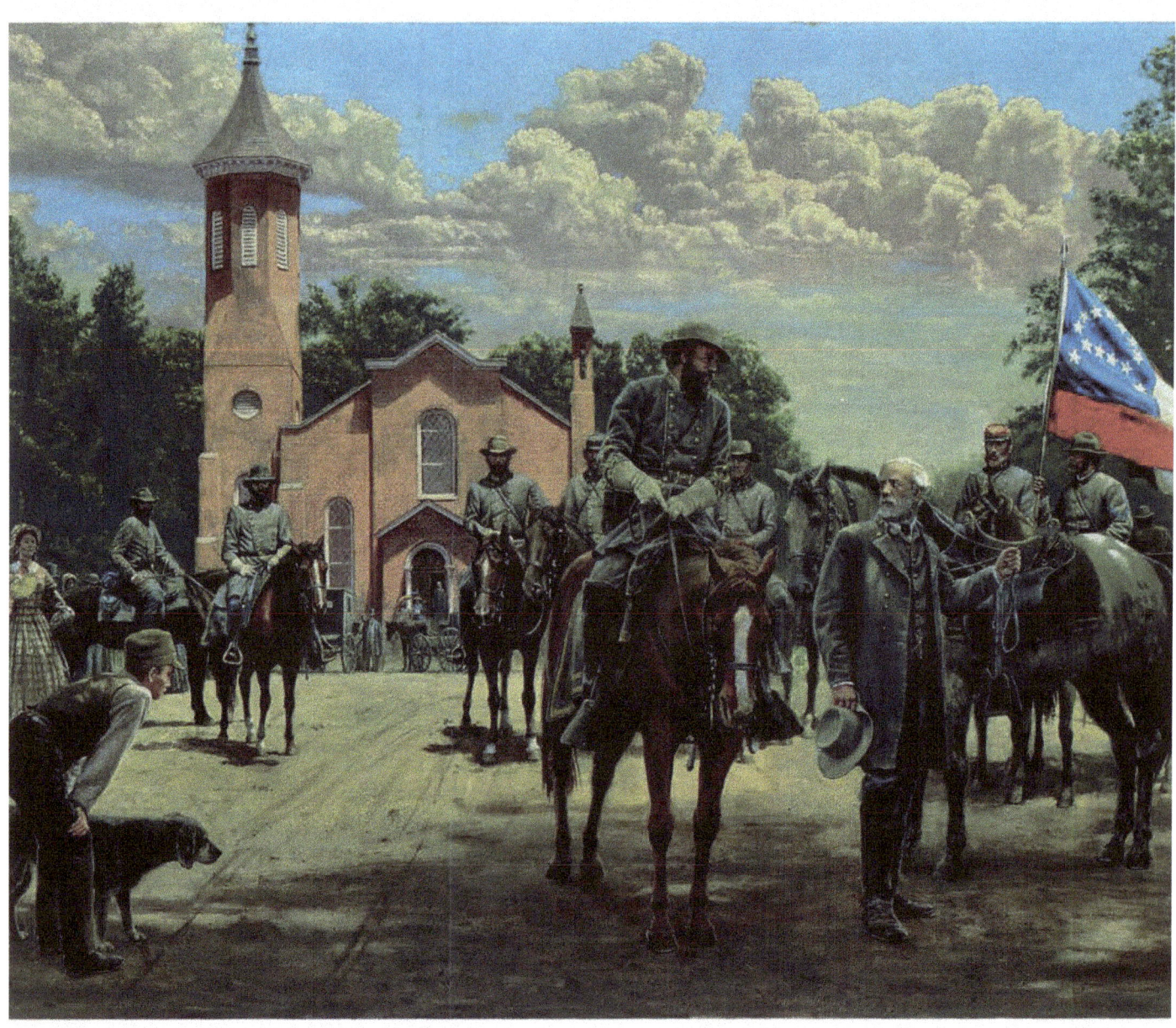

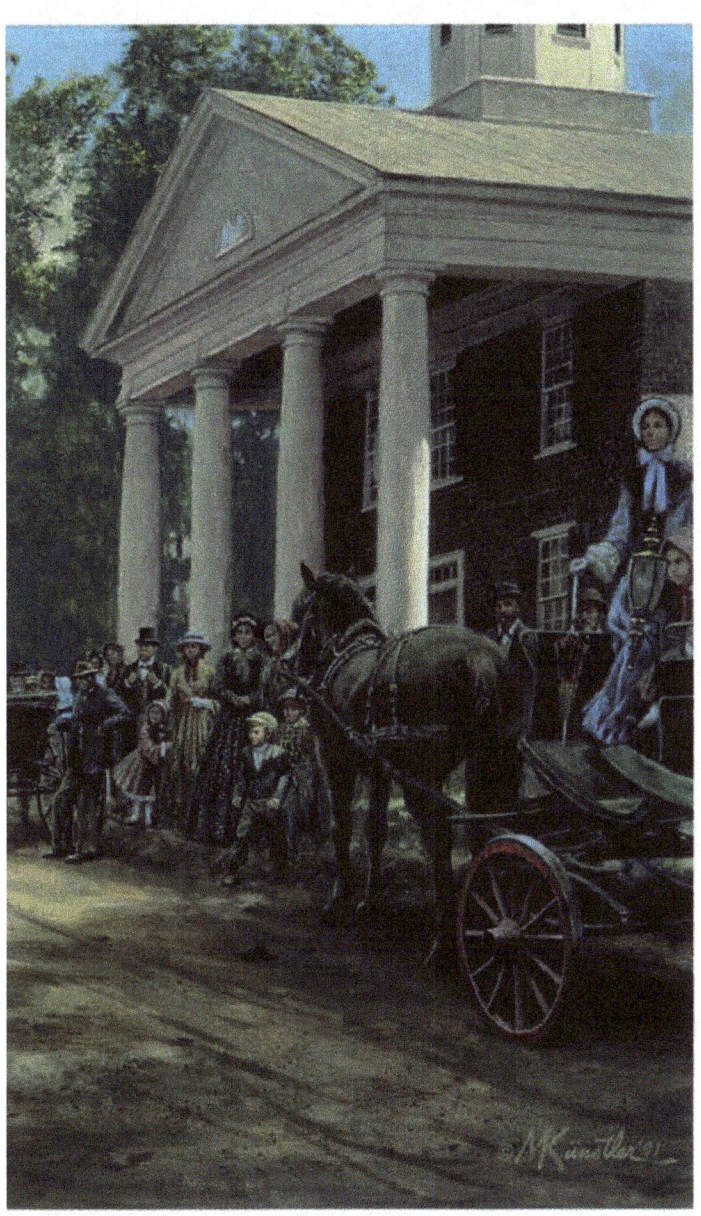

"God be with you" was the era's common benediction to believers. And Lee and his soldiers advanced with that benediction still fresh in their ears.

I learned of Berryville during a visit to Winchester, where Jerry Van Voorhis of Shenandoah University encouraged me to consider the town—which is rich in Civil War history—as a setting for a painting. When I visited the municipality, I was overwhelmed by the hospitality of the townspeople and impressed by Berryville's history and beauty.

The Reverend Dwight Brown showed me Grace Episcopal Church, which is in excellent condition and today appears much as it did during the war. I also learned the story of Lee and Longstreet's visit to the church during the Gettysburg campaign, when elements of the Army of Northern Virginia passed through the town. The Reverend Henderson Suter

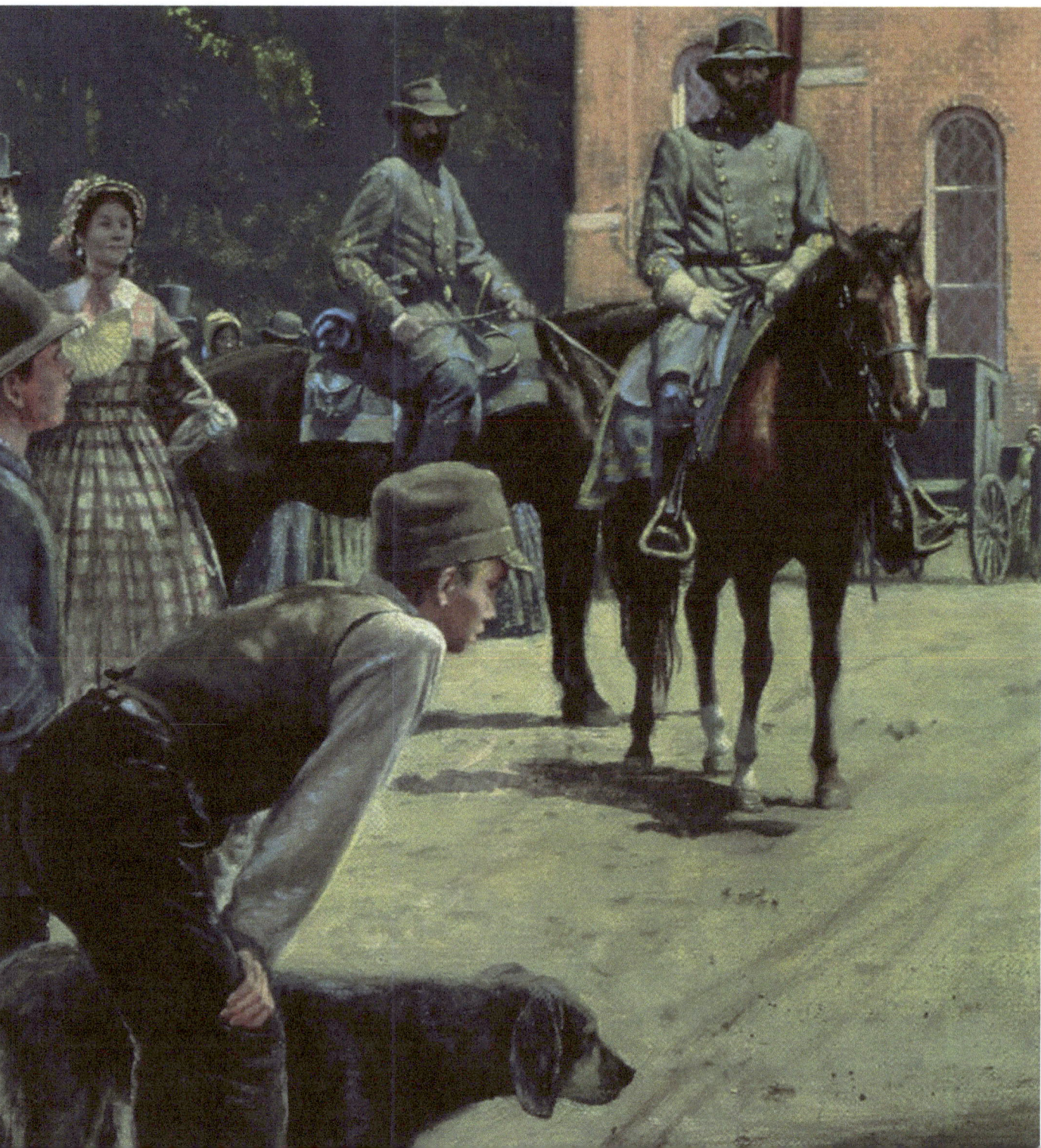

presided over the services, and Gen. William N. Pendleton, Lee's chief of artillery, delivered the sermon.

My visit to Berryville occurred during the same time of year—in June—and during the same time of day. Weather conditions were almost identical to that morning almost 150 years earlier. The Clarke County Courthouse, which was near the church, also dates from the Civil War, and it too remains almost unchanged. As soon as I saw those historical structures under almost identical conditions and considered the appeal of the historical event, I knew I had the setting for my painting.

The saddle seen on Traveller is based on the saddle in the collection of the Museum of the Confederacy in Richmond. The sun shines brightly on Lee's headquarters flag with its unusual star arrangement, which some historians believe may have been designed by the general's wife.

Many people in Berryville helped me research this painting, and I wish I could thank all of them. I received wonderful cooperation from John Sours of the Clarke County Economic Development Office. Clarke County Historical Association archivist Mary Thomason-Morris was invaluable in supplying the myriad details necessary to make the painting as authentic as possible.

Perhaps making this moment most worthy of commemoration is that this would be the last time Lee had an opportunity to worship in a church before his fateful date with destiny at Gettysburg. I like to think that his brief moment of worship and prayer in Berryville helped him to face the ordeal that lay ahead.

"MARYLAND, MY MARYLAND"

POTOMAC CROSSING, JUNE 25, 1863

2006, oil, 18 x 42

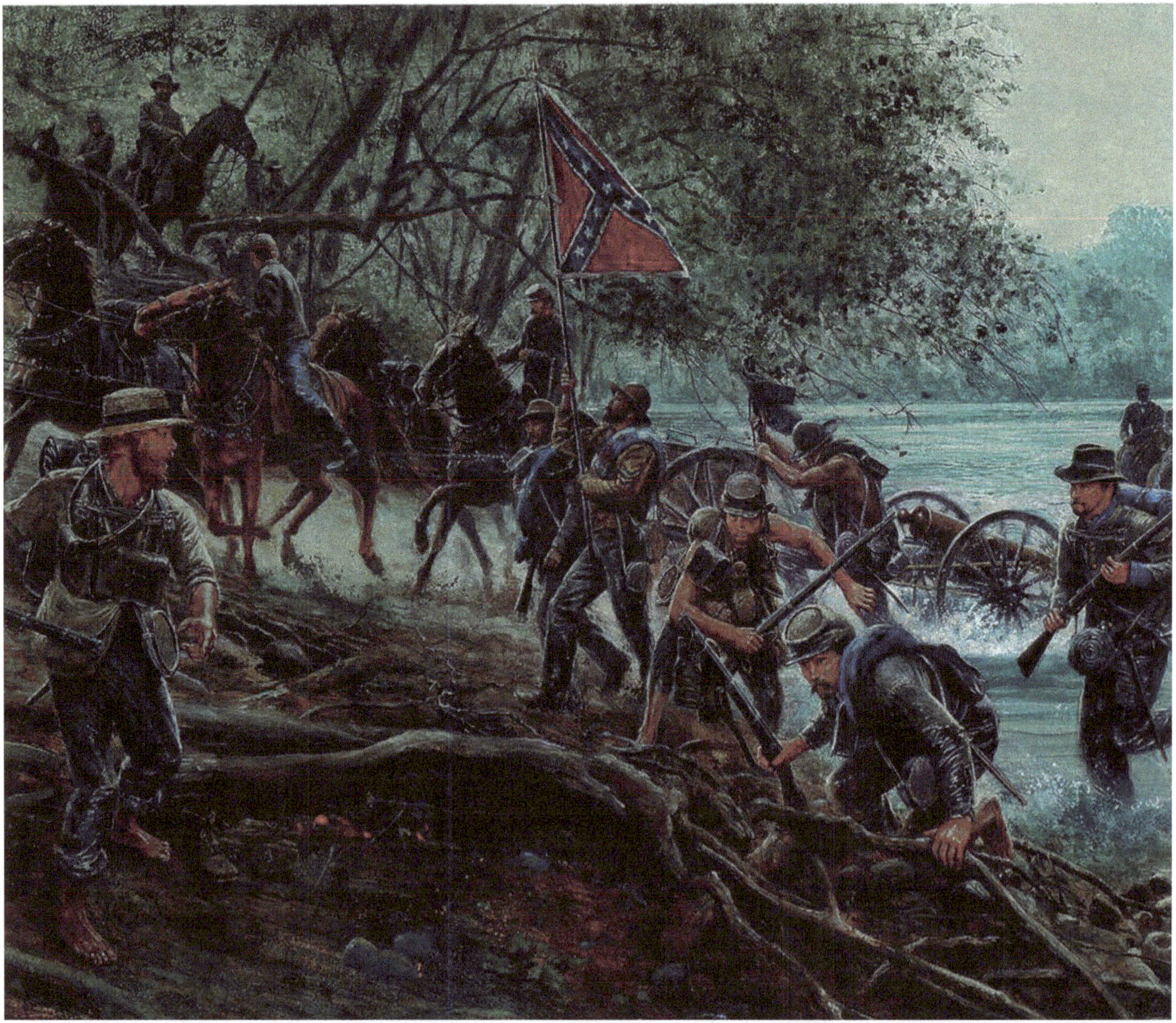

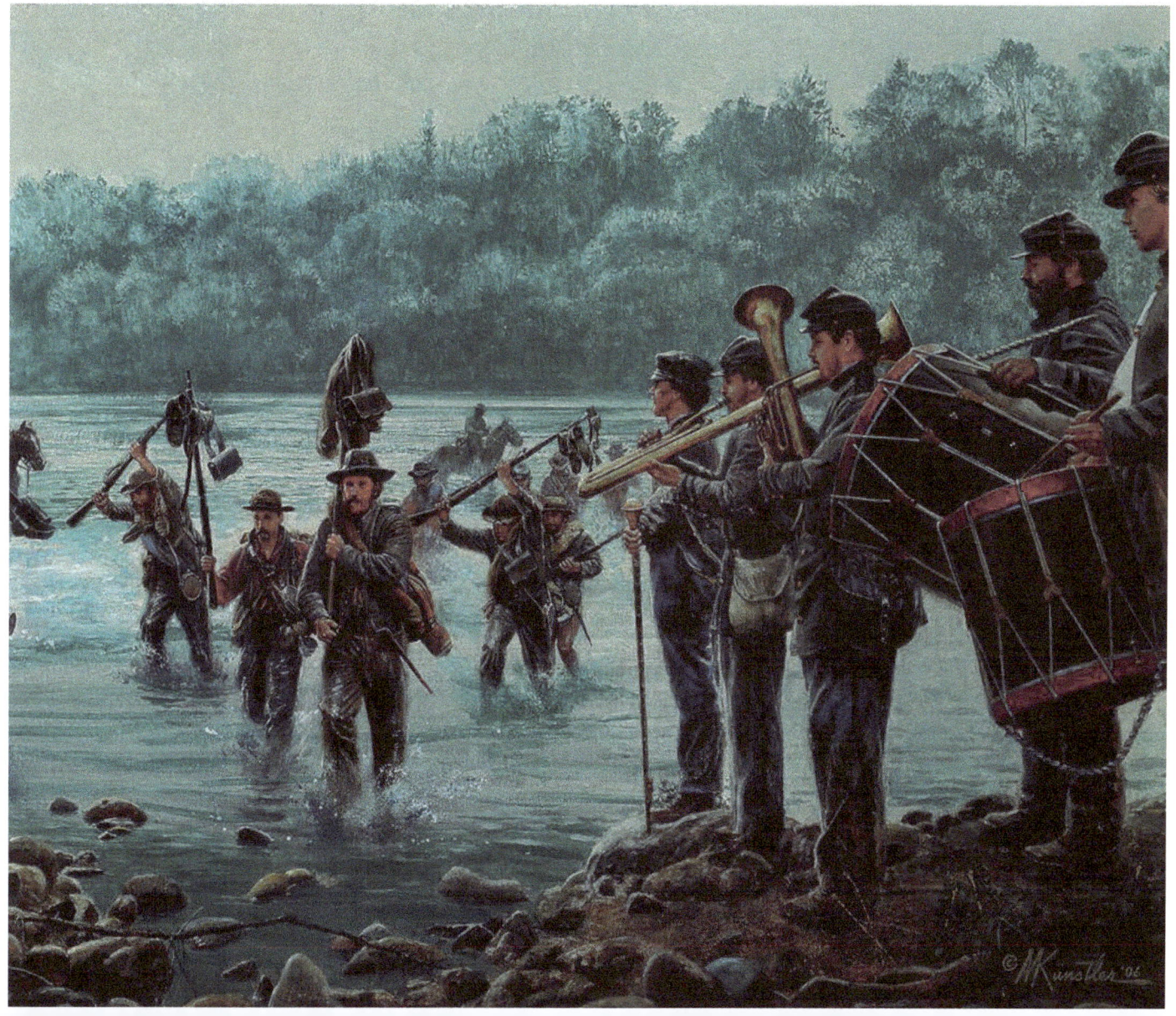

THE RIVER crossing was one of the war's most dramatic moments, and the men of Lee's army knew it: they were taking the war to the North. Less than a year earlier, the Army of Northern Virginia had ventured to the northern bank of the Potomac and been turned back at the battle of Antietam. Now Lee's legions again waded the river, crossing into Maryland and heading toward Pennsylvania.

On the morning of Thursday, June 25, Gen. James J. Pettigrew's brigade—part of A. P. Hill's Third Corps—forded the Potomac near Shepherdstown, Virginia. Here, at Boteler's Ford, the river was 150 yards wide, marked in spots by scattered boulders, and armpit-deep in places. Some men stripped to make the crossing; all kept their weapons dry.

On the Maryland shore they shouted the Rebel Yell, and someone in the Twenty-sixth North Carolina began singing "Maryland, My Maryland"—a poignant musical protest of the Federal occupation of the Old Line State. Other soldiers joined in the singing, and the poetic lament echoed over the broad river basin. An officer on Pettigrew's staff ordered the Twenty-sixth North Carolina regimental band to accompany the singing. The band—composed of accomplished musicians from the Moravian community in Salem, North Carolina—took up the tune and continued playing it until thousands of soldiers had crossed.

Pettigrew is seen in the upper left corner on horseback, accompanied by his staff, as he supervises the crossing and enjoys the singing.

An air of expectancy dominates the painting. When these men last crossed the Potomac—which I depicted in *Night Crossing*—it was during

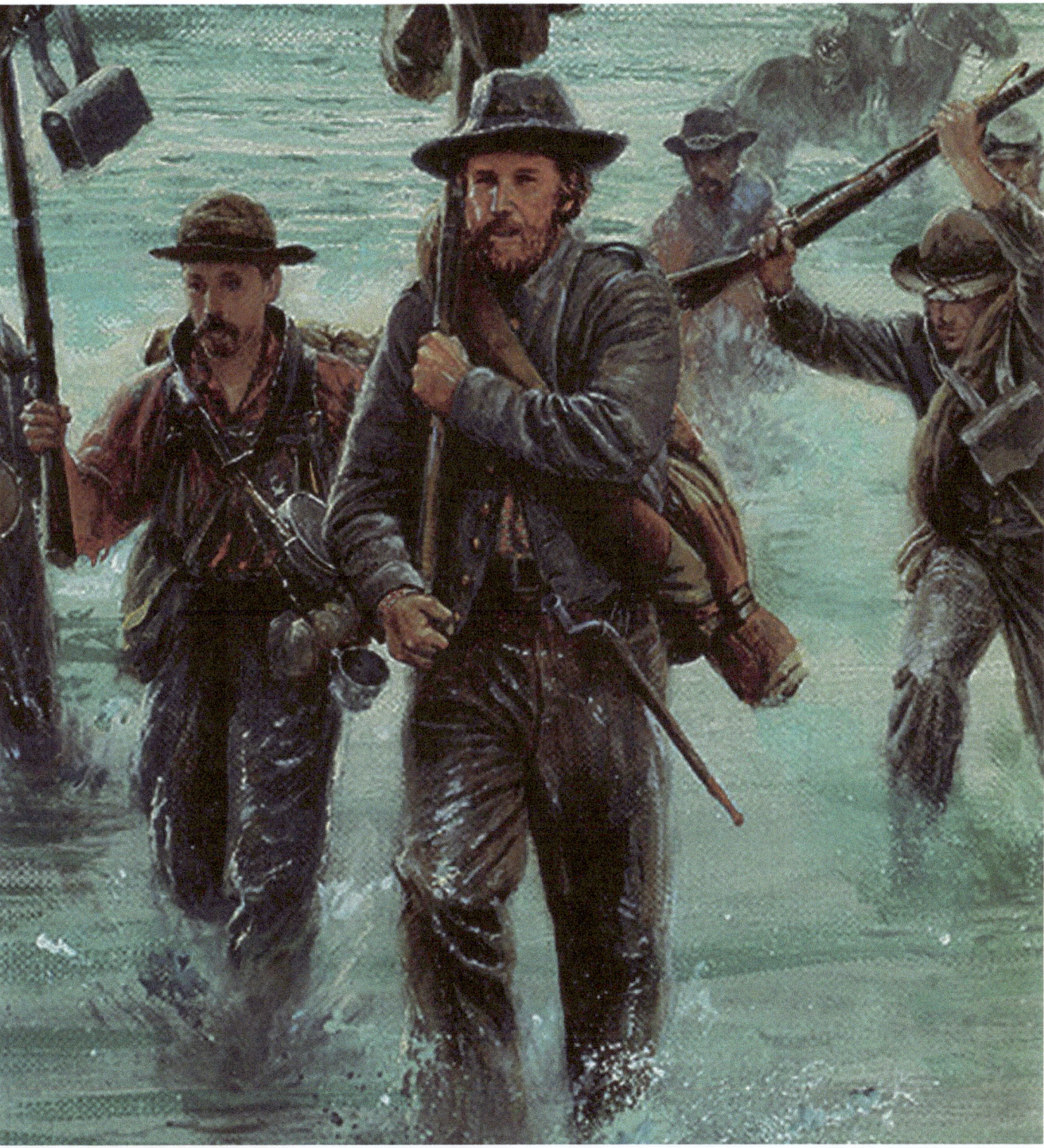

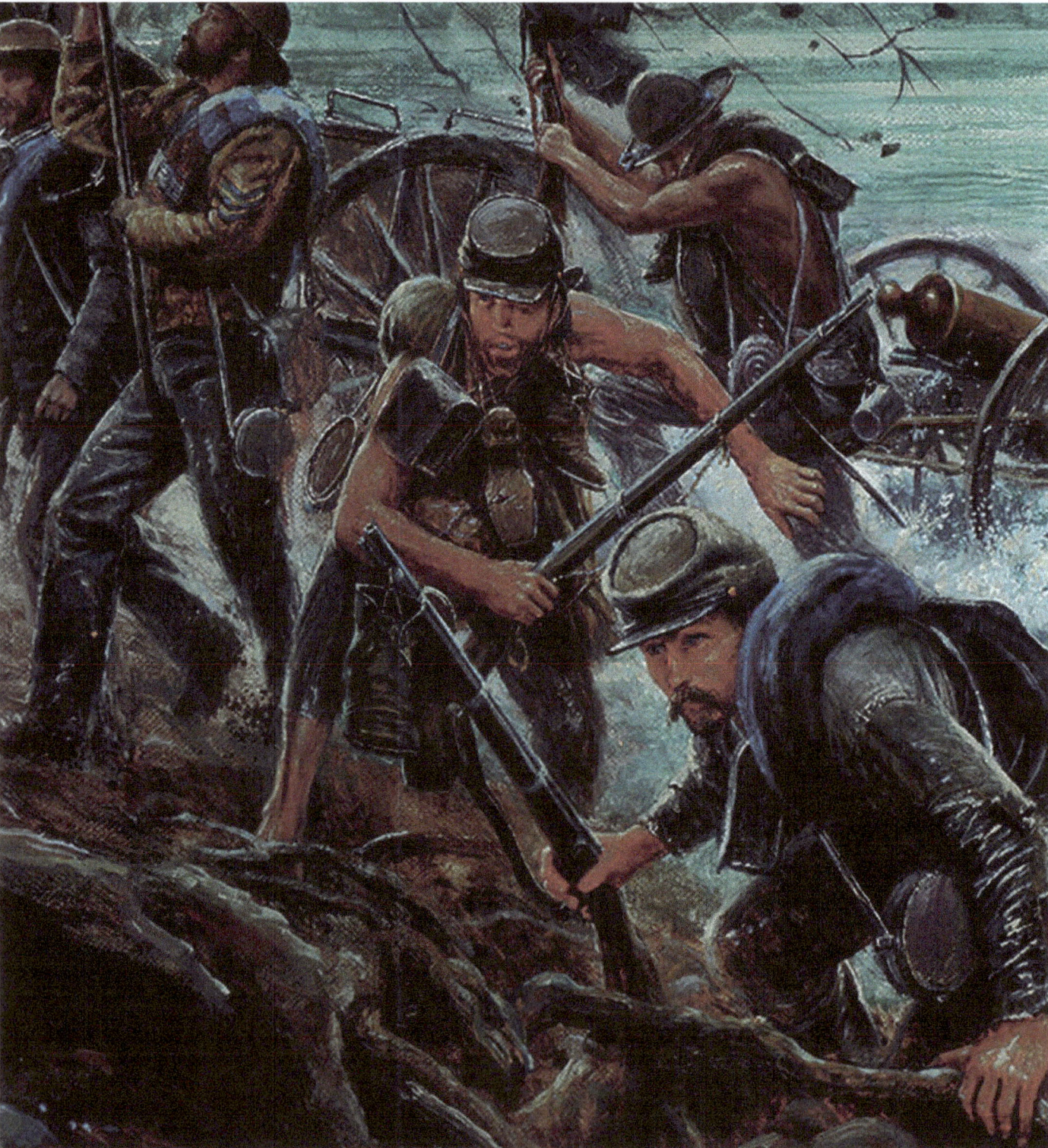

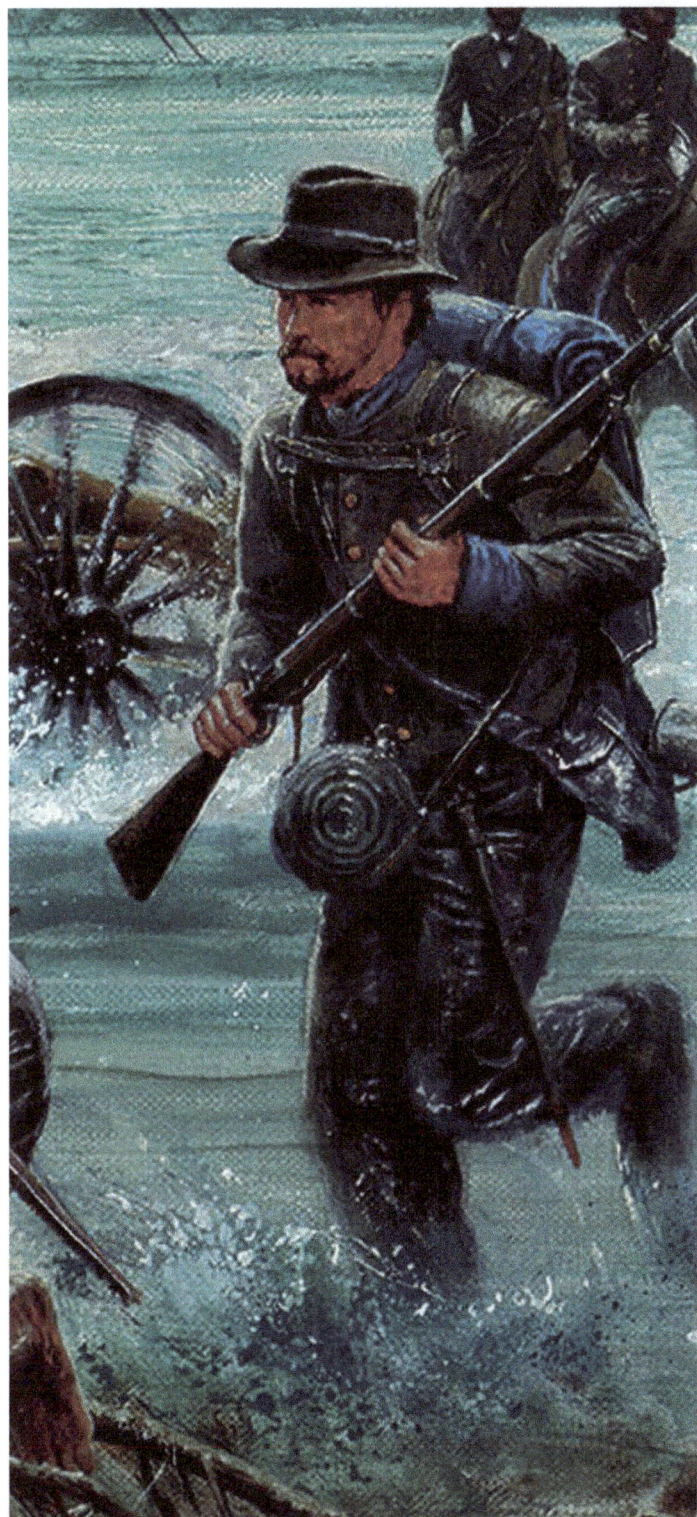

the evening, as part of a stealthy re-treat. Now, in broad daylight, they splash into the North. Still, they show great care in clambering out of the river and onto the northern bank. None knew exactly what lay ahead, but their faith in their commanders was steadfast.

I used the dark shapes of the band to frame the picture on the right and lead the viewer's eye to the center of the painting and the excitement of this momentous event. To the left, a clump of trees points the eye back to the crossing. The artillery teams are driven up the riverbank as the infantrymen scramble up from the water.

I visited Shepherdstown and went to the ford where the army waded into Northern territory. Standing there today, it's easy to imagine that remarkable scene. Such a colorful dis-play of fortitude and optimism! It gave me tremendous pleasure to re-search it and paint it.

AWARDS

1981

Brooklyn College Athletic Hall of Fame Award

1983

Secret Service Plaque of Appreciation

1985

Favell Museum in Klamath Falls, Oregon, Western Heritage Award for Excellence in Painting American History, Past and Present, from Caveman to Space Shuttle

1986

Pratt Institute, Brooklyn, NY, Alumni Achievement Award

Brooklyn College Alumni Association, New York, Distinguished Alumni Achievement Award in Art

Board of County Commissioners of Washington College, Maryland, Certificate of Appreciation

1989

PICA (Printing Industry of the Carolinas) Award for Excellence

1990

PICA (Printing Industry of the Carolinas) Award for Excellence

1992

PICA (Printing Industry of the Carolinas) Award for Excellence

1993

PICA (Printing Industry of the Carolinas) Award for Best of Category

1994

PICA (Printing Industry of the Carolinas) Special Judges Award

1995

House of Representatives, South Carolina, Certificate of Appreciation

Nassau County, New York, Annual Visual Artist Award

1997

Fredericksburg, Virginia, Proclamation and Key to the City

1998

County Executive of Nassau County, New York, Certificate of Appreciation

1999

Mort Künstler Day in the Commonwealth of Virginia, March 18, 1999
The Museum of the Confederacy in Richmond, Virginia, Commendation of Distinguished Service
Shenandoah University, Winchester, Virginia, Honorary Degree of Doctorate of Fine Arts

2000

Troy, Ohio, Key to the City

2001

The Order of the Stars & Bars, Henry Timrod Southern Culture Award

2002

Pratt Institute, Brooklyn, NY, Alumni Achievement Award
Fredericksburg Area Museum and Cultural Center Plaque of Appreciation

2003

Jefferson Davis Southern Heritage Award from the Military Order of the Stars and Bars
The Exchange Club of Capitol Hill, Plaque of Appreciation
Fuquay-Varina, North Carolina, Key to the City
Mort Künstler Day in City of Roanoke, Virginia, March 2, 2003
Mort Künstler Day in Bartow County, Georgia, November 15, 2003

2006

Hagerstown, Maryland, Commendation of Special Recognition

ART INDEX

ACKNOWLEDGMENTS

This book is a collaborative effort between many people and would not have been possible without their inspiration, advice, and dedication. Special thanks—

to Ron Pitkin and Ed Curtis of Cumberland House for their expertise. It has been a pleasure to work with them on this project.

to Dr. James I. Robertson Jr., the celebrated and highly esteemed author-historian for his superb foreword to this volume. I continue to treasure our friendship as the years go by.

to author-historian Rod Gragg, a colleague who has been one of my closest advisers for fifteen years as well as a dear friend.

to Richard Lynch, president of Hammer Galleries in New York City, for thirty years of friendship and guidance. Thanks also to Howard Shaw, vice president, and the rest of the staff at Hammer Galleries for all their efforts on my behalf, including the hosting of fifteen one-man exhibitions.

to Chris Brooks of American Spirit Publishing, the exclusive publisher of my limited-edition fine-art prints, for sharing his enthusiasm, knowledge, and friendship.

to my daughter, Jane Künstler Broffman, who as project manager met the daily challenges of compiling this book. I am delighted to have worked with her and admire her for the knowledge and creativity she brought to this volume.

to Paula McEvoy and Lissette Portillo of Künstler Enterprises for all their help and dedication in assembling and editing this book.

to my wife, Deborah, for her unwavering support of my work, her words of encouragement, and for making my life a joy in every way.

—Mort Künstler